Self-Control in Animals and People

AF737143

Self-Control in Animals and People

Michael Beran
Georgia State University, Atlanta, GA, United States

ELSEVIER

ACADEMIC PRESS
An imprint of Elsevier

Academic Press is an imprint of Elsevier
125 London Wall, London EC2Y 5AS, United Kingdom
525 B Street, Suite 1650, San Diego, CA 92101, United States
50 Hampshire Street, 5th Floor, Cambridge, MA 02139, United States
The Boulevard, Langford Lane, Kidlington, Oxford OX5 1GB, United Kingdom

Copyright © 2018 Elsevier Inc. All rights reserved.

No part of this publication may be reproduced or transmitted in any form or by any means, electronic or mechanical, including photocopying, recording, or any information storage and retrieval system, without permission in writing from the publisher. Details on how to seek permission, further information about the Publisher's permissions policies and our arrangements with organizations such as the Copyright Clearance Center and the Copyright Licensing Agency, can be found at our website: http://www.elsevier.com/permissions.

This book and the individual contributions contained in it are protected under copyright by the Publisher (other than as may be noted herein).

Notices

Knowledge and best practice in this field are constantly changing. As new research and experience broaden our understanding, changes in research methods, professional practices, or medical treatment may become necessary.

Practitioners and researchers must always rely on their own experience and knowledge in evaluating and using any information, methods, compounds, or experiments described herein. In using such information or methods they should be mindful of their own safety and the safety of others, including parties for whom they have a professional responsibility.

To the fullest extent of the law, neither the Publisher nor the authors, contributors, or editors, assume any liability for any injury and/or damage to persons or property as a matter of products liability, negligence or otherwise, or from any use or operation of any methods, products, instructions, or ideas contained in the material herein.

British Library Cataloguing-in-Publication Data
A catalogue record for this book is available from the British Library

Library of Congress Cataloging-in-Publication Data
A catalog record for this book is available from the Library of Congress

ISBN: 978-0-12-812508-3

For Information on all Academic Press publications
visit our website at https://www.elsevier.com/books-and-journals

ELSEVIER
Book Aid International
Working together to grow libraries in developing countries

www.elsevier.com • www.bookaid.org

Publisher: Nikki Levy
Acquisition Editor: Emily Ekle
Editorial Project Manager: Carly Demetre
Production Project Manager: Mohana Natarajan
Cover Designer: Matthew Limbert

Typeset by MPS Limited, Chennai, India

Contents

Acknowledgments

I have a lot of people to thank for helping this book come together, in terms of what it took to write it and what it took to get to a point in my own career where I was (I hope!) qualified to write it. At many points, a person or small number of people put me on this path, or kept me on it, and so without them, this book would not have been possible. I am grateful to one of my graduate mentors Duane Rumbaugh, for making me even begin the process of studying self-control. Despite going to graduate school to study numerical cognition across species, Duane wanted me to broaden my perspectives, and so he told me I had to do something different for my master's degree thesis project. From that prodding, combined with my interests in numerical cognition, I came across the work of Sally Boysen and the reverse-reward contingency task, and from there I was led to Walter Mischel's work with the marshmallow task and work on intertemporal choices, and many of the other things you will read about later. So, Duane kicked this whole thing off. Duane passed away while I was writing this book, and so he will not have a chance to read it. I think he would have liked it, and what I know is that any corrections he would have offered would have come gently and with real concern for my feelings and my growth as a scientist. Later, I had the support of David Washburn as my dissertation adviser and James Pate as another of my mentors. They helped shape and guide my development as a cognitive psychologist, and they taught me how to approach doing psychological science. Jim and David—any split infinitives in here are intentional, just to keep you sharp! David also provided countless hours of relaxed discussions of science, teaching, and mentoring, either in a plane or in a van on the way to or from a conference, or when I was routinely beating him at ping pong or racquetball (at least, that is how I remember those games going!). Except for the two times he almost got us arrested at the Canadian border, I am thankful for everything he has done to help me through my career.

During the many hours of data collection I did while thinking about self-control in animals, I was very fortunate to work with amazing people, both at Georgia State University and around the world. Ted Evans and I conducted more studies than I can even remember—some worked, some did not! But, without his help, I would not have been nearly as productive, and real insights would have been lost. Ted, for example, figured out how to see if the chimpanzees would self-distract during their own version of the marshmallow test, and when they did, I was really amazed. Crucial contributions were also made by Audrey Parrish, my first graduate student, who is now a professor at The Citadel. Audrey is perhaps the hardest working person I have ever been around, and countless times we both saw the same path forward on a project. She is a trusted colleague and a close friend, and I miss the chance to meet her in a coffee shop to talk data, science, and life. Audrey still ranks at the top of the list of funniest things I have ever seen someone do at a conference (but, I am sworn to secrecy on that!). Bonnie Perdue did her postdoctoral work with me and is now a professor at Agnes Scott College. Bonnie's creativity brought a whole new line of research to the lab, as she found a way to translate my fascination with sushi express lines to a method we could use to test self-control in monkeys. I still hope she will find a way to let us test elephants on delayed gratification (we once did try with otters, but that is a story for another day!). There was a time when Ted, Audrey, Bonnie, and I could never end a meeting in its allotted time, for two reasons: First, because we kept coming up with new ideas, and no one was willing to leave until we hashed those out, and second, because we liked being around each other so much. I think there is nothing better than being in a lab where you can work on a grant, look at new data, talk about new ideas, debate the best way to do a statistical test, and also shoot each other with Nerf guns. Those three people have moved on now from the Language Research Center (LRC), and I hope they know how much I miss them.

Fabio Palieri and Elsa Addessi, both at the Institute of Cognitive Sciences and Technologies in Rome, influenced my thoughts constantly over the past decade. They are wonderful colleagues, who share ideas and who are generous with their time. As I tell in more detail later, Fabio was the driving force behind the hybrid delay task, which we continue to use to great effect in studies with nonhuman animals. He and Elsa have made huge contributions to what we know about self-control across species, and their visits to Atlanta were truly wonderful times for me. In addition, it has been a pleasure to work with Bill Hopkins at Georgia State, who gave me the chance to see what a large group of chimpanzees might do on some of our delay of gratification tests, and to work with Erin Stromberg and Amanda Bania at the Smithsonian National Zoo where we tested orangutans' delay of gratification and other cognitive abilities. Other important colleagues over the years who have influenced my thinking about animal cognition and made doing science more fun include Christian Agrillo, Sarah Brosnan, Josep Call, Barbara Church, Jon Crystal, Gil Einstein, Tim Flemming, Rob Hampton, Lisa Heimbauer, Megan Hoffman, Andrew Kelly, Emily Klein, Rob Latzman, Tom Putney, Ken Sayers, Bennett Schwartz, David Smith, and Jeff Stevens.

When you work with animals, the most important people are the ones who take care of them. The LRC has always blended animal care with research efforts, because we believe you cannot separate how you care for the animals and how you hope to work with them in ways that let them show you the fullest capacities of their minds. John Kelly has been at the LRC longer than I have and has supported every project I ever undertook with his time and his ideas. He and Mattea Rossettie, Kathy Thompson, Julia Federov, and Dan Rice have taken care of our chimpanzees and monkeys for decades and helped make sure we could work with the animals productively. I have the chance to work with nonhuman primates because our care staff, research staff, and veterinarians make that happen. I am so grateful to them for all that they do.

I am also grateful to the other faculty in the Department of Psychology at GSU and to everyone at the LRC. There is nowhere else with as great a group of wacky, smart, weird, supportive, and at times wonderfully inappropriate people than we have at the LRC. Very special thanks go to Charles Menzel. Charlie and I have spent countless hours talking about ape cognition, and self-control, and future-oriented cognition. And, Duke basketball! I am indebted to him for all the time he has given to me from when I was a new graduate student up until now. Finally, we keep the bills paid (and the people paid!) because Pam Johnson always manages to do that for us, and so without her, none of this research would happen.

Our chimpanzees, Lana, Sherman, Austin, Panzee, and Mercury, are all gone now, with Sherman being the last (he died a week before I wrote this, at the age of 44, from chronic heart failure). I hardly know what to say about them. Until you spend time around chimpanzees, nothing prepares you for who they are, and after you spend time around them, nothing prepares you for when you cannot see them anymore. That they tolerated me as a naïve 22-year-old graduate student, and then worked with me for the next 22 years of our lives, amazes me each day when I think about it. I learned more than I ever thought possible from spending time with them. Working *with them* was one of the most amazing experiences of my life, and I appreciated all that they were willing to do to help me understand them a little better. It was a wonderful relationship, and we worked together in a truly rewarding way. I hope that maybe they felt the same way about that. I miss them all very much.

I am grateful to my current graduate students, Brielle James, Kristin French, and Molly Flessert, who have tolerated my absences on those days when I had to work on this book, although they may have seen those days as a blessing! They are three amazing young scientists, who I hope and expect will be writing their own books in the future on their own topics of interest. They each also probably owe me a paper right now, so I will be looking for those papers now that this book is done! Thanks also to Travis Smith, my recent former postdoc, for his excellent work in the lab during this process.

He is a behaviorist, so I just kept giving him a (gluten-free) cookie each time he did something well, and that seemed to do the trick.

I also want to express my thanks to everyone at Academic Press and Elsevier for their help with this book. Dennis McGonagle was the person who first approached me to see if I was interested, and he was the one who convinced me I could do this. Without his enthusiasm, I probably would not have taken the first big step of writing the proposal. Sarah Watson also helped me along the way, and Carly Demetre got us through to the end. During various stages, the following people kindly reviewed chapters and provided important insights, and often did so for more than one chapter: Bonnie Perdue, Sally Boysen, Desiree Brucks, Ted Evans, Andrew Kelly, Fabio Paglieri, Audrey Parrish, Travis Smith, and David Washburn.

Finally, to my family: My daughters Sam and Alex spent too many evenings and weekends hearing dad say "I just need to carve a little time to work on the book," and yet they persevered through to the end. My wife, Mary, helped carve out that time when she could, and made sure the girls only interrupted me every now and then on writing days. I hope they enjoy the book, but I know they will enjoy knowing that it is finished, and we can finally do more things together. Those three are the most important people in the world to me, and to them I offer my greatest thanks! And, my brother Matt, Aunt Janice, Aunt Parnell, and Uncle Scott often checked in to make sure I was still working, and kept asking when the book would be out. The process has certainly reflected an example of self-control (and quite a bit of impulsivity) in me. Now that it is finished, I am tempted to consider writing another, but then I remind myself (as you will read) about how bad we are with discounting the future, and I think I will instead eat a donut, have a nice glass of whisky, or perhaps light a good cigar. But just one...

Great is the art of beginning, but greater is the art of ending.

Henry Wadsworth Longfellow

Michael Beran

Chapter 1

What Is Self-Control and What Is It Good For?

Educate your children to self-control, to the habit of holding passion and prejudice and evil tendencies subject to an upright and reasoning will, and you have done much to abolish misery from their future and crimes from society.

Benjamin Franklin

I began working on this book about an hour after finishing an early dinner with my family while on vacation in Florida. It was the perfect time to begin work on a book about self-control because that day was filled with examples of what nearly all of us experience in our own lives, and something we experience nearly continuously—the struggle of "now versus later" and "good for future me versus really enjoyable for present me." The day started off right, with me putting in a run on the beach, in an effort to be healthy in general, but more specifically to lose weight and reach a goal I had set for the summer. What followed, however, was a series of choices that showed the difficulty I faced in trying to stick to that goal. I avoided butter on my bread for breakfast, but then also ate the extra slice (with jelly!) my daughter left on her plate. I had a healthy lunch, and avoided the candy dish at my father-in-law's house, but then dinner was my doom. Lobster mac-n-cheese, and then, for dessert, sharing a deep fried ice cream bowl, which was described on the menu as a "cannonball sized scoop of ice cream, dipped in batter, deep fried, and smothered with chocolate sauce, caramel, and whipped cream." There were six of us at dinner, and although we all said it seemed like something that one needed to try at least once in life, we all admitted to being too full from our dinner. Astonishingly, this was even true for my 10- and 6-year-old daughters. But, as we sat there, and talked more about what deep fried ice cream must taste like, we slowly began to convince ourselves we needed to have it. And, at one point, I declared that I would certainly try some, but it would require a team effort if we were to order it, so *I would only do it if everyone else did too.* Twenty minutes later, my wife scooped up the last bit of ice cream off the gigantic plate which delivered that cannonball of decadence, and we could not decide whether to celebrate or lament what we had

Self-Control in Animals and People. DOI: https://doi.org/10.1016/B978-0-12-812508-3.00001-3
© 2018 Elsevier Inc. All rights reserved.

just done! In that moment, our present selves largely wished we had not ordered and eaten it, and yet our past selves (just 20 minutes younger) had all hoped someone would give in and argue for ordering it, so we all could indulge.

When I got home that evening, I sat down in front of my laptop and looked over the collective notes that I had for this book. I also thought of a half dozen reasons yet again to put off the formal writing of this chapter. I thought about other emails that I could answer, or reviews I could complete quickly, or even what various games I could play on my smart phone that would provide me with a distraction and keep my mind off of the need to work on this book. I told myself that perhaps next week would be a better week to begin, because this week I was on vacation, and certainly I deserved time to relax. And, making things even worse, my wife and children came downstairs and announced they were going for a walk on the beach. That was incredibly tempting, and I almost agreed to join them, but I showed a rare glimpse of the self-control needed to accomplish the writing that you read here.

So, why was I successful in going for the run and eating the healthy lunch, and yet so wildly unsuccessful eating an unhealthy dinner and then making a choice for the unhealthy dessert? And, what allowed me to commit to the hours of writing that I needed to do rather than find yet another reason to engage in something more immediately pleasurable but more detrimental to my goal of finishing this book on time? The answer is that in some cases I exercised self-control. In other cases, my impulsivity overrode any sense of what was in my best long-term interests because I was only interested in satisfying my more immediate need for pleasure. In each of these situations in my day, I faced a conflict. And, a fairly simple conflict in terms of what I could choose from. There were two options in each case, one that was less enjoyable now, but served a greater purpose, and the other was the choice that felt best now, with little or no regard to the future.

This book is about self-control. The examples I gave you are all perfect ones for highlighting situations in which self-control is required, but often does not occur. People rely on self-control numerous times each day, sometimes succeeding and sometimes failing. Some of the most negative behaviors that people exhibit reflect failures of self-control, such as overeating, smoking, abusing drugs, problem gambling, physical aggression, and risky sexual behavior. And, the consequences from those behaviors are among some of the most severe, including poor health, poverty, and even loss of freedom or loss of life. In all of these cases, individuals can report that the behaviors they are currently choosing to engage in, such as gambling, smoking, or unsafe sex, are not in their long-term best interests, and yet they still feel compelled to engage in those behaviors because of how they feel now. Generating interventions to alleviate impulsivity, and to improve self-control, is arguably one of the most important goals for behavioral scientists who study how and why people make the choices that they do. Interventions that could improve self-control would be of great benefit to individuals who suffer from impulsivity, which leads to many deleterious consequences at the individual and societal levels (e.g., drug addiction, sexually transmitted behaviors, healthcare costs of obesity and smoking, and others). And yet, many attempts at interventions rarely succeed in the long term. In some cases, this is because they are based on faulty science, or they are simply a fad rather than an intervention based in scientific discovery. However, even in cases in which science has provided us with a clear set of guidelines for improving self-control, it is still difficult for people to put those guidelines into practice to help them improve self-control.

In fact, it is a striking example of human behavior that people understand, and often can clearly articulate, the best strategies and the best responses to make in a given situation, but then consistently fail to employ those strategies and make those choices. I knew at dinner that the deep fried ice cream was not in my best interest long term regarding my weight, and I even stated multiple times that I felt as if I should make the smart decision and avoid eating dessert. And yet, just a few minutes later, when it arrived at the table, I was thrilled and excited to engage in eating that dessert, with all thoughts about how my future self would feel about those extra calories quieted. I should have ordered coffee as a substitute, or better yet, got up and left the table, removing myself from the presence of the thing I needed to avoid. Or, I could have thought less about how it tasted, and more about the calories it contained, and how far one has to run to burn those off (probably 10 miles!). Those strategies all work. But, in the moment, they are less salient and less appealing than is a giant ball of fried ice cream. And, therein lies the dilemma of so many of our choices.

I have studied self-control for more than 20 years. Throughout this book, I will highlight my own journey in studying this topic, and how I first became interested in asking whether animals other than humans might also demonstrate self-control. You will learn about the research we do in my laboratory and in other laboratories around the world that study human and nonhuman choice behavior. To explain the studies that we do will require also learning about some of the special animals that I have worked with who have taught us that humans are not alone in facing now-versus-later decisions. Similarly, we are not alone in being able to anticipate a better future for ourselves, and in some cases work to make that future a reality. As part of this journey, I will tell you what I have learned along the way about the nature of studying psychological processes across species.

I am a comparative psychologist, which means I study psychology not just in humans, but in other species. I investigate how people and animals behave, to see how we differ, and how we might share with other animals some similar (and different) mechanisms that guide how we interact with the world around us. I believe the fullest description and understanding of human behavior comes from also studying nonhuman animals, and this is a perspective taken by many other excellent researchers and outlined more broadly in other sources (e.g., Call, 2017; Reznikova, 2007; Tomasello & Call, 1997; Zentall & Wasserman, 2012). Human behavior studied in isolation cannot allow us to disentangle various psychological processes to determine which are most critical or least critical in decision making and choice behavior. It is the broader perspective that takes into account evolutionary pressures, and evolved mechanisms for dealing with those pressures, that best describes who we are (e.g., Maestripieri, 2003; Shettleworth, 2009; Tomasello & Call, 1997; Vonk & Shackelford, 2012; Wasserman, 1993; see Additional Recommended Readings as well).

I will begin by talking about varieties of self-control. It is important, also, to explain what self-control is *not*, and to situate self-control behaviors within the broader behavioral domain known as inhibitory behavior. Thus, I will discuss when self-control may or may not be required, versus other psychological processes that guide choice and behavior. As part of this, I will talk about unique kinds of self-control that may not be about time-based decisions, but rather involve trade-offs in terms of effort or work. That said, most research into human decision-making that requires self-control involves intertemporal choices (e.g., Berns, Laibson, & Loewenstein, 2007; Green & Myerson, 2004; Loewenstein, Read, & Baumeister, 2003; Madden & Bickel, 2010; Rachlin, 2000; Stevens, 2014). These are simply choices between one thing more immediately, and one thing after a longer delay. These kinds of choices have dominated the literature on human choice behavior. I cannot give full recognition to that extensive literature, but will highlight what I think are the key issues and findings from the perspective of studying self-control not only in humans, but also in other animals. I will focus on what we have learned about how to improve self-control choices, or increase impulsive ones, and how those laboratory-based studies might be applied to real-life decisions.

Intertemporal choices have been studied extensively in other species, and I will provide an overview of work done with nonhuman animals. It was this research that first drew my attention, as I learned about how other animals, although typically impulsive, sometimes showed glimmerings of more self-controlled behavior. This is an important point, because it led me (and others) to ask new questions of animals, and those questions have led to a new conception of the decision-making abilities of animals when it comes to future-oriented, self-controlled choices. Prior to this work, there was the strong claim by many that what made humans unique was our ability to control our impulses, and to somehow rise above our "animal instincts." At some point in our history, perhaps before history was even being recorded, we came to elevate those who showed self-control and restraint in terms of their status, whereas we tend to look down upon those who consistently indulged their impulsive drives. We placed great value of those who avoided "acting like animals," and there remains a strong tendency to view people who make impulsive choices as being defective in their nature or personality. When seeing people who are obese, we think that they cannot control their impulse to eat. When seeing a smoker lighting a cigarette while attached to the oxygen canister designed to help him with smoking-induced emphysema, we shake our heads (and back away!) thinking about his failure of character to overcome his addiction and aid in his own health. In some cases, we laugh about failures of self-control, as when seeing children eat themselves sick again and again on popcorn or Halloween candy, and we talk about how they just cannot seem to remember and learn that they will pay a price for their gluttony. At the same time, we praise and elevate to high status those who "pinch pennies" and retire early, and we admire the disciplined athletes for their training regimens. We find examples of extolling the virtue of self-control in our most important historical writings, including the Bible and the Qur'an. For example, the story of Adam and Eve can be construed as a test of willpower over immediate gratification. We find examples in some of our most widely known myths such as the story of Odysseus, who was faced with a real test of self-control, where immediate gratification was so enticing, but also so deadly. The story of Odysseus anticipated what empirical research later showed about the self-controlled individual as being someone who wants to avoid temptation, recognizes the form of that temptation, and then puts into place a commitment to avoiding that temptation. Having oneself tied to the ship so as to avoid the call of the Sirens is much like locking away one's cookies or cigarettes in the modern-day version of Odysseus' solution (Fig. 1.1). Thus, as a society we know of this constant struggle, and we see it every day. I will provide some of the scientific data from studies of choices in the laboratory, and use those results to understand real-world choices such as I just described.

In many cases, elegant and yet simple tests have been designed that allow animals to show us their preferences for now-versus-later, and those tests can be presented without need of language to give instructions on how to engage the test. I will argue that some of those efforts have been misguided in terms of confusing prepotent responses with mechanisms of self-control, and that we must be careful in how to interpret some choices made by animals (or even people) when the context is such that it is unclear what may be guiding such choices. This discussion sets the stage for later suggestions on how to carefully design tests of intertemporal choice for animals. This is an exciting prospect, because the simplicity of these kinds of tests makes them easy to present to wide variety of animals, allowing us the chance to perhaps build one of the most complete "phylogenetic maps" of a behavioral capacity that has high relevance to understanding choice behavior.

I then will turn briefly to discussing one of the most famous experiments in all of psychology—the Marshmallow Test designed by Walter Mischel. It is a test that is well known, and that has been given its own justly deserved coverage (Mischel, 2014). It assesses a particular kind of self-control known

FIGURE 1.1 The kSafe. A product designed to lock away for some period of time things you may be tempted to use or consume more immediately. *Permission to use this image was granted by www.TheKitchenSafe.com.*

as delay of gratification, and the marshmallow test (and other variations of delay of gratification tests) is valuable because they allow us to study the constituent parts of self-control. I will outline those constituent parts, and how I think about the nature of self-control as evidenced in delay of gratification. My other goal, though, is to explain the value of this test not only for what it taught us about human self-control, but also in explaining why it and similar tests lend themselves so nicely to experiments with nonhuman animals. I will explain some of those other tests as well, which converged on the finding that human children show a wide variety of performances in delaying their gratification. And, how children perform on those tests when they are young has value in predicting how those same children will perform on various things later in life, like standardized tests, and how well those children will turn out in terms of employment, earning potential, and even criminal activity. Although, as recent research has shown, this relationship is more complicated than perhaps we thought in the past (Watts, Duncan, & Quan, 2018).

I will describe a series of experiments with nonhuman animals that adapted and extended delay of gratification tests to ask how long animals can wait to get a bigger, better reward. I will talk in detail about my own inspiration for conducting some of these tests, and in particular focus on a task known as the reverse-reward contingency task (Boysen & Berntson, 1995; Shifferman, 2009) that motivated me to study self-control in more detail. Delay of gratification tasks in animals are not nearly as well-known as those given to children, but I think the reader will find the results fascinating, and compelling, and some of those results may perhaps change the general perception that only humans anticipate a better, future outcome, and then structure their behavior to obtain that.

Toward the end of the book, I will discuss other tests of self-control given to animals, returning to the idea of how to best create fair tests of self-control that neither overestimate nor underestimate capacities in other species. A wide variety of new tests have been designed, but have never been presented in one place to show the range of capacities that other animals demonstrate. I offer that synthesis. As part of this, I will discuss the prominent but also controversial idea in human psychology that self-control is a limited resource, and one that may rely on a specific physiological mechanism that involves the metabolism of glucose (Baumeister, Vohs, & Tice, 2007; Gailliot & Baumeister, 2007; Hagger, Chantelle, Stiff, & Chatzisarantis, 2010; Muraven, Tice, & Baumeister, 1998). After explaining this hypothesis, and evaluating evidence for and against it in the human literature, I will discuss some fairly new studies with animals that have contributed to this debate.

Sometimes, in research settings, it can become easy to develop different tests that one assumes must be "tapping into" the same cognitive or behavioral mechanisms, but it is important to confirm that this is true. I will discuss some recent efforts to learn whether different experimental tasks called "self-control" tasks or "inhibition" tasks show consistent performances in the same people or animals who are given these tasks. The idea here is to see whether generalized self-control mechanisms may be at work in the behavior of people and animals. Alternately, it may be the case that a generalized self-control mechanism is not universally engaged in all contexts that would seem to require self-control, but rather individual and unique mechanisms that are part of a *suite of self-control mechanisms* are engaged (or not) depending very much *on the context*. The idea here is to use behavioral data to see whether the tasks we design all seem to tap into the same mechanisms, or do not. These data can tell us a lot about the nature of self-control, and perhaps also illuminate why we see strong inter-individual differences (e.g., differences between people or animals in the same context) and intra-individual differences (e.g., differences in self-control in the same people or animals when given different contexts in which choices are made). I will also talk about the rarely studied aspect of self-control or impulsivity as demonstrated in social contexts. We know that our choices are often affected strongly by who we are with when we make them, and whether we make choices in groups or by ourselves likely impacts when and how we engage in self-control (as with the fried cannonball of ice cream!). And yet this is an understudied topic in the developmental and comparative literatures on self-control.

Finally, a synthesis of two ideas that are popular in comparative research about animal cognition is presented. The idea of "mental time travel" and future-oriented cognition is discussed, and how those aspects of human behavior may also be evident in the behavior of some nonhuman animals. I will argue that these topics closely align with self-control research, and I will discuss how present and future work with children and animals is increasingly focused on the relation between prospective (future-oriented) cognition and self-control. After finishing this synthesis, I will discuss how past, present, and future efforts with tests designed for children, adults, and animals highlight how our own capacity to show self-control, and our own fallibilities, come from our evolutionary history and emerge through development.

In the chapters that follow, I often will focus fairly extensively on a smaller number of studies to highlight the main testing approach, or the main results. This is not to overlook the important data and implications from other studies on self-control, and at the end of each chapter I provide the reader not only with citations to the articles discussed in that chapter, but also with a list of other recommended readings for anyone who wants a broader and more complete overview of the literature surrounding the focus of that chapter.

Ultimately, this is a book about choice. What do we choose, and why do we choose? Some choices require no degree of self-control, and there is no threat of impulsive responding. For example, you likely chose the outfit you are wearing today on the basis of a number of factors, some of which you might not even have been aware of, but presumably you did not need to show any form of self-control (unless you really wanted to wear that t-shirt with the inappropriate slogan on the front to work today, but also wanted to keep your job!). Other choices are fascinating from a psychological perspective because of how simple things like product location or competing alternatives subtly influence what you decide to choose. The field of *behavioral economics* is largely focused on those kinds of choices, where framing effects play a large role in what we choose. For example, the bottle of wine you choose and the price you pay for it is partly determined by the price and quality of other wines around it (e.g., Hastie & Dawes, 2010), and your indecision between two sizes of popcorn containers at the movie theater can be eliminated by the choice of a third option you would never buy, but that leads you to choose one of the other two options (Ariely & Wallsten, 1995; Choplin & Hummel, 2005; Huber, Payne, & Puto, 1982; Pettibone & Wedell, 2000). However, those are again instances in which you are not comparing items on the basis of what you want right now versus what you know is a better, later choice in terms of it benefitting your future self (as in the case of deciding whether to have the giant tub of popcorn at the theater or stick to your diet). This book is about this last kind of choice, where self-control is needed, and impulsive urges must be overcome.

A critical aspect to choice behavior that involves the need for self-control is that the chooser has to know what his or her options are, and what the relative values of those choices are. In addition, the person (or animal) has to know what the time delays to each will be, and what the effort is to obtain those choices. Self-control research in all its approaches must be transparent to the individual being observed in terms of what can be gained, when it can be gained, and what effort is required to obtain it. And, there must be a way to objectively know that one of those two choices is *better in the longer term* even if the other choice is *more appealing in the shorter term*. A person who chooses a giant slice of chocolate cake for dessert because they just received an excellent health score on a physical examination and are thus celebrating that accomplishment is not behaving impulsively. One can make choices for the most hedonistic options and not be acting impulsively, if there is no clear reason or expectation that the individual has a longer term goal or objectively better outcome that comes from *not making the present choice*. These are the only requirements for testing self-control, whether in studying intertemporal choice, delay of gratification, or some other forms of behavioral inhibition that present competing choice options. For me, this was one of the attractive aspects of this line of inquiry—that as long as you designed tests around these requirements, you could study choice behavior in the face of the conflict one faces between what the present "self" wants, and what the future "self" would be better off having, and would choose to have, if no delay or requirement for greater effort was part of that choice. And, from such tests, we have learned about the nature of self-control, and a lot about the individuals (human and nonhuman) who make such choices.

REFERENCES

Ariely, D., & Wallsten, T. S. (1995). Seeking subjective dominance in multidimensional space: An explanation of the asymmetric dominance effect. *Organizational Behavior and Human Decision Processes*, *63*, 223–232.

Baumeister, R. F., Vohs, K. D., & Tice, D. M. (2007). The strength model of self-control. *Current Directions in Psychological Science*, *16*, 351–355.

Berns, G. S., Laibson, D., & Loewenstein, G. (2007). Intertemporal choice – Toward an integrative framework. *Trends in Cognitive Sciences*, *11*, 482–488.

Boysen, S. T., & Berntson, G. G. (1995). Responses to quantity: Perceptual versus cognitive mechanisms in chimpanzees (*Pan troglodytes*). *Journal of Experimental Psychology: Animal Behavior Processes*, *21*, 82–86.

Call, J. (Ed.), (2017). *APA handbook of comparative psychology*. Washington, DC: American Psychological Association.

Choplin, J. M., & Hummel, J. E. (2005). Comparison-induced decoy effects. *Memory & Cognition*, *33*, 332–343.

Gailliot, M. T., & Baumeister, R. F. (2007). The physiology of willpower: Linking blood glucose to self-control. *Personality and Social Psychology Review, 11*, 303–327.

Green, L., & Myerson, J. (2004). A discounting framework for choice with delayed and probabilistic rewards. *Psychological Bulletin, 130*, 769–792.

Hagger, M. S., Chantelle, W., Stiff, C., & Chatzisarantis, N. L. (2010). Ego depletion and the strength model of self-control: A meta-analysis. *Psychological Bulletin, 136*, 495–525.

Hastie, R., & Dawes, R. M. (2010). *Rational choice in an uncertain world: The psychology of judgment and decision making*. Los Angeles: Sage.

Huber, J., Payne, J. W., & Puto, C. (1982). Adding asymmetrically dominated alternatives: Violations of regularity and the similarity hypothesis. *Journal of Consumer Research, 9*, 90–98.

Loewenstein, G., Read, D., & Baumeister, R. F. (Eds.), (2003). *Time and decision: Economic and psychological perspectives of intertemporal choice*. New York: Russell Sage Foundation.

Madden, G. J., & Bickel, W. K. (2010). *Impulsivity: The behavioral and neurological science of discounting*. Washington, DC: American Psychological Association.

Maestripieri, D. (Ed.), (2003). *Primate psychology*. Cambridge, MA: Harvard University Press.

Mischel, W. (2014). *The marshmallow test: understanding self-control and how to master it*. New York: Random House.

Muraven, M., Tice, D. M., & Baumeister, R. F. (1998). Self-control as a limited resource: Regulatory depletion patterns. *Journal of Personality and Social Psychology, 74*, 774–789.

Pettibone, J. C., & Wedell, D. H. (2000). Examining models of nondominated decoy effects across judgment and choice. *Organizational Behavior and Human Decision Processes, 81*, 300–328.

Rachlin, H. (2000). *The science of self-control*. Cambridge, MA: Harvard University Press.

Reznikova, Z. I. (2007). *Animal intelligence: From individual to social cognition*. Cambridge, MA: Cambridge University Press.

Shettleworth, S. J. (2009). *Cognition, evolution, and behavior*. New York: Oxford University Press.

Shifferman, E. M. (2009). Its own reward: Lessons to be drawn from the reversed-reward contingency paradigm. *Animal Cognition, 12*, 547–558.

Stevens, J. R. (2014). Evolutionary pressures on primate intertemporal choice. *Proceedings of the Royal Society of London B: Biological Sciences, 281*, 20140499.

Tomasello, M., & Call, J. (1997). *Primate cognition*. New York: Oxford University Press.

Wasserman, E. A. (1993). Comparative cognition: Beginning the second century of the study of animal intelligence. *Psychological Bulletin, 113*, 211–228.

Watts, T.W., Duncan, G.J., & Quan, H. (in press). Revisiting the marshmallow test: A conceptual replication investigating links between early delay of gratification and later outcomes. *Psychological Science*, 0956797618761661.

Zentall, T., & Wasserman, E. (Eds.), (2012). *Oxford handbook of comparative cognition*. Oxford, UK: Oxford University Press.

FURTHER READING

Bekoff, M., Allen, C., & Burghardt, G. M. (2002). *The cognitive animal: Empirical and theoretical perspective on animal cognition*. Cambridge, MA: MIT Press.

Bitterman, M. E. (1960). Toward a comparative psychology of learning. *American Psychologist, 15*, 704–712.

De Waal, F. (2016). *Are we smart enough to know how smart animals are?* New York: WW Norton & Company.

Dewsbury, D. A. (2013). Comparative psychology in historical perspective. In D. K. Freedheim, & I. B. Weiner (Eds.), *Handbook of psychology, Vol. 1: History of psychology* (2nd ed, pp. 79–99). Hoboken, NJ: John Wiley & Sons.

Heyes, C., & Huber, L. (Eds.), (2000). *The evolution of cognition.* Cambridge, MA: MIT Press.

Kohler, W. (1925). *The mentality of apes.* London, UK: Routledge and Kegan Paul.

Roitblat, H. L., Bever, T. G., & Terrace, H. S. (1984). *Animal cognition.* Hillsdale, NJ: Erlbaum.

Roberts, W. A. (1998). *Principles of animal cognition.* New York: McGraw-Hill.

Tolman, E. C. (1932). *Purposive behavior in animals and men.* New York: Century.

Vonk, J., & Shackelford, T. K. (Eds.), (2012). *Oxford handbook of comparative evolutionary psychology.* Oxford, UK: Oxford University Press.

Washburn, D. A. (Ed.), (2006). *Primate perspectives on behavior and cognition.* Washington, DC: American Psychological Association.

Yerkes, R. M. (1907). *The dancing mouse: A study in animal behavior.* New York: The Macmillan Company.

Chapter 2

Varieties of Self-Control

When I first thought about writing this book, one of the key questions in my mind was how to accurately reflect the research and theories about self-control that already exist, and that I think are important, while also proposing something of a new framework for considering the many tasks that are used by those studying self-control and similar capacities. There has been a long-running debate about what we even mean when we say self-control (for recent reviews, see Beran, 2015; Eisenreich & Hayden, 2018; Inzlicht, Schmeichel, & Macrae, 2014). In everyday speech, and in much of the "pop psychology" that is freely available on the Internet and other places, *self-control* is a loosely used term. In those domains, people tend to call anything that requires some degree of behavioral restraint self-control. But, this is not always accurate, and such loose terminology when used in research settings hurts efforts to cleanly and clearly delineate different psychological and behavioral mechanisms that people and animals can engage to accomplish different kinds of tasks. In addition, lumping everything together as being self-control restricts how we can understand (and perhaps ultimately address) our fallibilities and shortcomings in our choices, and how we frame those choices. For example, a recent paper highlighted a clear relation between intelligence and what the authors called self-control (Meldrum, Petkovsek, Boutwell, & Young, 2017). However, their measures of "self-control" consisted of parent and teacher questionnaire ratings to the following questions: "Child bullies, is cruel, or mean," "Child does not feel guilty after misbehaving," "Child is impulsive or acts without thinking," "Child is restless, overly active, or cannot sit still," "Child is stubborn, sullen, or irritable," "Child has strong temper," "Child cheats or tells lies," "Child argues too much," and "Child has difficulty concentrating or cannot pay attention." I am not sure that any of those questions assess self-control as it is defined by most developmental or cognitive psychologists, and almost no one I know who studies self-control in animals would see a connection between their work and this type of measurement. This is not to suggest the data and implications of this study are uninformative. They are very informative, and this paper is important, but I think more so for highlighting the link between intelligence and a wide variety of reported behaviors in children. These survey questions measure executive attention, temperament, mood, and various forms of

Self-Control in Animals and People. DOI: https://doi.org/10.1016/B978-0-12-812508-3.00002-5
© 2018 Elsevier Inc. All rights reserved.

behavioral inhibition. These are not the same things as self-control, and so the conclusion that self-control is linked to intelligence is not necessarily supported by this effort (but see Shamosh et al., 2008; and the Further Reading section for this chapter). In other cases, researchers and theorists use terms other than self-control to refer to highly similar phenomena. For example, some refer to *effortful control* (e.g., Eisenberg et al., 2013; Kochanska, Murray, & Harlan, 2000). Because this is an important issue, to carefully define what is meant by self-control, I will offer a framework for what I think are or are not self-control tasks, and what mechanisms are engaged when people and some nonhuman animals make choices in those self-control tasks. I hope this framework will also lead you to think about the issue as being more than just "sometimes people show willpower, and sometimes they do not." I recognize and appreciate that not everyone will agree with my framework, but I hope it offers something to discuss, and perhaps can influence research teams to carefully consider the nature of the tasks they design, depending on what it is they want to claim they are assessing and studying. I also want to acknowledge that many of these ideas are not my own. I am particularly indebted to Fabio Paglieri, Ted Evans, and Jeff Stevens. I will discuss their contributions extensively throughout this book, and they have helped influence my thoughts on these issues through many stimulating conversations over many years (and perhaps a few beers). Many of their ideas are reflected in the framework I will outline in this chapter, although of course I am sure there are places where they would argue against what I have proposed.

DEFINING SELF-CONTROL

In an earlier commentary (Beran, 2015) I had defined self-control *as the ability or capacity to obtain an objectively more valuable outcome rather than an objectively less valuable outcome though tolerating a longer delay or a greater effort requirement in obtaining that more valuable outcome* (p. 2). I will modify that definition here because I think I left a few key aspects out of my previous effort. Now, I define self-control *as the ability or capacity to obtain a subjectively more valuable outcome rather than a subjectively less valuable outcome through choosing and then tolerating a longer delay or a greater effort requirement for obtaining that more valuable outcome.* Two things are changed in this new definition. First, I need to make clear that self-control must be a choice. This was an oversight in the definition in Beran (2015). Organisms forced to wait for delayed rewards, for example, are not engaging in self-control, any more than would people who are waiting in line for food when they are hungry and are in the only restaurant they can find. If, however, those people made the choice to stand in that line, because the wait was "worth it" for a particular meal they found more satisfying (perhaps in terms of better long-term health benefits) compared to the fast food options that they also could have chosen to satisfy their hunger, this would reflect self-control.[1]

Second, I think I was wrong to focus on objective valuation of options. There is no way to take any two outcomes and know which is the objectively more valuable one *for another person making the choice*. If offered $10 today or $100 in a week, it is not enough to know that $100 is 10 times more than $10, or that a week is 168 hours of delay. You also must know the circumstances of the person making the choice. If that person presently has no money and no way to eat, $10 now is going to be valued differently than if the person already has $100 and little to spend it on over the next week. The point is that each instance in which one chooses to take the more immediate, easier to obtain outcome, or chooses to wait for something larger or better (or work harder to gain that) can be different from all past similar circumstances. The context in which the choice is made is crucial because it interacts with the motivations of the chooser (see Lempert & Phelps, 2016). Paglieri (2013) noted this important point with a variety of examples in the real world. For example, he argued (and, I believe, rightfully so) that a person likely would not be inclined to stand in a line for 30 minutes in a store to receive $10 versus accepting $9 immediately. But, that same person might be willing to stay in the store, free to do as she pleases, for 30 minutes, and then receive the $10, rather than accept $9 immediately. The reason is that the first case requires waiting for reward, and the second consists of postponing reward. These are two different kinds of contexts. Paglieri, Addessi, Sbaffi, Tasselli, and Delfino (2015) argued that motivational confounds must be considered whenever one attempts to determine what a subject *should do* in a self-control test. They focused on different reward types offered to humans (blueberries or coins), and reported that people chose to wait more often for the larger amount of money than the larger amount of food even though in both cases, when there was no delay, they chose the larger amounts of both reward types (Fig. 2.1). A stronger preference for money over food was apparent even in the absence of delay. This is important for showing that the type of reward affects motivation, rather than delay tolerance. In this case, Paglieri et al. argued that people wait more for money simply because they value it more as a commodity in the context of the experiment, not because money makes them "more patient."

Paglieri (2016) outlined a number of additional reasons besides impulsivity why individuals might not always want to choose or be able to choose more delayed rewards, and reasons other than self-control for why they *may choose delayed rewards* (more on this in Chapter 9: How Do We Know Whether We Are Measuring Self-Control? Methodological Concerns Lead to

1. I think this example makes intuitive sense also because we know that part of the appeal of fast food is that it can be obtained more immediately, even if we would choose something else if the delays were equated.

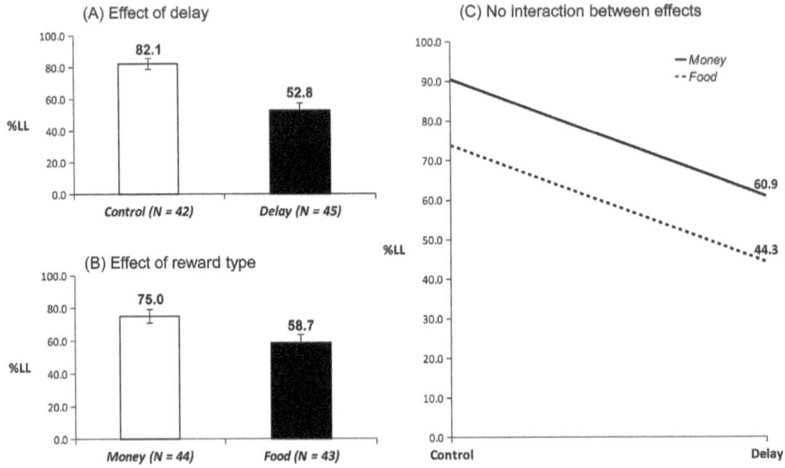

FIGURE 2.1 Results of Experiment 1 in Paglieri et al. (2015). Panel A shows the percentage of larger-later choices made by participants assigned to the control (no delay) and delay groups; data are averaged across food and monetary rewards. Panel B shows the percentage of larger later choices made by participants in the money and food conditions; data are averaged across delayed and immediate rewards. Panel C shows these data separated by reward type and delay. From Paglieri, F., Addessi, E., Sbaffi, A., Tasselli, M. I., and Delfino, A. (2015). Is it patience or motivation? On motivational confounds in intertemporal choice tasks. *Journal of the Experimental Analysis of Behavior, 103*, 196–217. *Reprinted with permission of Wiley.*

a New Test). Paglieri also reminded us that there are cases in which people show too much self-control, always making future-oriented choices with attendant delays, even in cases in which this is clearly detrimental to their current needs as well as never leading to actualized enjoyment of those delayed rewards. This is called temporal hyperopia, and is ideally represented in the character of Mr. Scrooge, before his eventful Christmas Eve adventures (Keinan & Kivetz, 2008; Kivetz & Keinan, 2006; Kivetz & Simonson, 2002). The point here is that it is never perfectly clear when self-control should be considered rational and when it should not. In this sense, choices to delay gratification or be impulsive are like many other economic decisions in terms of being subjective and contextual, with all of the attendant biases that occur in other choice domains (e.g., Kahneman & Tversky, 1984; Tversky & Kahneman, 1981). This is true not only for humans, but also for other animals (e.g., Stephens & Anderson, 2001; Stevens & Stephens, 2010).

In my definition offered here, there is a *capacity* for self-control in the sense that it is something one can demonstrate, through engagement of various behavioral and cognitive mechanisms, all of which lend themselves to choices to wait longer or to work more for the better outcome. Self-control is not a thing that we have or do not have in a certain amount. Rather, it is making and sustaining hard choices in the face of easier, more tempting options. By this definition, I also earlier noted that a self-control task has three essential features (Beran, 2015). First, there must be at least two known options available, and each outcome must be available to the subject at the moment of choice. By this, I do not mean that both can be obtained immediately, but rather than both are real and viable options. Second, those options each must be valuable to some extent but must be differentially preferred by the subject, if all else is the same (see Paglieri et al., 2015). In other words, one does not engage in self-control when choosing between taking the time to make a healthy salad versus just eating a rock. No one (that I know of!) would argue that eating a rock is a viable alternative to making a salad, even though it would be easy and quick to put a rock into your mouth. Eating a Twinkie for lunch instead of a salad, however, is a possibility, and one that could tempt a person on a diet who is comparing the time and effort it takes to make the salad (and be healthy) rather than to just enjoy eating the Twinkie.[2] Third, there must be a cost for obtaining the more preferred outcome. Typically, these costs have involved waiting longer for something better, but there are other costs one can experience. Choosing to work longer to earn more pay is an example of self-control, provided that leaving work earlier to do something fun or otherwise more immediately gratifying is a possibility. In some cases, effort and time are equivalent, and the cost is purely to the immediate sense of gratification and enjoyment. This is what happens when we reach into the refrigerator and take out a ready-made salad instead of a Twinkie. Both are immediately available, so time is a not a factor. Both are eaten at the same pace and satisfy hunger, so effort is not a factor. But assuming that you like Twinkies, that option is clearly more enjoyable in the immediate present! However, the more enjoyable option is not the best choice for good health due to its nutritional value, if good health is what one prefers in the long run. Thus, taking the salad out of the refrigerator instead of the Twinkie meets the criteria for being a self-control decision because it requires (1) comparing options on the basis of differential more immediate value and longer term value, (2) having a clear preference difference in which the self-control option is more preferred *all else being equal* (i.e., in this case, if we removed the more immediate pleasure of the taste of Twinkies and removed the delayed nature of the benefits gained from eating a healthy salad), and (3) having a greater immediate cost in that the salad cannot be enjoyed as much as the Twinkie would be in the present moment, and thus there must be a sacrifice of immediate pleasure for future benefit.

2. This was not even a possible self-control "test" during that awful period in American history when Twinkies were difficult to find (specifically, November 21, 2012 to July 15, 2013). Thankfully, this brief and dark period in world history was short lived—after all, even in a world overrun by zombies, we have some assurances that Twinkies can be found (that's a *Zombieland* reference, for those not into such movies).

The example above of working longer for more pay makes clear another important point. Because this example involves behaving more, this highlights that self-control and *behavioral inhibition* are not synonymous. Inhibition is the withholding of some behavior that otherwise one wants to do or tends to do, whether because it is pleasurable or it is prepotent (i.e., easier or more natural or more habitual). Of course, one could argue that the inhibition component in the job example is about inhibiting the desire to leave work early, but I think it is important to instead call this *choice with commitment*. There are two options here: to do more work for more pay, or do less work for less pay. The "temptation" is that leaving work now would feel best now. But, having more money later would feel better later. If, for some reason, that is not the case (for example, it is raining heavily outside, and you have nothing to do after work anyway), committing to work more is not an example of engaging in self-control.

In my perspective, *self-control is one form of behavioral inhibition*, but not all forms of behavioral inhibition require self-control. Fig. 2.2 presents a model of my thinking about how to conceptualize self-control (and tasks that assess self-control) within the broader context of motivational factors, perception, learning, cognition, and forms of behavioral inhibition. We begin with the idea (that I hope is not controversial!) that humans and nonhuman

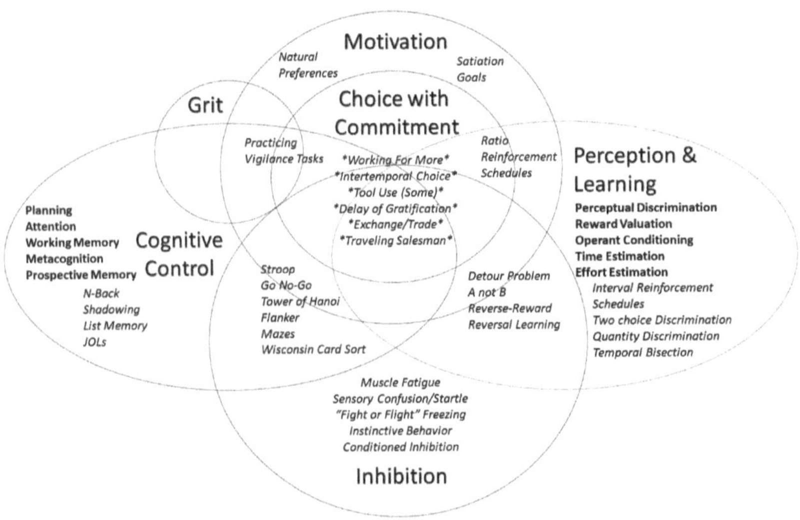

FIGURE 2.2 Mechanisms and tasks relevant to studying self-control. Each module in the model represents a system in large bolded letters (Motivation, Cognitive Control, Perception and Learning, Grit, Inhibition, and Choice with Commitment) as well as sub-systems (small bolded letters) in some cases. Points of overlap reflect areas in which different behavioral tests (in italics) may be relevant. Those highlighted with an * are self-control tasks, at least as I define self-control. See text for more details.

animals have perceptual experiences, are controlled at least partly by the constraints of perception and their ability to estimate time and space, and are controlled at least partly by well-established mechanisms of associative learning that control and affect behavior (called Perception & Learning in Fig. 2.2). There are also cognitive mechanisms available to at least some species that include so-called executive functions that deal with information manipulation and the engagement of memory processes as information is processed and used to guide responding (Cognitive Control in Fig. 2.2). And, there are motivational components that affect choice behavior (Motivation in Fig. 2.2), such as inherent preferences among stimuli, setting goals, experiencing levels of satiation, demonstrating curiosity, and showing perseverance. I think it is also uncontroversial to argue that motivation, perceptual processes, associative learning, and cognitive processing all can serve to inhibit automatic or prepotent response classes. When those mechanisms dictate stopping responses of organisms, we call that *behavioral inhibition*. From this conceptualization, one then can see a number of ways in which each of these factors might interact with behavioral inhibition and perhaps with each other to generate decisions and responses. The question is how to classify tasks within a framework that includes perception, learning, cognition, motivation, choice, and inhibitory control. I suggest the following framework for categorizing tasks and also for conceptualizing how different systems may interact to produce different kinds of behaviors.

SELF-CONTROL TASKS

In the center in the model are the key tasks, given the aims of this book. These are, to my mind, the clearest examples of self-control tasks. Here, motivation, perception and learning, cognition, and behavioral inhibition systems overlap. In intertemporal choice tasks, a participant is offered some form of smaller or less-preferred reward more immediately compared to some larger or more-preferred reward offered after a longer delay. In this case, the participant who chooses to wait is committing to waiting (or else, by definition, this form of intertemporal choice test is invalid; see Chapter 9: How Do We Know Whether We Are Measuring Self-Control? Methodological Concerns Lead to a New Test). Delay of gratification tests are also included as self-control tests. These tests all involve having to wait for something better or larger while constantly avoiding taking and consuming or otherwise enjoying things that one possesses during the delay. The most famous of these tests is the Marshmallow test (Mischel, 2014), which I will discuss in detail in Chapter 5 (Children's Delay of Gratification: How Long Would You Wait for Marshmallows?) as it has been used with humans. Other tests of delayed gratification also exist, such as the accumulation test, in which items accumulate during delay, as long as they are not taken and used or consumed. And, there are others, such as exchange tasks, in which lower preference items must be given in exchange for higher preference items. Many of these tests have been designed for use with nonhuman animals, because they do not require verbal instructions to teach the contingencies of waiting or giving up and taking what is available. I will cover many of these experimental approaches in Chapter 7, Would Animals Pass a Version of the Marshmallow Test?.

Humans use tools to accomplish many tasks, and in some of those cases, I think self-control is evident. One could, for example, smash the top of a beer bottle on a counter to more immediately get at some of the beer that would still be in that bottle, but choosing instead to ask for a bottle opener, and then opening the full bottle of beer is a more delayed, but certainly better outcome. This is a fairly trivial example in terms of time delays, but there are others that make the point even more convincingly. Every bridge built over water required time, energy, and money that otherwise could have been used more impulsively to spend on other things while swimming across a river or walking to a point where you could cross now even if it took longer now to do so. But, once the bridge was in place, it offered the clearly better long-term option. And, at any point, there would be agreement that having a bridge would be better than not having one, even if walking around the water source right now rather than spending weeks or months working on a bridge might be more appealing in the immediate present.

Animals also use tools (Beck, 1980; Seed & Byrne, 2010; Shumaker, Walkup, & Beck, 2011), and I think in some cases they too behave in a way that would seem to reflect self-control. For example, chimpanzees that gather hard-shelled nuts, and then search for a hammer stone to crack those nuts are investing time and energy to gain a better reward, but at the cost of a more immediate and certain opportunity to forage on available lower-calorie and less tasty foods that are plentiful. The travel paths that animals take also may reflect self-control, particularly when those paths are organized in such a way that more immediately available food or water resources are not the ones that are approached, because a more circumspect or longer trip leads to even better resources. Or, in the case of the traveling salesman problem, an organized path might involve foregoing close options (such as the next closest source or "door") because that allows for an overall more efficient and beneficial coverage of one's territory. In these cases, there is the more immediate gain that is present, and that is tempting to some degree, but the organism must instead structure its behavior on other than a what-is-closest algorithm. This requires the commitment to a travel path that is optimal in the long run, but not ideal for reaching the next closest reward as fast as possible. In some cases, an argument can be made that nonhuman animals who take such optimal travel paths or who organize their efforts to use tools may be engaging in future-oriented thought (Boesch-Achermann & Boesch, 1993; Byrne, Sanz, & Morgan, 2013; Janmaat, Polansky, Ban, & Boesch, 2014; Mulcahy & Call, 2006; Osvath & Osvath, 2008), perhaps even through "mental time travel" (Cheke & Clayton, 2010; Corballis, 2013; Suddendorf & Busby, 2003; Suddendorf & Corballis, 2007, 2010). I will discuss how future-oriented cognition may relate to self-control in Chapter 14, Mental Time Travel: What Is It, and How Does It Relate to Self-Control? For now, suffice it to say that I think certain problems that present themselves during travel through space or during tool use may tap into mechanisms that promote self-control.

Notice that I placed one self-control task just at the fringe of the Inhibition module, and that is the case of working more to obtain something better. I hinted at this type of situation earlier, with working more hours for more pay, instead of leaving early. I think it is fair to argue this is actually inhibition of the more prepotent response *all things considered equal*—which is to not do work when one could be relaxing or recreating. If this is how you think of the situation, then this is an example of self-control that requires inhibition. However, if the more motivating state is having more money later, but more effort is needed to realize that state, I think the individual who works more to gain more is exhibiting self-control without need of inhibitory mechanisms being at work. Other similar cases include practicing various skills (e.g., playing a musical instrument, practicing basketball free throws, and working on your golf swing), where more effort is needed now for a gain later in proficiency, and presumably there is the cost of time and energy directed toward the practice. I realize that this is perhaps one of the weaker "fits" in the model because these are cases not typically studied in traditional assessments of self-control. However, there is a growing and highly influential literature on "grit" that speaks directly to this aspect of human (and perhaps nonhuman[3]) behavior. Grit has been defined as passion and perseverance toward especially long-term goals (Duckworth, Peterson, Matthews, & Kelly, 2007). Grit has been shown to relate closely to other measures of self-control, and to predict in some cases success outcomes beyond what is predicted by general intelligence (e.g., Duckworth & Seligman, 2005; Duckworth et al., 2007). However, Duckworth and Gross (2014) noted important differences between self-control and grit. They defined self-control as the successful resolution of a conflict between two action impulses—one that corresponds to a goal that is more valued in the moment, and another that corresponds to a goal that is of a greater value at a

3. To my knowledge, no one has studied grit in animals, perhaps because much of what we might say qualifies is difficult to attribute to grit in animals rather than to some kind of instinctively programmed behavior. For instance, a human who sticks with a difficult building project and ends up with a very nice place to live, despite all of the problems would perhaps be seen as having a lot of grit. But, if a beaver showed continued effort to improve its dam and lodge, I am not sure if this is the same thing. The same is true for wild chimpanzees who often build large evening nests in trees, and those nests vary considerably in size and impressiveness as well as the time taken to complete them. Do the most impressive nests that take the longest to build reflect "grit" in chimpanzees?

later time, and that is more enduring. They contrasted this with grit, which involves a dominant goal and then a tenacious pursuit of that goal. The key issue here is that there is high motivation, and cognitive/behavioral mechanisms employed to achieve that goal, but there is no competing alternative that also has value (i.e., the alternative is to quit). Thus, in Fig. 2.2, grit is outside of the collection of self-control tasks, but I think still related.

As pointed out to me by Fabio Paglieri, one important consideration regarding grit is in its role with self-control. He offered the idea of working toward a college degree, in which the student must engage in consistent and prolonged self-control toward what is really only a long-term goal—the degree. However, he suggests that this kind of discrete goal does not offer much by way of "partial victories" when you do things like avoid partying all weekend to pass a specific test. After all, without a degree, any given exam score does not have much value. Instead, we tend to turn these long-term discrete goals into a number of smaller, more gradual goals, such as making the Dean's list in a given semester or doing well on mid-term exams. Our opportunities to celebrate these goals then afford the "push" we need to stay on track toward the true, longer term goal. And, it is perhaps the case that those with the strongest levels of grit are also those who best break down these long-term goals into shorter "victories" that are manageable.

SELF-REGULATORY INHIBITION TASKS

Other highly relevant tasks in this model are those in which perceptual processes, learning mechanisms, and/or cognitive processes sometimes generate behavioral inhibition. I think that a number of inhibitory tasks fall into this category *without being tasks of self-control*. Fig. 2.2 outlines some of these tasks, and they are often used in the self-control or self-regulatory literatures. I prefer calling these tasks of *self-regulatory inhibition*, because to me that term reflects that individuals are faced with competing response options (i.e., only one can be implemented), and they must choose or respond on the basis of only one response being "correct" both in terms of temporal reward or payoff and magnitude of reward or payoff. And, importantly, in these choices there is an easier, more prepotent, or more well-rehearsed behavior that must be inhibited to instead produce the appropriate response right now. In essence, what these tasks all share is the need for an organism to change what it is doing or would normally do. Most importantly, in these tasks the wrong outcome is not something that the organisms would otherwise accept as an outcome for their efforts, and as such there is not choice available in these tasks. An important point here is that I am defining choice in a more restrictive way than is sometimes the case in experimental psychology. Choice in this model is not about behaving in one of multiple possible ways, such as "choosing" to turn left in a maze instead of turning right. In this model, choice is about commitment to one of two (or more) possible outcomes, none of which are objectively "wrong" or undesirable. Thus, in the tasks that involve inhibition without need of self-control, there are negative outcomes, that are not desired. But, in self-control tasks, choice with commitment[4] is a crucial feature, as I described earlier. This is not true for self-regulatory inhibition.

At the simplest level, consider adjusting movement through space. When we walk down a sidewalk at a comfortable pace, and then recognize we are just about to step into a puddle, and quickly pull our shoe back up and awkwardly hop-step around the puddle, this is a type of behavioral inhibition, but it does not require self-control. When we see our cell phone in the gap between our car seat and the center panel of our car, and reach down and around under the seat to get it rather than reach directly toward it (where the gap is too small for our hand), this is also behavioral inhibition without need of self-control. In fact, this example has been adapted for one of the most common tasks that have been used with animals, called the detour task, sometimes with the unfortunate side effect that it is called a self-control task. I will talk more about that shortly. I will also talk in great detail in Chapter 6 (The Reversed-Reward Contingency Task—Why Pointing Away from What You Want is so Difficult for Animals) about a widely used task called the reverse-reward contingency task (Boysen & Berntson, 1995; Boysen, Berntson, Hannan, & Cacioppo, 1996; Shifferman, 2009), which has proven to be very difficult for many animal species to master. I will outline why this might be, and what we might be able to learn about self-control from our use of this task, even though it is not formally a self-control task as I am defining such tasks here.

COGNITIVE CONTROL TASKS

On the "cognitive" side of things, tasks of so-called executive functions that reflect control mechanisms involve inhibition. Perhaps the most famous is the Stroop test (Stroop, 1935), in which subjects must respond to stimuli on the basis of properties other than those that are typically most relevant and more readily apparent, such as trying to name the color of letters in a word

4. Fabio Paglieri once wrote this in an email exchange we had: "To me, self-control is (i) having a plan about oneself, and (ii) being able to execute that plan. Thus, behavioral inhibition is necessary for self-control, but not sufficient—you also need an overarching purpose, plan, or guiding idea." I think his ideas are exactly correct, and are what I am trying to capture in the notion of *choice with commitment*. This is the idea that there is an option to do one of two (or more things), all of which have value but only one of which is seen as better for the individual *in the long run*. Thus, self-control involves opting for the more effortful or delayed option with the purpose of seeing through that effort or time demand to achieve that outcome. As Fabio also noted in that email, the "having a plan about oneself" helps justify why the word "self" figures so prominently in "self-control." Note that none of this requires self-awareness or theory of mind in the individual in question, but rather is about a minimally future-oriented choice for the self.

rather than read the color name that the word spells (e.g., responding "Green" when seeing the word RED printed in green color). Stroop tests have been used in thousands of studies with humans (see MacLeod, 1991), and in some studies with animals (e.g., Beran, Washburn, & Rumbaugh, 2007; Washburn, 1994), to measure control processes and inhibition. Similar tests such as Go No-Go tasks involve stopping oneself from making a typical response when a specific kind of cue is experienced (Nosek & Banaji, 2001). Flanker tests involve ignoring cues that are highly salient but distract from the response goal (e.g., having to respond "right" when a central arrow in a row of arrows points right, but all others point to the left; Eriksen & Eriksen, 1974). Even performing mazes or the Tower of Hanoi task (Simon & Hayes, 1976; Simon, 1975), which require anticipating future moves and seeing points where one must go away from what appears to be a closer approximation of the goal to actually get closer to the goal, does not require self-control, but does require self-regulation and inhibition. Thus, cognitive tasks such as these also tap into basic mechanisms that are relevant to self-control choices, even if they are not self-control tasks themselves. The important point here is that one must be careful not to conflate all of these, simply because a subject in one of these tests inhibits responding at the right moment, toward achieving a goal.

There are tasks that measure cognitive control without need of inhibition, or that reflect perceptual and learning phenomena, again without need of inhibitory actions. Although these are not self-control tasks, they (and the processes that engage those tasks) are relevant to the more general capacities of humans and animals to deal with information as it may be presented in self-control contexts. For example, tasks assessing executive functions as evidence of cognitive control include N-back tasks, shadowing tasks, serial memory tasks, and judgments of learning (JOLs). The N-back task requires remembering a stimulus that was seen (or heard) N stimuli previously, so it measures working memory capacity. Shadowing tasks involve selective attention to one stream of information among others. Serial memory tasks involve structuring memory for different items in the same experience, and JOLs involve evaluating current states of knowledge against desired states of knowledge. Each of these capacities can easily be seen as relevant to an individual who is trying to weigh the value of two or more future outcomes against their delay to delivery, or as being relevant in how individuals might think about contingencies involved in temporal choice tasks. Other tasks that assess perceptual discrimination and learning such as quantity discrimination (i.e., "which is more" tasks), time estimation ("how long has it been" tasks), discrimination (which stimulus gets rewarded tasks) and general schedules of reinforcement (fixed and variable interval schedules) all lend themselves to showing us the capacities of individuals and species to be able to tell things apart in terms of their magnitudes, the required efforts to obtain those things, or temporal differences in general. Thus, I chose to include these tasks here as examples of well-known and widely used tests that I think do relate *at a broad level* to self-control by providing measures of some of the most fundamental processes involved in accurately structuring and representing a self-control test. Self-control is about choice and commitment, and that involves some level of understanding options, in terms of the amounts, delays, efforts, and hedonic values. Those choices and commitments require the ability to perceive, compare, remember, and perhaps even anticipate aspects of choice options, and thus are reliant on other basic perceptual, learning, and cognitive mechanisms.

What about the possibility of cognitive control tasks that involve motivational systems and the commitment to a course of action interacting with perceptual/learning systems but that do not require self-control or behavioral inhibition? I can think of some examples that I think fill these voids in the model. On the more purely cognitive side, vigilance tasks seem to qualify. An individual tracking and monitoring stimuli must sustain motivation to engage and commit to that task, but there is no external object or event that offers a tempting alternative because it occurs sooner or is more hedonically appealing. One can, of course, choose not to be vigilant, but not because the alternative is a preferred outcome (e.g., to miss a target item). The goal of vigilance tasks is to remain vigilant, and to commit to engaging attentional resources toward that goal. On the learning side of things, I think ratio schedules of reinforcement may be one example of tasks that involve commitment (to finish out the schedule by pressing, tapping, or otherwise responding in some way), but those schedules do not require self-control or inhibition. That said, I think these schedules and some types of interval schedules are important to consider, because they largely are adapted for presenting intertemporal choice tests, which do assess self-control, and which I will discuss in great detail in the next two chapters.

INHIBITORY BEHAVIOR

There is behavioral inhibition without any need to infer learning-based or cognitive contributions. When muscles fatigue, behavior decreases or stops. Some forms of instinctive responding are elicited by unconditioned stimuli in the environment, such as freezing behavior after a sensory experience linked to a predator, or the freezing that occurs when a sensory system is confused by signals or cannot gather information. Some forms of classical conditioning such as conditioned inhibition also lead to behavioral decreases or shifts, without need of learning through S-R associations or cognitive processes. One could argue about whether there are also operant learning processes at work in some of these cases, but that is not a discussion that is relevant to my aims here.

MOTIVATIONAL STATES

The motivational system generates preferences among things. For example, preferring apples to oranges requires no cognitive processing, no extended learning, and no inhibition. The same is true for many instance of mate preference for many species. Organisms prefer some things over others, and although that information can be used to design tests of self-control by using preferences to determine more immediate and more delayed rewards, those preferences do not emerge from other systems in the model. However, motivation is a key factor in the model when it interacts with other systems.

Examining Fig. 2.2, all of the self-control tasks fit my criteria outlined earlier. They all offer two or more viable and beneficial outcomes, meaning that none of them present the chooser with bad outcomes, or negative experiences, except as those experiences might be *relative to the other possible outcomes*. In the self-regulatory tasks, failure is negative. Stepping in the puddle is not a good thing. Reading the word in the Stroop test instead of naming the letter color is an error—not a good thing. Reaching toward your cell phone directly and not getting it is not a good thing. Taking the shortest immediate route that seems to lead to the goal of a maze even though it will dead end is not a good thing. Self-control tests offer two outcomes that are both beneficial, but to differing degrees. For instance, more money later versus less money now. Or, they can both be negative things, to differing degrees. For instance, foregoing a small number of calories each meal for a few months before a life insurance physical examination, or crash dieting 2 weeks before that physical examination. The point is that the outcomes are qualitatively of the same hedonic type (both positive or both negative) and are distinguished only on the basis of their delay or effort to be obtained.

In each of these self-control tasks, the available options are all valuable and would all be perfectly acceptable immediately and even ideal to accept if there was nothing else to consider. Receiving a small food reward after a short delay, eating one marshmallow now in the marshmallow test, keeping the first item you are given in an exchange task, settling for the easy-to-eat leaves and plants rather than an opened nut, or going to the closest house or food patch to make a sales pitch or eat or drink what is there are all acceptable outcomes. But, in each of those cases, something even better does exist (a bigger reward later, two marshmallows later, the better item you can exchange for, the cracked open high-calorie nut, or the overall more efficient sales route or foraging route). And, that something better requires a level of choice and commitment that comes with some kind of cost to the immediate self. Thus, to choose to delay for better rewards, or give up what you have, or work longer or harder for more reward, requires self-control.

The tasks I list in the center of Fig. 2.2 are not an exhaustive list of self-control tests (or an exhaustive list for any of the other areas in the model). Throughout the remainder of the book I will present many kinds of tests, and here I have simplified things somewhat by choosing broad task categories such as intertemporal choice tests and delay of gratification tests to include a variety of methods. The point is that these classes of tasks are those which I believe require self-control on the part of choosers, and that would engage behavioral and cognitive mechanisms that judge and generate inhibitory responses or choice responses that reflect comparing two positive (but quantitatively or qualitatively different) outcomes that vary on the basis of time or effort needed to obtain each. And, these are the kinds of tasks that are widely used across species.

Some situations present a real challenge to what is outlined in Fig. 2.2. Perhaps one of the examples I have struggled with the longest as I thought about how to define self-control is the example of a cheetah (or any stalking predator) crouched and waiting to begin its pursuit of a prey animal. Assuming the predator has some control over when it begins its charge, and that the longer it waits, the closer the prey will come (and the more likely the hunt will end with success), the scenario seems to fit my definition of one that requires engaging in self-control behavior. There are two options available (charge now or charge later), and the animal must commit to whatever course of action it takes (to charge or to wait). Presumably, there is a continual increase in anxiousness to release and charge that is satisfied when the charge begins, but only one outcome (waiting longer) provides the better chance to get the prey. So, there is a cost to waiting, as this anxiousness builds and the attractiveness of the prey item increases, especially if the distance between predator and prey decreases during this time. Despite this description, I struggle to see this as a case of self-control akin to the others I have discussed. Perhaps this is because this example feels more hard-wired, as predatory instinct. But, it is also easy to understand that a predator will learn, over repeated hunting experiences, that early charges are much less likely to lead to success, and so perhaps the learning component (i.e., Law of Effect) controls behavior almost entirely to the point that the predator no longer engages in an actual choice to charge or to wait. In other words, it could be that the decision is cued by environmental features nearly exclusively, and thus there is no real aspect of choice and commitment to this behavior. I am not sure, and so I think there is interesting work to be done to better understand whether these behaviors of animals are similar to those made in laboratory-based delay of gratification tests or intertemporal choice tests.

The framework I outline here shares some commonalities with that recently offered by Duckworth and Steinberg (2015). They argued that it is important to distinguish in the empirical literature two things: (1) the overt expression of self-control and (2) its underlying psychological processes. I have tried to model this in Fig. 2.2 as well. For them, the psychological processes are of two types: volitional processes that facilitate self-controlled behavior (what I am calling *choice with commitment* responses) and "impulsigenic processes" that lead individuals to accept immediately rewarding outcomes that are not in the best long-term interests of those individuals. These processes include reward sensitivity, sensation seeking, and domain-specific cravings. In my model, these processes are represented in the Perception and Learning module and the Motivation module. I would add to their ideas about impulsigenic processes the additional factors I mentioned earlier of accurately reflecting time, quantity, and value. I think these abilities are highly relevant to understanding the "pulls" toward impulsivity that individuals feel when faced with contexts in which self-control mechanisms could be engaged. These ideas all reflect the notion that organisms can experience situations in which they compare and contrast longer term goals and shorter term, more immediately enjoyable or beneficial outcomes.

Some have argued that what occurs in those situations is a competition between processes designed to achieve delayed outcomes versus those designed to produce satisfaction more immediately. This "dual-process" approach was espoused by Metcalfe and Mischel (1999) in their "hot/cool" conception of willpower and delay of gratification and in the dual motive approach of Fujita (2011) who argued that self-control is not just inhibiting impulsive responses but also involves behavior that advances distal versus proximate motivations (also see Fujita & Han, 2009). Others have offered dual-process approaches that include impulsive and reflective systems, for example, that frame the nature of the conflict felt by the individual faced with choices (e.g., Hofmann, Friese, & Strack, 2009). Or, frameworks in which there are future-oriented "planning selves" and short-sighted and impulsive "doing selves" (Thaler & Shefrin, 1981). The main idea behind these dual-process approaches is to recognize that there are dispositional and situational factors that can increase impulsivity or self-control, and that both need to be considered as they affect eventual choice. Much of the past research has focused on the impulsivity side of things (e.g., Madden & Bickel, 2010; Stevens, 2017), but more recent work has begun to focus on the reflective mechanisms that are sometimes available to lead individuals toward self-controlled responding, including executive functions and meta-cognitions (e.g., Bembenutty & Karabenick, 1998; Duckworth, Gendler, & Gross, 2014; Mischel & Mischel, 1983), as outlined in Fig. 2.2. As Hofmann et al. noted, this dual-systems approach highlights the "tug-of-war" between impulse and self-control.

Not everyone agrees that a dual-process approach appropriately captures the nature of choices that involve self-control. Shenhav (2017) outlined the nature of this debate, noting that there are those who argue that a dual process is not warranted when it comes to self-control (Kable & Glimcher, 2007). Part of this argument is that it is an oversimplification to consider that our choice conflicts come from only two driving forces. One can imagine many competing "pulls" on those faced with intertemporal choices, including those from motivational, perceptual, and cognitive systems. Another perspective is that self-control can be described by a value-based decision-making mechanism that operates in all kinds of choice situations, not just those requiring inhibition or the comparison of now versus later outcomes. Berkman, Hutcherson, Livingston, Kahn, and Inzlicht (2017) proposed that individuals faced with a choice, for example, of a high-calorie treat now or weight loss later are not engaging in controlled behavior by a "cool" system in the face of a competing "hot system" pulling toward eating the treat. Rather, one process calculates a value for each outcome option. This process integrates all the different aspects of the choice—its value, delay, effort, motivational properties, etc. The key issue is how attention is focused on each aspect of the choice, and thus individual differences in motivation and cognitive and attentional control influence what individuals choose. Engaging in self-distraction, for example, is a crucial aspect of self-control, as when someone chooses to put away a tempting treat or someone chooses to call a friend as a distraction when tempted to smoke a cigarette. This conception explains why self-control is related to executive functions (e.g., Hofmann, Schmeichel, & Baddeley, 2012), and why self-control is not the same thing as inhibition. Berkman et al. argued that choices might vary from time to time (sometimes we eat the treat, other times we stay on the diet) for reasons other than weakened self-control or failed cognitive control. Instead, each choice is unique and newly acquired information can lead to changes from one instance to another of the same choice options (see Fig. 2.3).

Each of these conceptualizations of what self-control is, *by way of processing mechanism(s)*, still highlights the situational and dispositional attributes of the choice and the chooser, but in dual-process theories there is conflict, and in value-based decision theories, there is accumulation of different aspects of each choice, resulting in the choice of greater value being selected. Shenhav (2017) noted that in some cases, the two theories are equally good at predicting and explaining choice, although there are clearly different implications for intervening to improve self-control that could emerge on the basis of whichever theory proves more accurate over time. I see value in the ideas of value-based decision models, but I also see the intuitive appeal of dual-process models that seem to better fit the experience of individuals faced with choices, in terms of competing "pulls." That said, Fig. 2.2 presents a single-process model, more in line with the value-based decision-making models, given that inputs from cognitive processes, motivational states, perceptual mechanisms, and learning processes are combined in determining choices. These systems are not in conflict, but may differentially contribute to choices, including in repeated instances of the same choice, through the differential selective engagement of each of these systems in that moment of choice.

Although much of the remainder of this book focuses on those tests that I think are assessments of self-control, and what we have learned from those tests, it is important to discuss at least briefly some of the tasks that may not fit my definition of self-control but that have been presented to various animal species to great effect. I think these tasks have a lot of value, even if I

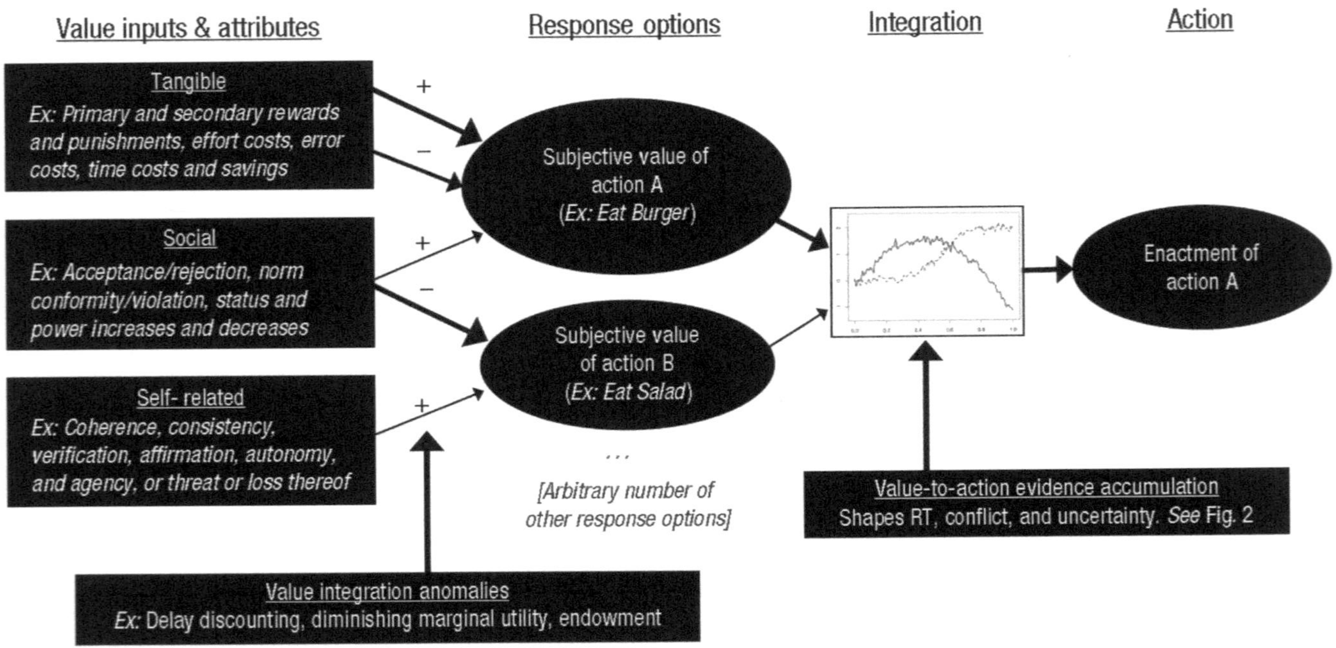

FIGURE 2.3 Value-based choice model of self-control in Berkman et al. (2017). The cumulative subjective value of each response option (middle column) is a weighted sum of value inputs based on the option's attributes (left column). Example attributes for a choice option include primary rewards, effort costs, social acceptance or rejection, and self-consistency and verification. The subjective value integration is not strictly rational but instead is modulated by a number of choice "anomalies" such as the tendency to discount delayed gains. Value accumulates dynamically and stochastically across time until a threshold is reached, and attention can influence the accumulation process by altering the relevant attributes. The option with the greatest value when the threshold is reached or time runs out is enacted. In Berkman, E. T., Hutcherson, C. A., Livingston, J. L., Kahn, L. E., and Inzlicht, M. (2017). Self-control as value-based choice. *Current Directions in Psychological Science, 26*, 422–428. *Reprinted with permission of Sage.*

would not call them self-control tests (Beran, 2015), because they give us additional insights into what animals can and cannot do when presented with challenges that require inhibiting responding. I think that these tasks, combined with the self-control tasks I will discuss, should continue to be administered broadly across species, toward the goal of better understanding the phylogenetic map of self-regulatory abilities.

One of the most famous tasks in comparative psychology that examines inhibitory control is called the detour task. Kabadayi, Bobrowicz, and Osvath (2018) summarized the more than 120-year history of this task, and so I will offer some highlights of their summary here. Discussion of the detour problem with animals goes back to Hobhouse (1901) who wrote about dogs running toward a door after seeing an owner through a window, rather than running through the window (although, I imagine quite a few dogs, and at least a few humans, have run through windows as well!). Thorndike (1911) used the detour problem extensively, with a variety of species including those rarely tested, such as chickens and fish, and he reported variable performance of these species. He also argued that success in the test would demonstrate responding on the basis of other than instinct, because instinct would drive an animal to take the most direct approach to what it wanted, even with a barrier in place. Köhler (1925) gave the test to dogs, chickens, and chimpanzees, arguing that success might reflect insight or prospection because those who succeeded had to "think through" the problem. Other early comparative psychologists also discussed the detour problem at length (Hull, 1938; Lewin, 1933; Tolman, 1932). Kabadayi et al. noted that since then, at least 127 additional studies with at least 96 other species have been conducted, and they very nicely outlined the key behaviors and cognitive processes that are likely involved in the detour problem (see their Table 1).

In the detour problem, the idea is that a direct approach to an item will not let you obtain it. Instead, you have to go around the barrier, moving away from the reward so as to get to it. A large variety of barriers have been used (Fig. 2.4), and there are two common versions of this task, one where the goal or reward remains visible on the other side of the barrier, and another where the goal or reward is shown but then is not visible during the time the animal (or child) moves to retrieve it. A number of factors seem to impact how readily and quickly subjects can move around the barrier (if they can at all). Visibility of the reward seems to create a real problem compared to when reward is not visible (chickens: Regolin, Vallortigara, & Zanforlin, 1994; dogs: Brucks, Marshall-Pescini, Wallis, Huber, & Range, 2017; human infants: Lockman & Adams, 2001; mice: Juszczak & Miller, 2016; birds: Miller & Tallarico, 1974), perhaps because of the prepotency of the reward, which naturally attracts attention and the desire to move toward that reward (Vallortigara & Regolin, 2002). Distance to the goal also seems to matter. When the goal is farther away, it appears to be easier to detour rather than going directly at the reward (Diamond & Gilbert, 1989; Junghans, Sterck,

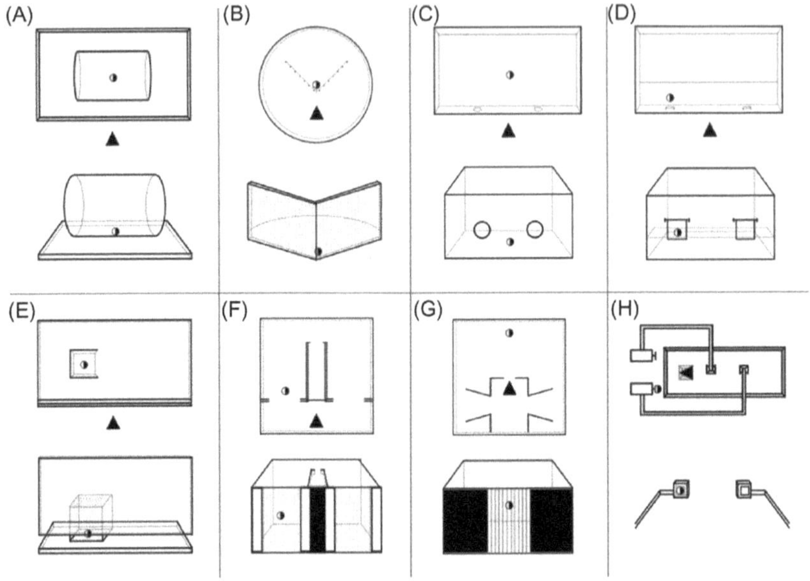

FIGURE 2.4 Examples of different detour problems as described in Kabadayi et al. (2018). Each setup comes with two symbols: a half-filled circle (a goal), and a filled triangle (a subject), and occupies a separate panel. Within each panel, the upper figure shows the bird-eye view, while the lower figure the first-person view. The setups belong to the following tasks: (A) the cylinder task requires a reaching detour through one of the side openings of the transparent cylinder. (B) Inward detour task requires locomotion detour around a V-shaped transparent/fence barrier. (C) Plexiglas-hole task requires a reaching detour through one of the two holes in a Plexiglas panel placed upright between the subject and the reward. (D) Swing-door task requires a reaching detour through the door that is furthest from the goal. The doors can only be opened by pushing them forward, and an attempt to open the door that is closer to the goal results in the goal falling backwards and becoming out of reach. (E) Detour reaching task (object-retrieval task) requires a reaching detour through the side opening of the transparent box. The box has only one opening, which allows changing the open side facing the subject across trials. (F) Delayed-detour task requires passing by an opaque corridor and in the end selecting between two paths, only one of which leads to the goal room. (G) Four-compartment box task requires the subject to turn its back to the goal and choose among four doors, only two of which lead to the goal room. (H) Detour-choice task requires the subject to turn its back to the goal that is placed on top of a tower, and select among two poles, only one of which leads to the tower where the goal is placed. From Kabadayi, C., Bobrowicz, K., and Osvath, M. (2018). The detour paradigm in animal cognition. *Animal Cognition, 21*, 21–35. *Reprinted with permission of Springer.*

Overduin de Vries, Evers, & De Ridder, 2016; Köhler, 1925; Lock & Collett, 1979; Regolin, Vallortigara, & Zanforlin, 1995). For versions of the test where the goal goes out of view, a large number of species seem to be successful, including octopi (Wells, 1964), spiders (Cross & Jackson, 2016), chickens (Regolin et al., 1995), and canaries, herring gulls and quail (Zucca, Antonelli, & Vallortigara, 2005).

The detour task was used in many cases to study learning, and specifically how individuals or species would improve with repeated experience (e.g., Lockman & Adams, 2001; Spigel, 1964; Thorndike, 1911; Vlamings, Hare, & Call, 2010; Wyrwicka, 1959). The main reason I am discussing it here, though, is that it also has been used as a measure of self-control by some research teams. MacLean et al. (2014) conducted an impressive and massive study, giving 36 species (29 mammals and 7 birds) a version of the detour task called the cylinder task. They reported that absolute brain size strongly predicted performance with the cylinder task, and they noted that the great apes were the best performers. They titled their paper "The evolution of self-control," and argued that their detour task and A-not-B task were measures of self-control. I argued they were not (Beran, 2015). Subsequent work by Kabadayi, Taylor, von Bayern, and Osvath (2016) also found that ravens, New Caledonian crows and Jackdaws matched the performance of the great apes on detour tasks, despite having much smaller brains. Subsequent to that report, however, Kabadayi et al. (2017) reported that parrots performed very poorly on the task, which seemed not to make much sense given the corvids' performances. In those later tests, and others, most research teams have returned to calling these detour problems tests of inhibitory control, rather than self-control. I think this is a good thing. Those tests require the inhibition presented in Fig. 2.2, as well as perceptual and learning contributions, but they lack the kind of choice aspect that is required for a self-control test.

Having now outlined my definition of self-control, and having classified tasks as being self-control tasks or not in the way that I think reflects this definition, it is time to narrow our focus to self-control tasks given to humans and nonhuman animals. The most widely used tasks are the intertemporal choice tasks, which are the focus of the next two chapters. Then, I will discuss the highly influential reverse-reward task and various tests of delayed gratification given to children and nonhuman animals. After finishing that part of the book, I hope the reader will have a thorough appreciation of the efforts of many research teams to document and understand the choice behaviors made in contexts in which variable rewards were available after variable delays or variable levels of effort.

REFERENCES

Beck, B. B. (1980). *Animal tool behavior: The use and manufacture of tools by animals*. New York: Garland STPM Press.

Bembenutty, H., & Karabenick, S. A. (1998). Academic delay of gratification. *Learning and Individual Differences*, *10*, 329–346.

Beran, M. J. (2015). The comparative science of "self-control": What are we talking about? *Frontiers in Psychology*, *6*, Article 51.

Beran, M. J., Washburn, D. A., & Rumbaugh, D. M. (2007). A stroop-like effect in color-naming of color-word lexigrams by a chimpanzee (*Pan troglodyte*). *The Journal of General Psychology*, *134*, 217–228.

Berkman, E. T., Hutcherson, C. A., Livingston, J. L., Kahn, L. E., & Inzlicht, M. (2017). Self-control as value-based choice. *Current Directions in Psychological Science*, *26*, 422–428.

Boesch-Achermann, H., & Boesch, C. (1993). Tool use in wild chimpanzees: New light from dark forests. *Current Directions in Psychological Science*, *2*, 18–21.

Boysen, S. T., & Berntson, G. G. (1995). Responses to quantity: Perceptual versus cognitive mechanisms in chimpanzees (*Pan troglodytes*). *Journal of Experimental Psychology: Animal Behavior Processes*, *21*, 82–86.

Boysen, S. T., Berntson, G. G., Hannan, M. B., & Cacioppo, J. T. (1996). Quantity-based interference and symbolic representations in chimpanzees (*Pan troglodytes*). *Journal of Experimental Psychology: Animal Behavior Processes*, *22*, 76–86.

Brucks, D., Marshall-Pescini, S., Wallis, L. J., Huber, L., & Range, F. (2017). Measures of dogs' inhibitory control abilities do not correlate across tasks. *Frontiers in Psychology*, *8*, Article 849.

Byrne, R. W., Sanz, C. M., & Morgan, D. B. (2013). Chimpanzees plan their tool use. In C. M. Sanz, J. Call, & C. Boesch (Eds.), *Tool use in animals. Cognition and ecology* (pp. 48–63). Cambridge: Cambridge University Press.

Cheke, L. G., & Clayton, N. S. (2010). Mental time travel in animals. *Wiley Interdisciplinary Reviews: Cognitive Science*, *1*, 915–930.

Corballis, M. C. (2013). Mental time travel: A case for evolutionary continuity. *Trends in Cognitive Sciences*, *17*, 5–6.

Cross, F. R., & Jackson, R. R. (2016). The execution of planned detours by spider-eating predators. *Journal of the Experimental Analysis of Behavior*, *105*, 194–210.

Duckworth, A. L., Gendler, T. S., & Gross, J. J. (2014). Self-control in school-age children. *Educational Psychologist*, *49*, 199–217.

Duckworth, A. L., & Gross, J. J. (2014). Self-control and grit: Related but separable determinants of success. *Current Directions in Psychological Science*, *23*(5), 319–325.

Duckworth, A. L., Peterson, C., Matthews, M. D., & Kelly, D. R. (2007). Grit: Perseverance and passion for long-term goals. *Journal of Personality and Social Psychology*, *92*, 1087–1101.

Duckworth, A. L., & Seligman, M. E. P. (2005). Self-discipline outdoes IQ in predicting academic performance of adolescents. *Psychological Science*, *16*, 939–944.

Duckworth, A. L., & Steinberg, L. (2015). Unpacking self-control. *Child Development Perspectives*, *9*(1), 32–37.

Eisenberg, N., Edwards, A., Spinrad, T. L., Sallquist, J., Eggum, N. D., & Reiser, M. (2013). Are effortful and reactive control unique constructs in young children? *Developmental Psychology*, *49*, 2082–2094.

Eisenreich, B. R., & Hayden, B. Y. (2018). Cognitive science: Persistent apes are intelligent apes. *Current Biology*, *28*, R160–R162.

Eriksen, B. A., & Eriksen, C. W. (1974). Effects of noise letters upon identification of a target letter in a non-search task. *Perception and Psychophysics*, *16*, 143–149.

Fujita, K. (2011). On conceptualizing self-control as more than the effortful inhibition of impulses. *Personality and Social Psychology Review*, *15*, 352–366.

Fujita, K., & Han, H. A. (2009). Moving beyond deliberative control of impulses: The effect of construal levels on evaluative associations in self-control conflicts. *Psychological Science*, *20*, 799–804.

Hobhouse, L. T. (1901). *Mind in evolution*. New York: The Macmillan Company.

Hofmann, W., Friese, M., & Strack, F. (2009). Impulse and self-control from a dual-systems perspective. *Perspectives on Psychological Science*, *4*, 162–176.

Hofmann, W., Schmeichel, B. J., & Baddeley, A. D. (2012). Executive functions and self-regulation. *Trends in Cognitive Sciences*, *16*, 174–180.

Hull, C. L. (1938). The goal-gradient hypothesis applied to some 'fieldforce' problems in the behavior of young children. *Psychological Review*, *45*, 271–299.

Inzlicht, M., Schmeichel, B. J., & Macrae, C. N. (2014). Why self-control seems (but may not be) limited. *Trends in Cognitive Sciences*, *18*, 127–133.

Janmaat, K. R., Polansky, L., Ban, S. D., & Boesch, C. (2014). Wild chimpanzees plan their breakfast time, type, and location. *Proceedings of the National Academy of Sciences*, *111*, 16343–16348.

Junghans, A. F., Sterck, E. H. M., Overduin de Vries, A., Evers, C., & De Ridder, D. T. D. (2016). Defying food—How distance determines monkeys' ability to inhibit reaching for food. *Frontiers in Psychology*, *7*, Article 158.

Juszczak, G. R., & Miller, M. (2016). Detour behavior of mice trained with transparent, semi-transparent and opaque barriers. *PLoS One*, *11*, e0162018.

Kabadayi, C., Bobrowicz, K., & Osvath, M. (2018). The detour paradigm in animal cognition. *Animal Cognition*, *21*, 21–35.

Kabadayi, C., Krasheninnikova, A., O'Neill, L., van de Weijer, J., Osvath, M., & von Bayern, A. M. (2017). Are parrots poor at motor self-regulation or is the cylinder task poor at measuring it? *Animal Cognition*, *20*, 1137–1146.

Kabadayi, C., Taylor, L. A., von Bayern, A. M., & Osvath, M. (2016). Ravens, New Caledonian crows and jackdaws parallel great apes in motor self-regulation despite smaller brains. *Royal Society Open Science*, *3*, 160104.

Kable, J. W., & Glimcher, P. W. (2007). The neural correlates of subjective value during intertemporal choice. *Nature Neuroscience*, *10*, 1625–1633.

Kahneman, D., & Tversky, A. (1984). Choices, values, and frames. *American Psychologist*, *39*, 341–350.

Keinan, A., & Kivetz, R. (2008). Remedying hyperopia: The effects of self-control regret on consumer behavior. *Journal of Marketing Research*, *45*, 676–689.

Kivetz, R., & Keinan, A. (2006). Repenting hyperopia: An analysis of self-control regrets. *Journal of Consumer Research*, *33*, 273–282.

Kivetz, R., & Simonson, I. (2002). Self-control for the righteous: Toward a theory of precommitment to indulge. *Journal of Consumer Research*, *29*, 199–217.

Kochanska, G., Murray, K. T., & Harlan, E. T. (2000). Effortful control in early childhood: Continuity and change, antecedents, and implications for social development. *Developmental Psychology*, *36*, 220–232.

Köhler, W. (1925). *The mentality of apes*. London: Kegan Paul, Trench, Trubner.

Lempert, K. M., & Phelps, E. A. (2016). The malleability of intertemporal choice. *Trends in Cognitive Sciences*, *20*, 64–74.

Lewin, K. (1933). Vectors, cognitive processes, and Mr. Tolman's criticism. *Journal of General Psychology*, *8*, 318–345.

Lock, A., & Collett, T. (1979). A toad's devious approach to its prey: A study of some complex uses of depth vision. *Journal of Comparative Physiology*, *131*, 179–189.

Lockman, J. J., & Adams, C. D. (2001). Going around transparent and gridlike barriers: Detour ability as a perception–action skill. *Developmental Science*, *4*, 463–471.

MacLean, E. L., Hare, B., Nunn, C. L., Addessi, E., Amici, F., Anderson, R. C., ... Boogert, N. J. (2014). The evolution of self-control. *Proceedings of the National Academy of Sciences*, *111*, E2140–E2148.

MacLeod, C. M. (1991). Half a century of research on the Stroop effect: An integrative review. *Psychological Bulletin*, *109*, 163–203.

Madden, G., & Bickel, W. (Eds.), (2010). *Impulsivity: The behavioral and neurological science of discounting*. Washington, DC: APA.

Meldrum, R. C., Petkovsek, M. A., Boutwell, B. B., & Young, J. T. (2017). Reassessing the relationship between general intelligence and self-control in childhood. *Intelligence*, *60*, 1–9.

Metcalfe, J., & Mischel, W. (1999). A hot/cool-system analysis of delay of gratification: Dynamics of willpower. *Psychological Review*, *106*, 3–19.

Miller, D. B., & Tallarico, R. B. (1974). On the correlation of brain size and problem-solving behavior of ring doves and pigeons. *Brain and Behavioral Ecology*, *10*, 265–273.

Mischel, H. N., & Mischel, W. (1983). The development of children's knowledge of self-control strategies. *Child Development*, *54*, 603–619.

Mischel, W. (2014). *The marshmallow test: Mastering self-control*. New York: Little, Brown.

Mulcahy, N. J., & Call, J. (2006). Apes save tools for future use. *Science*, *312*, 1038–1040.

Nosek, B. A., & Banaji, M. R. (2001). The go/no-go association task. *Social Cognition*, *19*, 625–666.

Osvath, M., & Osvath, H. (2008). Chimpanzee (*Pan troglodytes*) and orangutan (*Pongo abelii*) forethought: Self-control and pre-experience in the face of future tool use. *Animal Cognition*, *11*, 661–674.

Paglieri, F. (2013). The costs of delay: Waiting versus postponing in intertemporal choice. *Journal of the Experimental Analysis of Behavior*, *99*, 362–377.

Paglieri, F. (2016). Social choice for one: On the rationality of intertemporal decisions. *Behavioural Processes*, *127*, 97–108.

Paglieri, F., Addessi, E., Sbaffi, A., Tasselli, M. I., & Delfino, A. (2015). Is it patience or motivation? On motivational confounds in intertemporal choice tasks. *Journal of the Experimental Analysis of Behavior*, *103*, 196–217.

Regolin, L., Vallortigara, G., & Zanforlin, M. (1994). Perceptual and motivational aspects of detour behaviour in young chicks. *Animal Behaviour*, *47*, 123–131.

Regolin, L., Vallortigara, G., & Zanforlin, M. (1995). Object and spatial representations in detour problems by chicks. *Animal Behaviour*, *49*, 195–199.

Seed, A., & Byrne, R. (2010). Animal tool-use. *Current Biology*, *20*, R1032–R1039.

Shamosh, N. A., DeYoung, C. G., Green, A. E., Reis, D. L., Johnson, M. R., Conway, A. R., ... Gray, J. R. (2008). Individual differences in delay discounting relation to intelligence, working memory, and anterior prefrontal cortex. *Psychological Science*, *19*, 904–911.

Shenhav, A. (2017). The perils of losing control: Why self-control is not just another value-based decision. *Psychological Inquiry*, *28*, 148–152.

Shifferman, E. M. (2009). Its own reward: Lessons to be drawn from the reversed-reward contingency paradigm. *Animal Cognition*, *12*, 547–558.

Shumaker, R. W., Walkup, K. R., & Beck, B. B. (2011). *Animal tool behavior: The use and manufacture of tools by animals*. Baltimore, MD: JHU Press.

Simon, H. A. (1975). The functional equivalence of problem solving skills. *Cognitive Psychology*, *7*, 268–288.

Simon, H. A., & Hayes, J. R. (1976). The understanding process: Problem isomorphs. *Cognitive Psychology*, *8*, 165–190.

Spigel, I. M. (1964). Learning, retention, and disruption of detour behavior in the turtle. *Journal of Comparative and Physiological Psychology*, *57*, 108–112.

Stephens, D., & Anderson, D. (2001). The adaptive value of preference for immediacy: When shortsighted rules have farsighted consequences. *Behavioral Ecology*, *12*, 330–339.

Stevens, J. R. (2017). *Impulsivity: How time and risk influence decision making*. Cham, Switzerland: Springer.

Stevens, J., & Stephens, D. (2010). The adaptive nature of impulsivity. In G. Madden & W. Bickel (Eds.), *Impulsivity: The behavioral and neurological science of discounting* (pp. 361–387). Washington, DC: APA.

Stroop, J. R. (1935). Studies of interference in serial verbal reactions. *Journal of Experimental Psychology*, *18*, 643–662.

Suddendorf, T., & Busby, J. (2003). Mental time travel in animals? *Trends in Cognitive Sciences*, *7*, 391–396.

Suddendorf, T., & Corballis, M. C. (2007). The evolution of foresight: What is mental time travel, and is it unique to humans? *Behavioral and Brain Sciences*, *30*, 299–313.

Suddendorf, T., & Corballis, M. C. (2010). Behavioural evidence for mental time travel in non-human animals. *Behavioural Brain Research*, *215*, 292–298.

Thaler, R., & Shefrin, H. (1981). An economic theory of self-control. *Journal of Political Economy*, *89*, 392–406.

Thorndike, E. L. (1911). *Animal intelligence: Experimental studies*. New York: Macmillan.

Tolman, E. C. (1932). Lewin's concept of vectors. *Journal of General Psychology*, *7*, 3–15.

Tversky, A., & Kahneman, D. (1981). The framing of decisions and the psychology of choice. *Science*, *211*, 453–458.

Vallortigara, G., & Regolin, L. (2002). Facing an obstacle: Lateralization of object and spatial cognition. In L. J. Rogers (Ed.), *Comparative vertebrate lateralization* (pp. 383–444). Cambridge: Cambridge University Press.

Vlamings, P. H., Hare, B., & Call, J. (2010). Reaching around barriers: The performance of the great apes and 3–5-year-old children. *Animal Cognition*, *13*, 273–285.

Washburn, D. A. (1994). Stroop-like effects for monkeys and humans: Processing speed or strength of association? *Psychological Science*, *5*, 375–379.

Wells, M. (1964). Detour experiments with octopuses. *Journal of Experimental Biology*, *41*, 621–642.

Wyrwicka, W. (1959). Studies on detour behaviour. *Behaviour*, *14*, 240–264.

Zucca, P., Antonelli, F., & Vallortigara, G. (2005). Detour behaviour in three species of birds: Quails (*Coturnix* sp.), herring gulls (*Larus cachinnans*) and canaries (*Serinus canaria*). *Animal Cognition*, *8*, 122–128.

FURTHER READING

Boogert, N. J., Anderson, R. C., Peters, S., Searcy, W. A., & Nowicki, S. (2011). Song repertoire size in male song sparrows correlates with detour reaching, but not with other cognitive measures. *Animal Behaviour*, *81*, 1209–1216.

Bratman, M. (1987). *Intention, plans, and practical reason*. Cambridge, MA: Harvard University Press.

Diamond, A. (2013). Executive functions. *Annual Review of Psychology*, *64*, 135–168.

Diamond, A., & Gilbert, J. (1989). Development as progressive inhibitory control of action: Retrieval of a contiguous object. *Cognitive Development*, *4*, 223–249.

Duckworth, A. L. (2011). The significance of self-control. *Proceedings of the National Academy of Sciences*, *108*, 2639–2640.

Duckworth, A. L., Gendler, T. S., & Gross, J. J. (2016). Situational strategies for self-control. *Perspectives on Psychological Science*, *11*, 35–55.

Duckworth, A. L., Quinn, P. D., & Tsukayama, E. (2012). What no child left behind leaves behind: The roles of IQ and self-control in predicting standardized achievement test scores and report card grades. *Journal of Educational Psychology*, *104*, 439–451.

Güntürkün, O., Ströckens, F., Scarf, D., & Colombo, M. (2017). Apes, feathered apes, and pigeons: Differences and similarities. *Current Opinion in Behavioral Science*, *16*, 35–40.

Holton, R. (2009). *Willing, wanting, waiting*. Cambridge, MA: Oxford University Press.

Kabadayi, C., Jacobs, I., & Osvath, M. (2017). The development of motor self-regulation in ravens. *Frontiers in Psychology*, *8*, Article 2100.

Keren, G., & Schul, Y. (2009). Two is not always better than one: A critical evaluation of two-system theories. *Perspectives on Psychological Science*, *4*, 533–550.

Lockman, J. J. (1984). The development of detour ability during infancy. *Child Development*, *55*, 482–491.

Lucon-Xiccato, T., Gatto, E., & Bisazza, A. (2017). Fish perform like mammals and birds in inhibitory motor control tasks. *Scientific Reports*, *7*, 13144.

Lynam, D., Moffitt, T. E., & Stouthamer-Loeber, M. (1993). Explaining the relation between IQ and delinquency: Class, race, test motivation, school failure, or self-control? *Journal of Abnormal Psychology*, *102*, 187–196.

Marshall-Pescini, S., Virányi, Z., & Range, F. (2015). The effect of domestication on inhibitory control: Wolves and dogs compared. *PLoS One*, *10*, e0118469.

Mischel, W., & Ayduk, O. (2002). Self-regulation in a cognitive affective personality system: Attentional control in the service of the self. *Self and Identity*, *1*, 113–120.

Moffitt, T. E., Arsenault, L., Belsky, D., Dickson, N., Hancox, R. J., Harrington, H. L., ... Caspi, A. (2011). A gradient of childhood self-control predicts health, wealth, and public safety. *Proceedings of the National Academy of Sciences*, *108*, 2693–2698.

Moffitt, T. E., Poulton, R., & Caspi, A. (2013). Lifelong impact of early self-control. *American Scientist*, *101*, 352–359.

Petkovsek, M. A., & Boutwell, B. B. (2014). Childhood intelligence and the emergence of self-control. *Criminal Justice and Behavior*, *41*, 1232–1249.

Pongracz, P., Miklosi, A., Kubinyi, E., Gurobi, K., Topál, J., & Csányi, V. (2001). Social learning in dogs: The effect of a human demonstrator on the performance of dogs in a detour task. *Animal Behaviour*, *62*, 1109–1117.

Shamosh, N. A., & Gray, J. R. (2008). Delay discounting and intelligence: A meta-analysis. *Intelligence*, *36*, 289–305.

Smith, B. P., & Litchfield, C. A. (2010). How well do dingoes, *Canis dingo*, perform on the detour task? *Animal Behaviour*, *80*, 155–162.

Stahl, C., Voss, A., Schmitz, F., Nuszbaum, M., Tüscher, O., Lieb, K., & Klauer, K. C. (2014). Behavioral components of impulsivity. *Journal of Experimental Psychology: General*, *143*, 850–886.

Strack, E., & Deutsch, R. (2004). Reflective and impulsive determinants of social behavior. *Personality and Social Psychology Review*, *8*, 220–247.

Tangney, J. P., Baumeister, R. F., & Boone, A. L. (2004). High self-control predicts good adjustment, less pathology, better grades, and interpersonal success. *Journal of Personality*, *72*, 271–324.

Tsukayama, E., Duckworth, A. L., & Kim, B. E. (2012). Resisting everything except temptation: Evidence and an explanation for domain-specific impulsivity. *European Journal of Personality*, *26*, 318–334.

Tsukayama, E., Duckworth, A. L., & Kim, B. E. (2013). Domain specific impulsivity in school-age children. *Developmental Science*, *16*, 879–893.

Vernouillet, A., Anderson, J., Clary, D., & Kelly, D. M. (2016). Inhibition in Clark's nutcrackers (*Nucifraga columbiana*): Results of a detour reaching test. *Animal Cognition*, *19*, 661–665.

Wells, M. (1970). Detour experiments with split-brain octopuses. *Journal of Experimental Biology*, *53*, 375–389.

Wynne, C., & Leguet, B. (2004). Detour behavior in the Quokka (*Setonix brachyurus*). *Behavioural Processes*, *67*, 281–286.

Chapter 3

Human Intertemporal Choices: Choosing Between Now and Later

"I can pay you back the $100 I owe you right now, but if you can wait another month, I will pay you back $150."

"You can have one of those little cookies now, or a big slice of cake later tonight."

"You could buy the cheaper, shorter vacation right now with the cash you have, or make a down payment on the better, longer vacation that you still need to save more to get."

"You know, that cigarette you are smoking right now is going to kill you."

"A moment on the lips, a lifetime on the hips."

These are very common offers, and very common statements. And, they typify the kinds of things we are faced with numerous times each day. A choice between two outcomes. Something that would feel pretty good to have right now or at least to have more immediately versus something we can have later in time that is definitely better for us and more valuable. These are *intertemporal choices*. Two (or more) possible outcomes, of differing value and differing delay intervals until they appear. When people choose to wait for the more delayed, and better outcome, this is taken to be a *self-control* choice. When they choose the sooner item, which is less valuable when directly compared to the delayed item, this is called an *impulsive* response (Logue, 1988; Madden & Johnson, 2010). To many people, these are perhaps the most easily imagined self-control choices—deciding whether to forego that which can be had more immediately (and, that which you certainly want right now) for something that is more delayed and more valuable in the long term. A number of factors contribute to what choices people make in these situations, and there are important issues that help

Self-Control in Animals and People. DOI: https://doi.org/10.1016/B978-0-12-812508-3.00003-7
© 2018 Elsevier Inc. All rights reserved.

explain why it is that we sometimes choose the more impulsive options but other times choose the more delayed options. Impulsive choices in self-control tasks often are predictive of a variety of other negative behaviors, making them important to psychologists and educators. For example, drug users who tend to not think about future consequences are more likely to share needles in the present moment to get high (e.g., Odum, Madden, Badger, & Bickel, 2000), and a whole host of other long-term problems such as gambling troubles, alcoholism, risky sexual behavior, and even chronic tardiness is the result of people choosing more immediate pleasures over more delayed, but better outcomes (e.g., Rachlin, 2000). Such risks exist for children also. For example, Wulfert, Block, Santa Ana, Rodriguez, and Colsman (2002) gave high school students the chance to choose a small monetary reward right after participating in a research study, or wait to get a larger reward a week later. Those who chose the more immediate reward showed greater use of cigarettes, alcohol, and marijuana. They also demonstrated a poorer self-concept, and they underperformed academically compared to the students who chose to wait for the bigger reward. When Wulfert et al. gave the same kind of choice to middle-school students, they found the same general results. Those who chose the more immediate reward showed more negative behaviors in other areas. In another study, Kirby, Winston, and Santiesteban (2005) reported that there was a relation between undergraduate students' intertemporal choices and their college GPA. Thus, simple tests such as these can have predictive value on other meaningful aspects of children's lives, as we will also see in later chapters when we look in more detail at the marshmallow test and other tests of delayed gratification.

Intertemporal choice tests that assess self-control or impulsivity involve comparisons between something available more immediately and something that is more delayed, where one can objectively state that the more delayed outcome is the preferred outcome if time were not a relevant factor in the choice. Intertemporal choice tests have been used in psychological research for decades (e.g., Koriat & Nisan, 1978), and have provided us with extensive evidence about the nature of *delay discounting*, which is the process of devaluing future outcomes relative to more immediate outcomes. This process of devaluation can be estimated by collecting data on the choices people make when faced with different now-and-later outcomes, where those outcomes are varied in terms of the reward value or amount, and the delays to each of the choice options. From this effort, we can generate discounting functions that best fit choices among those different reward types and delay periods (Madden & Bickel, 2010). These functions help us understand how people value rewards in terms of their quality and amount. They also help us understand how people incorporate the passing of time (to the future) into their decisions, and whether such incorporation of time is faithful to the true delay interval or instead reflects a subjective aspect of future time (Madden & Johnson, 2010).

My goal in this chapter is not to cover all of the important research that has been done in this area of studying choice behavior. That would be impossible, because of the sheer number of studies that have been conducted. For example, my recent Google Scholar™ search returned 56,400 articles to the keywords self-control and intertemporal choice. "Delay discounting and self-control" returned 19,600 articles. In addition, there are already other excellent sources that focus nearly entirely on the issue of intertemporal choices, delay discounting, self-control, and impulsivity (e.g., Kable, 2013; Madden & Bickel, 2010; Rachlin, 2000; Stevens, 2017), and I have relied heavily on these sources to provide this far shorter summary. In this chapter, I focus on select studies that highlight how humans make intertemporal choices and what affects those choices, and in the next chapter I focus on this type of research with nonhuman animals.

When I talk about intertemporal choices, I am talking about a specific type of choice in which both outcomes are going to be realized, if they are chosen. What I mean is that these are choices in which the outcomes will happen, rather than only being probabilistic. For example, in the example above about $100 now versus $150 later, the two options would be guaranteed. In the real world, however, this might not be true. If the person offering $100 now is unreliable, or you just worry something unexpected may happen to them, the delayed $150 is not guaranteed, and then the choice is not as easy to make because you have to factor in the guaranteed $100 now versus the probability that $150 really will be there in a month. This is a very important point, for two reasons. First, when outcomes are only probabilistic, intertemporal choices are not necessarily reflections of self-control (or impulsivity), at least in the purest sense. Rather, they also reflect the chooser's sensitivity to risk. Those who are more *risk averse* will be more inclined to take the more guaranteed (and sooner) outcome whereas those who are more *risk tolerant* will be more inclined to wait, even if general capacities for self-control are equal in both kinds of choosers. In addition, risk has almost certainly played a large role in evolutionary selective pressures on many species' choice behavior (Green & Myerson, 2004; Patak & Reynolds, 2007; Platt & Heuttel, 2008; Rachlin, 2000; Rachlin, Logue, Gibbon, & Frankel, 1986; Stevens & Stephens, 2010). Thus, probability and risk sensitivity are crucial factors in human choice behavior (Kahneman & Tversky, 1979, 2000; Tversky & Kahneman, 1981, 1992), and especially intertemporal choices (Myerson, Green, Hanson, Holt, & Estle, 2003; Rachlin, Raineri, & Cross, 1991; see Heilbronner, Hayden, & Platt, 2009, for an excellent overview of these issues). However, given that my focus is on self-control, I will focus on studies in which both outcomes are guaranteed. Of course, in some ways, this means those tests have less relation to the real world, given that in the real world, any choice that involves delay must involve at least some degree of risk assessment, because at any moment future options can disappear. Most extreme in this idea is that, at any moment, the chooser could die (Stevens & Stephens, 2010), and thus it is true of the real world that anything that you cannot obtain right now cannot ever be truly guaranteed to be coming to you. But, setting that aside, I will briefly describe what we do know about choices that people make when they are as certain as they can be that a future outcome really will materialize at that later time.

What is clear from this massive literature is that people consistently discount the future. Perhaps this is exactly because of the reasons I just discussed, in which the future must be less certain than the present, and so this is an inherent and evolutionarily appropriate way (through discounting) to ensure that risk is accounted for somehow in all choices. Another possibility is that the future is discounted because time is not represented as it truly might elapse, but instead is represented in a way in which later events are overestimated in terms of how long they will take to arrive (e.g., Takahashi, 2005; Wittmann & Paulus, 2008). This is an important point that I will return to later, because it may explain not only why we discount the future, but also offer a potential route to making better choices if we can overcome our limitations for accurate time estimation.

In standard *intertemporal choice tasks* (or *delay discounting tasks*, as they also are called), the chooser is given two options. In one option, the reward is given after a shorter period of time, and is of a lesser quality or quantity than the other reward, which is given after a longer period of time. These options sometimes are offered as one-time choices, with a variety of different reward values and delay periods then being given across trials, so that a picture can emerge of choice behavior across varied time delays and reward outcomes.[1] Such tests can be given even to young children, using food rewards or nonfood rewards (e.g., Imuta, Hayne, & Scarf, 2014; Lemmon & Moore, 2007; Prencipe & Zelazo, 2005; Schwarz, Schrager, & Lyons, 1983; Thompson, Barresi, & Moore, 1997).

In other tests, one option is held constant, and the other option is varied across trials, until a point of equivalence between the two choices is found. So, for example, one might be offered $5 immediately, compared against a variety of different reward amounts offered in 24 hours, or compared against a $10 reward offered across a variety of other delays. Or, the smaller and sooner reward might be varied relative to a consistent larger, later reward. Or, the participant might be asked how much they would have to receive

1. It is important to note that individuals also can be given choices between aversive outcomes, such as a small shock more immediately versus a large shock later in time. In those cases, discounting still is seen in nearly all cases, but it occurs through choices to delay any outcome as long as possible since they are all negative. Of course, this means the negative event that comes later is more severe. So, for positive outcomes, there is discounting of future reward (and impulsive choice of more immediate gain), and for negative outcomes there is discounting of future aversive outcomes (and choice to avoid more immediate negative outcomes).

more immediately to lead them to choose that option over the delayed option (e.g., Reynolds & Schiffbauer, 2005; see Fig. 3.1). All of these approaches, with repeated choices of the same qualitative type, allow one to examine in the same subject the effects of reward magnitude, reward type, and delay interval on choice behavior (Green, Fry, & Myerson, 1994; Green & Myerson, 1993, 2004; Green, Myerson, & McFadden, 1997; Mazur, 1987; Rachlin et al., 1991). From these repeated responses, one can then generate a discounting function, which shows the best fitting curve for the subject's choices across all levels of the delay or reward magnitude that were varied (Doyle, 2013). Typically, what one sees is a steep drop in the value for the delayed option as a function of increasing delay lengths and then a shallower continuing drop as the delayed option gets farther and farther away in time. These discounting functions reflect the degree to which an individual made more impulsive choices or more self-controlled choices, although the functions themselves tell us nothing about the cause of the individual's impulsivity or self-control (e.g., Madden & Johnson, 2010).

Behavioral economists and psychologists have collected data on many types of intertemporal choices, leading to a robust database for examining the nature of discounting functions. Early arguments by economists were that such discounting should show an exponential character, in much the

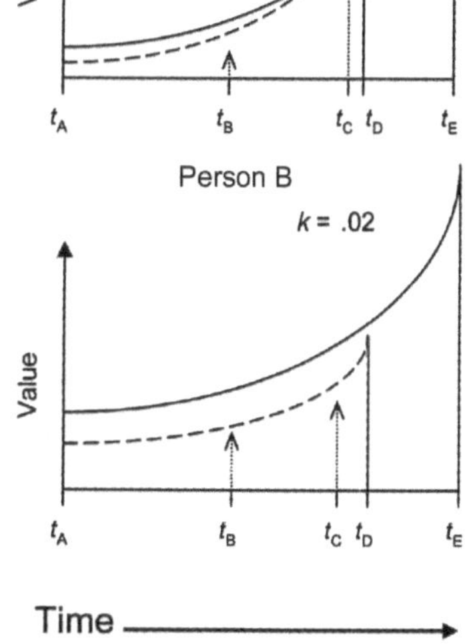

FIGURE 3.1 An example of a hyperbolic temporal discounting model (Reynolds & Schiffbauer, 2005). For both upper and lower panels, subjective value for rewards is shown to increase from left to right (curves) as the time to their delivery draws near. The top panel (Person A) represents a relatively impulsive individual whose preference shifts from a larger delayed reward to a smaller more immediate reward as it is about to become available. The bottom panel (Person B) represents a less impulsive individual whose preference does not shift from the larger delayed reward. *From Reynolds, B., & Schiffbauer, R. (2005). Delay of gratification and delay discounting: A unifying feedback model of delay-related impulsive behavior.* The Psychological Record, 55, *439–460, reprinted with permission of Springer.*

same way that there is exponential growth of capital when it is invested and saved in an interest-bearing account (e.g., Samuelson, 1937). The idea was that, over time, there should be compounding of discounting as well. In this exponential discounting function (Fig. 3.2; Kalenscher & Pennartz, 2008), the decline in value of a more delayed outcome is reflected by $V = Ae^{-kD}$, where V is the subjective value of the delayed reward, A is the amount of the delayed reward, D is the delay, and e is Euler's number. The parameter k determines the discounting rate at which value decreases with delay. The key point here is that a smaller value for k indicates shallower discounting (and reflects less impulsive choice) and a larger number indicates steeper discounting of the more delayed reward (and reflects more impulsive choice).

The exponential discounting model assumes that individuals will have time-consistent preferences and predicts that smaller/lesser rewards will always be valued less than larger/better rewards no matter the delay intervals to either outcome, and no matter the overall magnitudes of those rewards. However, what has been shown consistently is that reward magnitude and the delay intervals both can impact choice, and in a specific way. People show greater preference for the more immediate reward (i.e., they discount delayed rewards more steeply) when it occurs nearer in time compared to when it occurs further in time, even if the absolute temporal difference between choices remains the same (see Fig. 3.2; Kalenscher & Pennartz, 2008). Thus, in reality, the discounting functions for the smaller-sooner and larger-later options would cross as a function of delay time (Kirby & Herrnstein, 1995). A person who might prefer $10 now to $20 in a week will instead prefer $20 in 2 weeks compared to $10 in 1 week. In both cases, the doubled reward ($10 to $20) requires waiting a week longer from whenever the $10 reward can be had, but if both are already delayed by a week, the $20 is more frequently chosen. The exponential model would not predict this real-life example where people change their minds based upon how soon the smaller option is available. This led to the suggestion (e.g., Ainslie & Herrnstein, 1981; Mazur, 1987) that the best description of discounting functions was that of a hyperbola rather than being exponential (also see Ainslie & Haslam, 1992). As such, the value of delayed rewards was represented by $V = A/(1 + kD)$. However, even this better-fitting equation for most empirical results tends to over-predict subjective value at shorter delays while under-predicting it at longer delays (e.g., Green & Myerson, 2004; Odum, Baumann, & Rimington, 2006). As a result, other forms of hyperboloid models have been offered. For example, Myerson and Green (1995) proposed the equation $V = A/(1 + kD)^s$ where s is a free parameter that may reflect individual differences in the scaling of delay and/or amount (also see Green, Fristoe, & Myerson, 1994; Kirby & Marakovic, 1995; Loewenstein & Prelec, 1992; Rachlin, 1989). Other similar models based on hyperbolic discounting also have been proposed and tested (e.g., Rachlin, 2006). In all of these hyperbolic and hyperboloid models, k is a free parameter that reflects

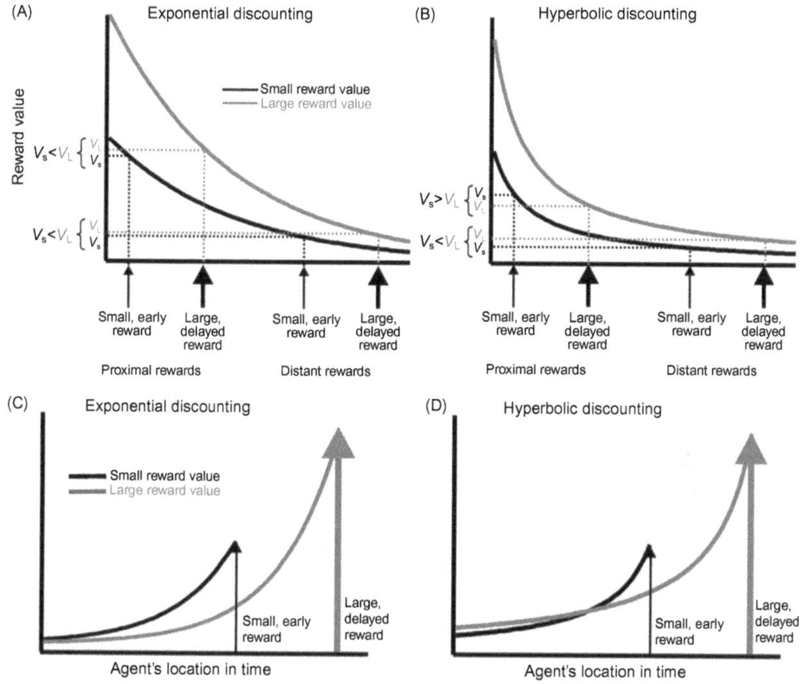

FIGURE 3.2 Preference reversals can be better explained by hyperbolic than exponential discounting. This figure depicts the situation where a subject first chooses between a small, early and a large, delayed reward (proximal rewards), and subsequently, both rewards are deferred in time by the same time interval (distant rewards), thus preserving the delay-difference between them. The figure plots the discounted value of a future reward (y-axis) as a function of reward amount and delay. Gray lines represent the discounted value of the large reward, black lines the value of the small reward. (A) The x-axis depicts the delay to the reward, fat arrows indicate a large, delayed reward, slim arrows a small, early reward. Due to constant discounting in the exponential function, the value of the large, delayed reward V_L is larger than the value of the small, early reward V_S when both rewards are temporally proximal, and also when they are deferred by the same time interval, so that always holds: $V_S < V_L$. (B) In hyperbolic discounting, the values of large and small rewards reverse when the rewards are deferred into the future: whereas $V_S > V_L$ when both rewards are relatively temporally proximal, $V_S < V_L$ when they are relatively distant. Often, this rationale is illustrated in a somewhat different fashion, as shown in (C) and (D). The x-axis depicts the temporal distance to the forthcoming reward from the perspective of the agent looking into the future, the attractiveness of the rewards increases with decreasing temporal distance. The x-axis displays the agent's position in time with respect to the temporally proximal and distant rewards. Long, fat arrows indicate a large reward, short, thin arrows a small reward. (C) Exponential discounting: the small reward value is continuously higher than the large reward value for distant and proximal rewards. (D) Hyperbolic discounting: when both rewards are temporally distant (left of the intersection of the lines), the value of the large reward (grey line) exceeds that of the small reward (black line), and subjects should consequently prefer the large over the small reward. Due to the crossover of the curves, the value of the small reward exceeds that of the large reward once the subject gets close in time to the small reward (right of the intersection), and they should now prefer the small over the large reward. *From Kalenscher, T., & Pennartz, C. M. (2008). Is a bird in the hand worth two in the future? The neuroeconomics of intertemporal decision-making.* Progress in Neurobiology, 84, *284–315, reprinted with permission of Elsevier.*

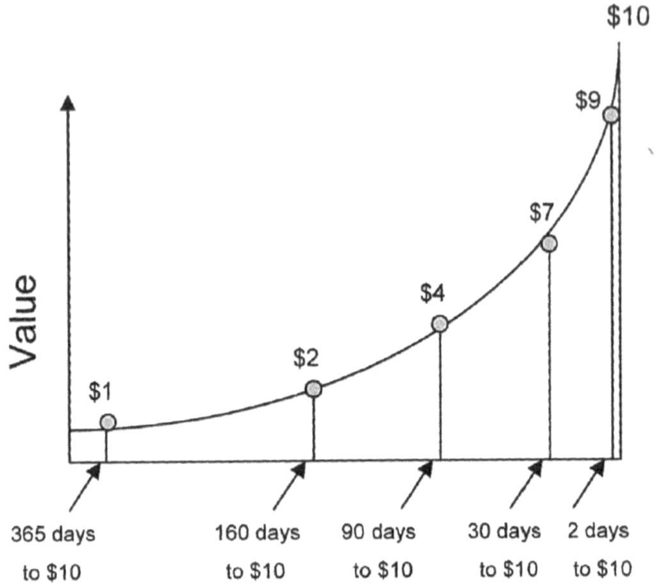

FIGURE 3.3 A hypothetical discounting function for monetary reward (Reynolds & Schiffbauer, 2005). Five different indifference points for money to be delivered after five specified delays (2, 30, 90, 160, and 365 days) are shown. Each indifference point represents the smallest amount of money a person chooses to receive immediately instead of waiting for the larger amount of money to be delivered after the specified delay. Such indifference points are plotted and fit to a curve-fitting function to derive *k*-values. *From Reynolds, B., & Schiffbauer, R. (2005). Delay of gratification and delay discounting: A unifying feedback model of delay-related impulsive behavior.* The Psychological Record, 55, *439–460, reprinted with permission of Springer.*

the individual differences component that accounts for why people choose differently (see Fig. 3.3 from Reynolds & Schiffbauer, 2005, to highlight this). And, *k* can say something about a person's relative self-control and impulsivity. That said, as I will discuss shortly, aspects such as the relative delays between outcomes and the magnitudes of those outcomes independently affect choice, and thus it is important to recognize those independent factors and perhaps reconsider how we use *k* (see Young, 2017).

My goal here is not to evaluate or even fully describe the different equations offered to best describe delay discounting functions (see Madden & Johnson, 2010; McKerchar et al., 2009; for more descriptions of these equations and what they reflect). Rather, I want to outline what we have learned when we give people choices between now and later outcomes, where we ensure that the later outcomes are objectively better, and would require self-control in choosing those outcomes. Generally, what we see is that choice data are better fit by hyperbolic models. For example, Green et al. (1997) had participants choose between immediate and delayed hypothetical rewards of different amounts of money ranging from $100 to $100,000. Hyperbolic functions better described the decrease in the subjective value of the delayed amounts of money as a function of how long it would be until that amount would be given. Green *et al.* (1994) also gave participants these kinds of choices, but when participants chose the smaller, sooner option, there was an additional constant delay added to both outcomes on future choices. This resulted in that reversal of preference I just noted, and there was evidence that the rate of discounting decreased with the increasing amount of the delayed reward. This shows that when both outcomes are more distant in time, the more delayed outcome is discounted less steeply, and larger delayed outcomes are also discounted less steeply.

That said, there are also important differences in what people choose as a function of the type of rewards that are offered. There are two primary ways this has been investigated. First, people have studied whether choice behavior (i.e., delay discounting) differs as a function of what outcomes are being offered. In general, it seems that certain kinds of things may be discounted more or less steeply by different kinds of people. In many cases, hedonic (pleasurable) delayed rewards are discounted more steeply than are monetary rewards. For example, cigarette smokers discount cigarettes more steeply than money (Bickel, Odum, & Madden, 1999), as do problem drinkers (Petry, 2001) and even recreational drinkers (Odum & Rainaud, 2003), cocaine users (Coffey, Gudleski, Saladin, & Brady, 2003), and heroin users (e.g., Madden, Petry, Badger, & Bickel, 1997). Madden, Bickel, and Jacobs (1999) reported that opioid-dependent participants who made choices between either monetary rewards or immediate or delayed heroin discounted heroin more steeply than money, meaning that they required smaller immediate heroin rewards than monetary rewards in order to choose the immediate option. We also know that individuals who are addicted to certain drugs are more likely to show steeper discounting functions in general across a variety of choices, reflecting their more impulsive tendencies (e.g., Kirby, Petry, & Bickel, 1999). It is not just problem behaviors that show greater discounting of delayed rewards. Delayed food rewards tend to be more steeply discounted compared to delayed monetary rewards, highlighting a key contributing factor to obesity and poor health as a result of diet choices. Navarick (1982) reported that even nonconsummable rewards such as access to playing video games were discounted more steeply than were monetary rewards, and Odum and Rainaud (2003) reported that people discounted food more steeply than money but at a level similar to how they discounted alcohol. Forzano, Michels, Sorama, Etopio, and English (2014) also reported that women discounted food reinforcers differently than they did video reinforcers, again highlighting that the reward type plays a major role in choice (also see Odum et al., 2006; see Fig. 3.4).

Another important question is whether hypothetical rewards lead to similar choice behavior compared to actual rewards. It seems that they typically

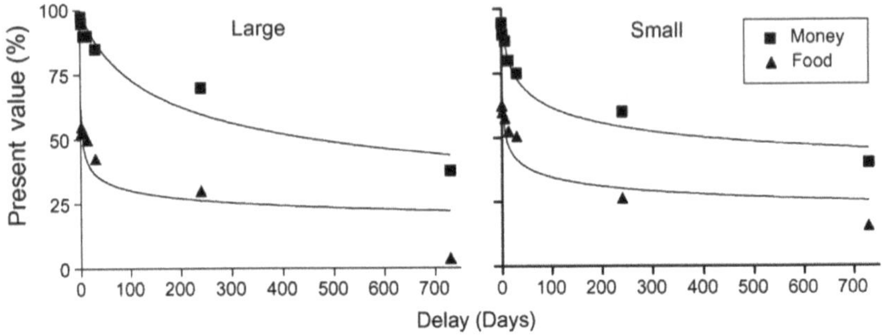

FIGURE 3.4 Temporal discounting functions for large amounts of money and food (left panel) and small amounts of money and food (right panel). Points show median indifference points for the outcomes as a function of delay, expressed as percentage of the delayed amount. Lines show the best-fitting discount functions generated by the hyperboloid model. *From Odum, A. L., Baumann, A. A. L., & Rimington, D. D. (2006). Discounting of delayed hypothetical money and food: Effects of amount.* Behavioral Processes, 73, *278–284, reprinted with permission of Elsevier.*

do, which is a good thing for giving us confidence that using hypothetical questions might generalize to real world choices. For example, Johnson and Bickel (2002) gave participants choices between real and hypothetical money rewards that ranged from $10 to $250. For nearly all participants, there was no difference in their choices depending on whether they chose between real and hypothetical rewards. Other studies also showed little or no difference between hypothetical and real rewards (e.g., Lagorio & Madden, 2005; Madden, Begotka, Raiff, & Kastern, 2003; Madden et al., 2004). This includes comparisons of hedonic rewards such as real and hypothetical food rewards (Robertson & Rasmussen, 2018). From this, it seems clear that one can assess intertemporal choices using either hypothetical or real rewards, with similar choice behavior emerging. This is important because it is not always possible (or affordable) to give participants real rewards, and so research with hypothetical rewards appears to be just as valid for understanding real world choices as would be using real rewards.

What remains is to consider *why* people make the choices they do. This gets beyond the way in which the future is discounted to instead focus on what aspects of the choice situation itself can lead to more self-controlled or more impulsive responses. I already noted the major roles that time and magnitude play in these choices. Lempert and Phelps (2016) outlined this issue succinctly by noting that reward magnitude seems to be the most salient factor that people consider (also see Ebert & Prelec, 2007). At the same time, people underweight time and duration (Ariely & Loewenstein, 2000). However, knowing this occurs also offers a chance for changing behavior. For example, when people are told to think about the time when the delayed reward will arrive, they more often choose the delayed reward when the delay is short. But, telling them to think about the magnitude of a future reward does not tend to change discounting behavior, which would seem to indicate they already were factoring in that aspect of the decision (Ebert & Prelec, 2007).

There are also broader contextual factors that affect intertemporal choice—such as framing, contrast, and highlighting certain aspects of the choices. Framing effects (Kahneman & Tversy, 2000) refer to how choice situations are "set up" with regard to other surrounding information, and they impact many kinds of decisions. When rewards are framed as rounded numbers rather than decimals, individuals tend to be more impulsive (Fassbender et al., 2014). So, being asked to choose between $5 now and $10 tomorrow is very different than being asked to choose between $5.65 now and $11.30 tomorrow. As Lempert and Phelps (2016) noted, one can also nudge people (Thaler & Sunstein, 2003) toward more delayed outcomes by explicitly noting what will be received or gained in each choice option at each time. For example, they noted that instead of asking a person if they wanted '$10 today OR $22 in 30 days' you could ask if they wanted '$10 today and $0 in 30 days OR $0 today and $22 in 30 days' (Radu, Yi, Bickel, Gross, & McClure, 2011). Dai, Grace, and Kemp (2009) highlighted another framing effect known as reward contrast. They compared how people made intertemporal choices for pairs of options that varied greatly in their magnitudes. People first either made choices about hypothetical $50 or $5,000 delayed reward options, and then they made choices about $500 delayed reward options. People who shifted from $5,000 to $500 showed steeper discounting functions compared to those who shifted from $50 to $500. This means that previous values of decisions impacted subsequent choices (Fig. 3.5).

Another way to impact choice behavior, and potentially to increase choices of more delayed outcomes is through steering people toward future-oriented thinking. Lempert and Phelps (2016) summarized that when episodic future thinking, or prospection, is triggered prior to choice, people tend to make more far-sighted choices, even if the content of the future thought is unrelated to the reward being offered (e.g., Kwan et al., 2015; Palombo, Keane, & Verfaellie, 2015; Peters & Büchel, 2010). This is a point I will discuss at length in Chapter 14, Mental Time Travel: What Is It, and How Does It Relate to Self-Control?, as it pertains to humans, and also to nonhuman animals. The estimation of time seems to play a number of roles in intertemporal choice. Specifically, how time is being presented changes how we feel about options. For example, describing future rewards on the basis of their calendar date of arrival instead of after an interval of some number of days leads to more choices of more delayed outcomes (DeHart & Odum, 2015; LeBoeuf, 2006; Read, Frederick, Orsel, & Rahman, 2005; see Fig. 3.6).

This issue of time estimation has been offered as a way to reconcile the general poor fit of exponential functions. Zauberman, Kim, Malkoc, and Bettman (2009) proposed that people's inability to accurately represent

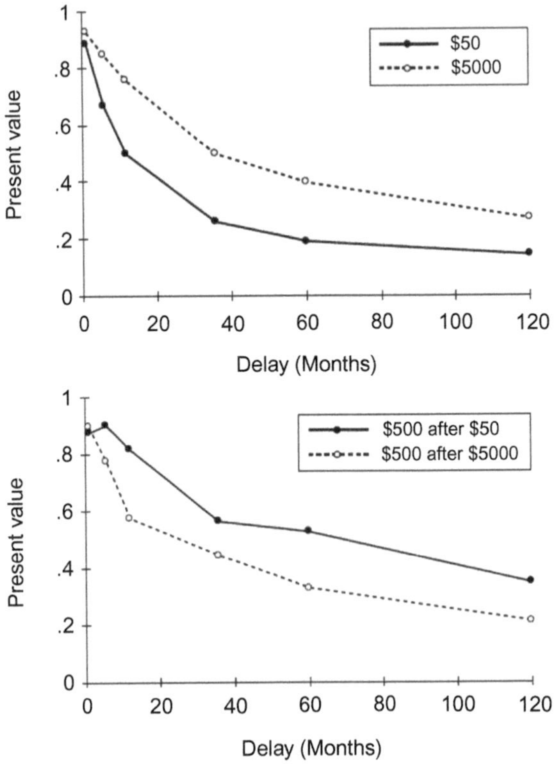

FIGURE 3.5 Average present value data for each question series from the delay-discounting task in Experiment 1 of Dai et al. (2009). The upper panel shows results from the first block, in which the amount was either $50 or $5,000 for different groups of subjects. The lower panel shows results from the second block, in which the amount was $500 for both groups. People discounted less steeply when starting with the $50 condition and then moving to the $500 condition than when starting with the $5,000 condition. *From Dai, Z., Grace, R. C., & Kemp, S. (2009). Reward contrast in delay and probability discounting.* Learning & Behavior, 37, *281–288, reprinted with permission of Springer.*

objective future time is an important component of intertemporal preferences and underlies hyperbolic discounting (also see Loewenstein & Prelec, 1992; Thaler, 1981). We know that people have a tendency to represent time logarithmically, rather than linearly. This means that the further away something is in time, the more compressed each additional time-unit is in the overall representation of that duration. In this way, time estimation is accounted for by Weber's Law, and such compression of estimated time has been well documented (e.g., Brannon & Roitman, 2003; Dehaene & Brannon, 2010; Gibbon, Malapani, Dale, & Gallistel, 1997; Killeen & Weiss, 1987). What I mean by compression is that thinking about the difference between 5 minutes from now and an hour and 5 minutes from now is not the same as thinking about the difference between 30 days from now and 30 days and 1 hour from now. In the first case, that time difference feels very large, but in the second case, it feels like basically the same point in the future, even though we know both examples involve two time periods separated by an hour. Across a long series of experiments, Zauberman et al. showed that people's subjective estimates of duration did not match objective time. Rather, they showed time estimates that were more logarithmic in nature than linear.

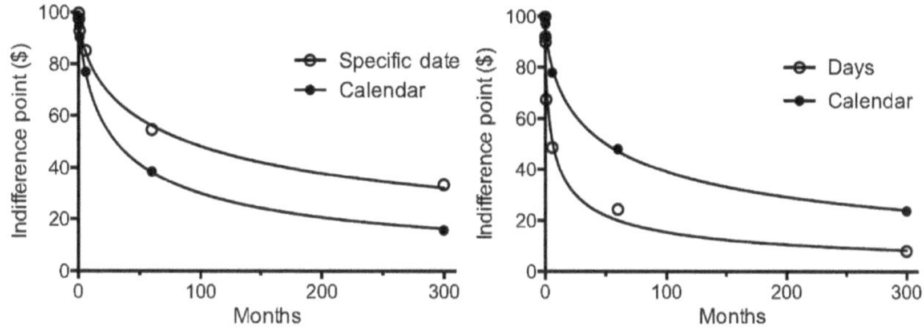

FIGURE 3.6 Left panel: Temporal discounting functions when delays were expressed as specific dates (open circles) and calendar units (filled circles). Points show median indifference points for $100 as a function of delay. Right panel: Temporal discounting functions when delays were expressed as days (open circles) and calendar units (filled circles). Points show median indifference points for $100 as a function of delay. In both panels, lines show the best-fitting discounting functions generated by the hyperboloid model. *From DeHart, W. B., &Odum, A. L. (2015). The effects of the framing of time on delay discounting.* Journal of the Experimental Analysis of Behavior, 103, *10–21, reprinted with permission of John Wiley & Sons.*

When participants' responses to intertemporal choices were plotted as a function of objective time delays, a hyperbolic function fit very well. However, if *subjective time* was included, with its compressed nature, then discount rates were fairly consistent across all time delays. This is an important point, and one that requires more research, because it may impact how we interpret discounting functions and the psychological processes that contribute to those functions (Takahashi, 2005). Humans' inability to represent time accurately may be crucial to understanding how we frame intertemporal choices in the same way that other framing effects I outlined are important, and in the same way that magnitude can affect intertemporal choice (see Killeen, 2015). This is an area in which comparative data could be highly informative, given all that we know about how animals estimate time. As it turns out, comparative psychologists already have spent decades studying intertemporal choices in animals, as I will describe in the next chapter, and those studies have offered important similarities and contrasts to the choice behavior of humans.

REFERENCES

Ainslie, E., & Herrnstein, R. J. (1981). Preference reversal and delayed reinforcement. *Animal Learning & Behavior, 9*, 476–482.

Ainslie, G., & Haslam, N. (1992). Hyperbolic discounting. In G. Loewenstein & J. Elster (Eds.), *Choice over time* (pp. 57–92). New York: Russell Sage Foundation.

Ariely, D., & Loewenstein, G. (2000). When does duration matter in judgment and decision making? *Journal of Experimental Psychology: General, 129*, 508–523.

Bickel, W. K., Odum, A. L., & Madden, G. J. (1999). Impulsivity and cigarette smoking: Delay discounting in current, never, and ex-smokers. *Psychopharmacology, 146*, 447–454.

Brannon, E. M., & Roitman, J. D. (2003). Nonverbal representations of time and number in animals and human infants. In W. H. Meck (Ed.), *Functional and neural mechanisms of interval timing* (pp. 143–182). Boca Raton, FL: CRC Press.

Coffey, S. F., Gudleski, G. D., Saladin, M. E., & Brady, K. T. (2003). Impulsivity and rapid discounting of delayed hypothetical rewards in cocaine-dependent individuals. *Experimental and Clinical Psychopharmacology, 11*, 18–25.

Dai, Z., Grace, R. C., & Kemp, S. (2009). Reward contrast in delay and probability discounting. *Learning & Behavior, 37*, 281–288.

Dehaene, S., & Brannon, E. M. (2010). Space, time, and number: A Kantian research program. *Trends in Cognitive Sciences, 14*, 517–519.

DeHart, W. B., & Odum, A. L. (2015). The effects of the framing of time on delay discounting. *Journal of the Experimental Analysis of Behavior, 103*, 10–21.

Doyle, J. R. (2013). Survey of time preference, delay discounting models. *Judgment and Decision Making, 8*, 116–135.

Ebert, J. E., & Prelec, D. (2007). The fragility of time: Time-insensitivity and valuation of the near and far future. *Management Science, 53*, 1423–1438.

Fassbender, C., Houde, S., Silver-Balbus, S., Ballard, K., Kim, B., Rutledge, K. J., & McClure, S. M. (2014). The decimal effect: Behavioral and neural bases for a novel influence on intertemporal choice in healthy individuals and in ADHD. *Journal of Cognitive Neuroscience, 26*, 2455–2468.

Forzano, L. B., Michels, J. L., Sorama, M., Etopio, A. L., & English, E. J. (2014). Self-control and impulsiveness in adult humans: Comparison of qualitatively different consumable reinforcers using a new methodology. *The Psychological Record, 64*, 719–730.

Gibbon, J., Malapani, C., Dale, C. L., & Gallistel, C. R. (1997). Toward a neurobiology of temporal cognition: Advances and challenges. *Current Opinion in Neurobiology, 7*, 170–184.

Green, L., Fristoe, N., & Myerson, J. (1994). Temporal discounting and preference reversals in choice between delayed outcomes. *Psychonomic Bulletin & Review, 1*, 383–389.

Green, L., Fry, A. F., & Myerson, J. (1994). Discounting of delayed rewards: A life-span comparison. *Psychological Science, 5*, 33–36.

Green, L., & Myerson, J. (1993). Alternative frameworks for the analysis of self-control. *Behavior and Philosophy, 21*, 37–47.

Green, L., & Myerson, J. (2004). A discounting framework for choice with delayed and probabilistic rewards. *Psychological Bulletin, 130*, 769–792.

Green, L., Myerson, J., & McFadden, E. (1997). Rate of temporal discounting decreases with amount of reward. *Memory & Cognition, 25*, 715–723.

Heilbronner, S. R., Hayden, B. Y., & Platt, M. L. (2009). Neuroeconomis of risk-sensitive decision making. In G. Madden & W. Bickel (Eds.), *Impulsivity: The behavioral and neurological science of discounting* (pp. 159–187). Washington, DC: American Psychological Association.

Imuta, K., Hayne, H., & Scarf, D. (2014). I want it all and I want it now: Delay of gratification in preschool children. *Developmental Psychobiology, 56*, 1541–1552.

Johnson, M. W., & Bickel, W. K. (2002). Within-subject comparison of real and hypothetical money rewards in delay discounting. *Journal of the Experimental Analysis of Behavior, 77*, 129–146.

Kable, J. W. (2013). Valuation, intertemporal choice and self-control. In P. Glimcher & E. Fehr (Eds.), *Neuroeconomics* (2nd ed., pp. 173–192). New York: Academic Press.

Kahneman, D., & Tversky, A. (1979). Prospect theory: An analysis of decision under risk. *Econometrica, 47*, 263–291.

Kahneman, D., & Tversy, A. (2000). *Choices, values, and frames*. Cambridge, UK: Cambridge University Press.

Kalenscher, T., & Pennartz, C. M. (2008). Is a bird in the hand worth two in the future? The neuroeconomics of intertemporal decision-making. *Progress in Neurobiology*, *84*, 284–315.

Killeen, P. R. (2015). The arithmetic of discounting. *Journal of the Experimental Analysis of Behavior*, *103*, 249–259.

Killeen, P. R., & Weiss, N. A. (1987). Optimal timing and the Weber function. *Psychological Review*, *94*, 455–468.

Kirby, K. N., & Herrnstein, R. J. (1995). Preference reversals due to myopic discounting of delayed reward. *Psychological Science*, *6*, 83–89.

Kirby, K. N., & Marakovic, N. N. (1995). Modeling myopic decisions: Evidence for hyperbolic delay-discounting within subjects and amounts. *Organizational Behavior and Human Decision Processes*, *64*, 22–30.

Kirby, K. N., Petry, N. M., & Bickel, W. K. (1999). Heroin addicts have higher discount rates for delayed rewards than non-drug using controls. *Journal of Experimental Psychology: General*, *128*, 78–87.

Kirby, K. N., Winston, G. C., & Santiesteban, M. (2005). Impatience and grades: Delay-discount rates correlate negatively with college GPA. *Learning and Individual Differences*, *15*, 213–222.

Koriat, A., & Nisan, M. (1978). Delay of gratification as a function of exchange values and appetitive values of the rewards. *Motivation and Emotion*, *2*, 375–390.

Kwan, D., Craver, C. F., Green, L., Myerson, J., Gao, F., Black, S. E., & Rosenbaum, R. S. (2015). Cueing the personal future to reduce discounting in intertemporal choice: Is episodic prospection necessary? *Hippocampus*, *25*, 432–443.

Lagorio, C., & Madden, G. J. (2005). Delay discounting of real and hypothetical rewards. III: Steady-state assessments, forced-choice trials, and all real rewards. *Behavioural Processes*, *69*, 173–187.

LeBoeuf, R. A. (2006). Discount rates for time versus dates: The sensitivity of discounting to time-interval description. *Journal of Marketing Research*, *43*, 59–72.

Lemmon, K., & Moore, C. (2007). The development of prudence in the face of varying future rewards. *Developmental Science*, *10*, 502–511.

Lempert, K. M., & Phelps, E. A. (2016). The malleability of intertemporal choice. *Trends in Cognitive Sciences*, *20*, 64–74.

Loewenstein, G., & Prelec, D. (1992). Anomalies in intertemporal choice: Evidence and an interpretation. *The Quarterly Journal of Economics*, *107*, 573–597.

Logue, A. W. (1988). Research on self-control: An integrating framework. *Behavioral and Brain Sciences*, *11*, 665–709.

Madden, G., & Johnson, P. S. (2010). A delay-discounting primer. In G. Madden & W. Bickel (Eds.), *Impulsivity: The behavioral and neurological science of discounting* (pp. 11–38). Washington, DC: American Psychological Association.

Madden, G. J., Begotka, A. M., Raiff, B. R., & Kastern, L. L. (2003). Delay discounting of real and hypothetical rewards. *Experimental and Clinical Psychopharmacology*, *11*, 139–145.

Madden, G. J., & Bickel, W. K. (Eds.). (2010). *Impulsivity: The behavioral and neurological science of discounting*. Washington, DC: American Psychological Association.

Madden, G. J., Bickel, W. K., & Jacobs, E. A. (1999). Discounting of delayed rewards in opioid-dependent outpatients: Exponential or hyperbolic discounting functions? *Experimental and Clinical Psychopharmacology*, *7*, 284–293.

Madden, G. J., Petry, N., Badger, G. J., & Bickel, W. K. (1997). Impulsive and self-control choices in opioid-dependent patients and non-drug-using control participants: Drug and monetary rewards. *Experimental and Clinical Psychopharmacology*, *5*, 256–262.

Madden, G. J., Raiff, B. R., Lagorio, C. H., Begotka, A. M., Mueller, A. M., Hehli, D. J., & Wegener, A. A. (2004). Delay discounting of potentially real and hypothetical rewards: II. Between-and within-subject comparisons. *Experimental and Clinical Psychopharmacology, 12*, 251–261.

Mazur, J. E. (1987). An adjusting procedure for studying delayed reinforcement. In M. L. Commons, J. E. Mazur, J. A. Nevin, & H. Rachlin (Eds.), *Quantitative analysis of behavior: Vol. 5. The effect of delay and of intervening events of reinforcement value* (pp. 55–73). Hillsdale, NJ: Erlbaum.

McKerchar, T. L., Green, L., Myerson, J., Pickford, T. S., Hill, J. C., & Stout, S. C. (2009). A comparison of four models of delay discounting in humans. *Behavioural Processes, 81*, 256–259.

Myerson, J., & Green, L. (1995). Discounting of delayed rewards: Models of individual choice. *Journal of the Experimental Analysis of Behavior, 76*, 235–243.

Myerson, J., Green, L., Hanson, J. S., Holt, D. D., & Estle, S. J. (2003). Discounting delayed and probabilistic rewards: Processes and traits. *Journal of Economic Psychology, 24*, 619–635.

Navarick, D. J. (1982). Negative reinforcement and choice in humans. *Learning and Motivation, 13*, 361–377.

Odum, A. L., Baumann, A. A. L., & Rimington, D. D. (2006). Discounting of delayed hypothetical money and food: Effects of amount. *Behavioral Processes, 73*, 278–284.

Odum, A. L., Madden, G. J., Badger, G. J., & Bickel, W. K. (2000). Needle sharing in opioid-dependent outpatients: Psychological processes underlying risk. *Drug and Alcohol Dependency, 60*, 259–266.

Odum, A. L., & Rainaud, C. P. (2003). Discounting of delayed hypothetical money, alcohol, and food. *Behavioural Processes, 64*, 305–313.

Palombo, D. J., Keane, M. M., & Verfaellie, M. (2015). The medial temporal lobes are critical for reward-based decision making under conditions that promote episodic future thinking. *Hippocampus, 25*, 345–353.

Patak, M., & Reynolds, B. (2007). Question-based assessments of delay discounting: Do respondents spontaneously incorporate uncertainty into their valuations for delayed rewards? *Addictive Behaviors, 32*, 351–357.

Peters, J., & Büchel, C. (2010). Episodic future thinking reduces reward delay discounting through an enhancement of prefrontal mediotemporal interactions. *Neuron, 66*, 138–148.

Petry, N. M. (2001). Delay discounting of money and alcohol in actively using alcoholics, currently abstinent alcoholics, and controls. *Psychopharmacology, 154*, 243–250.

Platt, M. L., & Heuttel, S. A. (2008). Risky business: The neuroeconomics of decision-making under uncertainty. *Nature Neuroscience, 11*, 398–403.

Prencipe, A., & Zelazo, P. D. (2005). Development of affective decision making for self and other: Evidence for the integration of first- and third-person perspectives. *Psychological Science, 16*, 501–505.

Rachlin, H. (1989). *Judgment, decision, and choice: A cognitive/behavioral synthesis*. New York: WH Freeman.

Rachlin, H. (2000). *The science of self-control*. Cambridge, MA: Harvard University Press.

Rachlin, H. (2006). Notes on discounting. *Journal of the Experimental Analysis of Behavior, 85*, 425–435.

Rachlin, H., Logue, A. W., Gibbon, J., & Frankel, M. (1986). Cognition and behavior in studies of choice. *Psychological Review, 93*, 33–45.

Rachlin, H., Raineri, A., & Cross, D. (1991). Subjective probability and delay. *Journal of the Experimental Analysis of Behavior, 55*, 233–244.

Radu, P. T., Yi, R., Bickel, W. K., Gross, J. J., & McClure, S. M. (2011). A mechanism for reducing delay discounting by altering temporal attention. *Journal of the Experimental Analysis of Behavior, 96*, 363–385.

Read, D., Frederick, S., Orsel, B., & Rahman, J. (2005). Four score and seven years from now: The date/delay effect in temporal discounting. *Management Science, 51*, 1326–1335.

Reynolds, B., & Schiffbauer, R. (2005). Delay of gratification and delay discounting: A unifying feedback model of delay-related impulsive behavior. *The Psychological Record, 55*, 439–460.

Robertson, S. H., & Rasmussen, E. B. (2018). Comparison of potentially real versus hypothetical food outcomes in delay and probability discounting tasks. *Behavioural Processes, 149*, 8–15.

Samuelson, P. A. (1937). A note on the measurement of utility. *Review of Economic Studies, 4*, 155–161.

Schwarz, J. C., Schrager, J. B., & Lyons, A. E. (1983). Delay of gratification by preschoolers: Evidence for the validity of the choice paradigm. *Child Development, 54*, 620–625.

Stevens, J. R. (2017). *Impulsivity: How time and risk influence decision making*. Cham, Switzerland: Springer.

Stevens, J. R., & Stephens, D. W. (2010). The adaptive nature of impulsivity. In G. Madden & W. Bickel (Eds.), *Impulsivity: The behavioral and neurological science of discounting* (pp. 361–387). Washington, DC: American Psychological Association.

Takahashi, T. (2005). Loss of self-control in intertemporal choice may be attributable to logarithmic time-perception. *Medical Hypotheses, 65*, 691–693.

Thaler, R. H. (1981). Some empirical evidence on dynamic inconsistency. *Economic Letters, 8*, 201–207.

Thaler, R. H., & Sunstein, C. R. (2003). Libertarian paternalism. *American Economic Review, 93*, 175–179.

Thompson, C., Barresi, J., & Moore, C. (1997). The development of future-oriented prudence and altruism in preschoolers. *Early Childhood Research Quarterly, 12*, 199–212.

Tversky, A., & Kahneman, D. (1981). The framing of decisions and the psychology of choice. *Science, 211*, 453–458.

Tversky, A., & Kahneman, D. (1992). Advances in prospect theory: Cumulative representation of uncertainty. *Journal of Risk and Uncertainty, 5*, 297–323.

Wittmann, M., & Paulus, M. P. (2008). Decision making, impulsivity and time perception. *Trends in Cognitive Sciences, 12*, 7–12.

Wulfert, E., Block, J. A., Santa Ana, E., Rodriguez, M. L., & Colsman, M. (2002). Delay of gratification: Impulsive choices and problem behaviors in early and late adolescence. *Journal of Personality, 70*, 533–552.

Young, M. E. (2017). Discounting: A practical guide to multilevel analysis of indifference data. *Journal of the Experimental Analysis of Behavior, 108*, 97–112.

Zauberman, G., Kim, B. K., Malkoc, S. A., & Bettman, J. R. (2009). Discounting time and time discounting: Subjective time perception and intertemporal preferences. *Journal of Marketing Research, 46*, 543–556.

FURTHER READING

Ainslie, G. (1975). Specious reward: A behavioral theory of impulsiveness and impulse control. *Psychological Bulletin, 82*, 463–496.

Berns, G. S., Laibson, D., & Loewenstein, G. (2007). Intertemporal choice–toward an integrative framework. *Trends in Cognitive Sciences, 11*, 482–488.

Frost, R., & McNaughton, N. (2017). The neural basis of delay discounting: A review and preliminary model. *Neuroscience & Biobehavioral Reviews, 79*, 48–65.

Green, L., & Myerson, J. (1996). Exponential versus hyperbolic discounting of delayed outcomes: Risk and waiting time. *American Zoologist, 36*, 496–505.

Green, L., Myerson, J., Lichtman, D., Rosen, S., & Fry, A. (1996). Temporal discounting in choice between delayed rewards: The role of age and income. *Psychology and Aging, 11*, 79–84.

Green, L., Myerson, J., & Macaux, E. W. (2005). Temporal discounting when the choice is between two delayed rewards. *Journal of Experimental Psychology: Learning, Memory, and Cognition, 31*, 1121–1133.

Green, L., Myerson, J., & Ostaszewski, P. (1999). Amount of reward has opposite effects on the discounting of delayed and probabilistic outcomes. *Journal of Experimental Psychology: Learning Memory and Cognition, 25*, 418–427.

Kable, J. W., & Glimcher, P. W. (2007). The neural correlates of subjective value during intertemporal choice. *Nature Neuroscience, 10*, 1625–1633.

Kable, J. W., & Glimcher, P. W. (2009). The neurobiology of decision: Consensus and controversy. *Neuron, 63*, 733–745.

Killeen, P. R. (2009). An additive-utility model of delay discounting. *Psychological Review, 116*, 602–619.

Lennings, C. J., & Burns, A. M. (1998). Time perspective: Temporal extension, time estimation, and impulsivity. *Journal of Psychology, 132*, 367–380.

Luhmann, C. C. (2013). Discounting of delayed rewards is not hyperbolic. *Journal of Experimental Psychology: Learning, Memory, and Cognition, 39*, 1274–1279.

Milkman, K. L., Rogers, T., & Bazerman, M. H. (2010). I'll have the ice cream soon and the vegetables later: A study of online grocery purchases and order lead time. *Marketing Letters, 21*, 17–35.

Mitchell, J. P., Schirmer, J., Ames, D. L., & Gilbert, D. T. (2010). Medial prefrontal cortex predicts intertemporal choice. *Journal of Cognitive Neuroscience, 23*, 857–866.

Odum, A. L. (2011). Delay discounting: Trait variable? *Behavioural Processes, 87*, 1–9.

Rachlin, H. (2016). Social cooperation and self-control. *Managerial and Decision Economics, 37*, 249–260.

Rung, J. M., & Young, M. E. (2015). Learning to wait for more likely or just more: Greater tolerance to delays of reward with increasingly longer delays. *Journal of the Experimental Analysis of Behavior, 103*, 108–124.

Shamosh, N. A., DeYoung, C. G., Green, A. E., Reis, D. L., Johnson, M. R., Conway, A. R., ... Gray, J. R. (2008). Individual differences in delay discounting: Relation to intelligence, working memory, and anterior prefrontal cortex. *Psychological Science, 19*, 904–911.

Thaler, R. H., & Shefrin, H. (1981). An economic theory of self control. *Journal of Political Economics, 89*, 392–406.

Weller, R. E., Cook, E. W., III, Avsar, K. B., & Cox, J. E. (2008). Obese women show greater delay discounting than healthy-weight women. *Appetite, 51*, 563–569.

Young, M. E., Webb, T. L., Rung, J. M., & Jacobs, E. A. (2013a). Sensitivity to changing contingencies in an impulsivity task. *Journal of the Experimental Analysis of Behavior, 99*, 335–345.

Young, M. E., Webb, T. L., Rung, J. M., & McCoy, A. W. (2014). Outcome probability versus magnitude: When waiting benefits one at the cost of the other. *PLoS One, 9*, e98996.

Chapter 4

Intertemporal Choices by Nonhuman Animals

This chapter continues on the topic of intertemporal choice but from the comparative perspective, outlining work with nonhuman animals that uses intertemporal choice tasks. Here, I will focus on what we know about how animals choose between smaller/sooner and larger/later rewards, and what can be done to "nudge" animals toward making more long-term choices that might reflect self-control.[1]

Many of the intertemporal choice tests that I outlined in the last chapter are well suited for using with other species, and particularly with traditional laboratory species that can press bars or peck keys to make discrete smaller-sooner or larger-later choices. And, there is an important reason to attempt such tests with animals. We know that impulsivity, and a general inclination to more steeply discount future rewards, is predictive of a number of problem behaviors in humans, such as gambling, drug addition, risky sexual behavior, and overeating. Thus, animal models of choice behavior that allow one to study self-control and impulsivity can provide the kind of controls and even interventions (e.g., drug trials or brain-based interventions) that allow researchers to make progress on human health-related issues. In addition, laboratory species such as pigeons, rats, and monkeys have been used extensively as a model specifically because they tend to show strong preferences for more immediate rewards compared to larger, more delayed rewards, thus allowing researchers to probe for conditions that might promote greater choice of delayed rewards (and perhaps stronger self-control behavior).

As with human studies, the animal studies are far too numerous for me to fairly or adequately document. So, I will offer the key outcomes from the decades of research that has been done, with some greater emphasis on more recent work. There are excellent other summaries of work in this area (e.g., Logue, 1988; Rachlin, 2000). And, there are important arguments that

1. Risk taking behaviors again are not a focus here, but they are important in understanding nonhuman animal choices more broadly (e.g., Hayden & Platt, 2007; Heilbronner, Rosati, Stevens, Hare, & Hauser, 2008; Kacelnik & Bateson, 1996; Marsh & Kacelnik, 2002; McCoy & Platt, 2005; Shafir, Wiegmann, Smith, & Real, 1999).

Self-Control in Animals and People. DOI: https://doi.org/10.1016/B978-0-12-812508-3.00004-9
© 2018 Elsevier Inc. All rights reserved.

can be made about the extent to which intertemporal choice tests actually reflect self-control and impulsivity in those individuals who make such intertemporal choices (see Hayden, 2016; Paglieri, 2013, 2016). For example, Hayden (2016) points out that the use of a consistent trial length during intertemporal choice tests can be problematic. Typically, in tests like these, each trial starts after the exact same duration from previous trials, independent of whether the subject just chose the SS or LL option. Otherwise, choosing a smaller, sooner reward also would net the benefit of getting the next trial started more quickly, and we would not want that unintended consequence to affect choice behavior. But, we cannot know that the animal subjects we test understand that their choices are not part of what determines the delay until the next trial. Without being certain of this, we cannot know that "impulsive" choices are not being made on the basis of assuming this will lead to faster next opportunities. We might expect that experience with the task helps with this problem, but we cannot know. And, those experiments that tried to more explicitly cue animals as to this issue found great shifts toward delayed rewards, suggesting that we might be underestimating self-control in some of these cases (see Blanchard, Pearson, & Hayden, 2013; Pearson, Hayden, & Platt, 2010). I will not review those critiques in any detail here, but I think this is an important point to keep in mind as you continue reading this chapter, as are other issues such as the external validity of some intertemporal choice tests that will be covered in Chapter 9, How Do We Know Whether We Are Measuring Self-Control? Methodological Concerns Lead to a New Test.

As a general rule, pigeons tend to choose impulsively during intertemporal choice tests (e.g., Logue & Peña-Correal, 1984, 1985). However, as with humans, preferences can shift more toward delayed rewards as a function of how the choice contingencies are presented. Ainslie and Herrnstein (1981) provided one early example of close similarity between human choice behavior and that of pigeons in a smaller-sooner (SS), larger-later (LL) task. When pigeons were offered a choice between 2 seconds of access to food or 4 seconds of access to food but delayed 4 seconds longer than the SS option, their choice of the LL option increased as the initial delay to both options increased. This means that pigeons were more likely to choose the LL option when the two delays were 12 seconds and 16 seconds than when they were 2 seconds and 6 seconds. In both cases, it is the same additional 4 seconds to the larger amount, but preference reversal occurred with longer delays, consistent with the idea that hyperbolic discounting better accounts for choice than exponential discounting (as I discussed in Chapter 3: Human Intertemporal Choices: Choosing Between Now and Later). King and Logue (1990) showed that, as with humans, pigeons' choices for the LL option could be increased by increasing the relative difference in reward preference between the SS and LL options. Logue and Chavarro (1987) showed that manipulating the amount of reward, the delay intervals, and the rates of reinforcement also affected pigeons' choices of SS and LL options (also see Chelonis, King, Logue, & Tobin, 1994).

The previous experiences of pigeons in similar choice tests also impacted SS and LL choices. For example, Mazur and Logue (1978) showed that pigeons that first learned to choose 6 seconds of access to grain after 6 seconds of delay versus only 2 seconds of access to grain after 6 seconds of delay chose the longer access period. This makes perfect sense because the delay was equated so all that had to be considered was how long food was available. What was interesting was that those birds later made more choices for 6 seconds of access after 6 seconds of delay compared to 2 seconds of access immediately. In other words, that early experience of having to wait no matter what allowed the birds to make more delayed choices later (also see Logue & Mazur, 1981; Logue, Rodriguez, Peña-Correal, & Mauro, 1984). This same effect was also shown for rats (e.g., van Haaren, van Hest, & van de Poll, 1988). Other studies, however, demonstrated that some manipulations seemed to have little or no effect on changing pigeons' choice behavior. Food deprivation, for example, seemed to have no effect on the delay discounting of pigeons (e.g., Logue & Peña-Correal, 1985).

Rats also have been tested extensively, with varying results. Some experiments have shown that rats make more choices of LL options compared to pigeons (e.g., van Haaren et al., 1988). However, as I noted, in that experiment the rats had some previous experience with tolerating delays. Other work indicated that rats were impulsive, tending to choose the SS outcomes most often (e.g., Tobin, Chelonis, & Logue, 1993).[2] Extensive work on rat choice behavior with SS and LL options has been done by Kirkpatrick and her colleagues. I think this research program nicely highlights some of the main outcomes of testing animals, and specifically testing them in ways that relate to how humans have been tested. Kirkpatrick has shown that impulsivity appears to be fairly stable within rats across different tests and across time (e.g., Galtress, Garcia, & Kirkpatrick, 2012; Marshall, Smith, & Kirkpatrick, 2014; Peterson, Hill, & Kirkpatrick, 2015) much like it is in humans (e.g., Jimura et al., 2011). For example, in one study, the same rats were tested twice with a 5-month delay in between, and there was strong consistency in the degree of impulsive choice shown by individual rats at each test time (Peterson et al., 2015). Rats also show consistency in their

2. I am writing as if all rats are the same. They are not, and especially when one looks at strain differences and intertemporal choices. Some research has shown that strain differences in impulsivity and self-control can be fairly large (e.g., Garcia & Kirkpatrick, 2013; Wilhelm & Mitchell, 2009), and so this must be considered as you read the more general findings that I am highlighting. Of course, individual differences can also be large in all species that we test, as can differences within the same individuals in different kinds of tests. Self-control is not a thing, and thus is not equally brought to bear on all tasks, in the same way, by all individuals or all species (or strains). This is an important point to remember as you read about the *general outcomes* that have been reported.

degree of delay discounting across a variety of different testing methods, which is important both for showing their value as an animal model of self-control and for providing comparative evidence of test–retest reliability not just as a function of time elapsing, but also as a function of the use of different assessment techniques (Peterson et al., 2015). Fig. 4.1 highlights this in terms of the discounting functions seen for two testing procedures used across four testing phases. The discounting curves are very similar in all cases, despite the changes in testing procedures.

Given the general degree of steep discounting of future rewards, it is a natural question as to whether rats can improve their self-control responses. They can! A key issue would seem to be giving them more experience with timing intervals and judging those intervals. We know that rats that are better at timing intervals are also those rats that make fewer impulsive choices (e.g., McClure, Podos, & Richardson, 2014), a finding which leads to the idea that improvements in choice could come from improvements in timing. For example, when rats were trained on a differential reinforcement of low rates task, where they had to wait beyond a set delay time between each

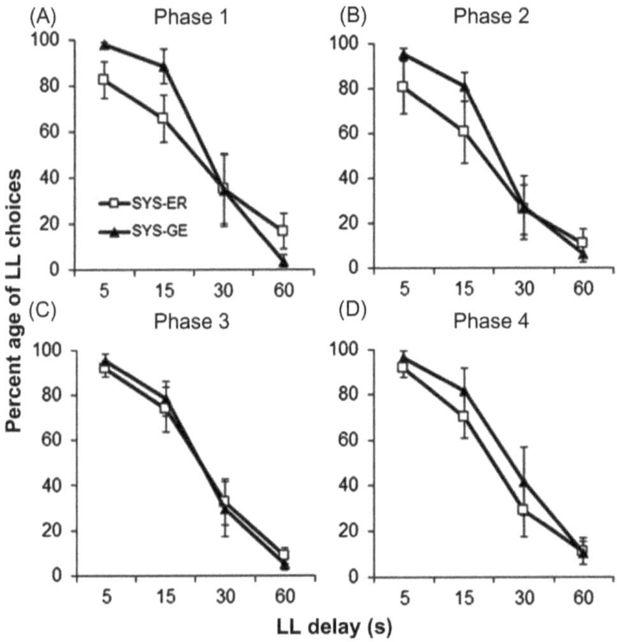

FIGURE 4.1 A demonstration of the consistent levels of choice of the LL option for rats in two conditions of four phases of the study in Peterson et al. (2015). *From Peterson, J. R., Hill, C. C., & Kirkpatrick, K. (2015). Measurement of impulsive choice in rats: Same-and alternate-form test–retest reliability and temporal tracking.* Journal of the Experimental Analysis of Behavior, 103, *166–179, reprinted with permission of John Wiley & Sons.*

response they made (and thus had to learn to wait to respond), they later showed more choices of LL options in an intertemporal choice test. And, it appears that these interventions also affect rats by making them more sensitive (and better) at timing intervals (Smith, Marshall, & Kirkpatrick, 2015). In another study (Marshall et al., 2014), some rats were trained to get better at making temporal bisection judgments (which are basically judgments of whether a light was presented for a long or short duration; Church & Delutty, 1977). Other rats were tested instead for their sensitivity in discriminating food magnitudes. The rats that were better at the time estimation task showed less impulsive responding, whereas there was no relation between magnitude sensitivity and impulsivity (but see Marshall & Kirkpatrick, 2016). Other research has confirmed this effect of temporal sensitivity training and impulsivity, and with older rats (Peterson & Kirkpatrick, 2016). This relationship relates back to a point I raised in Chapter 3 about the degree to which sensitivity to time may impact how one evaluates delayed rewards. These rat studies as well as other studies with humans (e.g., Cui, 2011; van den Broek, Bradshaw, & Szabadi, 1992; Wittmann & Paulus, 2008) suggest that temporal processing may be a key issue in impulsivity (Baumann & Odum, 2012; Takahashi, 2005). They also suggest that training better temporal estimation abilities may lead to greater self-control during intertemporal choices.

Another interesting finding is a connection between working memory and delay discounting. Working memory refers to our ability to hold and mentally manipulate information through a controlled cognitive process. We use working memory when we determine a sequence of events and then remember to do those in order, or when we try to remember all of the items that we wrote on a grocery list after we forget that list in our car and are now in the store. It turns out that poor working memory capacity is related to steeper delay discounting in humans (e.g., Shamosh et al., 2008), *and also in rats* (Renda, Stein, & Madden, 2014; but see Dellu-Hagedorn, 2006). If one improves the working memory of human participants, by giving them a training regimen to enhance their working memory, you also see a decrease in discounting delayed rewards (Bickel, Yi, Landes, Hill, & Baxter, 2011). And, if one improves working memory in rats, you also see decreases in delay discounting (Renda, Stein, & Madden, 2015).

Rat behavior parallels human behavior in other ways, as well. Both rats and humans show a strong relationship between impulsive choices and risky behaviors within individuals. This has led to the suggestion that these are actual trait variables in humans (e.g., Kirby, 2009; Odum, 2011; Ohmura, Takahashi, Kitamura, & Wehr, 2006) and in rats (e.g., Galtress et al., 2012; Garcia & Kirkpatrick, 2013). It seems to me that in both cases, taking risks and preferring more immediate reward are the result of difficulties with behavioral inhibition along with a general bias towards impulsive responding. And, of course, a person with this trait or these traits is going to be at greater risk for a whole host of problems in life because of their impulsive choices (de Wit, 2008; Perry & Carroll, 2008; Reynolds, 2006).

We also know that people who tend to eat a lot of fats and sugars also tend to respond more impulsively (Lumley, Stevenson, Oaten, Mahmut, & Yeomans, 2016). This relationship certainly is related to obesity levels because there is a negative feedback loop involved. The more you eat foods that are likely to make you gain weight, the more impulsive your future food choices may be, and impulsive food choices tend to be for less healthy foods. Turns out, rats show a similar relation. When rats were maintained on a diet high in sugar and fat (compared to control rats) they made more impulsive choices. However, when all rats were put on the same healthy diet later, this difference largely (but not entirely) disappeared (Steele, Pirkle, & Kirkpatrick, 2017).

The studies with rats and pigeons have helped situate human choice behavior in a better evolutionary perspective. Our shortcomings during intertemporal choices are shared with other species, and likely result, at least in part, from other fallibilities in our cognitive system. Certainly, timing mechanisms are highly relevant to choice behavior across species. And, it seems that, at least in mammals, there may even be shared traits within individuals of different species that generate risky behaviors and short-sighted decisions. However, the studies I have reviewed so far also show that there is room for improvement in terms of making better choices and opting for more delayed rewards. Rats clearly can do this in a number of ways and it may be that rats are better than pigeons at choosing more delayed rewards. This is interesting because rats show other cognitive capacities less frequently reported for pigeons. For example, rats have shown evidence of metacognition (Foote & Crystal, 2007, 2012; Kirk, McMillan, & Roberts, 2014; Templer, Lee, & Preston, 2017; Yuki & Okanoya, 2017) whereas the evidence is mixed for pigeons (Adams & Santi, 2011; Castro & Wasserman, 2013; Iwasaki, Watanabe, & Fujita, 2013, 2018; Sole, Shettleworth, & Bennett, 2003). And, as I will discuss in Chapter 14, Mental Time Travel: What Is It, and How Does It Relate to Self-Control?, there is good evidence that rats engage in prospective cognition, in terms of anticipating future events (Crystal, 2013; Wilson & Crystal, 2012; Wilson, Pizzo, & Crystal, 2013). Even comparing pigeons to rats for intertemporal choices already highlights the idea that species will differ in their ability to make more future-oriented responses, an important point when using data from animals to understand the evolution of human self-control. However, it is equally important to note that there have been very few direct comparisons of intertemporal choice tests across multiple species, and so we do not have a fully informed phylogenetic map of such choice behavior. Rather, we have largely isolated individual studies with different species, along with extensive work with pigeons and rats.

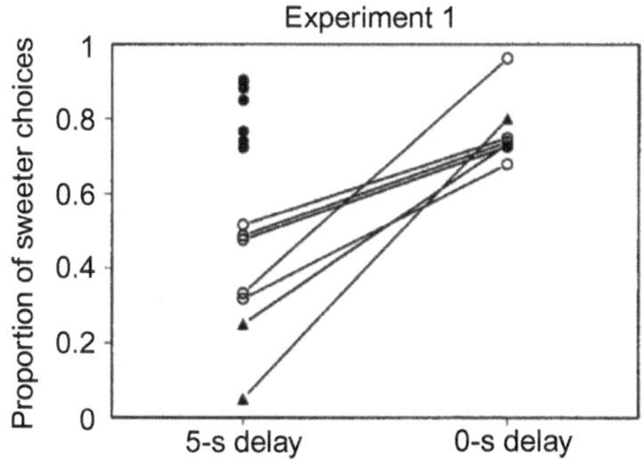

FIGURE 4.2 Proportion of choices of the sweeter reward by individual honeybees in Experiment 1. The left column indicates choices when the sweeter reward was delayed by 5 s. Filled circles indicate bees that significantly preferred the sweeter reward, open circles indicate bees that were indifferent between the two rewards, and triangles indicate bees that significantly preferred the less sweet reward. The right column indicates the choices of those bees that did not significantly prefer the delayed sweeter reward when offered both rewards without delay. *From Cheng, K. E. N., Peña, J., Porter, M. A., &Irwin, J. D. (2002). Self-control in honeybees.* Psychonomic Bulletin & Review, 9, *259–263, reprinted with permission of Springer.*

So, do other species tend to show better self-control than pigeons and rats? And, what might predict how well a given species does at choosing better, more delayed rewards? One hypothesis is that the degree of delay discounting should be negatively correlated with metabolic rate, where species with faster metabolic rates would be more inclined to discount future rewards more steeply (Tobin & Logue, 1994). However, a test with honeybees instead showed a high degree of self-control despite the high metabolic rate of this species. Many bees consistently chose the delayed rewards (Cheng, Peña, Porter, & Irwin, 2002; Fig. 4.2). Bees tend to work in a highly cooperative fashion, largely for the goal of hive survival, and so one might hypothesize that this places a higher premium on long-term goal maintenance rather than immediate satisfaction. And, bees forage for the best possible sources of energy, and so a better reward, even if delayed, might prove to be highly salient to that species. That said, in cases where bees reach a point of starving, self-control disappears (Mayack & Naug, 2015). Again, this makes sense, given that there must be cases in which immediate consumption is the better choice, or cases where failing to act on a more immediate reward could lead to injury or death (e.g., Stephens & Anderson, 2001). Another insect, the ant, also shows self-control behavior by traveling farther for a better food reward even though food is nearer in space (Wendt & Czaczkes, 2017; also see Mühlhoff, Stevens, & Reader, 2011, for a similar study with fish). In the case of the ants, time was represented also as distance, and there were multiple conditions. Most ants (69%) successfully traveled farther to get the better reward, and ignored the closer, poorer reward, when the differences in reward quality were large. But, when the far and the close rewards were of the same quality, then most of the ants went to the closer feeder, showing that they were sensitive to distance and quality of reward. In stark contrast to honeybees and ants are domestic chickens, which show little or no self-control choices, instead making impulsive choices except in cases where the delayed reward is massively large compared to the more immediate reward (Abeyesinghe, Nicol, Hartnell, & Wathes, 2005).

In recent years, primates have increasingly been the subjects of intertemporal choice tests. One of the first tests used macaque monkeys, with highly impressive results (Tobin, Logue, Chelonis, Ackerman, & May, 1996). When offered the SS and LL options, the two monkeys chose the LL options on more than 90% of trials. When the delay to the larger award was adjusted to find a point at which a monkey was indifferent between the SS and LL options, that point was close to a 1-minute delay for the larger reward compared to the immediate delivery of the smaller reward. This was a very promising outcome for future self-control tests with nonhuman species, and subsequent work verified that nonhuman primates can be excellent subjects for examining self-control and examining what affects choice behavior. A number of other primate species now have been given intertemporal choice tests, including lemurs (Stevens & Mühlhoff, 2012), cotton-top tamarins and common marmosets (Stevens, Hallinan, & Hauser, 2005), brown capuchins (Addessi, Paglieri, & Focaroli, 2011; Amici, Aureli, & Call, 2008), black-handed spider monkeys (Amici et al., 2008), long-tailed macaques (Amici et al., 2008), lowland gorillas (Amici et al., 2008), orangutans (Amici et al., 2008), and bonobos and chimpanzees (Rosati, Stevens, Hare, & Hauser, 2007). Stevens and Mühlhoff (2012) compared the outcomes of all of those studies and additional studies with nonprimate species, to reflect the large species differences that have been documented (Fig. 4.3).

A big question for researchers working with nonhuman primates is what accounts for these species differences? Stevens and Mühlhoff (2012) offered a number of possibilities, ranging from metabolic rate, body size, life span, and reward maximization theory. They argued that body size was a good predictor of choice (Fig. 4.4), although there are other possibilities. Amici et al. (2008) argued that species that undergo more fission (spreading out of group members) and fusion (coming back together) show greater delay tolerance, whereas Stevens et al. (2005) argued that perhaps diet plays an important role. In Stevens et al., common marmosets, who often have to wait to extract foods such as saps that exude from trees, showed more delay tolerance than did tamarins, who typically grab and consume moving prey items. This suggests that perhaps what accounts for species differences is feeding ecology, where those species that have to wait more often for their food would show greater delay tolerance during intertemporal or inter-spatial tasks such as those I have been describing (see Stevens & Stephens, 2009). This remains a highly engaging and productive debate, to determine what accounts for

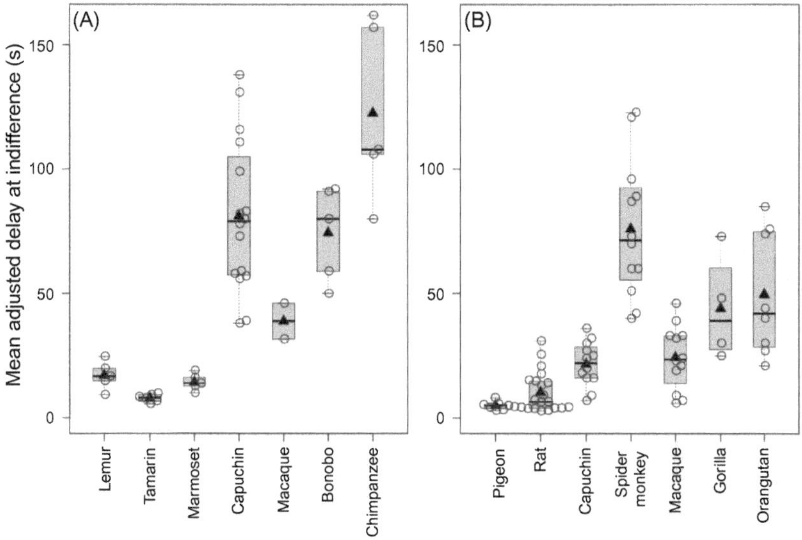

FIGURE 4.3 Intertemporal choice across animal species. (A) Seven species have been tested using the same adjusting-delay procedure with two versus six food items: lemurs (Stevens & Mühlhoff, 2012), cotton-top tamarins and common marmosets (Stevens et al., 2005), brown capuchins (Addessi et al., 2011), long-tailed macaques (Tobin et al., 1996), and bonobos and chimpanzees (Rosati et al., 2007). The mean adjusted delay at indifference for lemurs matched that found in common marmosets. (B) Other studies used similar but not identical adjusting-delay procedures for seven species: White Carneau pigeons (Green, Myerson, Shah, Estle, & Holt, 2007), Wistar rats (Perry, Larson, German, Madden, & Carroll, 2004), and brown capuchins, black-handed spider monkeys, long-tailed macaques, lowland gorillas, and orangutans (Amici et al., 2008). The capuchins and macaques are the same species in both panels, and some of the capuchin data are from the same individuals in both panels. In this figure, circles represent data points for individual subjects, triangles represent the mean, lines represent the median, boxes represent the interquartile range (25%–75%), and whiskers represent the range. *From Stevens, J. R., & Mühlhoff, N. (2012). Intertemporal choice in lemurs.* Behavioural Processes, 89, *121–127, with permission of Elsevier.*

differences in how animals[3] discount the future and value different outcomes on the basis of their magnitude, delay, and effort to acquire. I will discuss in more detail some of these primate studies in Chapter 9 when I outline some of the concerns that come from using intertemporal choices tasks that involve pointing toward response options, which has been the case for many of the tests given to nonhuman primates.

3. Recently, this research question has moved away from biological subjects. Paglieri, Parisi, Patacchiola, and Petrosino (2015) have created and evolved simulated robots that can be presented with different environments and different organismic features, such as having a metabolism or not. This allows for carefully controlled studies of the effects of these factors on intertemporal choices, and offers a nice comparison against the data collected with human and other animals.

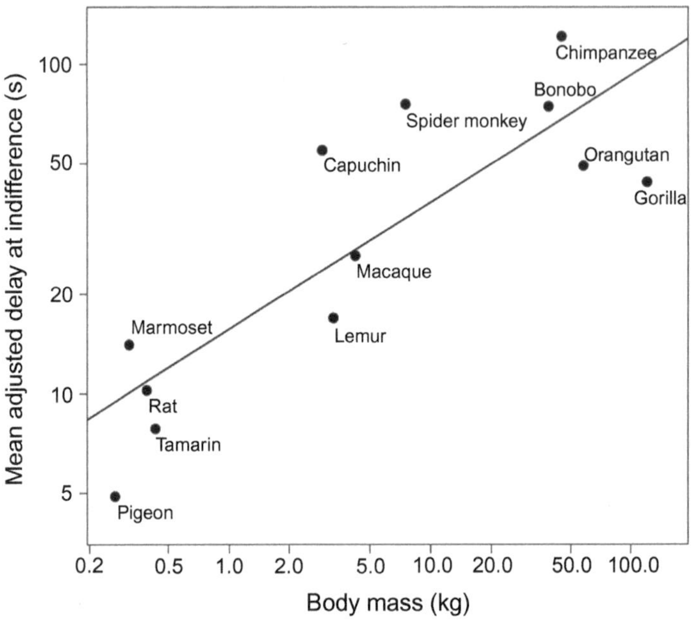

FIGURE 4.4 Body mass and intertemporal choice performance across species. These data are from Stevens and Mühlhoff. Data from all capuchin and macaque subjects were pooled to generate a single mean adjusted delay for each species. Both *x*- and *y*-axis are log scaled. *From Stevens, J. R., & Mühlhoff, N. (2012). Intertemporal choice in lemurs.* Behavioural Processes, *89, 121–127, with permission of Elsevier.*

There is one area in which humans seems to be quite different from other animals in terms of their intertemporal choices, and what impacts those choices. Humans typically show what is known as the *magnitude effect*. For the same temporal delays (to smaller or larger rewards), there is a shift toward less discounting of the more delayed reward when reward magnitudes are larger. So, a person who might chose $10 after a day rather than $50 after a week will be more likely to choose $500 after a week compared to $100 after a day (Green & Myerson, 2010). This is a robust effect in humans. It occurs for all kinds of rewards (money: Green, Myerson, & McFadden, 1997; Kirby & Marakovic, 1996; consumable rewards: Estle, Green, Myerson, & Holt, 2007; cigarettes: Baker, Johnson, & Bickel, 2003; heroin: Giordano *et al.* 2002; medical treatments: Chapman, 1996). It occurs in other cultures (Du, Green, & Myerson, 2002; Tan & Johnson, 1996). Rats and pigeons, however, show no such magnitude effect (Grace, 1999; Green, Myerson, Holt, Slevin, & Estle, 2004; Oliveira, Green, & Myerson, 2014). Primates also typically fail to show a magnitude effect. For example, in the study by Stevens et al. (2005) in which marmosets and tamarins were given a task where they had to move farther for a better reward, there was no increase in the likelihood of them making the longer movement when the amount of reward was increased. In some cases, one gets the *opposite effect* to humans, where larger rewards lead to increased choice of the SS option (De Petrillo et al., 2015; Ong & White, 2004; Orduña, Valencia-Torres, Cruz, & Bouzas, 2013; Richards, Mitchell, de Wit, & Seiden, 1997). Note that magnitude effects often are tested by increasing *both rewards* while keeping the delays to each at the same relative difference. Thus, nonhuman animals may be biased to attend more to magnitude when it increases for the more immediate outcome relative to what it had been. Animals certainly do attend to qualitative changes in reward type, and they do so in ways not seen for quantitative changes. For example, Freeman, Nonnemacher, Green, Myerson, and Woolverton (2012) reported that monkeys showed no change in their discounting of delayed rewards when those rewards were increased from being a 10% sucrose solution to a much sweeter 20% solution. However, the monkeys discounted delayed sucrose more than they discounted delayed heroin even when the delay intervals to SS and LL outcomes were the same for both reward types. Thus, reward quality plays a role in choice reversals for nonhuman animals, whereas to date it seems that reward magnitude is less relevant.

The final thing I want to highlight about these kinds of tests with nonhuman animals is, to me, the most interesting, and also had the largest impact on my career and my own research. In later chapters, I will talk about delay of gratification tests, including the famous marshmallow test given to children, as well as the varieties of other tests designed for use with children and with nonhuman animals. My research has largely been inspired more by delay of gratification tests than intertemporal choice tests such as those I described in this chapter and the last chapter, but a subset of those intertemporal choice tests with pigeons truly caught my attention. As I have noted, pigeons tend to be impulsive in most cases, choosing SS over LL options, and steeply discounting the future. And, as you will read later, some human children also discount future rewards. But, many do not, and in those cases, what one sees is that certain behavioral strategies clearly support better delay of gratification. In Chapter 1 I presented the kitchen safe as a tool for forcing oneself to tolerate a delay until something pleasant could be obtained. Locking away the cookies, or the rent money, or your smart phone, all *precommit* you to delaying gratification. This precommitment is highly effective, and in part because one can precommit at a time *before* the actual choice between a now or later reward is available. People put cookies into the kitchen safe when they are not interested in eating them so that, later, when they are really interested in eating them, they cannot. Turns out, pigeons will do that too, and learning this set me on a course to later studying how chimpanzees and other animals might approach delay of gratification tasks in similar strategic ways.

Rachlin and Green (1972) introduced a new stage to the two-option intertemporal choice test. In what they called "Choice Y" the pigeons could choose between 2 seconds of access to food immediately or 4 seconds of access to food, but delayed by 4 seconds. This is the usual kind of intertemporal choice I have been discussing. But, the pigeons also made "Choice X" first, which offered them either a delay of some number of seconds followed by the chance to make the "Choice Y" response or a delay of some number of seconds after which they *had to choose the delayed 4 seconds of food access*. So, in essence, the first choice was to either commit to making the delayed choice later, or to leave both the SS and LL options available for that second choice on each trial. The idea here was based, in part, on work showing that people would choose to commit themselves to locking away their cigarettes fairly often right after they have a cigarette, because the next cigarette is not that tempting. It is only later, when it is desired (but locked away) that a person would prefer to smoke it, but by then it is too late (Azrin & Powell, 1968). The pigeons frequently opted to commit themselves to the LL option when they could. Strikingly, whenever they had both options still available at "Choice Y," however, they chose the SS option! This seems very much like precommitting to a course of action that prevents an almost necessary impulsive response without such precommitment.

In another study (Ainslie, 1974), pigeons were given a small, immediate reward whenever they pecked a key that was colored red. But, if they refrained from pecking it for a period of time, they got a bigger reward. This was very difficult, however, and the pigeons consistently pecked at the key (~95% of the time). However, early in each trial they also had the chance to peck that key when it was instead green. If they did this, the key turned off and never came on as red during that trial, and thus never offered the temptation to peck it to get the small reward. Rather, the delayed, large reward became guaranteed. Three of 10 pigeons learned to turn off the red key that would almost definitely lead them to lose out on the delayed reward. And, when that earlier green key no longer functioned to *precommit* the pigeons to the delay, they stopped using it. To me, these results suggested that other species might be capable of the kinds of strategic behaviors that better afforded delayed gratification rather than impulsive choices. And, they provided a clear link with the large literature on children's delay of gratification, opening up new ideas for how to study strategic self-control across species. I will next outline that developmental research, and how a simple test with a marshmallow (or two) has taught us a lot about how children demonstrate self-control and adapt their behavior to delay with the frustration of delayed rewards.

REFERENCES

Abeyesinghe, S. M., Nicol, C. J., Hartnell, S. J., & Wathes, C. M. (2005). Can domestic fowl, *Gallus gallus domesticus*, show self-control? *Animal Behaviour, 70*, 1–11.

Adams, A., & Santi, A. (2011). Pigeons exhibit higher accuracy for chosen memory tests than for forced memory tests in duration matching-to-sample. *Learning and Behavior, 39*, 1–11.

Addessi, E., Paglieri, F., & Focaroli, V. (2011). The ecological rationality of delay tolerance: Insights from capuchin monkeys. *Cognition, 119*, 142–147.

Ainslie, G. W. (1974). Impulse control in pigeons. *Journal of the Experimental Analysis of Behavior, 21*, 485–489.

Ainslie, G. W., & Herrnstein, R. J. (1981). Preference reversal and delayed reinforcement. *Animal Learning & Behavior, 9*, 476–482.

Amici, F., Aureli, F., & Call, J. (2008). Fission-fusion dynamics, behavioral flexibility, and inhibitory control in primates. *Current Biology, 18*, 1415–1419.

Azrin, N. H., & Powell, J. (1968). Behavioral engineering: The reduction of smoking behavior by a conditioning apparatus and procedure. *Journal of Applied Behavior Analysis, 1*, 193–200.

Baker, F., Johnson, M. W., & Bickel, W. K. (2003). Delay discounting in current and never-before cigarette smokers: Similarities and differences across commodity, sign, and magnitude. *Journal of Abnormal Psychology, 112*, 382–392.

Baumann, A. A., & Odum, A. L. (2012). Impulsivity, risk taking, and timing. *Behavioural Processes, 90*, 408–414.

Bickel, W. K., Yi, R., Landes, R. D., Hill, P. F., & Baxter, C. (2011). Remember the future: Working memory training decreases delay discounting among stimulant addicts. *Biological Psychiatry, 69*, 260–265.

Blanchard, T. C., Pearson, J. M., & Hayden, B. Y. (2013). Postreward delays and systematic biases in measures of animal temporal discounting. *Proceedings of the National Academy of Sciences, 110*, 15491–15496.

Castro, L., & Wasserman, E. A. (2013). Information-seeking behavior: Exploring metacognitive control in pigeons. *Animal Cognition, 16*, 241–254.

Chapman, G. B. (1996). Temporal discounting and utility for health and money. *Journal of Experimental Psychology: Learning, Memory & Cognition, 22*, 771–791.

Chelonis, J. J., King, G., Logue, A. W., & Tobin, H. (1994). The effect of variable delays on self-control. *Journal of the Experimental Analysis of Behavior, 62*, 33–43.

Cheng, K. E. N., Peña, J., Porter, M. A., & Irwin, J. D. (2002). Self-control in honeybees. *Psychonomic Bulletin & Review, 9*, 259–263.

Church, R. M., & Deluty, M. Z. (1977). Bisection of temporal intervals. *Journal of Experimental Psychology: Animal Behavior Processes, 3*, 216–228.

Crystal, J. D. (2013). Remembering the past and planning for the future in rats. *Behavioural Processes, 93*, 39–49.

Cui, X. (2011). Hyperbolic discounting emerges from the scalar property of interval timing. *Frontiers in Integrative Neuroscience, 5*, 24.

de Wit, H. (2008). Impulsivity as a determinant and consequence of drug use: A review of underlying processes. *Addiction Biology, 14*, 22–31.

De Petrillo, F., Gori, E., Micucci, A., Ponsi, G., Paglieri, F., & Addessi, E. (2015). When is it worth waiting for? Food quantity, but not food quality, affects delay tolerance in tufted capuchin monkeys. *Animal Cognition, 18*, 1019–1029.

Dellu-Hagedorn, F. (2006). Relationship between impulsivity, hyperactivity and working memory: A differential analysis in the rat. *Behavioral and Brain Functions*, *2*, 10.

Du, W., Green, L., & Myerson, J. (2002). Cross-cultural comparisons of discounting delayed and probabilistic rewards. *Psychological Research*, *52*, 479–492.

Estle, S. J., Green, L., Myerson, J., & Holt, D. D. (2007). Discounting of monetary and directly consumable rewards. *Psychological Science*, *18*, 58–63.

Foote, A. L., & Crystal, J. D. (2007). Metacognition in the rat. *Current Biology*, *17*, 551–555.

Foote, A. L., & Crystal, J. D. (2012). "Play it again": A new method for testing metacognition in animals. *Animal Cognition*, *15*, 187–199.

Freeman, K. B., Nonnemacher, J. E., Green, L., Myerson, J., & Woolverton, W. L. (2012). Delay discounting in rhesus monkeys: Equivalent discounting of more and less preferred sucrose concentrations. *Learning & Behavior*, *40*, 54–60.

Galtress, T., Garcia, A., & Kirkpatrick, K. (2012). Individual differences in impulsive choice and timing in rats. *Journal of the Experimental Analysis of Behavior*, *98*, 65–87.

Garcia, A., & Kirkpatrick, K. (2013). Impulsive choice behavior in four strains of rats: Evaluation of possible models of Attention-Deficit/Hyperactivity Disorder. *Behavioural Brain Research*, *238*, 10–22.

Giordano, L. A., Bickel, W. K., Loewenstein, G., Jacobs, E. A., Marsch, L., & Badger, G. J. (2002). Mild opioid deprivation increases the degree that opioid-dependent outpatients discount delayed heroin and money. *Psychopharmacology*, *163*, 174–182.

Grace, R. C. (1999). The matching law and amount-dependent exponential discounting as accounts of self-control choice. *Journal of the Experimental Analysis of Behavior*, *71*, 27–44.

Green, L., & Myerson, J. (2010). Experimental and correlational analyses of delay and probability discounting. In G. J. Madden & W. K. Bickel (Eds.), *Impulsivity: The behavioral and neurological science of discounting* (pp. 67–92). Washington, DC: American Psychological Association.

Green, L., Myerson, J., Holt, D. D., Slevin, J. R., & Estle, S. J. (2004). Discounting of delayed food rewards in pigeons and rats: Is there a magnitude effect? *Journal of the Experimental Analysis of Behavior*, *81*, 39–50.

Green, L., Myerson, J., & McFadden, E. (1997). Rate of temporal discounting decreases with amount of reward. *Memory and Cognition*, *25*, 717–723.

Green, L., Myerson, J., Shah, A. K., Estle, S. J., & Holt, D. D. (2007). Do adjusting-amount and adjusting-delay procedures produce equivalent estimates of subjective value in pigeons? *Journal of the Experimental Analysis of Behavior*, *87*, 337–347.

van Haaren, F., van Hest, A., & van de Poll, N. E. (1988). Self-control in male and female rats. *Journal of the Experimental Analysis of Behavior*, *49*, 201–211.

Hayden, B. Y. (2016). Time discounting and time preference in animals: A critical review. *Psychonomic Bulletin & Review*, *23*, 39–53.

Hayden, B. Y., & Platt, M. L. (2007). Temporal discounting predicts risk sensitivity in rhesus macaques. *Current Biology*, *17*, 49–53.

Heilbronner, S. R., Rosati, A. G., Stevens, J. R., Hare, B., & Hauser, M. D. (2008). A fruit in the hand or two in the bush? Divergent risk preferences in chimpanzees and bonobos. *Biology Letters*, *4*, 246–249.

Iwasaki, S., Watanabe, S., & Fujita, K. (2013). Do pigeons (*Columba livia*) seek information when they have insufficient knowledge? *Animal Cognition*, *13*, 211–221.

Iwasaki, S., Watanabe, S., & Fujita, K. (2018). Pigeons (*Columba livia*) know when they will need hints: Prospective metacognition for reference memory? *Animal Cognition*, *21*, 207–217.

Jimura, K., Myerson, J., Hilgard, J., Keighley, J., Braver, T. S., & Green, L. (2011). Domain independence and stability in young and older adults' discounting of delayed rewards. *Behavioural Processes*, *87*, 253–259.

Kacelnik, A., & Bateson, M. (1996). Risky theories—The effects of variance on foraging decisions. *American Zoologist*, *36*, 402–434.

King, G. R., & Logue, A. W. (1990). Choice in a self-control paradigm: Effects of reinforcer quality. *Behavioural Processes*, *22*, 89–99.

Kirby, K. N. (2009). One-year temporal stability of delay-discount rates. *Psychonomic Bulletin & Review*, *16*, 457–462.

Kirby, K. N., & Marakovic, N. N. (1996). Delay-discounting probabilistic rewards: Rates decrease as amounts increase. *Psychonomic Bulletin & Review*, *3*, 100–104.

Kirk, C. R., McMillan, N., & Roberts, W. A. (2014). Rats respond for information: Metacognition in a rodent? *Journal of Experimental Psychology: Animal Learning and Cognition*, *40*, 249–259.

Logue, A. W. (1988). Research on self-control: An integrating framework. *Behavioral and Brain Sciences*, *11*, 665–679.

Logue, A. W., & Chavarro, A. (1987). Effect on choice of absolute and relative values of reinforcer delay, amount, and frequency. *Journal of Experimental Psychology: Animal Behavior Processes*, *13*, 280–291.

Logue, A. W., & Mazur, J. E. (1981). Maintenance of self-control acquired through a fading procedure: Follow-up on Mazur and Logue (1978). *Behaviour Analysis Letters*, *1*, 131–137.

Logue, A. W., & Peña-Correal, T. E. (1984). Responding during reinforcement delay in a self-control paradigm. *Journal of the Experimental Analysis of Behavior*, *41*, 267–277.

Logue, A. W., & Peña-Correal, T. E. (1985). The effect of food deprivation on self-control. *Behavioural Processes*, *10*, 355–368.

Logue, A. W., Rodriguez, M. L., Peña-Correal, T. E., & Mauro, B. C. (1984). Choice in a self-control paradigm: Quantification of experience-based differences. *Journal of the Experimental Analysis of Behavior*, *41*, 53–67.

Lumley, J., Stevenson, R. J., Oaten, M. J., Mahmut, M., & Yeomans, M. R. (2016). Individual differences in impulsivity and their relationship to a Western-style diet. *Personality and Individual Differences*, *97*, 178–185.

Marsh, B., & Kacelnik, A. (2002). Framing effects and risky decisions in starlings. *Proceedings of the National Academy of Sciences*, *99*, 3352–3355.

Marshall, A. T., & Kirkpatrick, K. (2016). Mechanisms of impulsive choice: III. The role of reward processes. *Behavioural Processes*, *123*, 134–148.

Marshall, A. T., Smith, A. P., & Kirkpatrick, K. (2014). Mechanisms of impulsive choice: I. Individual differences in interval timing and reward processing. *Journal of the Experimental Analysis of Behavior*, *102*, 86–101.

Mayack, C., & Naug, D. (2015). Starving honeybees lose self-control. *Biology Letters*, *11*, 20140820.

Mazur, J. E., & Logue, A. W. (1978). Choice in a "self-control" paradigm: Effects of a fading procedure. *Journal of the Experimental Analysis of Behavior*, *30*, 11–17.

McClure, J., Podos, J., & Richardson, H. N. (2014). Isolating the delay component of impulsive choice in adolescent rats. *Frontiers in Integrative Neuroscience*, *8*, 3.

McCoy, A. N., & Platt, M. L. (2005). Risk-sensitive neurons in macaque posterior cingulate cortex. *Nature Neuroscience*, *8*, 1220.

Mühlhoff, N., Stevens, J. R., & Reader, S. M. (2011). Spatial discounting of food and social rewards in guppies (*Poecilia reticulata*). *Frontiers in Psychology*, *2*, 68.

Odum, A. L. (2011). Delay discounting: Trait variable? *Behavioural Processes, 87*, 1–9.

Ohmura, Y., Takahashi, T., Kitamura, N., & Wehr, P. (2006). Three-month stability of delay and probability discounting measures. *Experimental and Clinical Psychopharmacology, 14*, 318–328.

Oliveira, L., Green, L., & Myerson, J. (2014). Pigeons' delay discounting functions established using a concurrent-chains procedure. *Journal of the Experimental Analysis of Behavior, 102*, 151–161.

Ong, E. L., & White, K. G. (2004). Amount-dependent temporal discounting? *Behavioural Processes, 66*, 201–212.

Orduña, V., Valencia-Torres, L., Cruz, G., & Bouzas, A. (2013). Sensitivity to delay is affected by magnitude of reinforcement in rats. *Behavioural Processes, 98*, 18–24.

Paglieri, F. (2013). The costs of delay: Waiting versus postponing in intertemporal choice. *Journal of the Experimental Analysis of Behavior, 99*, 362–377.

Paglieri, F. (2016). Social choice for one: On the rationality of intertemporal decisions. *Behavioural Processes, 127*, 97–108.

Paglieri, F., Parisi, D., Patacchiola, M., & Petrosino, G. (2015). Investigating intertemporal choice through experimental evolutionary robotics. *Behavioural Processes, 115*, 1–18.

Pearson, J. M., Hayden, B. Y., & Platt, M. L. (2010). Explicit information reduces discounting behavior in monkeys. *Frontiers in Psychology, 1*, 237.

Perry, J. L., & Carroll, M. E. (2008). The role of impulsive behavior in drug abuse. *Psychopharmacology, 200*, 1–26.

Perry, J. L., Larson, E. B., German, J. P., Madden, G. J., & Carroll, M. E. (2004). Impulsivity (delay discounting) as a predictor of acquisition of IV cocaine self-administration in female rats. *Psychopharmacology, 178*, 193–201.

Peterson, J. R., Hill, C. C., & Kirkpatrick, K. (2015). Measurement of impulsive choice in rats: Same-and alternate-form test–retest reliability and temporal tracking. *Journal of the Experimental Analysis of Behavior, 103*, 166–179.

Peterson, J. R., & Kirkpatrick, K. (2016). The effects of a time-based intervention on experienced middle-aged rats. *Behavioural Processes, 133*, 44–51.

Rachlin, H. (2000). *The science of self-control*. Cambridge, MA: Harvard University Press.

Rachlin, H., & Green, L. (1972). Commitment, choice and self-control. *Journal of the Experimental Analysis of Behavior, 17*, 15–22.

Renda, C. R., Stein, J. S., & Madden, G. J. (2014). Impulsive choice predicts poor working memory in male rats. *PLoS One, 9*, e93263.

Renda, C. R., Stein, J. S., & Madden, G. J. (2015). Working-memory training: Effects on delay discounting in male Long Evans rats. *Journal of the Experimental Analysis of Behavior, 103*, 50–61.

Reynolds, B. (2006). A review of delay-discounting research with humans: Relations to drug use and gambling. *Behavioural Pharmacology, 17*, 651–667.

Richards, J. B., Mitchell, S. H., de Wit, H., & Seiden, L. S. (1997). Determination of discount functions in rats with an adjusting-amount procedure. *Journal of the Experimental Analysis of Behavior, 67*, 353–366.

Rosati, A. G., Stevens, J. R., Hare, B., & Hauser, M. D. (2007). The evolutionary origins of human patience: Temporal preferences in chimpanzees, bonobos, and adult humans. *Current Biology, 17*, 1663–1668.

Shafir, S., Wiegmann, D. D., Smith, B. H., & Real, L. A. (1999). Risk-sensitive foraging: Choice behaviour of honeybees in response to variability in volume of reward. *Animal Behaviour, 57*, 1055–1061.

Shamosh, N. A., Deyoung, C. G., Green, A. E., Reis, D. L., Johnson, M. R., Conway, A. R., & Gray, J. R. (2008). Individual differences in delay discounting: Relation to intelligence, working memory, and anterior prefrontal cortex. *Psychological Science*, *19*, 904–911.

Smith, A. P., Marshall, A. T., & Kirkpatrick, K. (2015). Mechanisms of impulsive choice: II. Time-based interventions to improve self-control. *Behavioural Processes*, *112*, 29–42.

Sole, L. M., Shettleworth, S. J., & Bennett, P. J. (2003). Uncertainty in pigeons. *Psychonomic Bulletin and Review*, *10*, 738–745.

Steele, C. C., Pirkle, J. R. A., & Kirkpatrick, K. (2017). Diet-induced impulsivity: Effects of a high-fat and a high-sugar diet on impulsive choice in rats. *PLoS One*, *12*, e0180510.

Stephens, D. W., & Anderson, D. (2001). The adaptive value of preference for immediacy: When shortsighted rules have farsighted consequences. *Behavioral Ecology*, *12*, 330–339.

Stevens, J. R., Hallinan, E. V., & Hauser, M. D. (2005). The ecology and evolution of patience in two New World monkeys. *Biology Letters*, *1*, 223–226.

Stevens, J. R., & Mühlhoff, N. (2012). Intertemporal choice in lemurs. *Behavioural Processes*, *89*, 121–127.

Stevens, J. R., & Stephens, D. W. (2009). The adaptive nature of impulsivity. In G. J. Madden & W. K. Bickel (Eds.), *Impulsivity: The behavioral and neurological science of discounting* (pp. 361–387). Washington, DC: American Psychological Association.

Takahashi, T. (2005). Loss of self-control in intertemporal choice may be attributable to logarithmic time-perception. *Medical Hypotheses*, *65*, 691–693.

Tan, C., & Johnson, R. (1996). To wait or not to wait: The influence of culture on discounting behavior. In W. Loke (Ed.), *Perspectives on judgment and decision making* (pp. 297–305). Lanham, MD: Scarecrow Press.

Templer, V. L., Lee, K. A., & Preston, A. J. (2017). Rats know when they remember: Transfer of metacognitive responding across odor-based delayed match-to-sample tests. *Animal Cognition*, *20*, 891–906.

Tobin, H., Chelonis, J. J., & Logue, A. W. (1993). Choice in self-control paradigms using rats. *The Psychological Record*, *43*, 441–454.

Tobin, H., & Logue, A. W. (1994). Self-control across species (*Columba livia*, *Homo sapiens*, and *Rattus norvegicus*). *Journal of Comparative Psychology*, *108*, 126–133.

Tobin, H., Logue, A. W., Chelonis, J. J., Ackerman, K. T., & May, J. G. (1996). Self-control in the monkey *Macaca fascicularis*. *Animal Learning and Behavior*, *24*, 168–174.

van den Broek, M. D., Bradshaw, C. M., & Szabadi, E. (1992). Performance of impulsive and non-impulsive subjects on two temporal differentiation tasks. *Personality and Individual Differences*, *13*, 169–174.

Wendt, S., & Czaczkes, T. J. (2017). Individual ant workers show self-control. *Biology Letters*, *13*, 20170450.

Wilhelm, C. J., & Mitchell, S. H. (2009). Strain differences in delay discounting using inbred rats. *Genes, Brain and Behavior*, *8*, 426–434.

Wilson, A. G., & Crystal, J. D. (2012). Prospective memory in the rat. *Animal Cognition*, *15*, 349–358.

Wilson, A. G., Pizzo, M. J., & Crystal, J. D. (2013). Event-based prospective memory in the rat. *Current Biology*, *23*, 1089–1093.

Wittmann, M., & Paulus, M. P. (2008). Decision making, impulsivity and time perception. *Trends in Cognitive Sciences*, *12*, 7–12.

Yuki, S., & Okanoya, K. (2017). Rats show adaptive choice in a metacognitive task with high uncertainty. *Journal of Experimental Psychology: Animal Learning and Cognition*, *43*, 109–118.

FURTHER READING

Bateson, M., & Kacelnik, A. (1996). Rate currencies and the foraging starling: The fallacy of the averages revisited. *Behavioral Ecology*, *7*, 341–352.

Galtress, T., & Kirkpatrick, K. (2010). Reward magnitude effects on temporal discrimination. *Learning and Motivation*, *41*, 108–124.

Gibbon, J., Church, R. M., Fairhurst, S., & Kacelnik, A. (1988). Scalar expectancy theory and choice between delayed rewards. *Psychological Review*, *95*, 102–114.

Heilbronner, S. R., & Meck, W. H. (2013). Dissociations between interval timing and intertemporal choice following administration of fluoxetine, cocaine, or methamphetamine. *Behavioural Processes*, *101*, 123–134.

Jarmolowicz, D. P., Hudnall, J. L., Hale, L., Fowler, S. C., Bortolato, M., Lemley, S. M., & Sofis, M. J. (2017). Delay discounting as impaired valuation: Delayed rewards in an animal obesity model. *Journal of the Experimental Analysis of Behavior*, *108*, 171–183.

Killeen, P. R., Smith, J. P., & Hanson, S. J. (1981). Central place foraging in *Rattus norvegicus*. *Animal Behaviour*, *29*, 64–70.

Kirkpatrick, K., Marshall, A. T., Clarke, J., & Cain, M. E. (2013). Environmental rearing effects on impulsivity and reward sensitivity. *Behavioral Neuroscience*, *127*, 712–724.

Kirkpatrick, K., Marshall, A. T., & Smith, A. P. (2015). Mechanisms of individual differences in impulsive and risky choice in rats. *Comparative Cognition & Behavior Reviews*, *10*, 45.

Kirkpatrick, K., Marshall, A. T., Smith, A. P., Koci, J., & Park, Y. (2014). Individual differences in impulsive and risky choice: Effects of environmental rearing conditions. *Behavioural Brain Research*, *269*, 115–127.

Mazur, J. E. (2012). Effects of pre-trial response requirements on self-control choice by rats and pigeons. *Journal of the Experimental Analysis of Behavior*, *97*, 215–230.

Rachlin, H. (1995). Self-control: Beyond commitment. *Behavioral and Brain Sciences*, *18*, 109–159.

Stein, J. S., Smits, R. R., Johnson, P. S., Liston, K. J., & Madden, G. J. (2013). Effects of reward bundling on male rats' preference for larger-later food rewards. *Journal of the Experimental Analysis of Behavior*, *99*, 150–158.

Ventricelli, M., Focaroli, V., De Petrillo, F., Macchitella, L., Paglieri, F., & Addessi, E. (2013). How capuchin monkeys (*Cebus apella*) behaviorally cope with increasing delay in a self-control task. *Behavioural Processes*, *100*, 146–152.

Chapter 5

Children's Delay of Gratification: How Long Would You Wait for Marshmallows?

When I give presentations about self-control in humans and animals, or talk about delaying gratification with the students in my classes, or even when I get asked at a party what it is that I study, I know I have a "go to" response that will get nearly universal responses of knowing and understanding. I ask people "have you ever heard of the marshmallow test?" and when they nod their heads quickly and say "oh yeah, that is great," I tell them "well, I do stuff like that, only with animals."[1] Everyone knows the marshmallow test. And, the story of the marshmallow test has been told beautifully by the person who made it famous (Mischel, 2014). I would be a fool to try to do a better job, and so I would strongly encourage you to read that book (after you finish this one!). But, this book would be incomplete without at least covering the highlights of what the marshmallow test has taught us about self-control and delay of gratification. So, I will do that, highlighting those studies that were most influential to my own thinking, and to the subsequent development of animal tests of delayed gratification. I will also tell you a little bit about other ways that delay of gratification has been studied in children, because those approaches have taught us a lot about the ways in which children succeed and fail in monitoring their own short- and long-term desires and then make choices when faced with conflicts between those two things.

1. Although this is what I often do, it is not the only response I give. I have been lucky to have spent my whole career not only studying other animals, but also talking to them. Not like you might talk to your dog, but actually talking to them in ways they do understand. The chimpanzees I have worked with were language trained, from very early in life, and can use symbols to communicate with each other and with humans. Some of them even understood spoken English. So, if I do not want to strike up the conversation with the marshmallow test, I just say "I talk with chimpanzees" and the conversation usually carries on just fine from there!

Self-Control in Animals and People. DOI: https://doi.org/10.1016/B978-0-12-812508-3.00005-0
© 2018 Elsevier Inc. All rights reserved.

Mischel and Ebbesen (1970) stated perfectly the motivation and reasoning behind development of the marshmallow test:

> *Given that one has chosen to wait for a larger deferred gratification, how can the delay period be managed? The mechanisms that maintain goal-directed delay seem especially important, considering the fact that the ability to sustain self-imposed delay for the sake of larger but delayed consequences appears to be a chief component of most complex higher order human behavior. A main purpose of the present research, therefore, was to investigate the psychological processes that mediate sustained waiting behavior for delayed gratification. (p. 33)*

In other words, they wanted to devise tests that moved beyond just the dichotomous choice of so many intertemporal choice studies, where the choice phase was the only outcome measure one had (i.e., all that was recorded was whether the smaller-sooner or larger-later option was selected). Mischel and his colleagues cared as much about what happened *after one already had indicated the desire to wait for something better*. From this goal was born the marshmallow test, although it should be noted that marshmallows were only one of many different food rewards (or, in some cases, nonfoods) used as reward types.

Mischel and Ebbesen (1970) began this research effort with four conditions for children to experience: both rewards were present; neither reward was present; only the delayed reward was present; and only the immediate reward was present. In all cases, children were told that they could have the immediate reward as soon as they chose to end the trial, but the delayed reward was only given if they could wait for an experimenter to return. In this first study, they predicted that having the reward present, and therefore highly salient for the child, would work best for facilitating what is called *delay maintenance* (i.e., sustaining delay of gratification in the face of the alternate outcome of ending the trial). The results showed exactly the opposite. Children waited the longest when none of the rewards (in this case, pretzels and cookies) were present, and they did the worst when both were present. In fact, the difference was staggering: they waited approximately 11 minutes when nothing was present, but just over 1 minute when both foods were present. A follow-up study replicated this effect, only now the trials were terminated when the child pressed a bell, rather than eat a small piece of the less preferred food. Perhaps most importantly, Mischel and Ebbesen noted that a number of children engaged in fairly elaborate strategies, or even simple ones such as covering their eyes, and they commented that these strategies might be key to good performance. Subsequent research would certainly prove that to be true.

Mischel, Ebbesen, and Zeiss (1972) suggested that what is happening in the marshmallow test when food items are present is that children experience frustration, in the same way that Amsel (1958, 1962) had shown that frustration comes from nonreward. By this thinking, any attention paid to the rewards *as appealing items* would produce frustration, and decrease delay times because children would give in and ring the bell. However, efforts to either distract oneself from those rewards, or somehow minimize the appealing aspects of those rewards might help facilitate longer delay of gratification. This is exactly what they found in a long and fascinating series of experiments. Preschool-aged children were given the marshmallow test, but their experiences were different. Some children were given a toy to play with during the delay period, and they had to delay gratification by learning that a small pretzel could be taken immediately, but the marshmallow was only available after a delay. Other children just had the toy, and no delay task to perform. In the other conditions, children who were waiting for delayed rewards or not were also told to think about fun things while the experimenter was gone from the room. This was to generate cognitive distractions rather than physical ones. The results were striking (Fig. 5.1). Children with things to do waited longer, even when those things were self-generated. More importantly, these distractions were functional in the sense of improving self-control, not just in the sense of being distractions from the primary delay of gratification task. This is seen clearly in the data showing that kids who were not supposed to be waiting pressed the bell to end the session quickly, and why wouldn't they? They had no reason to be delaying, and thus the distractions served no real purpose.

Mischel et al. (1972) then focused on the nature of the thoughts that children were instructed to entertain. In a second experiment, the children were told to think about happy (nonfood-reward) things, to think about sad things, or to think about those rewards. Thinking about the rewards or about sad things both were detrimental to delay compared to thinking about happy things (Fig. 5.1). Next, Mischel et al. split a new group of children into those who were told to think of the rewards, or think of fun things, or were not given instructions on what to think. Now, however, the pretzel and marshmallow rewards were out of view. In this case, children who did not have anything that they were told to think about did well, as did kids having happy thoughts. But, the kids who were told to think of the rewards, even though those rewards were now out of view, struggled to wait very long (Fig. 5.1). Mischel et al. carefully considered what all of these results meant. At that time many ideas about self-control and inhibition included those from Freudian theory as well as learning theories. Mischel et al. concluded that these results most likely indicated that delay of gratification is at least based on avoiding or minimizing temptation to behave impulsively, and that there are multiple routes to doing that. Some efforts involve environmental manipulations, such as moving away from tempting items. Imagine yourself putting the cigarettes away from you, or closing the door to your office so that you do not see the box of donuts on the conference room table. Other efforts, however, can be self-generated or even "nudged" by those around you, and can involve cognitive interventions. If those donuts must stay in view all day at work, remind yourself about the fun movie you are going to see that evening, or remind yourself about how good it felt last time you got

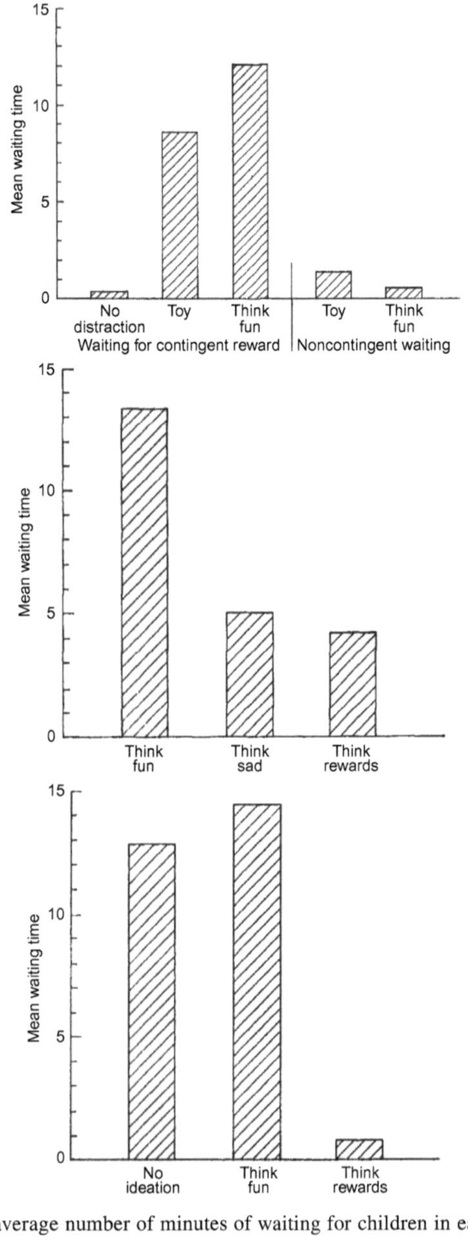

FIGURE 5.1 The average number of minutes of waiting for children in each of the conditions of Experiment 1 (top panel), Experiment 2 (middle panel), and Experiment 3 (bottom panel). *From Mischel, W., Ebbesen, E. B., & Zeiss, A. (1972). Cognitive and attentional mechanisms in delay of gratification.* Journal of Personality and Social Psychology, 21, *204–218, reprinted with permission of the American Psychological Association.*

on a scale and saw your weight loss. Or, allow other people to give you reminders to focus on thoughts that are not related to impulsive things that you are trying to avoid.

Subsequent work clarified things further. Mischel and Moore (1973) gave children the marshmallow task again, only now they showed some children images of the delayed reward during the delay maintenance phase. Other children saw images of unrelated things, and some children saw nothing, or saw only an illuminated, blank slide. In this case, children who waited the longest were those who saw pictures of the rewards that were part of their task. So, rather than being the case that any visual feedback about delayed rewards was detrimental to delay maintenance, this study showed that if that feedback was symbolic of the rewards, it could *help delay of gratification*. Thus, one can conclude that delay of gratification is not so much a function of what you see (or do not see) but rather a function of how you are thinking about relevant and nonrelevant aspects of the delay task. Attention to the consummatory, "hot" properties of the stimuli is likely to hurt delay maintenance, whereas attention to the "cool" properties can really help, as can distraction away from the hot properties (Metcalfe & Mischel, 1999; see below). Mischel et al. argued that we needed to think about stimuli from multiple perspectives when they were part of a marshmallow test (or, any delay of gratification situation). They would have both a motivating (consummatory, arousal) function and a cue (informative) function (also see Berlynes, 1960). This would explain why symbols of rewards worked well to aid delay maintenance, because those functioned as cues. However, real rewards have much stronger motivational properties, and will cause trouble, unless the individual can engage in some form of physical distraction, such as turning away, or some form of cognitive distraction, such as thinking of other things, or perhaps even cognitive *transformation*, which would involve changing how one thinks about an appetitive stimulus.

Mischel and Baker (1975) took this reasoning to its logical conclusion by having children think specific things about the nature of the delayed rewards. Some children were told to think about how good those items would taste, whereas other children were told to think about the physical properties of the stimuli, without thinking about their appetitive properties. For the children who were told to think about the consummatory properties, the script was almost cruel and unusual! I want you to think about how you would be imagining marshmallows after reading this (from Mischel and Baker, p. 257):

> *Look at the marshmallows. They are sweet and chewy and soft. When you look at marshmallows, think about how sweet they are when you eat them. When you look at marshmallows, think about how sweet they taste. Or you can think about how soft they are. When you look at marshmallows, think about how soft and sticky they are in your mouth when you eat them. Or you can think about how chewy they are. When you look at marshmallows, think about how chewy and fun they are to eat.*

Pretty tempting, right? For the other children, however, there was a different script:

> *Look at the marshmallows; they are round and white and puffy. When you look at marshmallows, think about how white and puffy they are. Clouds are white and puffy too—when you look at marshmallows, think about clouds. Or you can think about how round and white a marshmallow is. The moon is round and white. When you look at marshmallows, think about the moon. Or you can think about how round a marshmallow is on top. A ball is round. When you look at marshmallows, think about playing ball. (Mischel and Baker, 1975, p. 257)*

This clearly evokes very different feelings about marshmallows, and operated to generate very different delay times in the children. Children waited almost three times as long when they ideated about nonconsummatory features than consummatory features, and the consummatory condition led to shorter delays compared to the no-ideation condition while the nonconsummatory condition led to longer delays. Importantly, Mischel and Baker (1975) showed that it was not simply thinking "hot" thoughts about something that disrupted delay. When other children were told to think about consummatory features about things *other than the delayed rewards*, their delay times were much longer than students who were told to think about nonconsummatory features of things other than the delayed rewards. So, being in a more excited state, but one that is not related to things you must avoid attending to, actually aids delay of gratification. In fact, those children waited the longest. As I noted above, when the donut is the present temptation, thinking about how excited you are to later have popcorn at the movie theater may work well in aiding delay maintenance.

An important synthesis of these ideas and empirical results came from a highly influential paper by Metcalfe and Mischel (1999) in which they proposed a "hot/cool" framework for thinking about self-control and how it is manifest in delay of gratification. In this framework, there are two systems at work for controlling behavioral responses, and each of these processes situational information differently. The "cool" system is a cognitive system, that makes use of control mechanisms for attention allocation, stimulus cognitive transformation, and generally slower responding. It is specialized for complex spatiotemporal and episodic representation and thought. Metcalfe and Mischel also called it the "know" system. The "hot" system is emotional and is specialized for quick emotional processing and responding. It responds to the unconditional or conditional trigger features of stimuli, such as consummatory features in the case of food items. Metcalfe and Mischel also called it the "go" system. Some of the basic features of these systems are outlined in Table 5.1. The model offered by Metcalfe and Mischel is that of a neural network, and within this network there are hot and cool nodes that often can be connected, such that activation of a hot node can also potential activate a cool node. This would be, for example, what happens when one

TABLE 5.1 Characteristics of the "Hot" and "Cool" Systems Proposed by Metcalfe and Mischel (1999)

Hot System	Cool System
Emotional	Cognitive
"Go"	"Know"
Simple	Complex
Reflexive	Reflective
Fast	Slow
Develops early	Develops late
Accentuated by stress	Attenuated by stress
Stimulus control	Cognitive control

sees a potentially highly attractive food reward but then one thinks about the nonappetitive properties of that reward instead of the appetitive features. In this conception, environmental contexts that generate more states such as those in the column for the "hot" system in Table 5.1 are more likely to invoke impulsive responding, whereas those that are generated in ways like the "cool" column can lead to delayed gratification. This could include stress, for example. Other factors, such as developmental stage, personality traits, or pharmacological factors, also contribute to whether the hot or cool system dominates behavioral outputs in specific circumstances.

According to Metcalfe and Mischel (1999) the default state we are in is one in which the hot system dominates. Stimuli that appear that evoke the hot system are responded to by that system. We smoke that cigarette, eat that cookie, or otherwise do that which comes easiest and most naturally to us, and which is most motivating in the immediate present. However, when those prepotent stimuli are dampened or eliminated from perceptual systems, as with covering the rewards, or removing them, the cool system then activates in addition to the hot system. If the "hot" stimulus does stay within view, and remains salient in the environment, the cool system still can activate to somehow ignore or transform that stimulus in a way that allows for delay maintenance to continue. In these ways, the cool system dominates responding. Metcalfe and Mischel also noted that the emergence of the cool system occurs later in development, and might be, at least in part, reliant on the emergence of metacognition as well. Metacognitive abilities refer to how one knows that one knows, and the degree to which one is aware of potential fallibility. The delay of gratification paradigm is an ideal setting for this, because it could be that in order to shift attention or cognitively transform rewards requires knowing that one is at risk of behaving impulsively otherwise. And, metacognition lends itself to strategy choices that are adaptive.

So, what have we seen about knowledge of strategy effectiveness in children during delay of gratification? To this point, Mischel and others had guided children to do specific things that the investigators wanted to study—ideations, distractions, and so forth. But, did children have any sense of what strategies worked well, and what they should try to do to aid their own delay maintenance? And, at what age do children begin to understand at some level their own control over how well they can inhibit responding or delay gratification through recognition of the difficult nature of the task as it pertains to inhibiting behaviors? The ability to begin to deal with such potentially frustrating situations seems to emerge in the first two to three years of life. Vaughn, Kopp, Krakow, Johnson, and Schwartz (1986) studied the behaviors of such young children in an inhibitory test. When told not to touch a telephone, for example, while an experimenter was out of the room, those children who looked at the telephone or talked about it waited a shorter time before touching it. Those children who looked away from the telephone, or talked about other things, or engaged their hands in some other activity waited the longest. In a second experiment, children who chose to move the forbidden item away from them waited longer, although there was no evidence that these children (four years old and younger) explicitly were doing this as a strategic response. Instead, they may have simply moved the item away to reduce its frustrating effects on them, and as a result this led to longer delay. It might be later in development that this awareness of strategy effectiveness begins to emerge.

Mischel and Mischel (1983) also assessed strategy recognition and application by giving children the chance to decide whether rewards should stay present or be put out of sight. Around 6 years of age, children came to realize that out of sight was better. By this age, they also began to realize that engaging in tasks was better than talking about consummatory features of rewards. However, it took many more years (about age 12) before children understood that how they talked about rewards would affect their delay maintenance. In fact, Miller, Weinstein, and Karniol (1978) reported that third graders (children approximately 8 years of age) only outperformed kindergarten children in delay of gratification tests when there was no overt verbalization that was required during the delay. When task-oriented self-statements were made, both groups were equally good at delaying, and when reward-oriented self-statements were made, both groups suffered in their delay maintenance.

Yates and Mischel (1979) conducted four experiments in which children could control how often and for how long they saw the rewards during their tests. Those rewards sometimes were the real food items, sometimes were pictures of those items, and sometimes there were things present that had nothing to do with the delayed rewards for the delay of gratification test.

Preschool children spontaneously looked at the real rewards more than the symbols for those rewards. This was true whether they had to internally impose delay maintenance (i.e., they had to keep themselves from ending the trial) or delay was externally imposed (i.e., they had to wait for the trial to end no matter what they wanted). Yates and Mischel argued that this inability to redirect attention to the symbolic stimuli and away from the real rewards helps explain why children at this age may get frustrated by the delay. However, when first to third graders were given this test, they used better strategies, looking more at the symbolic stimuli (or, I suppose, they looked less at the real rewards is another way to consider this). This aided in how long they could wait.

Yates and Mischel (1979) also had contrasted older and younger children on their choice of strategies and the effectiveness of those choices. They found that younger children preferred looking at the real reward objects even when symbolic alternatives were available, and these preferences resulted in poorer delay maintenance. These children showed these preferences both when they had to maintain delay, and when a delay period was imposed on them (thus alleviating any need to engage in self-control behavior). Children in first, second, and third grades showed more selective preferences for the symbolic alternatives, especially when that was necessary to aid delay of gratification that was self-imposed. So, as children get older, the best ways to deal with the need to delay gratification seem to become clearer to them. There is certainly a maturational component to this, as the window during which self-control strategies become clear to children is also a developmental window in which seemingly related other cognitive capacities emerge, such as metacognition (e.g., Dunlosky & Metcalfe, 2009; Flavell, 1979; Flavell, Green, & Flavell, 1995, 2000). And, this is a point at which some forms of prospective cognition also emerge (see Chapter 14: Mental Time Travel: What Is It, and How Does It Relate to Self-Control? for more on this).

Other researchers also converged on the idea that children may recognize the best strategies or the most adaptive choices even before they can apply that knowledge to their own choices and cannot yet maintain delay of gratification themselves. For example, Koriat and Nisan (1977) gave fifth graders two hypothetical questions. In one, the child was asked to choose to pay less for a smaller chocolate bar now, or pay a little more for a larger chocolate bar later. In the other question, the offer was the same, but the child was deciding what a hypothetical smart kid would choose. Koriat and Nisan found that although about 75% of the kids were consistent in their choices in both scenarios (whether choosing immediate or delayed chocolate in both cases), for those cases where the answers differed, the children were three times as likely to choose the delayed option for the smart kid than they were to choose the delayed option for themselves! So, they knew what should be done, but that was not the same as what they would actually choose to do for themselves. Another study (Nisan & Koriat, 1977) showed the same basic outcome in even younger children, highlighting that even young children understand at some level the utility of delaying gratification, even if they do not always make that actual choice for themselves.

In later work, Nisan and Koriat (1984) showed that after allowing kindergarten children to choose a hypothetical delayed or immediate reward, and then telling them another hypothetical child had chosen the opposite, those kids sometimes changed their subsequent choices. But, this was only true when the children were asked to justify why the hypothetical other child chose differently from them, and then those children generated supportive reasons for that alternate choice. Simply being told that another child had chosen differently did not affect subsequent choices. In a second study, children were given either objective reasons or more emotional ones for why the hypothetical other child chose differently from them, and it was the objective perspective that led to the most switches to later delayed rewards for the focal subjects.

Other things are also related to the choices children make in the marshmallow test. One example is the ability to understand the nature of time. Children who can look at hourglasses with differing amounts of sand, and know which ones will run out faster, tend to delay gratification better than children who cannot pass these kinds of tests of time estimation (e.g., Zmyj, 2018). There is another interesting aspect to time and how the experience of time passing is affected by (and can affect) delay of gratification. Miller and Karniol (1976a) presented children with either an externally imposed delay to a reward (they simply were forced to wait), or an internally imposed delay (where the child decided whether to keep waiting or give up). Children were also asked to estimate how much time had passed while the experimenter was gone. The real duration was 4 minutes. Children in the internally imposed delay condition provided estimates that were about 50% longer (6 minutes) than children in the externally imposed delay condition, when the rewards remained visible during the delay. When the rewards were not in view, the time estimates were much closer to the true value although those children who had externally imposed delays estimated the time as being longer. Children in a control group who had not been told any reward was coming but were either told to just sit and wait (externally imposed) or to try to wait to press the button (internally imposed) also showed a large difference, but now the children who were trying to delay pressing the button estimated time as being shorter than those who were forced to sit and wait, for nothing. So, how one feels about the speed with which time is elapsing is determined by factors such as what you are waiting to get, and whether you are in control of that waiting period or simply have to tolerate it whether you want to or not.

Miller and Karniol (1976b) looked carefully at what children did when forced to wait through a delay versus when they chose to try to wait. These third grade children acted very differently depending on their test. If delay was forced on them, they attended a lot to the delayed rewards, and they did not engage much in self-distraction activities. But, if they had to maintain delay of gratification, they spent less time engaging the delayed rewards, and more time doing other things. For example, they played more with block toys that were nearby when they had to maintain delay than when they did not. The experimenters also provided a clock for the children in this case, and they found that those who had to self-impost the delay spent less time looking at the clock than those in the forced delay condition. When other children were told the delay until the experimenter's return would be even longer, those in the self-imposed maintenance condition decreased their attention to the rewards even more, whereas for those on whom the delay was forced this did not affect how much they looked at the rewards. Once again, the motivation and goal of the child when it included the need to inhibit a response led to very different behavior. And, those behaviors largely reflected "cool" states rather than the "hot" states more likely evoked by looking at the foods, or watching the clock slowly progress (Metcalfe & Mischel, 1999).

From these studies (and many others I do not have space to summarize) with the marshmallow test and other tests, Mischel and colleagues (e.g., Mischel, 1974, 1981; Mischel, Shoda, & Rodriguez, 1989) concluded that children are best able to deal with delaying gratification when they shift attention away from the delayed reward and the immediate reward, when they engage in other kinds of activities, whether physical in nature or forms of ideation that also are not focused on the rewards, or when they transform or focus on rewards in ways that make those things less consummatory as a result. Being reminded why they are waiting, and what they will get when they succeed, is also very helpful. But, they need to remind themselves infrequently, so as not to become too fixated on the immediate reward (which can tempt them) or the delayed reward (which can frustrate them because of its delay). These rules, of course, apply just as well to adult humans, and as I will discuss in the next chapter, they may even apply to some nonhuman animals.

The problem, of course, is that as you read this, you know full well that these prescriptions are right, and that employing them will help when you are forced with a situation where you need to delay gratification. But, it is in the moment of temptation that you forget to strategize ways around these temptations. Refrigerators have been stocked with vegetables and healthy foods while a homeowner again walks in with a bag of fatty take-out meals after a long day at work. Running shoes sit in closets, and gym equipment in basements serves solely as a place to hang coats on, while the homeowner sits on the couch eating potato chips. Local gyms consistently overbook new members on January 1, with no worries that by January 10 anyone will be complaining about overcrowding. This is because even with knowledge of what is best to do, we do not always do what is best. I have already discussed how temporal discounting plays a big role in this issue. In this chapter, I have related how maintaining delay also can be difficult, although there are clear strategies that do work to aid in self-control. That said, the marshmallow test, as creative and important as it is, does not reflect most real-world delayed gratification choices. Rather, in real life, the tiny pretzel is always around us (in the form of that donut, or cigarette, or extra beer, or chance to buy another pair of shoes you just saw but really do not need). The marshmallow in real life typically is a more abstract outcome (being healthy, losing weight, having more money for things we might really need, or staying out of trouble by not drinking too much). In the last chapter, I talk more about things we can do in our real lives to implement some of what has been learned from laboratory studies of delayed gratification (and, of course, read Mischel, 2014; for more ideas about this).

One of the reasons we all try harder to show more self-control and to delay gratification more often, is that we know it is good for us. This is true in the moment of choosing, of course, but there also seems to be something special about being the kind of person who can delay gratification. Intuitively, it feels like something that bestows clear benefits on those who can consistently show delayed gratification. In fact, as I have mentioned, we tend to hold in high esteem those who show patience, delay their rewards, and consider future benefits more so than current opportunities. As it turns out, there is a good reason for this. We now know that how children do on the marshmallow test, as simple as it is, can tell us a lot about the likelihood of their future successes (and failures) in the most meaningful aspects of their adult lives. How long you would wait for a marshmallow ends up being a pretty decent predictor of a lot of things about your later life.

Some of the first evidence of this came not long after the original series of studies by Mischel and his colleagues. Throughout that work, although there were clear variables that affected delay maintenance, there were also large individual differences in nearly all samples of children who were tested. Sometimes, no matter how beneficial the context (e.g., rewards out of sight, or children given toys to distract themselves), there were children who failed to wait. And, sometimes in the toughest conditions (rewards present, children told to think about consummatory features), some children still waited as long as they had to in order to get the better reward. So, these individual differences were of growing interest to the people testing the children, particularly with regard to whether performance differences were predictive of later life outcomes. Mischel, Shoda, and Peake (1988) followed up with children from the marshmallow studies about 10 years after they had been in those studies, to see what had happened with those children. Parental reports on a whole host of aspects of the child's life, at that later time, were provided. Broadly speaking, Mischel et al. found that how long children delayed was correlated with academic, social, and coping competence in adolescence, and this was true for both sexes. More specifically, they noted that

> *those who delayed longer are more verbally fluent; use and respond to reason; are attentive and able to concentrate; are planful and think ahead; are competent and skillful; are resourceful in initiating activities; are self-reliant and confident; become strongly involved in what they do; can be trusted and are dependable; are self-assertive; are curious, exploring, and eager to learn; and show concern for moral issues. These children also do not tend to go to pieces under stress or become rattled and disorganized; are less likely to appear unworthy or think of self as bad; are not shy and reserved or slow to make social contacts; are not stubborn; do not tease other children; do not revert to more immature behavior under stress; are not afraid of being deprived or concerned about getting enough; do not tend to be suspicious and distrustful; do not show mannerisms or rituals; are not unable to delay gratification or wait for satisfaction; are not jealous or envious; do not become rigidly repetitive or immobilized under stress; and do not withdraw or disengage when under stress. (pp. 690–691)*

Two things are striking about this list to me. First, these children sound exactly like the type of children we all wish we could raise. Second, these results come from seeing how children are, 10 years after they took a simple, short, test in which they either waited for marshmallows, or they did not.

A follow-up study by Shoda, Mischel, and Peake (1990) reported on additional children who were given the marshmallow task, and then were assessed again approximately 10 years later. In this case, special attention was paid to the specific variation of the marshmallow test that had been given: foods visible or not, and whether special instructions were given or not. In this case, in addition to survey responses, the investigators also collected SAT scores from these now much older children. What was interesting was that the condition of the marshmallow test was a predictor of later life outcomes. Not much was different among children who waited longer or shorter when rewards were not present, in terms of later test scores and survey responses. But, for those kids who were in the toughest task, where the rewards were present and ideation about those rewards could occur, it mattered a lot how long children waited in terms of other outcome factors. Among the findings were that children who delayed longer were rated as more likely to show self-control when frustrated by something, they were less likely to give in to temptation, they were more intelligent, and they were not as easily distracted when they were trying to concentrate on tasks. In this sense, what the marshmallow test showed about these children when they were 5 or 6 years old was also reflective of how well these children engaged in self-control when they were much older. And, many of the other traits I quoted above also were found for this sample of children, in the same pattern where longer delay in the marshmallow test predicted greater ratings of those positive traits and abilities when the children were older. For those children given the hardest version of the marshmallow test, there as a positive correlation of how long they waited, and their SAT scores years later: this correlation was 0.42 with SAT verbal scores and 0.57 with SAT quantitative scores. By way of reference, intelligence tests given to preschool-aged children only correlate at about 0.40 with the intelligence tests they are given as young adults! Importantly, when children had been given instructions on how to think about the rewards (or not think about them) during the marshmallow test, their performances in waiting did not correlate with these other outcome variables 10 years later. What this suggests is that being forced to determine how best to deal with delayed reward, in terms of strategies, and then being able to delay, predicts very well a number of important later life outcomes. This means that it is not simply being able to delay that is predictive, or even that choosing to try to delay is what we should measure as a predictor for late life outcomes. Rather, it is being good at delaying when you have to generate strategies on your own to cope with temptation.

Later studies showed even more benefits (or costs) to how children performed on the marshmallow test. Ayduk et al. (2000) reported that children who were good at delaying were less likely to engage in drug use or suffer from low self-esteem, and they were more protected from the effects of peer rejection. These results matched others that were emerging from studies that looked at broader measures of self-control and positive and negative life outcome measures. For example, self-control was positively correlated with healthy weights later in life as children transitioned into adolescence (e.g., Duckworth, Tsukayama, & Geier, 2010). In another study (Francis & Susman, 2009) that began with more than 1,000 children, the relation between self-control and BMI was assessed. Children were given a self-control task at age 3, in which they had to inhibit touching a highly salient toy, and then at age 5 were given a variation of the marshmallow test. They then were tracked and measured for height and weight also at 7, 9, 11, and 12 years of age. The results were very clear—performing poorly on one or the other self-control task was predictive of higher BMI scores, and performing poorly both times was predictive of the worst BMI status at each of the assessments after the self-control tests were given. Even more impressive is that a 30-year follow-up with the children in the original marshmallow studies still showed this relation of test performance and BMI (Schlam, Wilson, Shoda, Mischel, & Ayduk, 2013). In essence, this team found that each additional minute that a preschooler delayed gratification predicted a 0.2-point reduction in BMI in adulthood. What this suggests is the external validity of the marshmallow test as a measure of generalized self-control through delay of gratification abilities.

In addition, a new set of tests given to these same people 40 years after they were given the marshmallow test offered even more insights into the nature of individual differences in delaying gratification, and what those predict. Casey et al. (2011) gave nearly 60 people a new set of inhibitory tasks, where they had to inhibit responding to certain stimuli on a computer screen. The game involved making a "Go" or "No Go" response to each stimulus. The "cool" version of the test involved making those decisions for male and female faces (randomly assigned to be Go or No Go stimuli). The "hot" version used facial expression—smiling and fearfulness—as cues, and there was a trend for people who had performed more poorly on the marshmallow task to also struggle more to inhibit to these "hot" cues. These results, and others that have looked at other early-life measures of inhibition and self-control, and how they relate to later life outcomes (e.g., Moffitt et al., 2011) converge on the idea that having good inhibitory control and showing strong self-control through delay of gratification early in life is predictive of good things to come. For that reason, it has become important to begin to ask whether we can improve self-control in meaningful ways in children, through delay of gratification training or other similar efforts.

The answer is ... maybe. In one study by Murray, Theakston, and Wells (2016), children between 5 and 7 years of age were given attention training, to see if this would improve delay of gratification. All children were first given a test like the marshmallow test, where one food was available immediately, but the other required waiting 13 minutes. Then, for the next 4 days, some of the children performed the Attention Training Technique (Wells, 1990). This technique involves about 11 minutes of different sounds that are heard, with an instructor telling the listener how to control their attention by directing them to attend to specific things and ignore others. Those children who engaged in the training were 2.64 times more likely to wait through the entire delay when given another delay of gratification test, even though before training the two groups were equivalent (Fig. 5.2). Although this result was promising, we do not know whether the effect would last beyond the limited time scale of the study, and so more research is needed to see if children can maintain better delay of gratification over months and years after engaging in some type of intervention or training program.

One of my favorite studies, though, offers a different way to "boost" self-control and delay of gratification in children. Karniol et al. (2011) introduced the idea of superheroes as a way to supercharge delay of gratification. Rather than focus on getting children to cognitively transform the rewards, this study involved having the children transform themselves! In the first experiment, children performed a version of the marshmallow test while wearing a Superman cape or not wearing that cape. The key additional manipulation was that some children simply wore it, and others were told that it came with the power to help them be very patient and wait for the better reward. A 20-minute delay period then began, to see if children would

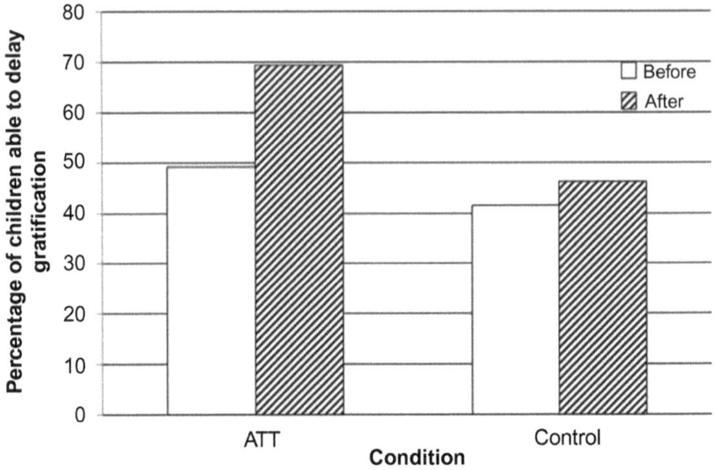

FIGURE 5.2 Proportion of children able to delay gratification in each condition. *From Murray, J., Theakston, A., & Wells, A. (2016). Can the attention training technique turn one marshmallow into two? Improving children's ability to delay gratification.* Behaviour Research and Therapy, 77, *34–39, reprinted with permission of Elsevier.*

wait that long for the better reward. Only 2 of 22 children in the no cape condition waited the whole time, whereas 8 of 22 did so with the cape only, and 15 of 22 did so with the cape and the information that it would give them super powers to be patient. Children in the control condition without capes waited for about 5 minutes on average. Children with the cape but no reminders of superpowers waited about 12 minutes, and the children who were told how the cape was magical waited nearly 17 minutes. Superman really is the Man of Steel when it comes to patience!

In a second experiment, Karniol et al. (2011) gave children one of two superhero capes. Some again got Superman's cape, which brought magical powers of patience. Others got Dash's cape, and Dash was an impulsive character. Otherwise, the test was the same for both groups. Of those wearing the Superman cape, 11 of 22 waited the entire delay interval, and averaged almost 14 minutes of delay overall. Only 4 of 21 waited the entire delay interval in the Dash cape, and those children averaged only a delay of 9.5 minutes. In Experiment 3, no actual capes were used, but the children were told to pretend they were Superman or an unknown character named Danny. In both cases, the children were again told that this character had excellent self-control abilities. Other children just watched a video of Superman, without being told anything else before doing the marshmallow test. Invoking Superman again led to the best delays in this experiment. These experiments seemingly highlight one way to intervene in children's choice behavior and to steer more decisions toward delayed, better rewards, and that is to offer children reference points that exhibit the desired characteristic of waiting for things. Again, it is not known if this type of manipulation would generate long-lasting effects, but it might, especially if it is ingrained in many routines in the child's day. I think about some of the other routines that have come to be established and that seem to generate and sustain certain favorable behaviors from children. One example is the Elf on the Shelf during Christmas season, who needs to be discussed only infrequently but that seems to act as a fairly consistent monitor or scaffold for general good behavior by children. Between superheroes and statement of goodness such as repeating "good children are those who wait," we see that environmental cues can be offered that generate other spontaneous and internally imposed delay of gratification in children. Of course, the world of behaving children (and adults) is not this simple, and so there are certainly many other factors that matter a great deal in good temporal choices. Even the Marshmallow test, and its reported relationship with life outcomes, has come to be challenged recently (Watts, Duncan, & Quan, 2018), and so more research is certainly needed to truly generate a full understanding of how delay of gratification works, and how it affects other aspects of psychological life.

Other important tests also have been designed for developmental assessments of self-control and delay of gratification. I cannot describe all of those, but many of the more recent approaches are focused on looking at the role of future-oriented cognition and self-control. This is an issue that is the focus of Chapter 14, and so I will discuss those tasks in detail in that chapter. I want to conclude this chapter by asking whether the marshmallow test is ultimately a measure of self-control, or whether its predictive value comes not from measuring self-control but perhaps because it is sensitive to something else about participants who do well or do poorly on the marshmallow test (again, see Watts et al., 2018, for a very recent assessment of exactly this question).

Duckworth, Tsukayama, and Kirby (2013) noted that in all of this research with the marshmallow test, it might be difficult to know what a child is doing when they show good delay maintenance. They could be demonstrating strong self-control as they control impulses to take the immediate reward. Or, they might not be that tempted in the first place. These two perspectives, then, might inform us differently about people who later in life are good students, do not use drugs, etc. They could either (1) be very good an inhibiting doing things they want to do that are impulsive (i.e., they have good self-control) or (2) they just may not be that tempted by such things in general. In their first study, Duckworth et al. gave fifth graders a version of the marshmallow test with larger delayed amounts of a preferred food versus a small amount of that food that could be had as soon as the participant ended the trial. Teacher ratings of the children's self-control and personality traits were also collected and children completed three scales that assessed how susceptible they were to reward-related impulses. And, children completed the Raven's Progressive Matrices and the Junior version of the Mill Hill Vocabulary Scale (Raven, Raven, & Court, 1988). These scales are untimed tests of nonverbal and verbal intelligence, respectively. What is nice about this study was that a diverse range of students were tested, in terms of racial and ethnic background and socioeconomic status (I would note that this has not always been the case in past work, which is a real limitation on a full understanding of delay of gratification in children).

What Duckworth et al. (2013) found was that children who performed better on the delay of gratification task were reported to be more self-controlled according to teacher ratings. Delay time was not associated with self-reported reward-related impulses, including reward responsiveness. In this study, delay time was unrelated to either nonverbal or verbal intelligence, although the authors noted that their sample showed a fairly restricted range of scores on the IQ tests. Duckworth et al. then also looked at the much larger database of nearly 1,000 children who had done the marshmallow test when they were four years old, and who also had been given rating by teachers and parents on a number of behavioral tendencies that included aspects of self-control behavior and impulsivity. These children also had completed a number of IQ tests at that time, and their academic performance scores were also available when they were in eighth grade. In ninth grade they all completed additional assessments of their academic abilities. At that time, these students were measured for their BMI scores, and they also gave responses to a questionnaire designed to assess their risk-taking behavior. Consistent with other studies I described, delay time at age 4 was related to each of the outcomes assessed in adolescence. Children who delayed longer had higher GPAs, higher standardized achievement test scores, healthier BMI scores, and they engaged in less risky behavior. Delay times were not closely associated with reward-related impulses, however. Thus, delay of gratification performance related most closely to self-control, rather than to how tempting rewards were to these children in general. Through a series of modeling efforts (see Fig. 5.3 for the results), Duckworth et al. concluded that preschool delay performance was most closely associated with concurrently measured self-control and intelligence. Through these connections, delay of gratification performance relates to outcomes about health, smart choices, and school performance. They concluded that the marshmallow test predicts life outcomes because it measures self-control, rather than general intelligence or reward-related impulses, and thus it is a good test of self-control. They said the task works because (1) the child is working for a preferred treat, which maximizes temptation, but the food amounts are not so large that hunger is dominant in the decisions to behave, (2) the task is done in a quiet, isolated place, ensuring that the child is fully immersed in the test context that is desired, namely one in which they must keep evaluating what they want to do, (3) the child is also left to her or his own devices, and own choices, as the experimenter does not place any demand on the child as to

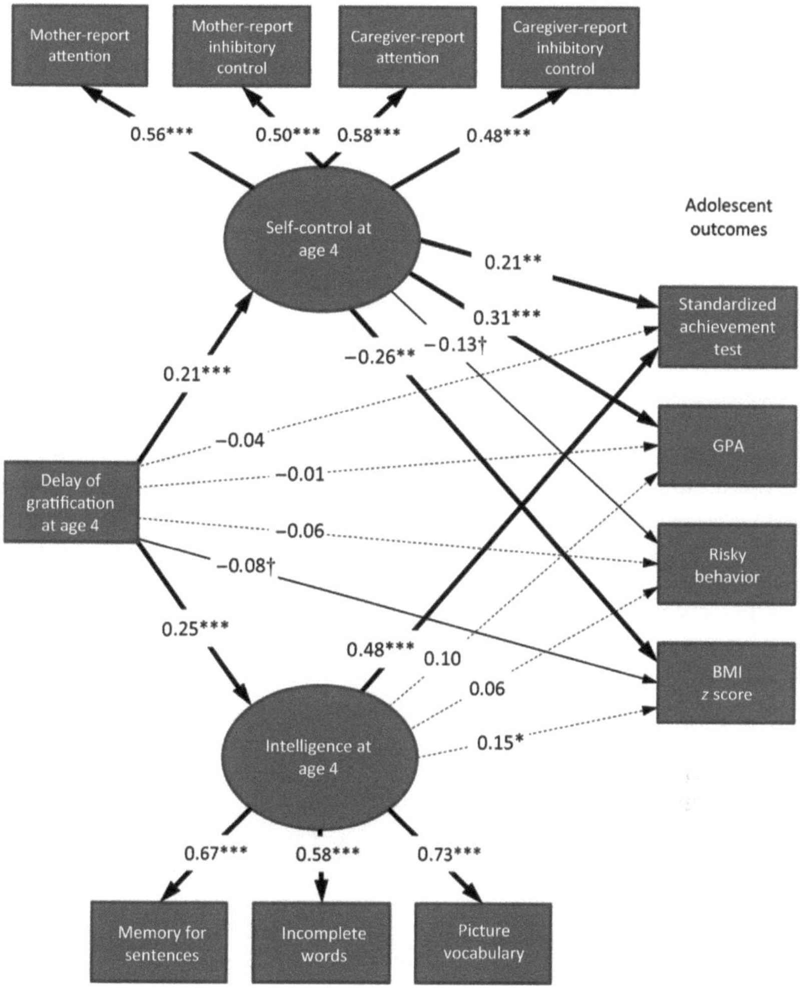

FIGURE 5.3 The model of the relation of self-control, intelligence, and delay of gratification testing from Duckworth et al. (2013). The covariates of gender, age, ethnicity, log-transformed income-to-needs, and maternal education, as well as error variances, and disturbances, are not displayed. Also not shown is the correlation between self-control and verbal intelligence, $r = 0.38$. Bold lines indicate significant relationships, normal lines indicate marginal relationships at $P < 0.10$, and dotted lines indicate nonsignificant paths or paths significant in the non-predicted direction. $^{\dagger}P < 0.10$. $^{*}P < 0.05$. $^{***}P < 0.001$. *From Duckworth, A. L., Tsukayama, E., & Kirby, T. A. (2013). Is it really self-control? Examining the predictive power of the delay of gratification task.* Personality and Social Psychology Bulletin, 39, *843–855, reprinted with permission of Sage.*

what they are supposed to do, and (4) the task has a crucial maintenance component, allowing for more information to be gathered about what is occurring through the delay interval that may impact ongoing choices to maintain delay or give up.

What all of these tests seem to show, now after nearly 50 years of research efforts, is that willpower, or delay of gratification, or self-control, should not be thought of as a unitary thing that one has or does not have. Rather, the value of the marshmallow test and other tests is that they showed us the incredible role that context plays. Those tests also showed us that even when children (and adults) choose to self-impose delaying gratification, they may not do it the most effective way, thereby conflating the ideas of "having self-control" and "properly exhibiting self-control." The marshmallow test also shows us that simple manipulations can have powerful predictions for future behavior. But, even then caution is needed. Despite many correlations existing between marshmallow test performance and later life outcomes, those correlations often account for only a small minority of the variance seen in those later life outcomes. Delaying gratification well as a child is no guarantee of a happy, healthy, productive life, nor is failing a marshmallow test when you are 5 years old a reason to give up on the rest of your life (or your child's life). Rather, childhood tests of self-control and delay of gratification, such as tests of attention, or memory, or verbal ability, are predictors of what might be coming, but with a whole host of other intervening factors also sure to come into play. That said, I think if you had to choose to be good or bad at the marshmallow test, you should choose to be good at it. The benefits are clearly present for such abilities to delay gratification, and those benefits are seemingly entrenched in other cognitive capacities in our species. The question next is whether this is true only for our species, or whether we might share with other species many of these capacities for delaying gratification and other forms of self-control.

REFERENCES

Amsel, A. (1958). The role of frustrative nonreward in noncontinuous reward situations. *Psychological Bulletin, 19S8*, 102–119.

Amsel, A. (1962). Frustrative nonreward in partial reinforcement and discrimination learning. *Psychological Review, 69*, 306–328.

Ayduk, O., Mendoza-Denton, R., Mischel, W., Downey, G., Peake, P. K., & Rodriguez, M. (2000). Regulating the interpersonal self: Strategic self-regulation for coping with rejection sensitivity. *Journal of Personality and Social Psychology, 79*, 76–92.

Berlyne, D. E. (1960). *Conflict, arousal, and curiosity*. New York: McGraw-Hill.

Casey, B. J., Somerville, L. H., Gotlib, I. H., Ayduk, O., Franklin, N. T., Askren, M. K., & Glover, G. (2011). Behavioral and neural correlates of delay of gratification 40 years later. *Proceedings of the National Academy of Sciences, 108*, 14998–15003.

Duckworth, A. L., Tsukayama, E., & Geier, A. B. (2010). Self-controlled children stay leaner in the transition to adolescence. *Appetite, 54*, 304–308.

Duckworth, A. L., Tsukayama, E., & Kirby, T. A. (2013). Is it really self-control? Examining the predictive power of the delay of gratification task. *Personality and Social Psychology Bulletin*, *39*, 843–855.

Dunlosky, J., & Metcalfe, J. (2009). *Metacognition*. Los Angeles, CA: Sage.

Flavell, J. H. (1979). Metacognition and cognitive monitoring: A new area of cognitive-developmental inquiry. *American Psychologist*, *34*, 906–911.

Flavell, J. H., Green, F. L., & Flavell, E. R. (2000). Development of children's awareness of their own thoughts. *Journal of Cognition and Development*, *1*, 97–112.

Flavell, J. H., Green, F. L., & Flavell, E. R. (1995). Young children's knowledge about thinking. *Monographs of the Society for Research in Child Development*, *60*, 1–96.

Francis, L. A., & Susman, E. J. (2009). Self-regulation and rapid weight gain in children from age 3 to 12 years. *Archives of Pediatric Adolescent Medicine*, *163*, 297–302.

Karniol, R., Galili, L., Shtilerman, D., Naim, R., Stern, K., Manjoch, H., & Silverman, R. (2011). Why Superman can wait: Cognitive self-transformation in the delay of gratification paradigm. *Journal of Clinical Child & Adolescent Psychology*, *40*, 307–317.

Koriat, A., & Nisan, M. (1977). The nature of the conflict in delay of gratification. *The Journal of Genetic Psychology*, *131*, 195–205.

Metcalfe, J., & Mischel, W. (1999). A hot/cool-system analysis of delay of gratification: Dynamics of willpower. *Psychological Review*, *106*, 3–19.

Miller, D. T., & Karniol, R. (1976a). The role of rewards in externally and self-imposed delay of gratification. *Journal of Personality and Social Psychology*, *33*, 594–600.

Miller, D. T., & Karniol, R. (1976b). Coping strategies and attentional mechanisms in self-imposed and externally imposed delay situations. *Journal of Personality and Social Psychology*, *34*, 310–316.

Miller, D. T., Weinstein, S. M., & Karniol, R. (1978). Effects of age and self-verbalization on children's ability to delay gratification. *Developmental Psychology*, *14*(5), 569–570.

Mischel, H. N., & Mischel, W. (1983). The development of children's knowledge of self-control strategies. *Child Development*, *54*, 603–619.

Mischel, W. (1974). Processes in delay of gratification. In L. Berkowitz (Ed.), *Advances in experimental social psychology* (pp. 249–292). New York: Academic Press.

Mischel, W. (1981). Objective and subjective rules for delay of gratification. In G. d'Ydewalle, & W. Lens (Eds.), *Cognition in human learning and motivation* (pp. 33–58). Hillsdale, NJ: Erlbaum.

Mischel, W. (2014). *The marshmallow test: Mastering self-control*. New York: Little, Brown.

Mischel, W., & Baker, N. (1975). Cognitive appraisals and transformations in delay behavior. *Journal of Personality and Social Psychology*, *31*, 254–261.

Mischel, W., & Ebbesen, E. B. (1970). Attention in delay of gratification. *Journal of Personality and Social Psychology*, *16*, 329–337.

Mischel, W., Ebbesen, E. B., & Zeiss, A. (1972). Cognitive and attentional mechanisms in delay of gratification. *Journal of Personality and Social Psychology*, *21*, 204–218.

Mischel, W., & Moore, B. (1973). Effects of attention to symbolically presented rewards on self-control. *Journal of Personality and Social Psychology*, *28*, 172–179.

Mischel, W., Shoda, Y., & Peake, P. K. (1988). The nature of adolescent competencies predicted by preschool delay of gratification. *Journal of Personality and Social Psychology*, *54*, 687–696.

Mischel, W., Shoda, Y., & Rodriguez, M. L. (1989). Delay of gratification in children. *Science*, *244*, 933–938.

Moffitt, T. E., Arseneault, L., Belsky, D., Dickson, N., Hancox, R. J., Harrington, H., ... Ross, S. (2011). A gradient of childhood self-control predicts health, wealth, and public safety. *Proceedings of the National Academy of Sciences*, *108*, 2693–2698.

Murray, J., Theakston, A., & Wells, A. (2016). Can the attention training technique turn one marshmallow into two? Improving children's ability to delay gratification. *Behaviour Research and Therapy*, *77*, 34–39.

Nisan, M., & Koriat, A. (1977). Children's actual choices and their conception of the wise choice in a delay-of-gratification situation. *Child Development*, *48*, 488–494.

Nisan, M., & Koriat, A. (1984). The effect of cognitive restructuring on delay of gratification. *Child Development*, *55*, 492–503.

Raven, J., Raven, J. C., & Court, J. H. (1988). *Manual for Raven's progressive matrices and vocabulary scales*. San Antonio, TX: Harcourt Assessment.

Schlam, T. R., Wilson, N. L., Shoda, Y., Mischel, W., & Ayduk, O. (2013). Preschoolers' delay of gratification predicts their body mass 30 years later. *The Journal of Pediatrics*, *162*, 90–93.

Shoda, Y., Mischel, W., & Peake, P. K. (1990). Predicting adolescent cognitive and self-regulatory competencies from preschool delay of gratification: Identifying diagnostic conditions. *Developmental Psychology*, *26*, 978–986.

Vaughn, B. E., Kopp, C. B., Krakow, J. B., Johnson, K., & Schwartz, S. S. (1986). Process analyses of the behavior of very young children in delay tasks. *Developmental Psychology*, *22*, 752–759.

Watts, T. W., Duncan, G. J., & Quan, H. (2018). Revisiting the marshmallow test: A conceptual replication investigating links between early delay of gratification and later outcomes. *Psychological Science*, in press.

Wells, A. (1990). Panic disorder in association with relaxation induced anxiety: An attentional training approach to treatment. *Behavior Therapy*, *21*, 273e280.

Yates, B. T., & Mischel, W. (1979). Young children's preferred attentional strategies for delaying gratification. *Journal of Personality and Social Psychology*, *37*, 286–300.

Zmyj, N. (2018). The relationship of delay of gratification and time comprehension in 4-year-old children. *International Journal of Behavioral Development*, *42*, 434–438.

FURTHER READING

Bandura, A., & Mischel, W. (1965). Modifications of self-imposed delay of reward through exposure to live and symbolic models. *Journal of Personality and Social Psychology*, *2*, 698–705.

Johnson, W. G., Parry, W., & Drabman, R. S. (1978). The performance of obese and normal size children on a delay of gratification task. *Addictive Behavior*, *3*, 205–208.

Kidd, C., Palmeri, H., & Aslin, R. N. (2013). Rational snacking: Young children's decision-making on the marshmallow task is moderated by beliefs about environmental reliability. *Cognition*, *126*, 109–114.

Mauro, C. F., & Harris, Y. R. (2000). The influence of maternal child-rearing attitudes and teaching behaviors on preschoolers' delay of gratification. *The Journal of Genetic Psychology*, *161*, 292–306.

Mischel, W., & Ayduk, O. (2004). Willpower in a cognitive-affective processing system: The dynamics of delay of gratification. In R. F. Baumeister, & K. D. Vohs (Eds.), *Handbook of self-regulation: Research, theory, and applications* (pp. 99–129). New York: Guilford.

Mischel, W., & Gilligan, C. (1964). Delay of gratification, motivation for the prohibited gratification, and responses to temptation. *The Journal of Abnormal and Social Psychology*, *69*, 411–417.

Mischel, W., & Metzner, R. (1962). Preference for delayed reward as a function of age, intelligence, and length of delay interval. *The Journal of Abnormal and Social Psychology*, *64*, 425–431.

Mischel, W., & Patterson, C. J. (1976). Substantive and structural elements of effective plans for self-control. *Journal of Personality and Social Psychology*, *34*, 942–950.

Putnam, S. P., Spritz, B. L., & Stifter, C. A. (2002). Mother–child coregulation during delay of gratification at 30 months. *Infancy*, *3*, 209–225.

Schack, M. L., & Massari, D. J. (1973). Effects of temporal aids and frustration on delay of gratification. *Developmental Psychology*, *8*, 168–171.

Sethi, A., Mischel, W., Aber, J. L., Shoda, Y., & Rodriguez, M. L. (2000). The role of strategic attention deployment in development of self-regulation: Predicting preschoolers' delay of gratification from mother-toddler interactions. *Developmental Psychology*, *36*, 767–777.

Silverman, I. W. (2003). Gender differences in delay of gratification: A meta-analysis. *Sex Roles*, *49*, 451–463.

Yates, G. C. R., Yates, S. M., & Beasley, C. J. (1987). Young children's knowledge of strategies in delay of gratification. *Merrill Palmer Quarterly*, *33*, 159–169.

Chapter 6

The Reversed-Reward Contingency Task—Why Pointing Away from What You Want Is So Difficult For Animals

My career in working with nonhuman animals began in 1995. I came to Georgia State University to work at the Language Research Center, to see what nonhuman primates could show us about their cognitive abilities, and to try to understand how and why they make the choices that they do. My intention was to focus on numerical cognition across species, something I have studied for many years (e.g., Beran, 2017; Beran, Parrish, & Evans, 2015). This is one of the oldest area of inquiry in comparative psychology, stretching back well more than 100 years (see Boysen & Capaldi, 1993; Davis & Perusse, 1988), and it is an area with its own fascinating history that I will not be able to cover here (see the Further Reading list for this chapter for more information, if you are interested). At that time, the focus was on learning more about whether animals could count, and whether their counting-like behavior really qualified as being similar to what human children learn to do sometime around the age of 5. There were a lot of interesting projects, including at the Language Research Center, where chimpanzees and rhesus monkeys had learned how to use Arabic numerals in different ways, comparing them to each other (Washburn & Rumbaugh, 1991) and using them as symbols for how many items to collect (Beran & Rumbaugh, 2001). I worked on these questions during my graduate study, adding new data to our understanding of how animals use numerosity and quantitative information (e.g., Beran, 2001, 2004; Beran & Beran, 2004).

That year (1995) also saw the publication of one of the most fascinating papers I have ever read. Sally Boysen, a psychologist at Ohio State University, worked with chimpanzees also, and she had reported some of the strongest evidence of counting-like abilities in those apes (e.g., Boysen & Berntson, 1989). But, it was a different test that really opened my eyes to a new line of research, about self-control, inhibition, and choice. Professor Boysen had undertaken to test her chimpanzees in pairs, to assess their

Self-Control in Animals and People. DOI: https://doi.org/10.1016/B978-0-12-812508-3.00006-2
© 2018 Elsevier Inc. All rights reserved.

numerical competence in a new way, when she realized something very striking, and very limiting, in their choice behavior. She had two chimpanzees sit near each other, and one was the subject, whereas the other was there just to receive food. The subject was given the choice of one of two sets of candies, and had to point to one of those sets. Now, normally, chimpanzees and a whole host of other animals are very good at pointing at the larger set of items, in what we call a relative quantity discrimination task—basically, a choice of "which is more." For example, we have seen that chimpanzees can choose the larger set of visible food items when two piles of cereal pieces are presented to them, even for difficult choices between eight and nine pieces (Dooley & Gill, 1977). Chimpanzees can see four sets of items, and have to combine each of two pairs and then decide which pair holds more total food, and they succeed with this (Rumbaugh, Savage-Rumbaugh, & Hegel, 1987). And, if you drop items, one at a time, into opaque containers, so that the chimpanzees never see all items at once, and instead have to rely on memory for the number of items they saw individually, they can do this (Beran, 2001, 2004) as can other great apes. Chimpanzees also do this when two or more sets are added to each container—for example, they might see one person drop two items in one container, and then four items in the other. Then, a second person adds three more items to the first container, and two more to the second. If you are lost, that makes five items in the first container, and six in the second! Chimpanzees keep this straight (Beran, 2004), and they even keep track of accumulating items when it takes up to 20 minutes to keep adding them, one at a time, to a container (Beran & Beran, 2004). Other apes make these quantity judgments of food items as well (Anderson, Stoinski, Bloomsmith, & Maple, 2007; Anderson et al., 2005; Call, 2000; Hanus & Call, 2007), and so can a variety of other species including sea lions, whales, and dolphins (Abramson, Hernández-Lloreda, Call, & Colmenares, 2011, 2013), fish (e.g., Agrillo, Dadda, Serena, & Bisazza, 2008), frogs (Stancher, Rugani, Regolin, & Vallortigara, 2015), coyotes (Baker, Shivik, & Jordan, 2011), parrots (Al Aïn, Giret, Grand, Kreutzer, & Bovet, 2009), robins (Garland, Beran, McIntyre, & Low, 2014), elephants (Perdue, Talbot, Stone, & Beran, 2012), and different species of primates (e.g., Barnard et al., 2013; Evans, Beran, Harris, & Rice, 2009).

As I noted earlier, some apes, such as Boysen's chimpanzees, even can experience looking at sets of things and then provide a symbolic label for the total number of items they saw. Boysen showed this in her earlier work where chimpanzees walked to one location in her laboratory, looked at a number of food items, then walked to another location, saw another set of items, and then returned to the start point to touch the Arabic numeral that represented the summed total (Boysen & Berntson, 1989). They were very good at this, suggesting that they added or summed the total number of items, and held in memory that number until they could tell the experimenter what they had seen. Other animals can also label such sets of items, such as the Grey parrot Alex, who was famous for his ability to announce the number of items he saw presented on a tray (Pepperberg, 1994, 2006, 2012). So, it seemed pretty clear during this time that animals were capable of using numerical and quantitative cues, and that in particular they were good at choosing more food over less food.

But, there was a trick in this new game that Sally Boysen was using. In all of the studies I discussed above where choices had to be made, the game was fair in the sense that the animal subject was given options, and it pointed to one of those, and it received what it pointed at. Now, however, the set that the subject chose was *given away* to the other chimpanzee, and the (unchosen) set that remained went to the subject. So, to be successful in getting more food meant being successful at pointing to less food. Boysen's chimpanzees just could not figure it out when two food sets were present. They kept pointing to the bigger set, and kept watching it being given away, and then they received the smaller set. They just could not do it. At least, not in that situation, with real food items. Later, I will explain what it takes to get them to improve.

Being a first-year graduate student, and seeing the things our chimpanzees could do, I just knew this had to be wrong. So, I tried this test with our chimpanzees Sherman, Lana, Mercury, and Panzee. Well, it was not wrong! They consistently pointed to the larger set of treats, and got the smaller set. Hundreds of trials, no improvement. I tried all manner of things—I gave them huge differences in numbers, such as sets of 10 versus 2 items. I gave them qualitative differences in food type, such as a big banana slice versus a small sliver of celery. No matter how I presented it, they nearly always pointed to the thing that I knew they most wanted. They saw that go away (or be given away to a partner chimpanzee), and they got what was left. This kept happening, and at no point did I see any improvement. It was a clear replication of Boysen's result, and a striking "failure." From it, I learned two things—this really is a very hard test for them, and it is not any fun to be the experimenter who consistently "disappoints" large chimpanzees by giving away what they just told you they wanted!

Over the next 20 years, a lot of other researchers also learned how hard this reversed-reward contingency (RRC) test could be, for a variety of species (see Shifferman, 2009; for an excellent review of this work, and from which I borrowed heavily in reporting some of the studies that were conducted). Largely, after Boysen and Berntson's (1995) report, the search was on for demonstrating what species *could solve* the task, although it is important to note that this was never the goal for Boysen in her original studies. Her subsequent work showed some of the important contextual factors that changed performance (Boysen, Berntson, Hannan, & Cacioppo, 1996; Boysen, Mukobi, & Berntson, 1999; see below), and it was against this background that other research teams sought to demonstrate what species could pass the test (i.e., point to smaller amounts of food) and what it took to generate success. Silberberg and Fujita (1996) first replicated the original result

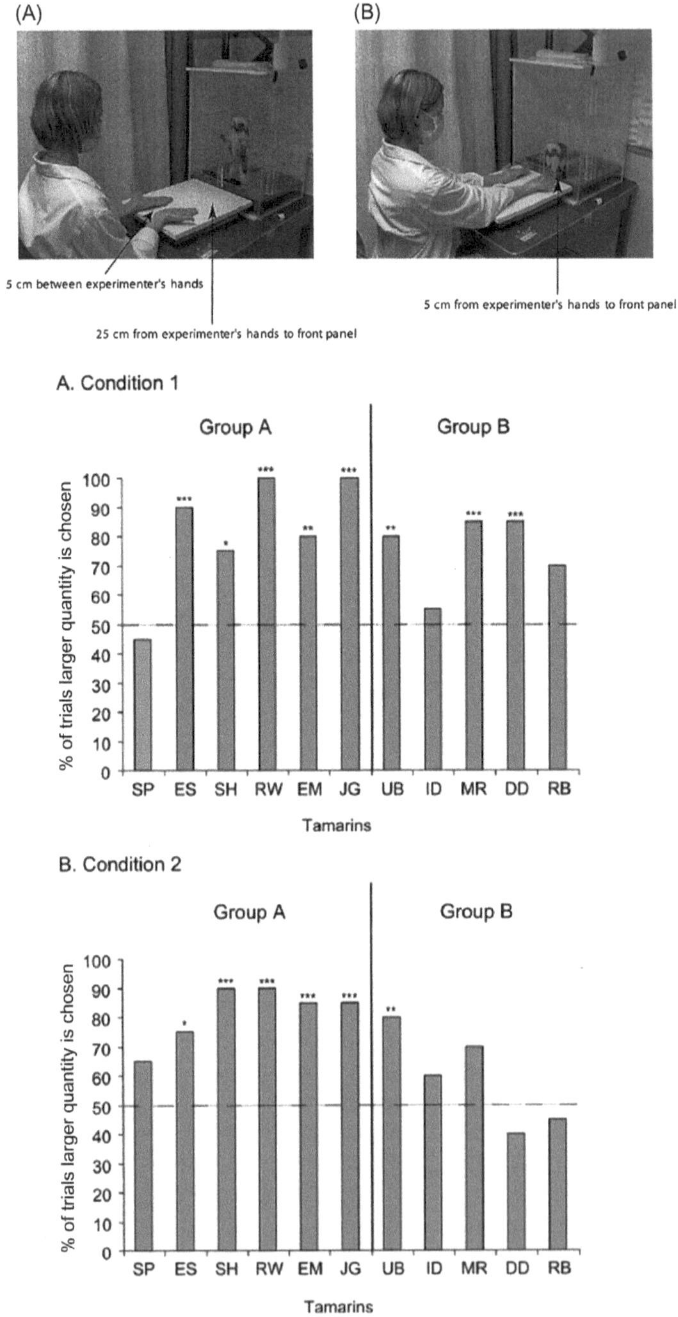

FIGURE 6.1 The top image shows the test apparatus and general presentation procedure in Kralik et al. (2002). (A) Each trial began with the experimenter placing her hands on the edge of the white platform. (B) After the tamarin has looked at the two alternatives for approximately

(*Continued*)

when they found that Japanese macaques repeatedly failed to point to one raisin when it was offered against four raisins. Hundreds of trials showed no improvement. However, in one of the crucial modifications that have been used over the years, they then changed the contingencies so that a point to four raisins led to no food delivery, and a point to one raisin led to gaining the four raisins. That produced a fairly rapid change in which the monkeys then came to point to the single raisin. From this, Silberberg and Fujita argued that something else (or in addition to) an inability to inhibit pointing to bigger amount of food much be at work when animals fail the RRC task. If that was true, the replacement of one raisin for pointing at the set of four with *no raisins* when the set of four was chosen should not have affected actual choice behavior.

Silberberg and Fujita instead (1996) argued that failure in the original version of the RRC task was the result of both choices leading to some degree of reward which therefore could not act as directly on subsequent choice behavior as would a purer means of differential reinforcement as in the case of getting four raisins or getting none. They argued that these data were at odds with the claims of Boysen et al. that chimpanzees struggled because they could not go against their desire to reach toward more food, a form of perceptual imperative. However, although these monkeys and then later rhesus macaques (Kralik, 2012) were successful in pointing to less food when pointing to more food led to no reward, other monkeys continued to fail even with this zero-reward contingency in place. Kralik, Hauser, and Zimlicki (2002) reported three experiments with cotton-top tamarins in which even large rewards for pointing to the small food set, and no reward for pointing to the large food set, still led to consistent points to the large set (i.e., failure to point at smaller to get any reward) or chance level performance (Fig. 6.1). Other experiments with squirrel monkeys also showed that they consistently failed, even when no food was given for points to the larger set, and success only emerged when the same trial was presented repeatedly until the monkeys finally changed their choice (Anderson, Awazu, & Fujita, 2000; also see Anderson, Awazu, & Fujita, 2004). Lemurs performed slightly better, although they, too, could not pass the RRC task under the original

---

◀ 3 s, the experimenter moved her hands up to the front panel. The tamarin made its selection by touching the fingers of one of the hands. The graphs show performance. Group A was under the rule "pick larger quantity, receive smaller quantity," and group B was under the rule "pick larger quantity, receive nothing." Condition 1 used a correction procedure, whereas the quantities were presented randomly in Condition 2. For each tamarin, the *y*-axis plots the percentage of trials in which the larger quantity was chosen, averaged over the last two sessions of the condition. *From Kralik, J., Hauser, M. D., & Zimlicki, R. (2002). The relationship between problem solving and inhibitory control: Cotton-top tamarins (*Saguinus oedipus*) performance on a reversed contingency task.* Journal of Comparative Psychology, 116, *39–50. Reprinted with permission from the American Psychological Association.*

conditions of receiving the set that was not selected (Genty, Palmier, & Roeder, 2004) unless they received a large number of trials, and even then the majority of the lemurs still failed (Genty, Chung, & Roeder, 2011). Murray, Kralik, and Wise (2005) also reported that rhesus monkeys came to point to the smaller set to receive the larger set, without need of the zero-reward modification, but it took many hundreds of trials before performance was significantly above chance levels in pointing to the smaller set. Subsequent work with all of the great apes also showed variability in performance, although there were occasional successes, even without need of modification of the original task (e.g., Uher & Call, 2008; Vlamings, Uher, & Call, 2006).

What is interesting in addition to the wide variability in outcomes outlined above is that there does not appear to be any clear explanation for the species differences that are documented. As already noted, chimpanzees struggle with the RRC task, as do some New and Old World primate species, whereas others can succeed, especially when the modification to use a no-reward outcome for pointing to larger sets is in place. As one looks at the performances of nonprimate species that have been tested, the picture gets even cloudier. Genty and Roeder (2006) gave the RRC task to sea lions, and three of four passed the test, even when choices of the larger set led to receiving the small set (Fig. 6.2). This is the most impressive outcome documented yet in a nonhuman species, and yet it is hard to understand why sea lions would be capable of doing this. Perhaps the best explanation is that the sea lions pressed levers to make choices, rather than respond directly to food items, and so in some ways this was not a true RRC task. Although Genty and Roeder suggested that the sea lions performed as they did because in their natural habitat there was no need to behave impulsively, I would argue that, in fact, the key issue in RRC tasks are direct responses toward stimuli for which prepotent (naturally attractive) features exist, and such a feature was not present for the sea lions. The sea lions could not directly access their food sets, and so some of the impulsive and prepotent characteristics of the primate version of this test were not present. These little design features can have big effects, and likely did with the sea lions, in much the same way that I outlined how changes in delay of gratification tests with children (and adults) can radically change what people choose to do.

An interesting and compelling test involved presenting cleaner wrasse with the RRC task (Danisman, Bshary, & Bergmüller, 2010). These fish serve "client" fish by cleaning them, and they do so in a situation in which they experience a conflict. Clients want to be cleaned of parasites, but the cleaner wrasse prefer the mucus from clients that they can only get by biting (something the clients appear to not like, as they will retaliate; Bshary & Grutter, 2002; Grutter & Bshary, 2003). Thus, we see a natural test of

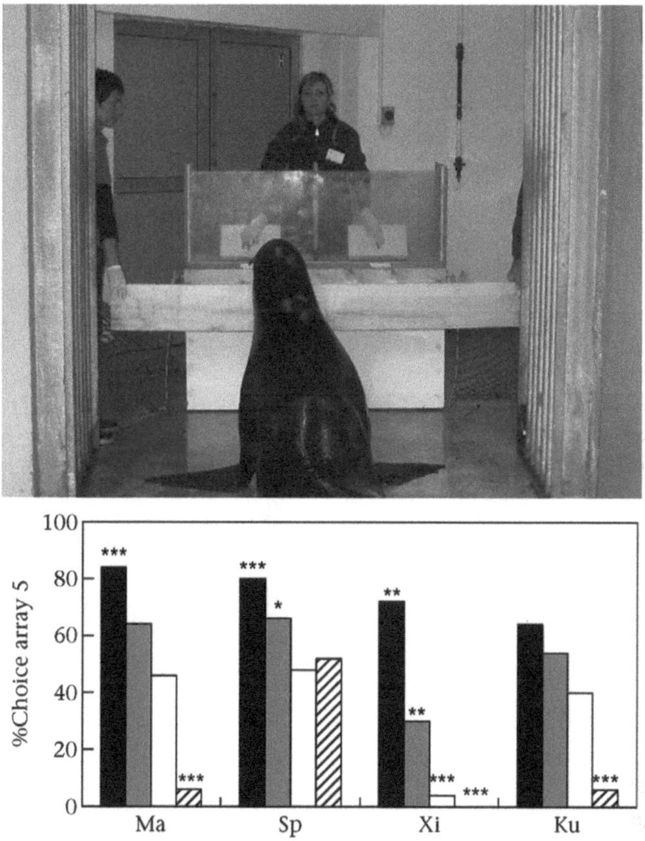

FIGURE 6.2 The top image shows a sea lion faced with a choice between two quantities of food after different delays to delivery. The bottom panel shows the results as the percentage of trials on which the larger of two quantities of food was chosen for each individual over four successive blocks of 50 trials. *$p < 0.05$; **$p < 0.01$; ***$p < 0.001$. *From Genty, E., & Roeder, J. J. (2006). Self-control: Why should sea lions,* Zalophus californianus, *perform better than primates?* Animal Behaviour, 72, *1241–1247, with permission from Elsevier.*

self-control: cleaners can choose to bite mucus now for a good reward now, but at the risk of losing clients, a long-term problem. Given that they do show inhibition from biting (Bshary & Grutter, 2006; Grutter & Bshary, 2003), they seem an ideal species to also show success on the RRC task. But, they do not succeed! They consistently chose the preferred item over the nonpreferred item or responded at chance levels (Fig. 6.3). With the no-reward contingency in place, one fish then solved the task, but the clear outcome is that the RRC task is not any easier for a species that shows clear evidence in other contexts of inhibition of responses that serve only short-term interests but not long-term interests.

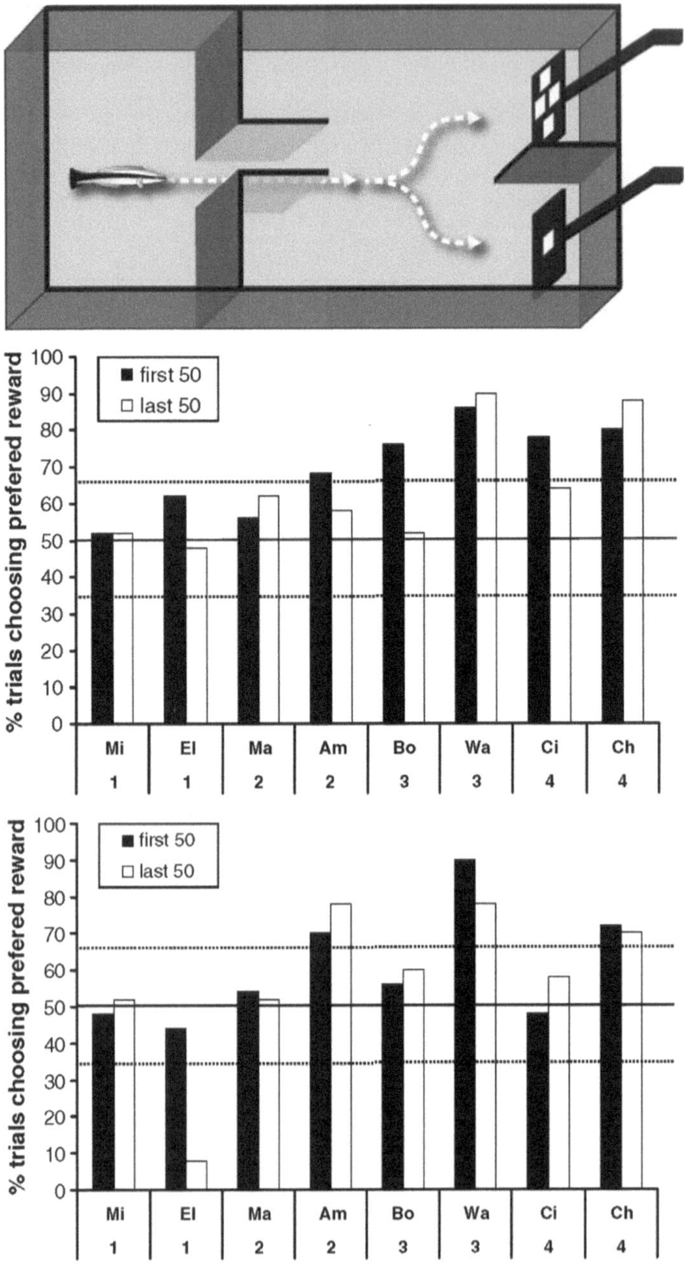

FIGURE 6.3 The top image shown the experimental aquarium used in Danisman et al. (2010). It was divided into a back compartment (left) and the test compartment (right) with help of an opaque PVC partition. Two plates with different quantities (indicated by the number of white

(Continued)

The picture becomes even more confused when looking at choices between qualitatively different foods rather than quantitative differences. For example, Anderson, Hattori, and Fujita (2008) reported that capuchin monkeys could point to a lower preference food to thus obtain the higher preference item that was the other choice option, whereas the quantitative comparisons (like those described earlier) did not lead to success. However, these successes were not consistent across tests, and not all individuals showed any success. So, it is not enough to change types of food rather than quantities of food to get success, probably because in both cases there is still the strong desire to reach toward or grab what one wants, rather than to reach toward or grab something that one does not want.

Thus, it is convincingly clear that nonhuman animals struggle with the RRC task. In some cases, successes are reported, but in the original version with real food rewards, in nearly all cases the contingencies create trouble for nonhumans animals. Those difficulties persist until a large number of trials are presented, a modification such as zero-reward is introduced, the choices differ in terms of their quality instead of quantity, or the stimuli are made less salient and prepotent by making them symbolic or by making them more traditional response modes (such as levers) that are associated with reward amounts. These results clearly begged data from humans, for comparison, and especially from children. The first such effort was conducted by Carlson, Davis, and Leach (2005) with 3- and 4-year-old children. They presented sets of candies to the children and found that age was related to how well children could learn to point to the smaller amount to get the larger one. Both age groups, however, showed the capacity to pass the test. What I find most interesting is that performance on the RRC task also was related to verbal ability and to executive function in these children. In particular, there were strong correlations between performance on the RRC task and standard tests of conflict executive function and delay executive function. This means that the RRC task appears to tap into the same resource or resources that are used when individuals must deal with conflicting stimuli

---

◀ patches) or qualities of food were introduced into the test compartment. The fish could move into the test compartment through a slot followed by a corridor when an opaque partition in front of the corridor (not displayed) at the side of the back compartment was pulled up. The middle figure shows the percentage of trials in which individuals chose the preferred reward during the first 50 trials (filled bars) and during the last 50 trials (open bars) in the reverse-reward contingency test where the unchosen set was the set given to the fish and the chosen set was not given. The 50% line corresponds to random choice. Dotted lines at 66% and 34% indicate threshold values for significant deviation from chance responding. Letters are individual codes for the test subjects. The bottom figure shows the same information, but for the condition where choice of the larger set led to no food being given. In nearly all cases, fish either chose the set that they could not obtain, or chose at random levels *From Danisman, E., Bshary, R., & Bergmüller, R. (2010). Do cleaner fish learn to feed against their preference in a reverse reward contingency task?* Animal Cognition, 13, *41–49, reprinted with permission of Springer.*

(presumably by inhibiting responses to some of those) and must deal with delay of gratification. These data from children add a lot to that story, and to me, this provides another nice example of how comparative approaches to cognition and behavior can generate new tests that useful in area of cognitive and developmental psychology focused on human thought and behavior.

In my laboratory, we have recently used a version of the RRC task with preschool-aged children, but without using food. Instead, we gave children a game in which they had to fill a sticker sheet as quickly as they could, and then gave them repeated choices of 1 versus 3 sticker sets. The fastest way to fill the sheet, of course, was to point at one sticker, but this was not always easy for them to do. However, by age 5, most kids figure out the rule most of the time. These results match those from an earlier study with 3- to 4-year-olds who were competing for stickers in a game (Apperly & Carroll, 2009). To gain stickers most efficiently required these children to point to an empty box that the other player would receive in order to obtain stickers for themselves. Sometimes, as in the original RRC task (Boysen & Berntson, 1995), the baited box contained actual stickers, and in this case children showed a strong tendency to point at that box with the stickers in it. This error was diminished, however, when the number of stickers to be won was represented with some kind of a symbol such as a number word, or a quantity of dots to represent the stickers that could be given for that box. For those children who improved on the RRC when symbols were presented, performance remained good even when they went back to nonsymbolic conditions with real stickers in the boxes. This indicates that symbols aided the children, and may have "scaffolded" their learning in a way that they then could leverage even in the original, harder version of the game. This is a key point—symbolic representation, transformation of rewards into less "hot" version of themselves, and removal of primary rewards from test situations seem to consistently be valuable aids for improving self-control and increasing inhibitory control. I will return to this point when I describe the various ways that delay of gratification and other forms of self-control are assessed across species.

This also returns us to the question—what does it take to get success with chimpanzees, the original subjects who experienced the RRC task? Boysen found that answer, eventually, with her chimpanzees, and it was the same result I just outlined for the work with children in the stickers task (Apperly & Carroll, 2009). Boysen and Berntson's (1995) original result, and all of those replications and extensions I outlined earlier with so many species, seemed to argue that animals were basically impulsive creatures that could not control even their simple pointing responses unless strong prohibitions against such pointing were in place (such as zero-reward outcomes) or unless massive experience was given so that the correct choices could slowly emerge. It is true that many research teams reported eventual success on the RRC task, but an examination of those reports shows that (1) typically performance was better than chance, but not at ceiling, (2) success occurred in a minority of individuals tested within the groups that were given the RRC task, and (3) success did not necessarily transfer from one condition to another, even though the changes to those conditions might be fairly minor. So, when real food items are presented, and animals must inhibit pointing toward the larger set, they struggle. This seems to be a strong limitation on their inhibitory capacities, given that even with experience failure is often still the outcome. Although it is true that this experience pales in comparison to perhaps a decades long life in which reaching toward what one wants is the natural (and rewarded) behavior that emerges, animals learn many arbitrary and sometimes complex relations in other domains that do not require such inhibition. Here, however, they appear to be highly deficient.

But, this picture of animal behavior is at odds with a lot of what we otherwise know about things that animals can do that seemingly reflect control of impulses. Anecdotally, I had seen this in the chimpanzees I worked with. A male chimpanzee would begin to get agitated, begin to go into what is called "display" behavior that usually culminated in loud banging, or spitting water, or worse! But, then, that individual would find some distraction, or somehow break that usual building pattern of rocking, vocalizing, and then displaying. Often, I had seen that this was when such behavior was not going to be good for the chimpanzee, as during feeding time, or testing time, when the human on the other end of that display might walk away and not return for some time. In other cases, I had seen a chimpanzee be offered a smaller piece of food that it had to hand to a lower ranking individual, in which case I would offer a larger piece. Although this was not always successful, often they would place the smaller piece on the ground and allow it to be taken, and then wait as I handed the larger piece. Other, much more systematic work had shown even greater degrees of self-control and inhibition, as I will describe in future chapters. So, the evidence of possible inhibitory control was available, even if the RRC task seemed to be one of the harder assessments of that.

In the 1960s and 1970s, the primatologist Emil Menzel conducted many groundbreaking studies of chimpanzee behavior and intelligence (Menzel, 1960, 1961, 1972, 1975). Among those was one of my favorites, in which he assessed how well chimpanzees could remember where food items were hidden in a large outdoor area (Menzel, 1973). In one such test (Menzel, 1974), he allowed a young female chimpanzee named Belle to watch as he moved around, hiding food items in various places in the outdoor compound that she frequently visited. Then, when Belle was released, he recorded where she went and what she did. He found that her memory for the location of hidden items was quite good, but it was a series of tests that involved more than one chimpanzee that highlighted a naturalistic setting in which to see self-control. Sometimes, Belle was released into the yard with other chimpanzees, and she would lead them to the food, where it was shared.

However, one male chimpanzee, Rock, came to monopolize the reward, and this led Belle to begin to inhibit retrieving the food from where it was located. Rock seemed to realize this, and would displace her from wherever she sat and paused for a while, which led Belle to then stop moving all of the way to the hiding location. Rock countered that effort by looking all around the area where Belle sat, so Belle began sitting farther and farther away. This escalated to other seemingly highly deceptive behaviors such as Rock making it seem as if he was looking away, and with Belle sometimes going in directions away from the food in what appeared to be an attempt to get to Rock to look in the wrong places. The key point here is in looking at what Belle tried to do—inhibit herself from going right to the food, even though she certainly must have wanted to do that, until she could perhaps find a time to trick Rock and obtain at least some of the reward for herself. To me, this is a striking example of a future-oriented instance of self-control. Of course, there are also elements of learning in this, from her past experiences with Rock, and there is a role for conditional cues (Rock's orientation, gaze, etc.) that partially controlled Belle's actions. But through all of those, she had to inhibit going directly to what she wanted in order to have any hope of obtaining and keeping it.

What Sally Boysen found in her modified tests supported these last observations that inhibition was possible. After seeing her chimpanzees fail again and again at pointing to the smaller set of items, she tried something new (Boysen & Berntson, 1995). She replaced the real candies with two Arabic numerals. As I noted, her chimpanzees had learned the corresponding quantities that were associated with some numerals, and so now the game involved pointing to a numeral that would lead to the partner (the lucky chimpanzee who just got free food) getting that number of items, whereas the subject got the number of food items that matched the unselected Arabic numeral. In this test, success! And not only that, but success immediately! A profound shift in performance, and one that tells us a lot about the nature of how chimpanzees process different kinds of stimuli, and what those stimuli mean.

Changing to numerals led to the Boysen's chimpanzees pointing to the smaller numeral, and thereby getting the bigger number of candies. Importantly, after this success, however, a return to the version of the game with real candies to be pointed at led to poor performance once again. And, even the use of nonsymbolic but also inedible items such as rocks seemed to create more problems for the chimpanzees than did the numerals (Boysen et al., 1996). But—if numerals were compared to candies, a surprising result emerged in that now the chimpanzees would point to a numeral that was smaller in value than the number of candies in the other choice option (Boysen et al., 1999). This is a crucial result because it directly compared the prepotency of candy stimuli with the symbolic nature of the numerals, and in this case, the symbolic stimuli came to control responding through inhibition of reaches toward food. Symbols changed everything in terms of performance when they were used, but these results still stand in contrast to the work with children I discussed. Recall that Apperly and Carroll (2009) reported that children who needed symbols to learn to make the correct response in the RRC task then could go back to the original version of the game and succeed, whereas the chimpanzees could not (Boysen et al., 1996, 1999). However, there is an important caveat to that proposed big difference between animals and humans, and it is that Apperly and Carroll used nonedible "primary" rewards, unlike nearly all of the animal studies. Thus, it remains to be seen whether children who struggle with a food-based version of the RRC task, and who then learn to succeed in the task when symbols are introduced, can then return to the food-based version and continue to succeed. If they can, this may reflect an important species difference. It would be one that makes sense—symbolic representation, although present in some nonhuman species (Pepperberg, 2006; Rumbaugh, 1977; Rumbaugh & Washburn, 2003; Savage-Rumbaugh et al., 1993; Savage-Rumbaugh, 1986), is clearly a defining feature of human existence. Such symbols operate to fundamentally change not only how humans interact with each other, but also how they represent the world. Thus, being "symbol-minded" may afford humans with unique behavioral patterns that can be engaged during situations of cognitive conflict or impulsivity. But, if animals such as Boysen's chimpanzees can use symbols in such choice situations, their performance also can reflect inhibition over impulsivity. At the same time, if symbols uniquely aid the self-control of those who can use them, then other symbol-using animals might provide crucial data in determining whether it is symbolic representation or humanness that explains strong self-control. This is a point that will be discussed in more detail later.

Boysen's thoughts on why her chimpanzees could succeed with the symbols so much better than with real food items was interesting in light of what was known about how children show facilitated self-control and delay of gratification. In previous chapters, I described research showing that transforming the nature of the situation to something in which the stimuli you are responding to, or what you are thinking, is less about the "hot" aspects of those stimuli or that situation and more about "cool" aspects (e.g., Metcalfe & Mischel, 1999). Boysen's chimpanzees sometimes were in a "hot" situation with real foods that they had to reach toward, whereas in this modified test the numerals allowed them to approach the decision in a "cooler" framework. Of course, other possibilities existed for why the task was difficult with real food items. Those chimpanzees, and many other animals that have been tested on the RRC task had long histories of pointing and reaching toward what they wanted, and being rewarded nearly always for that by obtaining those items. This was the reason Silberberg and Fujita (1996) argued that manipulating that reinforcement history could eventually shift choice behavior, to where animals would point at the smaller amounts because their most recent history of reward was tied only to that response.

Even still, the RRC, and what we have learned about what it takes to be successful with it, highlights that prepotent stimuli can be troubling when the goal of a task is not to make the most natural response. If other stimuli can be introduced that act as symbols or otherwise decrease the aspect of "prepotency" that leads to more impulsive responding, greater success can be seen in the RRC. For example, Kralik et al. (2002) trained monkeys to associate colors with outcomes, and this seemed to improve performance. Addessi and Rossi (2011) also trained monkeys with symbolic stimuli. In their task, monkeys were given the RR task when real foods were presented, when tokens were presented where each token was exchangeable for one food item (what they called low-symbolic distance tokens), and tokens each represented a different quality (and value) food type (what they called high-symbolic distance tokens). Nearly all monkeys were below chance or at chance in choosing the smaller set of real foods or smaller set of low-symbolic distance tokens, but three of eight learned to point to the smaller valued token in the high-symbolic distance condition. With additional experience, more of the capuchins then passed the food-based condition and the high-symbolic token version of the tests. These data show that for monkeys, symbolic stimuli can serve as a kind of "bridging" stimulus to better performance in the RR task. This general idea that changing the nature of the stimuli that one reacts to can change how well one can show inhibition relates directly to many delay of gratification tasks, where preferred items are right in front of you (such as those marshmallows for the children) or preferred behaviors are available and appealing right now (such as that cigarette, or piece of chocolate cake). What is required to show restraint and wait for the better, later outcome often is a means of transforming the situation, or self-distracting, or reframing the choice in the way that Sally Boysen did with her chimpanzees so that they could point to smaller numerals in order to get larger sets of candies.

I have known Sally Boysen for many years, and I had the chance to ask her some questions about the RR task while I was working on this chapter. I wanted to include some of her comments and thoughts, because I think they very nicely summarize what this task has contributed to understanding self-control, and other aspects of animal behavior. I first asked her what she thinks is the key cognitive ability needed to succeed, and whether she liked the "hot/cool" framework that has been offered. I also asked her whether she thought this framework made sense especially as it pertained to her chimpanzees, and their interesting successes when numerals were used. She responded:

> *I do like this framework, as it still allows for what I perceive to be an involuntary, pre-potent perceptual response to quantity/mass, which is an impulsive, "hot" system that is highly adaptive in most naturalistic cases. Under lab conditions, however, one solution to assist in overriding such impulsivity and assist with inhibition of a pre-wired response system is to bootstrap the*

processing system by eliminating some of the perceptual features of the stimuli by representing them with other stimuli that lessen the impact on the perceptual system. This means trying to represent quantity, for example, without using iterations of the items, but instead, allowing a symbol to represent quantity. This highjacks the perceptual imperative, and moves the processing to the "slower" system (in terms of the immediacy of the perceptual demands of the choice) that allows/requires cortical processing. This system, though slower, in terms of neural activity, is more efficient for problem-solving under artificial conditions such as the RRC task (which I am still trying to have it become known as the "Boysen effect" (ha)).

I then asked her what she thought was the most important take-home message from her work with the chimpanzees on the RRC task and all of the subsequent work that was inspired by her work. She answered:

To tell you the truth, I never expected a body of experiments to come from the original tasks. At least with respect to the candy/numeral phase of the study, I think that the overwhelming power of symbols to allow us to override powerful, biological dictates is the most important take-home message, which emphasizes whenever/however that incredible evolutionary shift occurred that allowed the hominid line to begin to represent its work was the one of the most significant changes in our evolutionary trajectory. However, had we not stood up, remaining quadrupedal like the apes, human language would not have been possible, and human culture, as we know, would simply not have emerged. Becoming upright eventually allowed for powerful, voluntary control over expired air and subsequent vocalizations, emerging into human speech and language. Without this initial preliminary representational capacity, all other forms of accumulated culture would not have been forthcoming.

Finally, I really wanted to ask Sally about anecdotes from her early tests with the chimpanzees, and their struggles. Every time I have tried this test with my chimpanzees, their reactions are interesting, to say the least, and sometimes even downright funny. Her response was more than I could have hoped to get. She said:

Without thinking anything of it, I tested [chimpanzee] Sarah first on the task. As you probably know, she was bequeathed to me by David Premack when he closed his lab in 1987, when she was 28. Sarah began working on a variety of tasks about 2 months after she arrived, and we quickly noted, although she could usually learn new things, she was a bit more distractible than the other chimps, except Kermit, who was 'ADD,' even for a chimpanzee. Sarah seemed to have similar attention issues, although we attributed some of it to her age, and perhaps her own perception that she was the Queen of Chimpanzee Comparative Cognition, and thus had earned to the right to NOT participate, if she so chose. It was clear from the start of testing with her that she didn't seem to "get it," which we had seen with her on other tasks. I gave it the old college try, however, and ran her through the initial trials, which I think compared something like 2 vs 1 or so. I keep increasing the disparity between the candy arrays in subsequent sessions hoping that the loss of huge amounts of candy when she chose the larger array consistently might shake her up enough to pay attention to what was going on. We even had to watch ourselves so that we didn't start to brace ourselves and hold on to the apparatus we were using. It had a metal frame and wooden flat surface which we could just push up against the front of Sarah's home cage and present the two arrays. Sarah was getting so frustrated after each choice that she started to grab and shake the apparatus violently. After we ran the 1 vs 6 trial sessions, I gave up with her.

But at that time, we weren't sure if it was just Sarah not getting it, or something weird going on with the task. How could the most highly-trained, highly taught chimpanzee in the world at the time NOT understand how her choice was impacting on the rewards she was getting (mostly NOT getting). Moreover, how come she could not LEARN how to get the most for her decision? She would make the same choice, over and over, and pound/shake the metal frame of the apparatus, grimace, and whine, and then 10 seconds later, make the same WRONG choice, trial after trial (I think we did 6–8 trials per session, for 2 sessions, and then changed the disparity (1 vs 2, 1 vs 4, 1 vs 6)), and still NOTHING made a difference. When we finished with Sarah, I remembered something that I think is attributed to Skinner, "If you find something interesting, drop everything else and study that." So, that's what I did, and we immediately ran Sheba on the task—with exactly the same findings. After Sheba, I now knew that it wasn't just a quirk of Sarah, but all our chimps were not "getting it." Since the chimps had been using numbers for some time, I immediately thought we could "subtract" the features of the candy arrays, and see if they could learn the task using numerals. Imagine my surprise when I discovered that they didn't have to "learn" the task at all—they just needed a cognitive conduit for expressing the optimal choice.

After reading all of this early work with chimpanzees and other animals on the "Boysen task," it made me wonder about other ways in which animals might show self-control. As I noted, these experiments emerged and were highly influential on the literature as I was beginning graduate school, and so they led me to begin reading about human and nonhuman animal intertemporal choice tests, and then the work of Mischel and others that I described earlier. There was a long history of giving animals intertemporal choice tests like those given to humans, but I was particularly curious to see if people had tried to make tests like the marshmallow task for nonhuman animals, and when I found that they had, I was immediately drawn to seeing what I could try with the chimpanzees in my laboratory. That began a now decades long effort in my lab to study delay of gratification, and most recently, it has led us to return to the RRC, with some new ideas about what may or may not aid chimpanzees (and other animals) in succeeding in this task and other tasks. Before we get to that, though, I need to describe the delay of gratification tasks that are used with animals, and how we adopted one of the tasks used first with children to look at many of the same questions about contextual factors in self-control and delay of gratification by chimpanzees and other animals.

REFERENCES

Abramson, J. Z., Hernández-Lloreda, V., Call, J., & Colmenares, F. (2011). Relative quantity judgments in South American sea lions (*Otaria flavescens*). *Animal Cognition, 14*, 695–706.

Abramson, J. Z., Hernández-Lloreda, V., Call, J., & Colmenares, F. (2013). Relative quantity judgments in the beluga whale (*Delphinapterus leucas*) and the bottlenose dolphin (*Tursiops truncatus*). *Behavioural Processes, 96*, 11–19.

Addessi, E., & Rossi, S. (2011). Tokens improve capuchin performance in the reverse-reward contingency task. *Proceedings of the Royal Society B: Biological Sciences, 278*, 849–854.

Agrillo, C., Dadda, M., Serena, G., & Bisazza, A. (2008). Do fish count? Spontaneous discrimination of quantity in female mosquitofish. *Animal Cognition, 11*, 495–503.

Al Aïn, S., Giret, N., Grand, M., Kreutzer, M., & Bovet, D. (2009). The discrimination of discrete and continuous amounts in African grey parrots (*Psittacus erithacus*). *Animal Cognition, 12*, 145–154.

Anderson, J. R., Awazu, S., & Fujita, K. (2000). Can squirrel monkeys (*Saimiri sciureus*) learn self-control: A study using food array selection tests and reverse-reward contingency. *Journal of Experimental Psychology: Animal Behavior Processes, 26*, 87–97.

Anderson, J. R., Awazu, S., & Fujita, K. (2004). Squirrel monkeys (*Saimiri sciureus*) choose smaller food arrays: Long-term retention, choice with nonpreferred food, and transposition. *Journal of Comparative Psychology, 118*, 58–64.

Anderson, J. R., Hattori, Y., & Fujita, K. (2008). Quality before quantity: Rapid learning of reverse-reward contingency by capuchin monkeys (*Cebus apella*). *Journal of Comparative Psychology, 122*, 445–448.

Anderson, U. S., Stoinski, T. S., Bloomsmith, M. A., & Maple, T. S. (2007). Relative numerousness judgment and summation in young, middle-aged, and old adult orangutans (*Pongo pygmaeus abelii* and *Pongo pygmaeus pygmaeus*). *Journal of Comparative Psychology, 121*, 1–11.

Anderson, U. S., Stoinski, T. S., Bloomsmith, M. A., Marr, M. J., Smith, A. D., & Maple, T. S. (2005). Relative numerousness judgment and summation in young and old Western lowland gorillas. *Journal of Comparative Psychology, 119*, 285–295.

Apperly, I. A., & Carroll, D. J. (2009). How do symbols affect 3-to 4-year-olds' executive function? Evidence from a reverse-contingency task. *Developmental Science, 12*, 1070–1082.

Baker, J. M., Shivik, J., & Jordan, K. E. (2011). Tracking of food quantity by coyotes (*Canis latrans*). *Behavioural Processes, 88*, 72–75.

Barnard, A. M., Hughes, K. D., Gerhardt, R. R., DiVincenti, L. J., Bovee, J. M., & Cantlon, J. F. (2013). Inherently analog quantity representations in olive baboons (*Papio anubis*). *Frontiers in Psychology, 4*, 253.

Beran, M. J. (2001). Summation and numerousness judgments of sequentially presented sets of items by chimpanzees (*Pan troglodytes*). *Journal of Comparative Psychology, 115*, 181–191.

Beran, M. J. (2004). Chimpanzees (*Pan troglodytes*) respond to nonvisible sets after one-by-one addition and removal of items. *Journal of Comparative Psychology, 118*, 25–36.

Beran, M. J. (2017). Quantitative cognition. In J. Call (Ed.), *APA handbook of comparative psychology* (Vol. 2, pp. 553–578). Washington, DC: APA Press.

Beran, M. J., & Beran, M. M. (2004). Chimpanzees remember the results of one-by-one addition of food items to sets over extended time periods. *Psychological Science, 15*, 94–99.

Beran, M. J., Parrish, A. E., & Evans, T. A. (2015). Numerical cognition and quantitative abilities in nonhuman primates. In D. Geary, D. Berch, & K. Mann Koepke (Eds.), *Evolutionary origins and early development of number processing* (pp. 91–119). San Diego, CA: Elsevier.

Beran, M. J., & Rumbaugh, D. M. (2001). "Constructive" enumeration by chimpanzees (*Pan troglodytes*) on a computerized task. *Animal Cognition, 4*, 81–89.

Boysen, S. J., & Capaldi, E. J. (Eds.). (1993). *The development of numerical competence: Animal and human models*. Hillsdale, NJ: Erlbaum.

Boysen, S. T., & Berntson, G. G. (1989). Numerical competence in a chimpanzee (*Pan troglodytes*). *Journal of Comparative Psychology, 103*, 23–31.

Boysen, S. T., & Berntson, G. G. (1995). Responses to quantity: Perceptual versus cognitive mechanisms in chimpanzees (*Pan troglodytes*). *Journal of Experimental Psychology: Animal Behavior Processes, 21*, 82–86.

Boysen, S. T., Berntson, G. G., Hannan, M. B., & Cacioppo, J. T. (1996). Quantity-based interference and symbolic representations in chimpanzees (*Pan troglodytes*). *Journal of Experimental Psychology: Animal Behavior Processes, 22*, 76–86.

Boysen, S. T., Mukobi, K. L., & Berntson, G. G. (1999). Overcoming response bias using symbolic representations of number by chimpanzees (*Pan troglodytes*). *Animal Learning and Behavior, 27*, 229–235.

Bshary, R., & Grutter, A. S. (2002). Parasite distribution on client reef fish determines cleaner fish foraging patterns. *Marine Ecology Progress Series, 235*, 217–222.

Bshary, R., & Grutter, A. S. (2006). Image scoring and cooperation in a cleaner fish mutualism. *Nature, 441*, 975–978.

Call, J. (2000). Estimating and operating on discrete quantities in orangutans (*Pongo pygmaeus*). *Journal of Comparative Psychology, 114*, 136–147.

Carlson, S. M., Davis, A. C., & Leach, J. G. (2005). Less is more: Executive function and symbolic representation in preschool children. *Psychological Science, 16*, 609–616.

Danisman, E., Bshary, R., & Bergmüller, R. (2010). Do cleaner fish learn to feed against their preference in a reverse reward contingency task? *Animal Cognition, 13*, 41–49.

Davis, H., & Perusse, R. (1988). Numerical competence in animals: Definitional issues, current evidence, and a new research agenda. *Behavioral and Brain Sciences, 11*, 561–615.

Dooley, G. B., & Gill, T. (1977). Acquisition and use of mathematical skills by a linguistic chimpanzee. In D. M. Rumbaugh (Ed.), *Language learning by a chimpanzee: The LANA project* (pp. 247–260). New York: Academic Press.

Evans, T. A., Beran, M. J., Harris, E. H., & Rice, D. (2009). Quantity judgments of sequentially presented food items by capuchin monkeys (*Cebus apella*). *Animal Cognition, 12*, 97–105.

Garland, A., Beran, M. J., McIntyre, J. M., & Low, J. (2014). Relative quantity judgments between discrete spatial arrays by chimpanzees (*Pan troglodytes*) and New Zealand robins (*Petroica longipes*). *Journal of Comparative Psychology, 128*, 307–317.

Genty, E., Chung, P. C., & Roeder, J. J. (2011). Testing brown lemurs (*Eulemur fulvus*) on the reverse-reward contingency task without a modified procedure. *Behavioural Processes, 86*, 133–137.

Genty, E., Palmier, C., & Roeder, J. J. (2004). Learning to suppress responses to the larger of two rewards in two species of lemurs, *Eulemur fulvus* and *E. macaco*. *Animal Behaviour, 67*, 925–932.

Genty, E., & Roeder, J. J. (2006). Self-control: Why should sea lions, *Zalophus californianus*, perform better than primates?. *Animal Behaviour, 72*, 1241–1247.

Grutter, A. S., & Bshary, R. (2003). Cleaner wrasse prefer client mucus: Support for partner control mechanisms in cleaning interactions. *Proceedings of the Royal Society of London B: Biological Sciences, 270*, S242–S244.

Hanus, D., & Call, J. (2007). Discrete quantity judgments in the great apes (*Pan paniscus, Pan troglodytes, Gorilla gorilla, Pongo pygmaeus*): The effect of presenting whole sets versus item-by-item. *Journal of Comparative Psychology, 121*, 241–249.

Kralik, J. D. (2012). Rhesus macaques (*Macaca mulatta*) spontaneously generalize to novel quantities in a reverse-reward contingency task. *Journal of Comparative Psychology, 126*, 255–262.

Kralik, J. D., Hauser, M. D., & Zimlicki, R. (2002). The relationship between problem solving and inhibitory control: Cotton-top tamarins (*Saguinus oedipus*) performance on a reversed contingency task. *Journal of Comparative Psychology, 116*, 39–50.

Menzel, E. W., Jr. (1960). Selection of food by size in the chimpanzee, and comparison with human judgments. *Science, 131*, 1527–1528.

Menzel, E. W., Jr. (1961). Perception of food size in the chimpanzee. *Journal of Comparative and Physiological Psychology, 54*, 588–591.

Menzel, E. W., Jr. (1973). Chimpanzee spatial memory organization. *Science, 182*, 943–945.

Menzel, E. W., Jr. (1974). A group of young chimpanzees in a one acre field. In A. M. Schrier & F. Stollnitz (Eds.), *Behaviour of non-human primates* (Vol. 5, pp. 83–153). New York: Academic Press.

Menzel, E. W., Jr. (1975). Purposive behavior as a basis for objective communication between chimpanzees. *Science, 189*, 652–654.

Metcalfe, J., & Mischel, W. (1999). A hot/cool-system analysis of delay of gratification: Dynamics of willpower. *Psychological Review, 106*, 3–19.

Murray, E. A., Kralik, J. D., & Wise, S. P. (2005). Learning to inhibit prepotent responses: Successful performance by rhesus macaques, *Macaca mulatta*, on the reversed-contingency task. *Animal Behaviour, 69*, 991–998.

Pepperberg, I. M. (1994). Numerical competence in an African grey parrot (*Psittacus erithacus*). *Journal of Comparative Psychology, 108*, 36–44.

Pepperberg, I. M. (2006). Grey parrot numerical competence: A review. *Animal Cognition, 9*, 377–391.

Pepperberg, I. M. (2012). Further evidence for addition and numerical competence by a grey parrot (*Psittacus erithacus*). *Animal Cognition, 15*, 711–717.

Perdue, B. M., Talbot, C. F., Stone, A., & Beran, M. J. (2012). Putting the elephant back in the herd: Elephant relative quantity judgments match those of other species. *Animal Cognition, 15*, 955–961.

Rumbaugh, D. M. (Ed.). (1977). *Language learning by a chimpanzee: The LANA Project*. New York: Academic Press.

Rumbaugh, D. M., & Washburn, D. A. (2003). *Intelligence of apes and other rational beings*. New Haven, CT: Yale University Press.

Rumbaugh, D. M., Savage-Rumbaugh, E. S., & Hegel, M. T. (1987). Summation in the chimpanzee (*Pan troglodytes*). *Journal of Experimental Psychology: Animal Behavior Processes, 13*, 107–115.

Savage-Rumbaugh, E. S. (1986). *Ape language: From conditioned response to symbol*. New York: Columbia University Press.

Savage-Rumbaugh, E. S., Murphy, J., Sevcik, R. A., Brakke, K. E., Williams, S., & Rumbaugh, D. M. (1993). Language comprehension in ape and child. *Monographs of the Society for Research in Child Development, 58*, 1–222.

Shifferman, E. M. (2009). Its own reward: Lessons to be drawn from the reversed-reward contingency paradigm. *Animal Cognition, 12*, 547–558.

Silberberg, A., & Fujita, K. (1996). Pointing at smaller food amounts in an analogue of Boysen and Berntson's (1995) procedure. *Journal of the Experimental Analysis of Behavior, 66*, 143–147.

Stancher, G., Rugani, R., Regolin, L., & Vallortigara, G. (2015). Numerical discrimination by frogs (*Bombina orientalis*). *Animal Cognition, 18*, 219–229.

Uher, J., & Call, J. (2008). How the great apes (*Pan troglodytes, Pongo pygmaeus, Pan paniscus, Gorilla gorilla*) perform on the reversed reward contingency task II: Transfer to new quantities, long-term retention, and the impact of quantity ratios. *Journal of Comparative Psychology, 122*, 204–212.

Vlamings, P. H. J. M., Uher, J., & Call, J. (2006). How the great apes (*Pan troglodytes, Pongo pygmaeus, Pan paniscus*, and *Gorilla gorilla*) perform on a reversed contingency task: The effects of food quantity and food visibility. *Journal of Experimental Psychology: Animal Behavior Processes, 32*, 60–70.

Washburn, D. A., & Rumbaugh, D. M. (1991). Ordinal judgments of numerical symbols by macaques (*Macaca mulatta*). *Psychological Science, 2*, 190–193.

FURTHER READING

Adachi, I., Anderson, J. R., & Fujita, K. (2011). Reverse-reward learning in squirrel monkeys (*Saimiri sciureus*): Retesting after 5 years, and assessment on qualitative transfer. *Journal of Comparative Psychology, 125*, 84–90.

Beran, M. J. (2007). Rhesus monkeys (*Macaca mulatta*) enumerate large and small sequentially presented sets of items using analog numerical representations. *Journal of Experimental Psychology: Animal Behavior Processes, 33*, 55–63.

Beran, M. J., & Parrish, A. E. (2016). Going for more: Discrete and continuous quantity judgments by nonhuman animals. In A. Henik (Ed.), *Continuous issues in numerical cognition: How many or how much* (pp. 175–192). San Diego, CA: Academic Press.

Beran, M. J., Perdue, B. M., & Evans, T. A. (2015). Monkey mathematical abilities. In R. Cohen Kadosh & A. Dowker (Eds.), *Oxford handbook of mathematical cognition* (pp. 237–257). Oxford, UK: Oxford University Press.

Boysen, S. T. (1992). Counting as the chimpanzee views it. In W. K. Honig & J. G. Fetterman (Eds.), *Cognitive aspects of stimulus control* (pp. 367–383). Hillsdale, NJ: Erlbaum.

Boysen, S. T., Berntson, G. G., Shreyer, T. A., & Hannan, M. B. (1995). Indicating acts during counting by a chimpanzee (*Pan troglodytes*). *Journal of Comparative Psychology, 109*, 47–51.

Boysen, S. T., & Hallberg, K. I. (2000). Primate numerical competence: Contributions toward understanding nonhuman cognition. *Cognitive Science, 24*, 423–443.

Brannon, E. M., & Terrace, H. S. (2000). Representation of the numerosities 1-9 by rhesus macaques (*Macaca mulatta*). *Journal of Experimental Psychology: Animal Behavior Processes, 26*, 31–49.

Cantlon, J. F., & Brannon, E. M. (2006). Shared system for ordering small and large numbers in monkeys and humans. *Psychological Science*, *17*, 401–406.

Cantlon, J. F., & Brannon, E. M. (2007). How much does number matter to a monkey (*Macaca mulatta*)? *Journal of Experimental Psychology: Animal Behavior Processes*, *33*, 32–41.

Genty, E., & Roeder, J. J. (2007). Transfer of control in black (*Eulemur macaco*) and brown (*Eulemur fulvus*) lemurs: Choice of a less preferred food item under a reverse-reward contingency. *Journal of Comparative Psychology*, *121*, 354–362.

Kralik, J. D. (2005). Inhibitory control and response selection in problem solving: How cotton-top tamarins (*Saguinas oedipus*) overcome a bias for selecting the larger quantity of food. *Journal of Comparative Psychology*, *119*, 78–89.

Menzel, E. W., Jr. (1972). Spontaneous invention of ladders in a group of young chimpanzees. *Folia Primatologica*, *17*, 87–106.

Menzel, E. W., Jr. (1985). Chimpanzee (*Pan troglodytes*) spatial problem solving with the use of mirrors and televised equivalents or mirrors. *Journal of Comparative Psychology*, *99*, 211–217.

Pepperberg, I. M. (1999). *The Alex studies: Cognitive and communicative abilities of grey parrots*. Cambridge, MA: Harvard University Press.

Rumbaugh, D. M., Hopkins, W. D., Washburn, D. A., & Savage-Rumbaugh, E. S. (1989). Lana chimpanzee learns to count by "NUMATH": A summary of a videotaped experimental report. *Psychological Record*, *39*, 459–470.

Chapter 7

Would Animals Pass a Version of the Marshmallow Test?

Mischel's marshmallow test is arguably one of the most famous tests in psychological science. When I teach one of my classes, or give a presentation at a conference, and I just mention the marshmallow test, many heads nod in recognition. In fact, even talking to nonstudents and nonresearchers often leads to the same response. People love the test, they love to watch the many videos online that show children going through the test, and they love hearing about what helps and what hurts the performance of children. I think in large part this is because people can easily empathize with what the children are going through, with that tempting and delicious treat in front of them, but also with the desire to get another treat, if they can. I think the marshmallow test is also so appealing to people because it clearly highlights the nature of the struggle between Now and Later that we all feel at various points each day, and because it reflects such a fundamental developmental milestone for children, as they slowly learn how to control their impulses, or at least we hope that they do.

I think another reason people enjoy seeing the marshmallow test is because it reflects an area of human choice behavior and intelligence that we hold sacred—the ability to think of the future, to anticipate what we will want later, and to "rise above" our animal impulses. That last part is the key issue for this chapter—are we alone in being able to do this? We already discussed that although we *can* delay gratification, we are not necessarily good at it, and even for those who can do it, it is not easy. Self-control of this sort, where we have to put off something we really want now, feels like one of those sophisticated abilities that would make our species unique, in much the same way as we consider the use of language, higher mathematics and engineering, cooperation of large groups in projects that benefit many individuals at once, and long-term planning to be unique to our species. But, of those things, I think most people would agree that delay of gratification is the biggest daily struggle. We take for granted after the first few years of life our ability to use language to communicate, and in industrialized societies (where most psychological research is conducted) we are immersed in using products of math and engineering, and participating in economic structures

Self-Control in Animals and People. DOI: https://doi.org/10.1016/B978-0-12-812508-3.00007-4
© 2018 Elsevier Inc. All rights reserved.

that govern how we buy and sell things and coordinate with other people to move about in daily life. We even take for granted that we can know what we need to accomplish, and then set goals toward that end, as long as those goals do not conflict too much with what we want right now. But, skipping that donut (or second donut!) at breakfast, or putting more money toward retirement rather than spending it now, or going for that run instead of watching television are all difficult choices for many of us, even if our longer-term goals are clear to us.

When we do these things, though, and we show restraint, and we make the choice to do more now, or wait to get something better, we feel as if we have really accomplished something. And, because of how hard that choice may have felt, and how impressed we might be that we "did the right thing," we want to consider this an important feat. Because impulsivity is seen to underlie so many negative aspects of human behavior, our morality and ethics seem tied to self-control. We elevate those who show restraint, and self-control, whereas we denigrate those who seem to respond impulsively. We want to be more like Benjamin Franklin, and less like Homer Simpson. And from this, we create what is perhaps a false dichotomy between impulsive and controlled people, where the truth is that no one is completely impulsive or completely self-controlled, as was discussed earlier. But, we want to believe that we are controlled in our choices, and that this separates what we, as humans, can do over and above the actions of animals.

However, is this really true? Are animals blindly impulsive, inclined (or even predisposed) to always take what they can get now, rather than to wait to get something better? We saw that for intertemporal choice tests, this was not always true. Animals such as rats and pigeons tend to discount the future much more steeply than do humans, that is true, but in some cases, they appear to choose the better, more distant outcome. And, in some cases, they appear to behave in ways that suggest they might even be able to precommit to the delayed but better outcome, if such precommitment is available. Recall that in some cases, pigeons were shown to do this by pecking a key that only functions to then force them to the choose the larger-later reward from among two other stimuli to peck (e.g., Rachlin & Green, 1972). When no such precommitment was possible, the pigeons tended to choose the smaller, more immediate reward, suggesting limited self-control. But, when they could precommit, they sometimes forced themselves away from that impulsive response, and perhaps in a way that is analogous to a person hiding away the cigarettes, or not buying them in the first place so that later they could not be smoked. Perhaps this is like the runner-in-training, who signs up for a 5K race a month in advance so that later he or she is committed to the race, and will therefore train for it. Perhaps this precommitment response is like our fictional friend from Chapter 1, who bought the kitchen safe so that, when he was not hungry, he could lock away the brownies and therefore ensure that later, when he was hungry, he could not get at those brownies. This might be a stretch, of course, and there are alternate explanations for why the pigeons pecked that precommitment key. They may have learned through trial and error that pecking that key later led to a lot of food, and thus when it was the only thing available this was all that they remembered or associated with that stimulus, and so they pecked it. This would be very different from the example of the kitchen safe from Chapter 1, or from the smoker who actively avoids purchasing cigarettes. But, the point is that these older studies, and others, set the stage for asking new questions about whether other animals might also delay gratification in meaningful ways.

The "marshmallow test" and other similar approaches in developmental psychology drew attention from those working with animal models of self-control behavior, to the point that studies emerged with animal-friendly "marshmallow-like" tasks. In an impressive paper with pigeons that really highlighted the value of animal models of delayed gratification, the birds again made choices between smaller-sooner and larger-later rewards as I described for other intertemporal choice tests (Grosch & Neuringer, 1981). However, this new version of a self-control test offered the pigeons the continuous chance to peck one key, and get a low preference reward immediately. But, if they waited through a delay interval, they got access to a more preferred reward. This was a wonderful design to then test a lot of the same things in pigeons that had made big impacts on delay of gratification in children. First, Grosch and Neuringer assessed whether the visibility of rewards impacts behavior in the way it does with children (Mischel & Ebbesen, 1970). It did. Like with children, the pigeons waited more often for the delayed reward when both rewards were not present than when they were present. Next, pigeons were given something else to do during trials, to see whether options to distract oneself or engage in another activity might promote greater self-control and longer delay of gratification, as had been seen with children (Mischel, Ebbesen, & Zeiss, 1972). This was not exactly the same as the test with children, given that pigeons are not going to play with toys, like the kids did. But, they were given another key they could peck, in addition to the immediate reward key and the delayed reward if that key was not pecked. At first, pigeons could get occasional pellet rewards if they pecked the "toy" key often enough. However, in a later condition, that key did nothing but offer an alternative to the key that led to the immediate, lower preference reward, and of course loss of the delayed, better reward. The results again showed at least a surface similarity to what children did with toys—the pigeons waited longer. This was true even when they got nothing for pecking that new key. Other subsequent tests did things like prefeed the pigeons to see if that affected how well they waited, or even attempted to get pigeons to focus more on the delayed rewards (or not) by illuminating the hoppers where the different grains were located. In one of my favorite variations (which, as far as I know, has otherwise never been tried with animals), the researchers looked at how past experiences with future-based rewards affected self-control. As in the studies of by Mischel and Staub (1965) and Mahrer (1956), Grosch and Neuringer (1981) tried to give pigeons different experiences before the delay of gratification test. The children had been told on one day they would receive a prize the next day, but only some of them saw that come to reality, whereas the others did not get the promised prize. Those who got what was promised performed better later in terms of choosing and waiting for delayed rewards than did those who did not get a promised reward. The pigeons were given analogous circumstances. In one case, they had some preliminary trials where they got the preferred reward after only a short time (which was supposed to be analogous to the positive expectation case in children). In another case, the pigeons never got that preferred reward and could only get the less preferred reward (analogous to the negative expectation). The positive experiences led to better self-control in the standard test that was used throughout this study compared to the negative expectation. This indicated that pigeons, like humans, show better self-control when they have some experience that waiting is actually a good thing to do. When I read this paper, I became more interested in designing a test for chimpanzees that could also look at many of the phenomena seen in children, only in a nonverbal, nonhuman species. Grosch and Neuringer showed that such efforts might lead to really interesting results.

As I noted in the last chapter, it was first and foremost the reverse-reward task that drew my attention specifically to studying self-control in the chimpanzees I worked with each day. The growing number of reports about how difficult the RR task was for so many species, and how symbolic rewards really helped some animals (e.g., Boysen & Berntson, 1995; Boysen, Berntson, Hannan, & Cacioppo, 1996; Boysen, Mukobi, & Berntson, 1999) overcome what appeared to be a strong case of impulsivity, fascinated me. I was also reading about the marshmallow task, and other tests of delayed gratification in children, and so I began to think about how one could test chimpanzees in a marshmallow-like task. It was then when I learned of the approach taken by Grosch and Neuringer (1981), which really impacted how I thought about giving chimpanzees a "marshmallow" test. This turned into my Masters thesis project, after my adviser, Duane Rumbaugh, strongly pushed me to move away from numerical cognition research, at least for a bit, and pursue another line of research. I read the other attempts to make marshmallow-like tests for animals, but wanted to try to come up with something more like what a child experienced when he or she sat in that chair with one marshmallow right there, and another promised, but only if he or she could wait. After a few aborted attempts at things, I came up with an idea that led to our version of the marshmallow test for chimpanzees (Beran, Savage-Rumbaugh, Pate, & Rumbaugh, 1999).

Chimpanzees, of course, cannot verbally announce when they are done waiting, unlike the children. But, they can make other kinds of discrete choices and responses. So, I designed a simple apparatus that had a door bell button mounted on one side, and the button was accessible to the chimpanzee inside his or her testing enclosure, whereas I could place food items or other things on top of the apparatus and out of reach. The apparatus was about three feet long, allowing me to put items either right on top of where the button projected out to within reach of the chimpanzee, or down at the other end of the bench. All I needed to do was to train the chimpanzees that when they pressed the button, a long melodic chime would sound, and I would hand them whatever was right on top of the button. This was just about the easiest thing I have ever taught a chimpanzee! They all were naturally curious about the button, and like so many rats, birds, and other animals before them in various operant chambers, it was no problem to quickly establish a schedule for pushing that button! Then, it was time to teach them the rules about item location, and outcome. I introduced the *immediate* bowl, which was right on top of the button, and the *delayed* bowl, on the other end of the bench. Training trials with delayed rewards involved placing the food item at the other end of the bench, and an empty bowl above the button. Now, a button press led to that food reward going away, and an empty bowl being given to the chimpanzee. It took a little work, and some trials of explicitly telling the chimpanzees not to touch the button, to get them to learn that *doing nothing* was another response option. In this way, they learned to wait through a delay period, and then a timer sounded, and they learned that I would then give them the bowl (and whatever was in it) from the far end of the bench. Once they learned this, I could then slowly build their tolerance for delays until I was able to present trials that were 3 minutes long, and food items could go into either or both of the bowls. When the button was pushed, the chimpanzees received the immediate bowl, but if they waited three minutes, they received the other bowl, and whatever was in it.

In the formal "marshmallow test" for chimpanzees, I used three conditions. In one, real food items (one more preferred and one less preferred) were placed into the bowls. Sometimes, the better food was available immediately, but other times it was the delayed reward. These foods always stayed in view. At the time, I thought this was going to be a difficult condition, and that the presence of a highly preferred food would lead the chimpanzees to want to do something—like press the button. So, based on all that I had learned about symbolic rewards in children, and in Sally Boysen's tests with chimpanzees in the RR task, I included some symbolic conditions as well. In one, I used photographs of those food items, rather than the items themselves. These chimpanzees readily match photos to their real world objects, and so the idea here was to convert the task to a more "cool" version of what I thought would be a "hot" version with real foods. And, because some of these chimpanzees also knew lexigram symbols that represented food items (but did not look at all like those items; Rumbaugh, 1977; Savage-Rumbaugh, 1986), I had a condition with lexigrams in bowls, and whatever those lexigrams (or photos) represented would be what the chimpanzees received, depending on how they behaved.

The task was not easy for any of the chimpanzees, and as one might expect, they tended to press the button frequently. Of course, when the immediate reward was the better reward, the chimpanzees pressed the button on nearly all trials (215 of 216 trials). When the better reward was in the delayed bowl, that changed. All three chimpanzees did show trials where they waited through the entire delay period, which could be as long as 5 minutes in some cases, when real food items were presented (see Table 7.1). Only Sherman showed any strong evidence of delayed gratification when photographs were used, and only Sherman and Lana made use of lexigrams to aid in getting the better rewards (Table 7.1). This last outcome made sense, because chimpanzee Mercury had never been trained to use or understand lexigrams, so he could not possibly know what to do when they were presented. But, the results were most striking because the chimpanzees seemed to do best when real food items were present. This was in stark contrast to the role of visibility of real food items during the marshmallow test with children, as well as the general finding with children that symbolic

TABLE 7.1 Chimpanzees' Performance in the Test of Beran et al. (1999)

	Condition		
Chimpanzee	Foods	Photographs	Lexigrams
Mercury			
Total	9 of 48	0 of 48	1 of 48
Delay = 180 s	6 of 14	0 of 48	1 of 48
Delay = 240 s	3 of 34		
Lana			
Total	21 of 48	2 of 48	9 of 48
Delay = 180 s	6 of 14	2 of 48	9 of 48
Delay = 240 s	6 of 6		
Delay = 300 s	9 of 28		
Sherman			
Total	12 of 48	13 of 48	20 of 48
Delay = 180 s	12 of 48	13 of 48	14 of 31
Delay = 240 s			6 of 17

Note: The values reflect the number of trials in each condition, and at each delay for which the chimpanzees waited through the full delay to collect the delayed reward when it was the more preferred reward. These data are from Table 2 in Beran et al. (1999).

rewards are more conducive to supporting delay maintenance than are real rewards (e.g., Mischel & Ebbesen, 1970; Mischel & Moore, 1973). For children, paying attention to real rewards is a bad strategy, but this test with chimpanzees perhaps suggested something different. However, at the time, I could not yet say whether this was a fundamental difference between adult chimpanzees and human children, or whether perhaps this use of symbolic stimuli (photographs and lexigrams) was not equivalent to how such symbols were used with children. Although the chimpanzees could match these stimuli to real world referents, their use was different from many of the symbolic tasks given to children, as I described those tests in the last chapter. But, the take-home story from this first effort with chimpanzees was that they could, in fact, inhibit ending a trial for a lower preference outcome in order to get a higher preference outcome later. And, we also saw something interesting on those trials in which the chimpanzees failed to wait for the better, more delayed reward—they were trying to wait. Fig. 7.1 illustrates this, and perhaps best for Mercury with food items, and for Sherman with photographs and lexigrams. In these cases, and others, even though the chimpanzee failed to wait through the delay and receive the better reward, they waited longer before pushing the button than on those trials where the better reward was in the immediate bowl. This showed that although delay of gratification was not sufficient to reach the goal of receiving the better reward, the

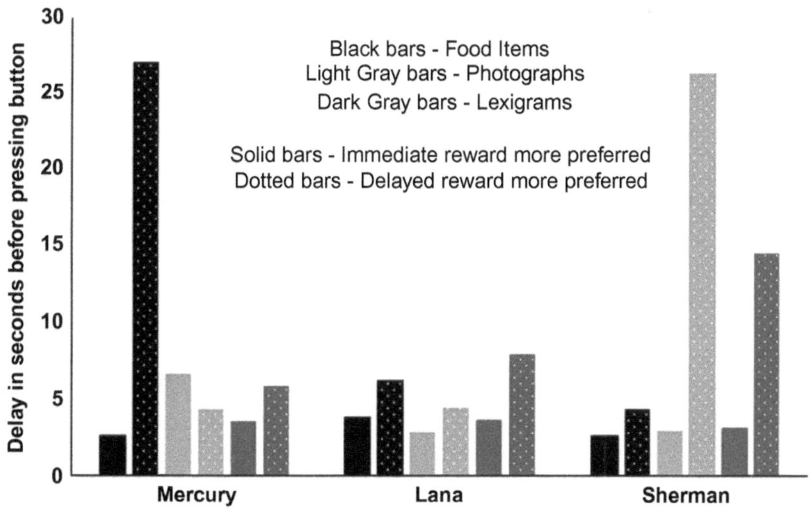

FIGURE 7.1 Delay times for chimpanzees as a function of stimuli (food items, photographs, or lexigrams presented) and trial condition (whether the better reward was in the immediate bowl or the delayed bowl). The comparisons to be made here are between adjacent bars of the same color, but comparing solid bars to dotted ones. *These data are redrawn from Table 3 in Beran et al. (1999).*

chimpanzees were trying to wait on those trials, much as do children when faced with the present, single marshmallow that they can take at any time.

Given these results, I conducted a second experiment (Beran, 2003) with some modifications. First, I wanted to remove the presence of an experimenter during trials. This always helps increase confidence that whatever an animal is doing, that behavior is not based on some kind of external inhibitory factor such as an experimenter being nearby, and who might be influencing behavior. So, I wanted a task with no person present. I trained two chimpanzees (Lana and Panzee) to move into a small transport box that was used to move them to separate caging areas, and to remain in that box while I presented the relevant stimuli for a trial. In this test, the rules were a little more intuitive. Some food items were left outside of the enclosure (and out of reach of the chimpanzee) whereas other food items were placed into the enclosure (Fig. 7.2). In that case, nothing prevented the chimpanzees from sliding open the door to the box they were in, and walking to those items and eating them. But, if they did, they learned that I would return and take away the food item that was outside of the enclosure. So, the immediate reward was the one that the chimpanzees could go retrieve whenever they wanted, and the delayed reward required them to stay in the box until I returned. I was in a room that kept the chimpanzees from seeing me, but I could observe their behavior, and thus could know that they had ended a trial early, or I would return when a 4-minute interval had passed. In addition, I video recorded these trials, to see what behaviors the chimpanzees might engage in while they were in the test box, to see if there was any evidence of a relation between their attention to the rewards or other things and how long they were able to maintain delay of gratification in those trials where the better reward was the delayed reward. I again found interesting results. Both chimpanzees clearly waited longer before leaving the box (or, they waited the full four minutes and received the delayed reward) when the delayed reward was better (Fig. 7.2). Even when they failed to wait long enough to get the delayed reward, they clearly were trying. This suggested that perhaps *what they were doing* might impact how well they could wait. What I found was that both chimpanzees again attended to the delayed reward *more* throughout those trials in which they did wait long enough to get the delayed reward. This again seemed counterintuitive to the developmental research. However, I also found that one chimpanzee (Panzee) waited longer when she manipulated parts of the test box, which presumably turned her attention to something else to do. She also performed worse, in terms of waiting, when she was manipulating the door she needed to open to move out of the test box and go retrieve the immediate reward. This would suggest a type of difficulty in which she was already beginning the behavior (of leaving the box) that would terminate the trial without the good reward. However, the other chimpanzee, Lana, showed the opposite pattern! The more she manipulated the door (without leaving), the more likely she would

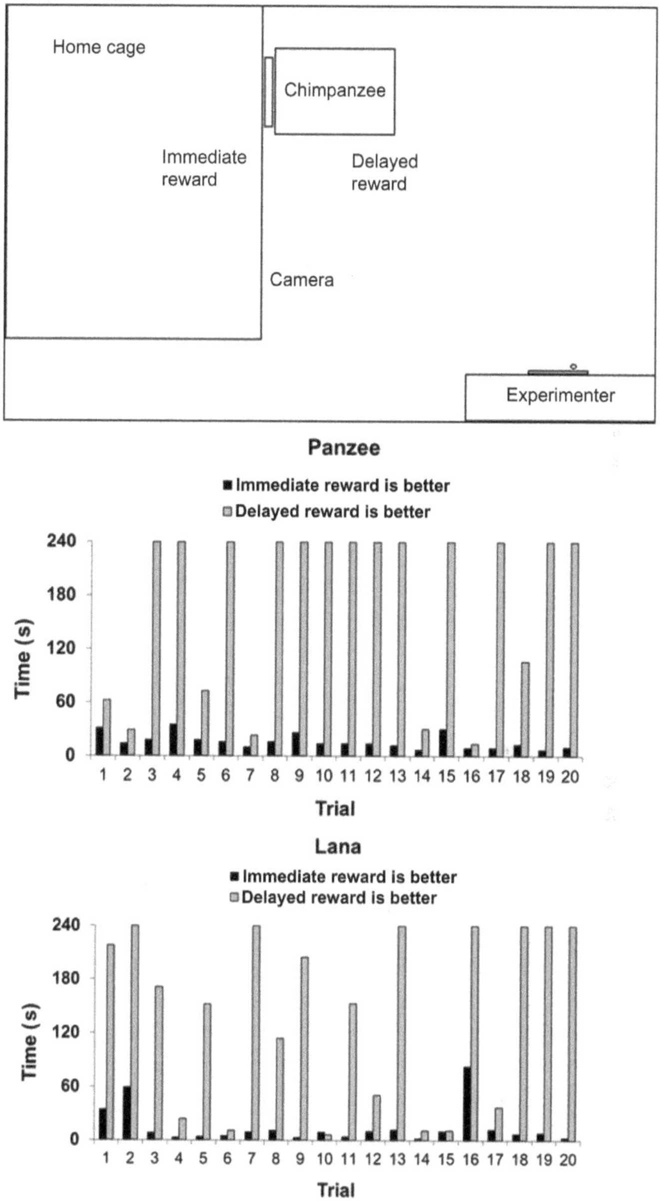

FIGURE 7.2 The top panel is a schematic of the test setting for the Beran (2002) study. The performance of Panzee (middle panel) and Lana (bottom) panel is shown as a function of how long the chimpanzees remained in the test box before leaving and taking the immediate reward. The maximum delay of 240 seconds, so those bars reflect trials in which the delayed reward was given to the chimpanzees. Trials are shown in the paired blocks that occurred in which on one trial the better reward was immediately available and on the other trial the better reward was delayed. The order of these trials was randomized and is presented here as immediate and then delayed for ease of comparison. *The data are redrawn from those in Beran (2002).*

wait through the whole delay period. So, there was not a clear answer as to how behavior strategies might have impacted chimpanzee self-control through their ability to delay gratification.

What about other species? These kinds of "one thing now, or another thing later" tests are fairly simple to present to nonhuman animals, and so many species could be tested. One species for which there is now a lot of interest in comparative cognition research is the domestic dog. Dogs are intriguing in terms of self-control research for the reason that they have been bred largely to tolerate situations in which impulse control is required. Hunting dogs, for example, must track and contain prey species without attacking them directly. Retrievers must take into the mouth freshly killed prey but not damage those prey animals as they are retrieved. These both seem like situations of strong behavioral inhibition. And, if you think about the family dog, always around human food, or around small children, one imagines constant efforts of those dogs to not take food (especially from small children!). Thus, it seems like they would be a good candidate species for self-control research, and I think that there is good reason to have high expectations for them. Brucks, Soliani, Range, and Marshall-Pescini (2017) gave dogs a series of tasks that I think are highly similar to the tasks I just outlined with chimpanzees. Brucks et al. had noted that perhaps dogs inhibit those kinds of behaviors I just noted not through engaging in self-control mechanisms, but through mechanisms of social inhibition, which are exactly the kinds of mechanisms that would have been artificially selected for during domestication by humans. They argued that it would be important in assessing self-control in dogs to ensure that any inhibition of eating items would not be solely the result of human presence and influence. So, they designed a task to see how dogs tolerated having to forego eating one continuously available reward for the chance to later get a better reward. And, they performed this task without people present, so there was no concern that the presence of humans led directly to a more socially based inhibition of action. In their test, one bowl was always within reach, with a food item in it. Another bowl was out of reach, and if the dogs avoided eating the item in the bowl within reach, eventually the bowls would exchange, and the second item would come within reach (Fig. 7.3). The dogs were taught that the second bowl eventually would arrive, and that it would hold a qualitatively better reward, or a larger quantity of the same reward available in the immediate bowl. Thus, the dogs, like the children in the marshmallow test, or the chimpanzees in the tests above, had to wait and not eat what was right in front of them, in order to get the later, better reward. And, many of them could do this, for fairly long delays (Fig. 7.3). They seemed to do a little better when the delayed reward was qualitatively better rather than simply more of the same food type, but in both cases dogs would wait multiple minutes. And, some dogs showed some of the same behavioral patterns children had shown. They looked away from the food, laid down, or even moved away

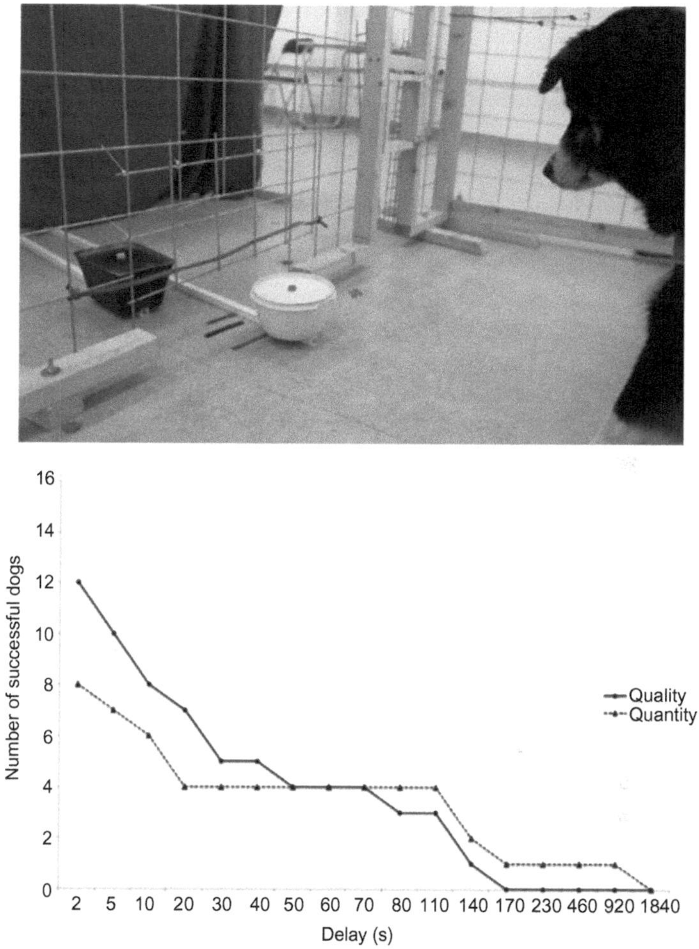

FIGURE 7.3 Test setup for quality condition in Brucks et al. (2017). The dog is waiting for the black bowl, which contains the high value reward (in this case sausage) and resists from eating the low value reward (in this case dry food) from the white bowl. The figure shows the number of successful dogs that waited for a minimum of 3 trials for the delayed reward option per delay in the quantity condition and quality condition. *From Brucks, D., Soliani, M., Range, F., & Marshall-Pescini, S. (2017). Reward type and behavioural patterns predict dogs' success in a delay of gratification paradigm.* Scientific Reports, 7, *42459, Open Access article, reprinted with permission.*

from the test area. All of those behaviors predicted better waiting, and more successful retrieval of the delayed reward. I think these are impressive results, highlighting what may be a strategic performance pattern by dogs that matches that seen in chimpanzees (a point I will return to later in this chapter). What I also found very interesting is that the dogs' owners reported their own perceptions of the dogs' impulsivity, using a questionnaire, but those results were not predictive of performance in the task. I do not think this has been done with nonhuman primates, where such caregiver ratings also could be given. It would be interesting if, in those species also, there is no real relation between performance and others' ratings of how impulsive individuals might be. In some ways, this makes sense, because we know that general tendencies toward impulsivity or self-control do not always predict what one might do in a particular context, and I doubt that many of these dogs' owners had ever given their dogs this kind of situation to deal with, where they could see clearly that waiting was going to bring a better reward. I think this is a key aspect to the good performance, because the subject animal could understand the nature of the task, and understand why waiting would be beneficial. This point leads to my next comments, on how another test of self-control with animals also makes use of an intuitive test environment to probe delay of gratification abilities.

Around the time I was finishing my own first studies with tests based on the marshmallow test, I came across a series of papers testing children that led me to a new approach to studying self-control in animals. Toner and Smith (1977) reported a variation of delayed gratification test, in which there was not a dichotomous set of outcomes, but rather a continuous and changing situation for the child throughout a trial. Mischel's marshmallow task and its variants presented the child with one thing now (and through the delay), and then something better if a child waited long enough. Toner wanted the reward to change throughout the delay, and to improve. So, in this task, children observed as candies accumulated in front of them, and as long as they did not take and eat those candies, more would be coming. I like to think of this task as being similar to what someone might go through when putting money into a savings account to spend later on a big purchase. At the start, there is little or nothing to spend, but with each passing day, not only is the accumulation of money growing, but presumably the appeal of that growing accumulation also increases, as it is worth more and more until it is taken. So, Toner's task is more dynamic than some other tests of delayed gratification, because throughout the trial the immediate reward is changing. What Toner and Smith did was to present preschool and elementary school girls with this task, and also with some specific instructions about what they needed to say aloud each time a candy was added to the set. The neutral condition just involved saying number words, whereas the "hot" condition involved talking about how good the candy would taste, and the "cold" condition involved talking about how good it was to wait instead of taking the candies. Toner and Smith found that this was a big issue—what one says: those girls who talked about how good the rewards would taste waited significantly shorter periods before taking the candies, but the girls who talked about how good it is to wait for rewards waited significantly longer. So...what you say when trying to wait through a delay period can impact what you do.

Subsequent work showed many of the same environmental effects on delay of gratification that Mischel had shown with the marshmallow paradigm. Toner, Lewis, and Gribble (1979) reported that children's statements during trials of the accumulation task affected how long they would wait before taking those accumulations. Children who focused on reward, no matter whether they talked about that reward in positive or negative terms, performed less well in accumulating items compared to children who made no verbal statements (see also Toner, 1981). These results aligned nicely with other tasks, but for me the task itself was most interesting, because it seemed so relevant to nonhuman animal experiences, and fairly easy to implement with nonhuman primates.

My first effort at doing this involved testing the four LRC chimpanzees and an orangutan who also lived at the LRC, named Madu. In the first test (Beran, 2002), I acted in pretty much the same role as the experimenters in the Toner studies. Each ape was tested alone, and I placed a bowl on the ground so that they could pull it in any time they wanted, but I could also place items into the bowl. This made it pretty clear that I was adding things, and they could take them as they wished. I tried this for a couple of trials on the first day, and the results were encouraging! On the very first time seeing the task, they all did exactly what you might expect, if you remember that I had no way to tell them the basic rules of the game. I came in to the area with a bowl of food items, and as soon as I put the first one in their bowl, they pulled it in and ate it. So, I walked away with the rest. That got their attention, in ways one normally does not like attention from apes! There was some banging on the mesh, and some other forms of mild "protest." But, when I came back a while later and tried it again, all five waited for many more items than on the first trial. Once they realized I was there to keep transferring food from my possession to their possession, the rules of the game became clear.

In the first formal study (Beran, 2002), I presented the apes with up to 20 candy rewards, transferred at different speeds. I started transferring at 3 seconds per item, then increased the delay between items to 6 seconds, and then finally to 9 seconds. In that last phase, I also put the supply pile of candies (those not yet transferred) some distance away, so that I had to leave the ape and walk over to retrieve the items one at a time. This was to see whether my presence, or lack of presence, in the immediate area had any effect on the apes. The results were clear—all apes were fairly good at waiting for the items to accumulate, and some were nearly perfect (Fig. 7.4). The orangutan, Madu, was the least proficient, but later work with other orangutans would show them to be quite capable in the task as well, as I describe later.

The other aspect to this first "accumulation test," as it has come to be called, involved recording videos of the apes as they waited. I again was interested in any strategies, or any indication that certain behaviors aided or hurt delay maintenance, while the apes were waiting for the items to be

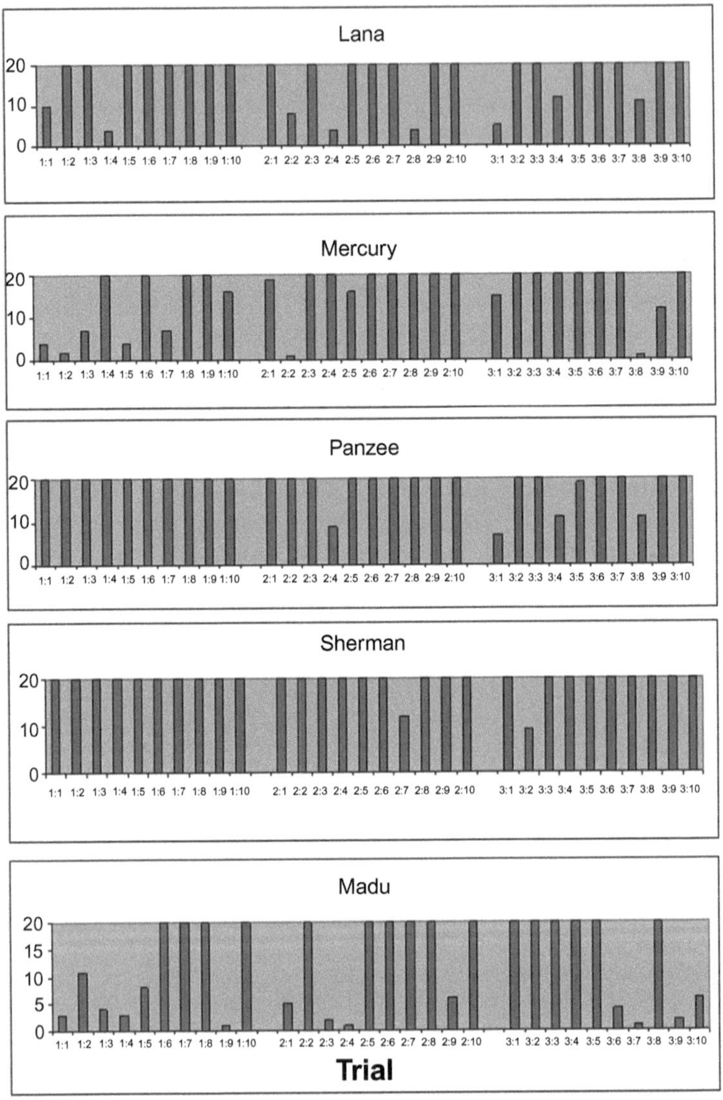

FIGURE 7.4 The performance of four chimpanzees and one orangutan on the first accumulation test presented to great apes. In each panel, the *x*-axis shows each trial, with the first number designating the phase (Phase 1 total trial delay = 60 seconds; Phase 2 = 120 seconds; Phase 3 = 180 seconds) and the trial number within that phase. *From Beran, M. J. (2002). Maintenance of self-imposed delay of gratification by four chimpanzees (*Pan troglodytes*) and an orangutan (*Pongo pygmaeus*).* Journal of General Psychology, 129, *49–66, reprinted with permission from Taylor & Francis Ltd: http://www.informaworld.com.*

transferred. So, in this test I scored how often they touched the bowl or the candies, thinking that attention to those rewards would certainly predict shorter delay times. But, once again, I was wrong. There was great variability among the apes in the number of times they touched the bowl or candies, but the main outcome was that those who touched a lot (Sherman touched the bowl 74.5% of the coded intervals), or even frequently, performed as well as the other apes, and the number of bowl touches on each trial was not significantly correlated with the number of food rewards received on that trial. Attention to the delayed rewards just did not seem to be a problem for adult apes. The overall results of this study, however, led me to trying many more studies like this, and varying the accumulation task in new ways.

One of the things I first wanted to move away from was having an experimenter present. So, in the next study, Ted Evans joined the project and built a computerized apparatus with dispenser which allowed us to remove any need for an experimenter in the test area. Ted had just joined the LRC, and part of his previous research while completing his Master's degree involved a very creative test with capuchin monkeys looking at self-control that I discuss in the next chapter. So, he and I began a long series of tests with the LRC apes and monkeys that occupied the next 10 years of our lives. In the first series (Beran & Evans, 2006), we made the transition to this computerized method. First, we wanted to look at other environmental features of the manual task to see how they might affect the chimpanzees. So, we varied the visibility of the supply source of the foods to be transferred, thinking that having those out of view might make it harder for the chimpanzees to delay gratification until all items were transferred. It did not. Then, we moved to using the automated system. In this version of the task, a computer cart is in front of the chimpanzees' enclosure, and a dispenser holding the rewards is mounted on top. Those items, when they are dispensed, slide down a long tube that attached at the bottom to a collection container that can be detached by the chimpanzees from the tube because it is inside the enclosure with them. So, the computer controls the dispenser, and the chimpanzees take the rewards whenever they want. The experimenters then could leave the test area, and observe from another, out-of-view location by watching closed circuit television. In this way, if the chimpanzees took the container and ate the accumulated rewards, we would stop the trial remotely.

With this system in place, we still saw excellent performance from three of four chimpanzees (Fig. 7.5), with delays of approximately 3 minutes before all 36 items would be dispensed. We pushed the temporal limits of the task by increasing the time between each item, and found that in this experiment some chimpanzees would wait longer than 10 minutes to get all of the food that they could. However, we continued to see little by way of evidence that behavior during these trials affected how long the chimpanzees would wait. For each trial in which the tube was inserted into the chimpanzee's enclosure, and food treats could be taken, we paired another trial (on

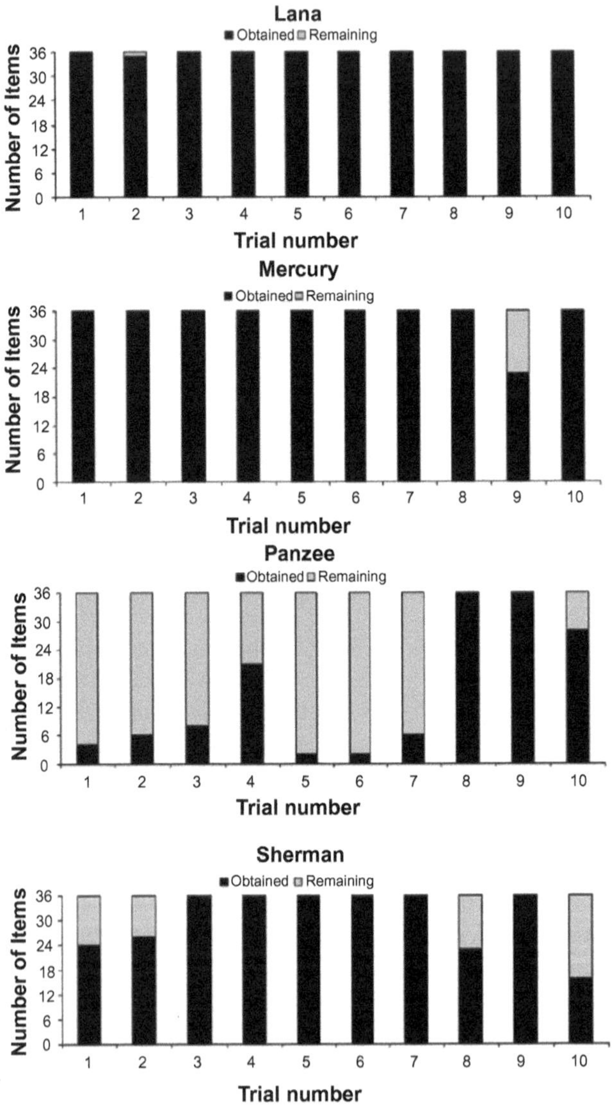

FIGURE 7.5 Performance of the chimpanzees in the internally imposed delay condition in Beran and Evans (2006). The black section of each bar indicates the number of candies obtained, and the gray section indicates the number of candies remaining at the end of the trial (after the chimpanzee pulled in the collection container). *From Beran, M. J., & Evans, T. A. (2006). Maintenance of delay of gratification by four chimpanzees (*Pan troglodytes*): The effects of delayed reward visibility, experimenter presence, and extended delay intervals.* Behavioural Processes, 73, *315–324, reprinted with permission from Elsevier.*

another day) that perfectly matched that trial in terms of the trial length and number of items dispensed. So, for example, if a chimpanzee waited for 16 items on one day when the chimpanzee controlled when they could take it, the next trial would also dispense 16 items at the same rate, but now the container where those items collected was out of reach. The first situation we called the *internally imposed* delay condition, and the second was *externally imposed*. From the videos, we examined whether behavior differed in the two situations, thinking that perhaps when the chimpanzees had to show self-control because the foods were available whenever they wanted to take them, certain behaviors might be more evident, and certain behaviors might be more predictive of how long the chimpanzees waited. We looked at self-scratching behavior, which often is taken as a sign of frustration, self-grooming behavior, which we thought might be a form of self-distraction, and vocalizations. Despite high hopes that this might show us something interesting, it did not. Instead, we saw that once again the overt behaviors of the chimpanzees hardly varied between internally imposed and externally imposed trials (Fig. 7.6). However, we had not yet tried to directly manipulate how the chimpanzees might interact with things in a way they let them direct attention, either toward or away from the accumulating reward.

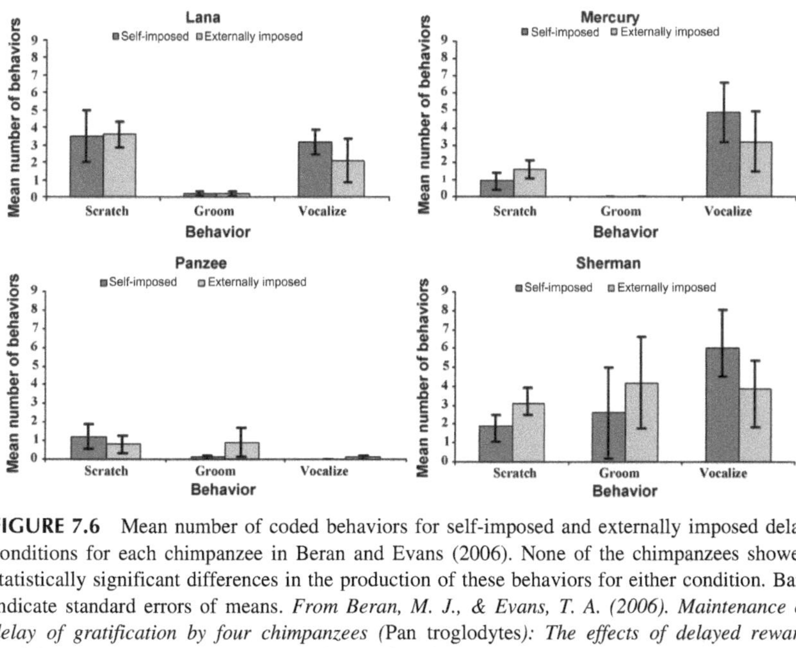

FIGURE 7.6 Mean number of coded behaviors for self-imposed and externally imposed delay conditions for each chimpanzee in Beran and Evans (2006). None of the chimpanzees showed statistically significant differences in the production of these behaviors for either condition. Bars indicate standard errors of means. *From Beran, M. J., & Evans, T. A. (2006). Maintenance of delay of gratification by four chimpanzees (*Pan troglodytes*): The effects of delayed reward visibility, experimenter presence, and extended delay intervals.* Behavioural Processes, 73, *315–324, reprinted with permission from Elsevier.*

That came next, in the form of our own efforts to introduce toys to the test, as Grosch and Neuringer (1981) had tried many years earlier.

By this point, the chimpanzees were used to sitting with the tube with accumulating items in front of them. So, we continued to use that approach, with the automated dispensing, and no people in the test area. But, now we introduced toys, in two different conditions (Evans & Beran, 2007a). We also had baseline trials, in which no toys were present, and the chimpanzees simply had to wait as items accumulated in front of them. The toys were a variety of chimpanzee favorites, such as magazines, crayons, toothbrushes, and other items that they like to manipulate. A subset of those things were given to the chimpanzees before the accumulation started. In one condition, the tube with the accumulating rewards also was available to the chimpanzees, in another *internally imposed* situation. In the other condition, with *externally imposed* delay, the trial last the same amount of time, and the same number of items accumulated before they were given to the chimpanzee. So, in one case, they had toys and needed to maintain they own imposed delay of gratification, and in the other case, they had toys, the same delays and items accumulated, but it was out of their control as to when they could take those accumulated items.

We had two questions. First, did having toys make a difference? If it did, the chimpanzees should wait longer on internally imposed trials with toys than on internally imposed trials without toys. We found that this was true (Fig. 7.7). Toys aided delay of gratification. But, this might be a rather trivial result. Having something to do might have led to the chimpanzees doing that

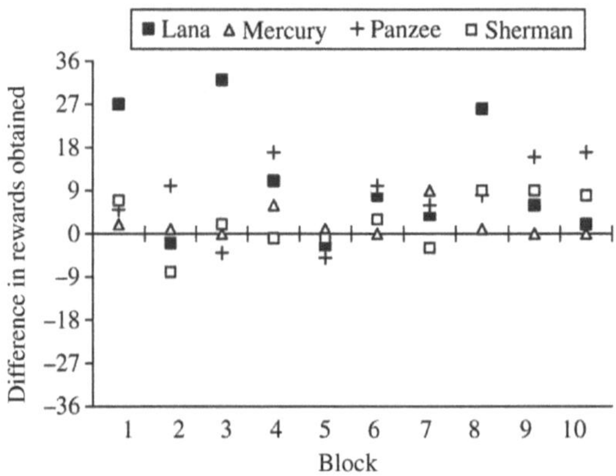

FIGURE 7.7 Difference in performance on the basis of the experimental condition. Data points represent the arithmetic difference between rewards obtained when toys were available versus when they were not, and the chimpanzees were in the *internally imposed* condition in both cases. Points above the central line indicate paired trials where more rewards were earned with toys than without toys in that block. *From Evans, T. A., & Beran, M. J. (2007). Chimpanzees use self-distraction to cope with impulsivity.* Biology Letters, 3, *599–602, reprinted with permission of The Royal Society.*

activity, and this might have coincidentally distracted them from the accumulating rewards. In this case, it would be like someone else distracting you from what you are waiting to get, thereby helping you to wait. But, to demonstrate that the chimpanzees were more strategic in their behavior, and were choosing to self-distract during delay, we needed to examine the paired trials with internally imposed and externally imposed delays and the toys available. If the chimpanzees were self-distracting, to gain more rewards, the toys should be more useful (and more used) in the internally imposed condition than the externally imposed condition. This is exactly what we found, for three of four chimpanzees (Fig. 7.8). Those chimpanzees used the toys not simply because they were there, but when they were needed as a means to aid in delay maintenance. To us, this was a striking similarity to what had been reported with children (e.g., Mischel et al., 1972; see also Miller & Karniol, 1976), and suggested that some nonhuman animals are capable of experiencing some sense of possible failure, and adjusting behavior to avoid that failure. This ability to deal with fallibility by changing behavior (such as playing with toys) feels fairly sophisticated. It makes good sense that chimpanzees would be one species that could show this, given many of their other apparent capacities for dealing with fallibility, such as the reports showing metacognitive abilities in great apes and some other primates that have been summarized in other places (Beran, Smith, & Perdue, 2013; Beran et al., 2015; Call, 2010; Call & Carpenter, 2001; Marsh & MacDonald, 2012; Smith, 2009; see Further Reading for more on nonhuman primate metacognition). This type of self-distraction would seem to be a good example of a form of cognitive control (Beran, 2015) in a nonhuman species, and perhaps a capacity evident in other species also, as I describe later.

In the next chapter, I will discuss a range of other really intriguing tests that are used to assess delayed gratification in nonhuman animals, and the accumulation test has been in that set for a number of years. In general, it seems to be a harder task for monkeys to master compared to all of the great apes. The first orangutan we tested, Madu, seemed to have more trouble with the task compared to our chimpanzees, but subsequent tests showed that orangutans could wait for quite some time, and in some cases for as many as 50 food rewards to accumulate (Parrish et al., 2014). And, another great apes species, bonobos, also would wait for rewards to accumulate (Stevens, Rosati, Heilbronner, & Mühlhoff, 2011). Stevens et al. also assessed for the first time in apes the issue of expectancies and delaying gratification, inspired by work with children (Mahrer, 1956) and work I described earlier with pigeons (Grosch & Neuringer, 1981). In the Stevens et al. study, an unreliable experimenter sometimes first offered a bonobo a treat but withdrew it before it was consumed, and then that bonobo took an accumulation test. Reliable experimenters, however, did not behave badly in this way, and instead conducted a normal trial after giving the treat. This seemed to make little difference to some bonobos, as they waited about the

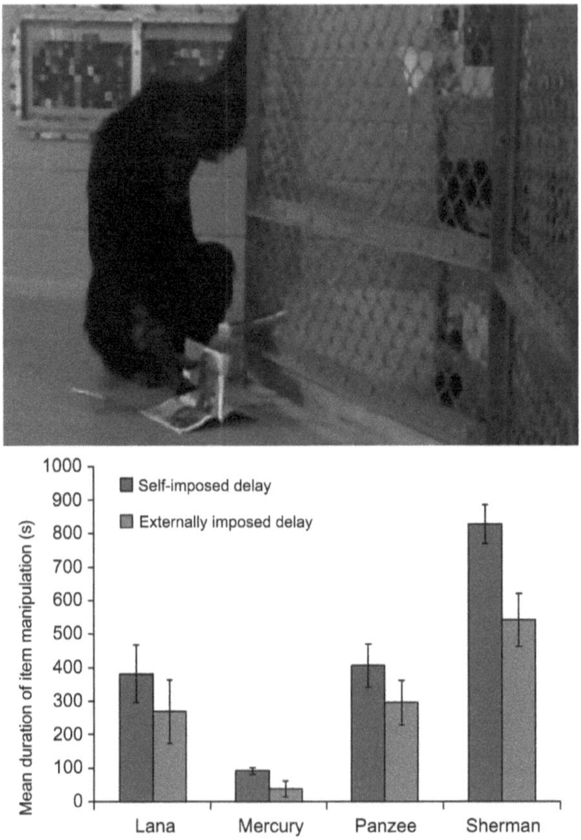

FIGURE 7.8 Illustration of the experimental setup and results from Evans and Beran (2007a). Panel (A) shows chimpanzee Sherman with some toys he could use for self-distraction during the accumulation test. It also shows the automated dispenser that delivered the food items one at a time. Panel (B) shows the mean cumulative duration of item manipulation for each chimpanzee. Error bars indicate standard errors of the mean. Delay maintenance was either self-imposed which means that the chimpanzees had to refrain from taking the food items in order for more to accumulate or externally imposed which meant the tube with the food items was placed out of reach but was still visible. Three chimpanzees, Mercury, Panzee, and Sherman, showed a statistically greater level of item manipulation in the self-imposed condition than the externally imposed condition. *From Beran, M. J. (2015). Chimpanzee cognitive control.* Current Directions in Psychological Science*, 24, 352–357, reprinted with permission of Sage.*

same amount of time no matter the reliability or past actions of the experimenter working with them (this experimenter was the one transferring the accumulated items). And, most bonobos did not seem to be affected much in their own delay of gratification even if the experimenter first offered them a treat, but instead *gave it to another nearby bonobo*. In principle, this should have been very frustrating for the subject ape, and yet the results showed little or no effect on delay time, except for one bonobo, who began to wait shorter periods of time when unreliability was evident. What did make a big difference for the group was when the experimenter sometimes took items *out of the accumulation*, and this unreliability led to shortened delay on the part of bonobos who experienced it. This makes sense, of course, because if an accumulation suddenly gets smaller, it might be time to take the rewards.

I think this last study by Stevens et al. (2011) is important because it gets at an often overlooked aspect of real-world situations that might involve delaying gratification—namely that delays come with their own risks independent of the internal conflict or struggle of the delaying individual to keep delaying. For humans, there are many examples. Imagine the gardener who slowly watches, day after day, as a watermelon or other slow growing fruit or vegetable slowly increases toward the ideal size to pick and prepare. Each day, the impulse to pick it now, and take it as it is, gets stronger, but this is not an unfounded or irrational impulsiveness if one is aware that an animal (or other hazard) may befall the beautiful watermelon, leaving the gardener with nothing. This seems unlikely to be a humanly unique experience, and in fact one can imagine many foraging species that make such decisions about when to move in and consume various grasses, plants, fruits, or other food sources (see Kalenscher & Pennartz, 2008; Stephens & Krebs, 1986; Stevens & Stephens, 2010). So, I think a crucial aspect to defining self-control contexts is to ensure that delayed, better outcomes (or outcomes that require more work to obtain) are guaranteed. These may be fewer than we imagine, perhaps restricted to things that are in the real world more contractual, such as savings accounts, retirement plans, or other vehicles in which guarantees really can be offered for waiting or maintaining some kind of behavior in the face of a competing interest to stop doing that, and do something else more immediate in its consequence.

Returning to the accumulation test, as a possible analog of a savings account for animals, tests with monkeys showed marked differences from most of those with apes. We first attempted to give rhesus macaques the accumulation test, and learned quickly that much more work would be required to see results even remotely like those from the apes. Ted Evans and I first gave the monkeys the chance to wait while food items accumulated in containers attached to their housing enclosures. We saw quickly that most monkeys were unable to wait more than a few seconds or to accumulate more than a couple of items. To help the monkeys improve, we had to make the accumulation consist of mostly lower preference items with the high preference items late in the sequence, in which case some monkeys (but not all!) finally allowed food to accumulate in front of them (Evans & Beran, 2007b). But, overall, we concluded from that first study that self-control in terms of delaying gratification during food accumulation was not as prevalent for monkeys as it had been for chimpanzees and for most human children.

However, one has to be careful about making such broad claims about species, because much of the work in comparative psychology relies on small numbers of animal subjects, and sometimes very different laboratory environments. A strong example of this comes from accumulation tests given to parrots. Vick, Bovet, and Anderson (2010) were the first researchers I know of to give parrots an accumulation test. In their version, sunflower seeds were placed within reach of African Grey parrots until they were taken, and the birds initially received 10 trials per day for 30 daily sessions. They barely accumulated any items, even with this fairly heavy experience, although there was some indication that they improved a little over time. However, when only one trial was given per day, performance was very poor, even though the total delay time was only 5 seconds to get all five seeds. Despite other efforts to aid delay maintenance, there was not much improvement throughout this study. However, before one could conclude that parrots just cannot get it, another study offered a striking contract in performance. Irene Pepperberg has been working with African Grey parrots for decades, and she has shown some of the most sophisticated abilities in these birds (see Further Reading for more on her work with numerical cognition in parrots and other cognitive abilities. To study delay of gratification, Koepke, Gray, and Pepperberg (2015) presented their version of a "marshmallow" task to a parrot named Griffin in which the experimenter placed one treat in a location immediately available to Griffin but another treat (more preferred) was kept in view, but out of reach (Fig. 7.9). As in the marshmallow test, the parrot had to not eat the treat in front of him in order to gain (later) the more preferred treat. Sometimes, the delayed reward was even taken out of view, leaving only the immediate reward as something the parrot could see. Delays intervals varied up to 15 minutes, and there were control trials in which sometimes the best food was the one immediately available (the parrot always took that food quickly in those cases). The results were impressive—Griffin obtained more than 90% of the delayed rewards (Fig. 7.9). And, Griffin showed what I think are clear examples of self-distracting behaviors. Koepke et al. reported that Griffin did things like move the cup away from him or even throw the cup containing the less favored treat across the room, perhaps to move it out of view and make it less tempting. He sometimes preened extensively, and even appeared to drift to sleep on occasion (something I have occasionally seen in the chimpanzees during long accumulation trials). I find these descriptions fascinating, and even if it is difficult to know how intentional they were, they merit additional study, in parrots, and other animals.

Overall, the results from Griffin, and some of the other results with various birds such as cockatoos and corvids that I will discuss in later chapters (e.g., Auersperg, Laumer, & Bugnyar, 2013; Dufour, Wascher, Braun, Miller, & Bugnyar, 2012; Hillemann, Bugnyar, Kotrschal, & Wascher, 2014) suggest that birds might show good delay of gratification, provided the

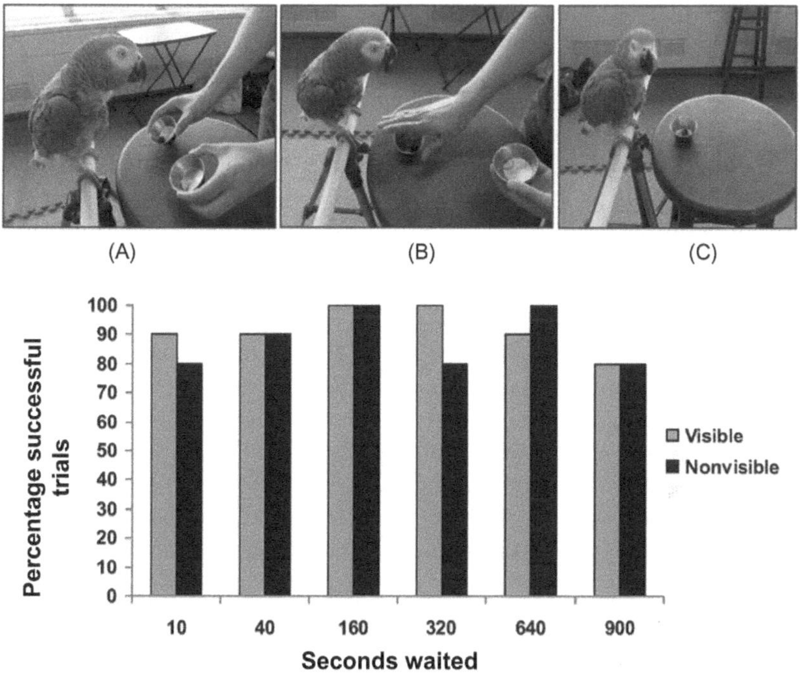

FIGURE 7.9 Griffin and his delay of gratification test. The top panel shows how trials worked. (A) The experimenter placed one treat in each cup and showed each to Griffin. (B) The experimenter positioned cup with one treat (less-preferred in noncontrol trials; more-preferred in control trials), and briefly covered it with her hand as she said, "Wait." (C) For each trial/condition, the experimenter either stood several feet away, showing treat (visible condition) or left room with treat (not-visible condition). The bottom panel shows the percentages of trials at each time delay for which Griffin waited or failed to wait in the two conditions. *From Koepke, A. E., Gray, S. L., & Pepperberg, I. M. (2015). Delayed gratification: A Grey parrot (*Psittacus erithacus*) will wait for a better reward.* Journal of Comparative Psychology, 129, *339–346, reprinted with permission of the American Psychological Association.*

correct task is presented to them. Perhaps the accumulation test is not a fair test for birds. One possibility is that any test that involves an experimenter moving toward the reward pile may bias the subject (whether bird, monkey, or other type of animal) to immediately take what is available, not because of impulsivity, but because of uncertainty about that reward remaining available. This is a limitation of any accumulation test that keeps a conspecific or a human experimenter in the test area. With the chimpanzees, we originally worried that our presence might *overestimate* self-control because we inhibited the chimpanzees from taking the rewards while we were right there (after all, we were the ones who worked with them every day, and they were used to us delivering their treats). But, the opposite concern is that self-control might be *underestimated* if experimenter activities produce uncertainty, confusion, or anxiety on the part of subjects about what is happening to accumulating or otherwise delayed reward. More research is certainly needed to help us better understand these relations.

I want to talk about two last points as they pertain to self-control and efforts to use accumulation tasks. Both relate back to what was discussed in the last chapter. First, recall that Sally Boysen's chimpanzees given the reverse-reward task with symbolic stimuli performed much better than with real food items. This connects to another finding with nonhuman animals—namely that token stimuli often produce very interesting results. I cannot fully (or fairly) outline all of the work that has been done with tokens (see Further Reading for some of those papers), but I want to highlight a few studies. Tim Hackenberg and his colleagues have worked a lot with pigeons and using tokens in place of primary reinforcers like food, and sometimes even comparing pigeons and humans directly (e.g., Andrade & Hackenberg, 2012; Hackenberg, 2009). In one of the first such studies (Jackson & Hackenberg, 1996), pigeons were offered the kinds of intertemporal choices that I discussed earlier, and token reinforcers seemed to affect choice behavior in a number of ways (see also Hackenberg & Vaidya, 2003). In subsequent work, tokens were used with pigeons in an accumulation task, where the birds had the same kinds of choices as the other animals given accumulation tests, but now for token stimuli (Yankelevitz, Bullock, & Hackenberg, 2008). Pigeons chose between one key that produced tokens (lights that illuminated to indicate future reward delivery) and another that effectively "cashed" in those tokens if the pigeons pecked that key often enough. Up to 12 tokens could be earned, and the results showed that pigeons would accumulate tokens. And, as expected, they accumulated fewer when they had to work harder (more pecks) to earn each one, and they accumulated more tokens when it was more effortful to cash those in for the food rewards (Fig. 7.10). Perhaps most interesting was that the token condition showed generally better overall levels of self-control compared to when tokens were not used.

More ambiguous results have been seen with some primates and token stimuli, although in general it does not seem that tokens necessarily provide the support to self-control in the accumulation task that was seen in the reverse-reward task. Evans, Beran, Paglieri, and Addessi (2012) reported that capuchin monkeys did not perform better when accumulating tokens versus real food items in the accumulation test (Fig. 7.11), and chimpanzees either were equally good with food items and tokens or actually (in one case) performed better when accumulating real food items than tokens. However, there has not been as much research with tokens and primates using self-control tests like the accumulation task, and so this issue is not resolved at all. I suspect that if a stronger token economy was established (one that was instantiated beyond just the single studies in which new tokens are trained), the results might be different.

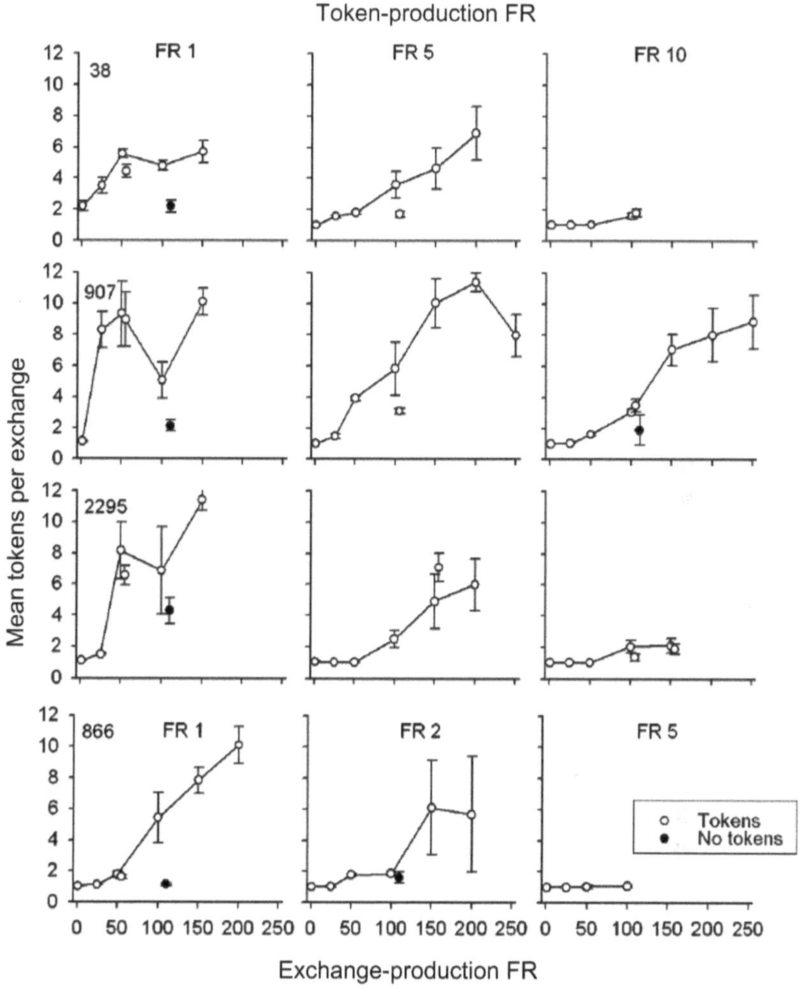

FIGURE 7.10 Mean tokens per exchange as a function of token-production and exchange-production ratios for each pigeon across the final five sessions of each condition in Yankelevitz et al. (2008). Token-production ratios are depicted across columns, and exchange-production ratios within columns. Replications are represented by detached, unfilled points, and no-token conditions by detached, filled points. *From Yankelevitz, R. L., Bullock, C. E., & Hackenberg, T. D. (2008). Reinforcer accumulation in a token-reinforcement context with pigeons.* Journal of the Experimental Analysis of Behavior, *90, 283–299, reprinted with permission of Wiley.*

Another thing that we have learned is that experience seems to help in some of these tasks. For example, although capuchin monkeys often failed to accumulate many items in versions of the accumulation task, we did find in one study that with extensive experience, they could improve. We worked with seven capuchin monkeys that were tested in the accumulation task with

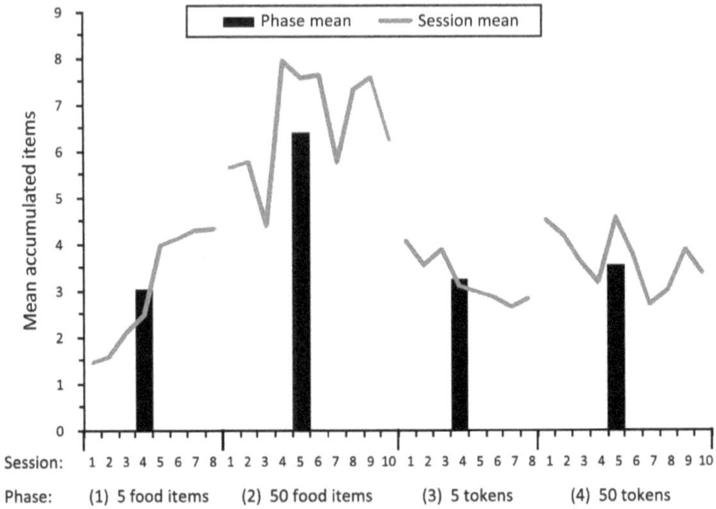

FIGURE 7.11 Mean capuchin monkey accumulation performance in Evans et al. (2012; Experiment 1). Black vertical bars represent the mean of monkeys' performance in each phase of the experiment. Gray lines represent the mean of monkeys' performance over individual sessions of each phase. *From Evans, T. A., Beran, M. J., Paglieri, F., & Addessi, E. (2012). Delaying gratification for food and tokens in capuchin monkeys (*Cebus apella*) and chimpanzees (*Pan troglodytes*): When quantity is salient, symbolic stimuli do not improve performance.* Animal Cognition, *15, 539–548, reprinted with permission from Springer.*

a gap of about five years between tests, and found that in the second test (Beran, Perdue, et al., 2016) the monkeys' accumulation abilities improved 92%–515% when given comparable tests. If you look at Fig. 7.12 Phase 4 data compared to Fig. 7.11, you can see this marked improvement. So, more experience can definitely help, although it is also clear that some species like chimpanzees may not need as much experience as do others, such as capuchin monkeys.

And, finally, to summarize the main issues of this chapter and the last chapter, I want to outline a recent study we conducted that combined the key aspects of the accumulation task in a new way of looking at the reverse-reward task (Beran, James, Whitham, & Parrish, 2016). Recall that chimpanzees struggle to point to one set of food to get another, and yet seem quite proficient at waiting for food items to accumulate within reach. In the latter case, this means they refrain from reaching toward or taking those items. So, we wondered what it was about the RR task that made it so difficult, and whether it was truly the case that chimpanzees struggled to point toward smaller amounts when also faced with larger amounts, or whether it was something more about the *contingencies* for those points that affected choice behavior. To assess this, we gave our chimpanzees a long sequence of experiments. First, we gave them the RR task, and we

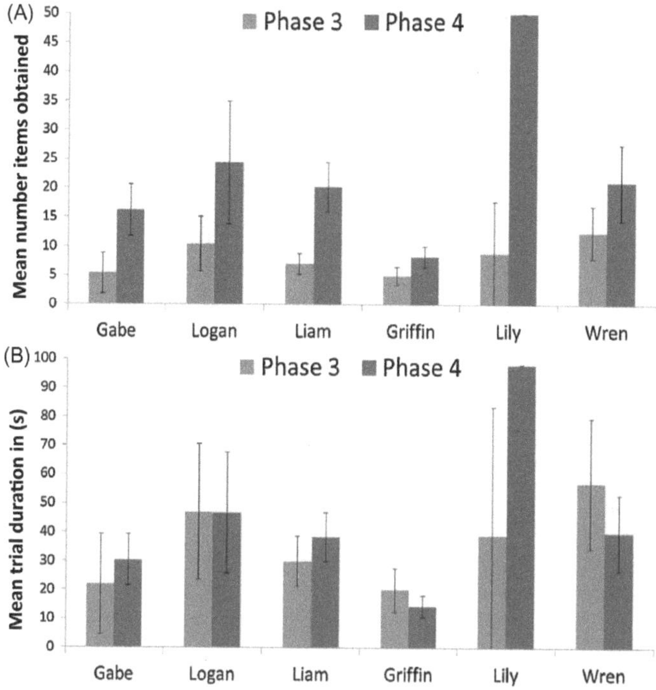

FIGURE 7.12 (A) Mean number of items obtained (out of 50) during the accumulation task for two phases of Experiment 3 in Beran, Perdue, et al. (2016). (B) The mean delay duration for those same phases. The key point here is to compare the improvement shown in this figure (in Phase 4) to that in Fig. 7.11, where the tasks were basically identical. *From Beran, M. J., Perdue, B. M., Rossettie, M. S., James, B. T., Whitham, W., Walker, B., ... Parrish, A. E. (2016). Self-control assessments of capuchin monkeys with the rotating tray task and the accumulation task.* Behavioural Processes, 129, *68–79, reprinted with permission from Springer.*

found that they pointed to the larger amount (and thus received the smaller amount) on nearly 100% of the trials. So, total failure. Then, we did something new. We presented them with a single food item, and an empty bowl. They pointed, of course, to the food item, but instead of giving it to them, we placed it into the bowl. We added another single item to the test board, so now they could point to that one item, or they could point to the bowl. If they pointed to the single item, it went into the bowl also. If they pointed to the bowl, they got whatever was in it. In this way, each point to a single item led to that item going into the bowl, and pointing to the bowl ended the trial (forfeiting all remaining single items that might have been offered). The best way to respond in this task was thus to keep pointing to the single item, and not to the bowl, which would progress from having 1 to 10 items in it, at which point nothing else was offered on the single-item side. Here is the key point—to get all 10 items, the chimpanzees would have to consistently point *at less food* (the single item) and not at more food (from 2 to 9 items in the bowl). Not only could the chimpanzees do this, they did it very well. This was a surprising result if the problem with the RR task is just about pointing to less to eventually get more. But, it is not surprising if you consider that the RR task leads to an immediate outcome (either getting the larger set or smaller set) whereas this new task led to chimpanzees accumulating their own pile of reward, which they could "cash out" whenever they chose to do that. Their success showed that in such cases as choosing to accumulate rewards, and deciding when to collect that accumulation, pointing was optimal even though it was toward less food rather than more food. By the way, we returned the chimpanzees to the usual variation of the RR task after this, and they again failed miserably. But, when we gave them other variations of the accumulation test where they had to point to single items to add those to the accumulation, they succeeded (e.g., with the remaining items not visible, with differing types of food). But, if they had to choose between *adding* one or three items to the accumulation by pointing to the *other set* (i.e., under RR contingencies), they again struggled! From these results, it seems that what makes the RR task difficult is that the two choices are both things that will be delivered or accumulated but under contingencies that reverse, with the selected set disappearing. In other words, it seems like losing what one points to is difficult to deal with, whereas keeping what one points to (even if it is delayed in its delivery) makes it easier for chimpanzees to point to less food when more food is visually available and is an option to choose.

My hope is that we can try this task with other species, and see whether this result generalizes to their performance too, because I think if it does, it would generate new ideas about the nature of choice behavior under nonintuitive contingencies. Perhaps the RR task is difficult for animals to perform because they are faced with a choice they want (the greater number of items) but when they point to it they get something else that was not their focus. If making the less appealing item (e.g., the single item in the test by Beran, Perdue, et al., 2016), become part of the more appealing option (the accumulating set), this may "reframe" the choice. If so, we could think about how to apply this to real world situations of impulsivity and self-control. For example, it is difficult to imagine cases where people have to choose something they do not want to have to instead be given immediately something they do want. But, it is easy to think about choosing something you want to put away for later, while also leaving the later, accumulating reward, alone (e.g., putting cash earned into a savings account to earn interest and grow toward a future purchase). Thus, considering how tasks are framed will provide new insights into what affects choices, even if those choices seem to be highly similar in their nature.

REFERENCES

Andrade, L. F., & Hackenberg, T. D. (2012). Saving the best for last? A cross-species analysis of choices between reinforcer sequences. *Journal of the Experimental Analysis of Behavior, 98*, 45–64.

Auersperg, A. M. I., Laumer, I. B., & Bugnyar, T. (2013). Goffin cockatoos wait for qualitative and quantitative gains but prefer 'better' to 'more'. *Biology Letters, 9*, Article 20121092.

Beran, M. J. (2002). Maintenance of self-imposed delay of gratification by four chimpanzees (*Pan troglodytes*) and an orangutan (*Pongo pygmaeus*). *Journal of General Psychology, 129*, 49–66.

Beran, M. J. (2003). Studying delay of gratification in animals. In S. P. Shohov (Ed.), *Advances in psychology research* (Vol. 24, pp. 161–179). New York: Nova Science.

Beran, M. J. (2015). Chimpanzee cognitive control. *Current Directions in Psychological Science, 24*, 352–357.

Beran, M. J., & Evans, T. A. (2006). Maintenance of delay of gratification by four chimpanzees (*Pan troglodytes*): The effects of delayed reward visibility, experimenter presence, and extended delay intervals. *Behavioural Processes, 73*, 315–324.

Beran, M. J., James, B. T., Whitham, W., & Parrish, A. E. (2016). Chimpanzees can point to smaller amounts of food to accumulate larger amounts but they still fail the reverse-reward contingency task. *Journal of Experimental Psychology: Animal Learning and Cognition, 42*, 347–358.

Beran, M. J., Perdue, B. M., Futch, S. E., Smith, J. D., Evans, T. A., & Parrish, A. E. (2015). Go when you know: Chimpanzees' confidence movements reflect their responses in a computerized memory task. *Cognition, 142*, 236–246.

Beran, M. J., Perdue, B. M., Rossettie, M. S., James, B. T., Whitham, W., Walker, B., ... Parrish, A. E. (2016). Self-control assessments of capuchin monkeys with the rotating tray task and the accumulation task. *Behavioural Processes, 129*, 68–79.

Beran, M. J., Savage-Rumbaugh, E. S., Pate, J. L., & Rumbaugh, D. M. (1999). Delay of gratification in chimpanzees (*Pan troglodytes*). *Developmental Psychobiology, 34*, 119–127.

Beran, M. J., Smith, J. D., & Perdue, B. M. (2013). Language-trained chimpanzees name what they have seen, but look first at what they have not seen. *Psychological Science, 24*, 660–666.

Boysen, S. T., & Berntson, G. G. (1995). Responses to quantity: Perceptual versus cognitive mechanisms in chimpanzees (*Pan troglodytes*). *Journal of Experimental Psychology: Animal Behavior Processes, 21*, 82–86.

Boysen, S. T., Berntson, G. G., Hannan, M. B., & Cacioppo, J. T. (1996). Quantity-based interference and symbolic representations in chimpanzees (*Pan troglodytes*). *Journal of Experimental Psychology: Animal Behavior Processes, 22*, 76–86.

Boysen, S. T., Mukobi, K. L., & Berntson, G. G. (1999). Overcoming response bias using symbolic representations of number by chimpanzees (*Pan troglodytes*). *Animal Learning and Behavior, 27*, 229–235.

Brucks, D., Soliani, M., Range, F., & Marshall-Pescini, S. (2017). Reward type and behavioural patterns predict dogs' success in a delay of gratification paradigm. *Scientific Reports, 7*, 42459.

Call, J. (2010). Do apes know that they could be wrong? *Animal Cognition, 13*, 689–700.

Call, J., & Carpenter, M. (2001). Do apes and children know what they have seen? *Animal Cognition, 4*, 207–220.

Dufour, V., Wascher, C. A. F., Braun, A., Miller, R., & Bugnyar, T. (2012). Corvids can decide if a future exchange is worth waiting for. *Biology Letters, 8*, 201–204.

Evans, T. A., & Beran, M. J. (2007a). Chimpanzees use self-distraction to cope with impulsivity. *Biology Letters, 3*, 599–602.

Evans, T. A., & Beran, M. J. (2007b). Delay of gratification and delay maintenance by rhesus macaques (*Macaca mulatta*). *Journal of General Psychology, 134*, 199–216.

Evans, T. A., Beran, M. J., Paglieri, F., & Addessi, E. (2012). Delaying gratification for food and tokens in capuchin monkeys (*Cebus apella*) and chimpanzees (*Pan troglodytes*): When quantity is salient, symbolic stimuli do not improve performance. *Animal Cognition, 15*, 539–548.

Grosch, J., & Neuringer, A. (1981). Self-control in pigeons under the Mischel paradigm. *Journal of the Experimental Analysis of Behavior, 35*, 3–21.

Hackenberg, T. D. (2009). Token reinforcement: A review and analysis. *Journal of the Experimental Analysis of Behavior, 91*, 257–286.

Hackenberg, T. D., & Vaidya, M. (2003). Determinants of pigeons' choices in token-based self-control procedures. *Journal of the Experimental Analysis of Behavior, 79*, 207–218.

Hillemann, F., Bugnyar, T., Kotrschal, K., & Wascher, C. A. F. (2014). Waiting for better, not for more: Corvids respond to quality in two delay maintenance tasks. *Animal Behaviour, 90*, 1–10.

Jackson, K., & Hackenberg, T. D. (1996). Token, reinforcement, choice, and self-control in pigeons. *Journal of the Experimental Analysis of Behavior, 66*, 29–49.

Kalenscher, T., & Pennartz, C. M. (2008). Is a bird in the hand worth two in the future? The neuroeconomics of intertemporal decision making. *Progress in Neurobiology, 84*, 284–315.

Koepke, A. E., Gray, S. L., & Pepperberg, I. M. (2015). Delayed gratification: A grey parrot (*Psittacus erithacus*) will wait for a better reward. *Journal of Comparative Psychology, 129*, 339–346.

Mahrer, A. R. (1956). The role of expectancy in delayed reinforcement. *Journal of Experimental Psychology, 52*, 101–106.

Marsh, H. L., & MacDonald, S. E. (2012). Orangutans (*Pongo abelii*) "play the odds": Information-seeking strategies in relation to cost, risk, and benefit. *Journal of Comparative Psychology, 126*, 263–278.

Miller, D. T., & Karniol, R. (1976). The role of rewards in externally and self-imposed delay of gratification. *Journal of Personality and Social Psychology, 34*, 310–316.

Mischel, W., & Ebbesen, E. B. (1970). Attention in delay of gratification. *Journal of Personality and Social Psychology, 16*, 329–337.

Mischel, W., Ebbesen, E. B., & Zeiss, A. (1972). Cognitive and attentional mechanisms in delay of gratification. *Journal of Personality and Social Psychology, 21*, 204–218.

Mischel, W., & Moore, B. (1973). Effects of attention to symbolically presented rewards on self-control. *Journal of Personality and Social Psychology, 28*, 172–179.

Mischel, W., & Staub, E. (1965). Effects of expectancy on working and waiting for larger rewards. *Journal of Personality and Social Psychology, 2*, 625–633.

Parrish, A. E., Perdue, B. M., Stromberg, E. E., Bania, A. E., Evans, T. A., & Beran, M. J. (2014). Delay of gratification by orangutans (*Pongo pygmaeus*) in the accumulation task. *Journal of Comparative Psychology, 128*, 209–214.

Rachlin, H., & Green, L. (1972). Commitment, choice, and self-control. *Journal of the Experimental Analysis of Behavior, 17*, 15–22.

Rumbaugh, D. M. (Ed.), (1977). *Language learning by a chimpanzee: The LANA Project*. New York, NY: Academic Press.

Savage-Rumbaugh, E. S. (1986). *Ape language: From conditioned response to symbol*. New York, NY: Columbia University Press.

Smith, J. D. (2009). The study of animal metacognition. *Trends in Cognitive Sciences, 13*, 389–396.

Stephens, D. W., & Krebs, J. R. (1986). *Foraging theory*. Princeton, NJ: Princeton University Press.

Stevens, J. R., Rosati, A. G., Heilbronner, S. R., & Mühlhoff, N. (2011). Waiting for grapes: Expectancy and delayed gratification in bonobos. *International Journal of Comparative Psychology, 24*, 99–111.

Stevens, J. R., & Stephens, D. W. (2010). The adaptive nature of impulsivity. In G. J. Madden & W. K. Bickel (Eds.), *Impulsivity: The behavioral and neurological science of discounting* (pp. 361–388). Washington, DC: American Psychological Association.

Toner, I. J. (1981). Role involvement and delay maintenance behavior in preschool children. *Journal of Genetic Psychology, 138*, 245–251.

Toner, I. J., Lewis, B. C., & Gribble, C. M. (1979). Evaluative verbalization and delay maintenance behavior in children. *Journal of Experimental Child Psychology, 28*, 205–210.

Toner, I. J., & Smith, R. A. (1977). Age and overt verbalization in delay-maintenance behavior in children. *Journal of Experimental Child Psychology, 24*, 123–128.

Vick, S. J., Bovet, D., & Anderson, J. R. (2010). How do African grey parrots (*Psittacus erithacus*) perform on a delay of gratification task?. *Animal Cognition, 13*, 351–358.

Yankelevitz, R. L., Bullock, C. E., & Hackenberg, T. D. (2008). Reinforcer accumulation in a token-reinforcement context with pigeons. *Journal of the Experimental Analysis of Behavior, 90*, 283–299.

FURTHER READING

Addessi, E., Crescimbene, L., & Visalberghi, E. (2007). Do capuchin monkeys (*Cebus apella*) use tokens as symbols? *Proceedings of the Royal Society of London, 274*, 2579–2585.

Addessi, E., Crescimbene, L., & Visalberghi, E. (2008). Food and token quantity discrimination in capuchin monkeys (*Cebus apella*). *Animal Cognition, 11*, 275–282.

Addessi, E., Mancinia, A., Crescimbene, L., Ariely, D., & Visalberghi, E. (2010). How to spend a token? Trade-offs between food variety and food preference in tufted capuchin monkeys (*Cebus apella*). *Behavioural Processes, 83*, 267–275.

Basile, B. M., Schroeder, G. R., Brown, E. K., Templer, V. L., & Hampton, R. R. (2015). Evaluation of seven hypotheses for metamemory performance in rhesus monkeys. *Journal of Experimental Psychology: General, 144*, 85–102.

Beran, M. J. (2015). Chimpanzee cognitive control. *Current Directions in Psychological Science, 24*, 352–357.

Beran, M. J., Brandl, J., Perner, J., & Proust, J. (Eds.). (2012). *Foundations of metacognition*. Oxford, UK: Oxford University Press.

Beran, M. J., & Evans, T. A. (2009). Delay of gratification by chimpanzees (*Pan troglodytes*) in working and waiting situations. *Behavioural Processes, 80*, 117–121.

Beran, M. J., Evans, T. A., & Hoyle, D. (2011). Numerical judgments by chimpanzees (*Pan troglodytes*) in a token economy. *Journal of Experimental Psychology: Animal Behavior Processes, 37*, 165–174.

Brown, E. K., Templer, V. L., & Hampton, R. R. (2017). An assessment of domain-general metacognitive responding in rhesus monkeys. *Behavioural Processes, 135*, 132–144.

Dufour, V., Pele, M., Neumann, M., Theirry, B., & Call, J. (2009). Calculated reciprocity after all: Computation behind token transfers in orangutans. *Biology Letters*, *5*, 172–175.

Evans, T. A., & Beran, M. J. (2007b). Chimpanzees use self-distraction to cope with impulsivity. *Biology Letters*, *3*, 599–602.

Evans, T. A., Beran, M. F., & Addessi, E. (2010). Can nonhuman primates use tokens to represent and sum quantities? *Journal of Comparative Psychology*, *124*, 369–380.

Kileen, P. R., Smith, J. P., & Hanson, S. J. (1981). Central place foraging in *Rattus norvegicus*. *Animal Behavior*, *29*, 64–70.

Kornell, N. (2009). Metacognition in humans and animals. *Current Directions in Psychological Science*, *18*, 11–15.

Lagorio, C. H., & Hackenberg, T. D. (2009). Ricky choice in pigeons and humans: A cross-species comparison. *Journal of the Experimental Analysis of Behavior*, *93*, 27–44.

Mulcahy, N. J. (2016). Orangutans (*Pongo abelii*) seek information about tool functionality in a metacognition tubes task. *Journal of Comparative Psychology*, *130*, 391–399.

Pepperberg, I. M. (1987). Evidence for conceptual quantitative abilities in the African grey parrot: Labeling of cardinal sets. *Ethology*, *75*, 37–61.

Pepperberg, I. M. (1994). Numerical competence in an African grey parrot (*Psittacus erithacus*). *Journal of Comparative Psychology*, *108*, 36–44.

Pepperberg, I. M. (2002). Cognitive and communicative abilities of grey parrots. *Current Directions in Psychological Science*, *11*, 83–87.

Pepperberg, I. M. (2006). Grey parrot numerical competence: A review. *Animal Cognition*, *9*, 377–391.

Pepperberg, I. M. (2013). Abstract concepts: Data from a grey parrot. *Behavioural Processes*, *93*, 82–90.

Pepperberg, I. M., Koepke, A., Livingston, P., Girard, M., & Hartsfield, L. A. (2013). Reasoning by inference: Further studies on exclusion in grey parrots (*Psittacus erithacus*). *Journal of Comparative Psychology*, *127*, 272–281.

Rachlin, H., Castrogiovanni, A., & Cross, D. (1987). Probability and delay in commitment. *Journal of the Experimental Analysis of Behavior*, *48*, 347–353.

Ritchie, F. K., & Toner, I. J. (1984). Direct labeling, tester expectancy and delay maintenance behavior in Scottish preschool children. *International Journal of Behavioral Development*, *7*, 333–341.

Smith, J. D., Beran, M. J., & Couchman, J. J. (2012). Animal metacognition. In T. Zentall & E. Wasserman (Eds.), *Oxford handbook of comparative cognition* (pp. 282–304). Oxford, UK: Oxford University Press.

Smith, J. D., Couchman, J. J., & Beran, M. J. (2014). The highs and lows of theoretical interpretation in animal-metacognition research. In S. M. Fleming & C. Frith (Eds.), *The cognitive neuroscience of metacognition* (pp. 87–114). Berlin: Springer-Verlag.

Tan, L., & Hackenberg, T. D. (2015). Pigeons' demand and preference for specific and generalized conditioned reinforcers in a token economy. *Journal of the Experimental Analysis of Behavior*, *104*, 296–314.

Toner, I. J., & Ritchie, F. K. (1984). American-Sign-Language statements and delay of gratification in hearing-impaired and nonhandicapped children. *Journal of General Psychology*, *110*, 155–164.

Yates, B. T., & Mischel, W. (1979). Young children's preferred attentional strategies for delaying gratification. *Journal of Personality and Social Psychology*, *37*, 286–300.

Chapter 8

Other Tests of Self-Control and Delay of Gratification in Animals

The Marshmallow task and other tests originally used with children were redesigned or reimagined so that animal-friendly, similar tests could be used, as I discussed in the last chapter. And, as I noted earlier, intertemporal choice tests have been used for many decades with animals, and sometimes those tests were used *first* with animals, and then adapted or presented to humans for comparative analyses. However, these are not the only kinds of tests used with animals, and in this chapter I want to highlight some of the very creative and valuable tests that people have come up with to show that a given animal or species will opt for a better reward after a longer delay, or after more effort. I cannot hope to cover all of these approaches in the detail they deserve, but I do hope to impress upon the reader that there are many converging lines of evidence that nonhuman animals will choose to impose delays upon themselves, or engage in more effortful action to gain greater rewards.

One of the most commonly used approaches to studying delayed gratification is the exchange task. The idea here is a simple one. Imagine that I hand you a slice of apple, and then ask you to return that for a piece of chocolate. Assuming you like chocolate more than apple, then you have to avoid eating the apple until that time when you can hand it back for the chocolate. Or, imagine I hand you a small piece of chocolate, and then let you give that back to me for a much larger piece. Same rule—eat what you have, or return it for something else. If the "something else" is something you would rather have in a situation where both were offered to you at the same time, and in this exchange task you choose to return the less valuable reward for the more valuable one, this is commonly taken to be an example of self-control through delayed gratification. And, this simple test is easy to use with many species, and in principle could be used with any species that has the capability to possess something and then return it. Hands like those of nonhuman primates are ideal in this sense, but other species can be given tests like this as well. And, this kind of test nicely approximates all of the key elements of the marshmallow test, except that it now also requires not only inhibiting eating or otherwise taking what is right in front of you, but also actively

Self-Control in Animals and People. DOI: https://doi.org/10.1016/B978-0-12-812508-3.00008-6
© 2018 Elsevier Inc. All rights reserved.

returning that item to an experimenter so as to initiate an exchange. For these reasons, a number of researchers have used this approach, and they have varied things such as the duration of the delay before exchange, and the type of exchange. In the latter case, what I mean is the apple-for-chocolate exchange would be an example of a qualitative exchange (one type of thing for another type of thing) whereas the smaller-for-larger chocolate exchange would be an example of a quantitative exchange (one amount exchanged for another of the same reward type).

The types of exchange tasks that I will focus on in this chapter are those that I think reflect degrees of self-control because of the nature of what must be exchanged (or given up) to get something else. But, it is important to note that exchange as a behavior itself has a long history in tests of animals, and has been used to assess a number of social and cognitive phenomena. Those are not the focus of this book, but some of that work has served to inspire the self-control designs that make use of exchange. For example, many people have used tasks that involve tokens to examine when and how nonhuman primates such as chimpanzees and capuchin monkeys will exchange those tokens for various kinds of rewards. Some of the earliest such studies are now nearly 100 years old, such as the report of Nissen and Crawford (1936) in which chimpanzees learned to insert tokens into an apparatus to get food rewards, and in some cases either shared the food or shared tokens with other chimpanzees. From these reports, people such as Frans De Waal at Emory University began to ask questions about whether nonhuman primates would exchange tokens with human experimenters, or with other animals, to obtain rewards. For example, after discovering that capuchin monkeys sometimes passively or even actively would share food with each other (De Waal, 1997), investigators asked whether monkeys would selectively exchange tokens for food based not solely on the reward type, but on the basis of the *relative reward value* that one animal received for exchanges compared to another animal. My colleague at Georgia State, Sarah Brosnan, has conducted many studies like this. In one of the first (Brosnan & De Waal, 2004), a subject monkey and a partner monkey were in adjoining test compartments where they could see each other, and everything that happened. The subject then received a token, and giving that token back to the experimenter led to a food reward. That reward was present in a bowl that both monkeys could see. Sometimes, it was a high value reward like a grape, whereas in other cases it was a low value reward like a cucumber. In general, monkeys chose to exchange tokens for any kind of food, at least in the basic task where they both were getting the same thing. But, if there was a difference in terms of who got what, then the monkey getting the less preferred item was way less keen to trade a token. Or, if there was a difference in the amount of effort that went into getting the same food, such as one monkey having to exchange while the other received food for free, then the monkey doing the work was more likely to refuse to exchange. This makes sense, if the monkey sees the exchange as inequitable in terms of the outcome that the partner monkey gets for the same effort and activity. These early results led to many more studies of inequity and exchange behavior in nonhuman primates (Brauer, Call, & Tomasello, 2009; Brosnan, Schiff, & De Waal, 2005; Neiworth, Johnson, Whillock, Greenberg, & Brown, 2009; Price & Brosnan, 2012; Roma, Silberberg, Ruggiero, & Suomi, 2006; Silberberg, Crescimbene, Addessi, Anderson, & Visalberghi, 2009; Talbot, Freeman, Williams, & Brosnan, 2011) and other species such as dogs (e.g., Horowitz, 2012; Range, Horn, Viranyi, & Huber, 2009; Range, Leitner, & Virányi, 2012) and even humans (Hachiga, Silberberg, Parker, & Sakagami, 2009). Much of this work has focused on better understanding what mechanisms might underlie refusals to exchange (see Further Reading for some of those papers). For our present purposes, these tasks set the stage for efforts to use exchange not as a means to study social cognition, social learning, or inequity aversion, but to study self-control.

One of the first studies to use exchanges to assess self-control in nonhuman primates was with capuchin monkeys. Drapier, Chauvin, Dufour, Uhlrich, and Thierry (2005) allowed the monkeys to trade low-valued objects for high-valued objects or to trade smaller amounts of a food item for larger amounts. To establish the basic exchange behavior, the experimenter handed a monkey a lower preference item such as a piece of carrot, and if the monkey immediately handed that back to the experimenter, the higher preference reward was given (Fig. 8.1). Then, the experimenters introduced a delay. Between handing the item back and getting the better item was a 5 second delay. Although this may seem fairly short in comparison to some of the other work that has been discussed, this is an important manipulation because it means that the monkey had to experience that time as time during which it had nothing, and that was right after it did have something it could have eaten. As you might expect, when the relative value of the item the monkey first received and the delayed reward was large (i.e., the immediate reward was much lower preference), there were a lot of exchanges, but it was more difficult for monkeys to inhibit eating and then given back a medium preference item for a high preference one. And, what I really loved about this study was that the authors noted that many times even successful exchanges came with the caveat that the monkey might take just a little nibble out of the less preferred item before exchanging it! This makes me think of some of the marshmallow task videos I have seen where a child might take a tiny taste of the marshmallow during the delay interval. Another interesting aspect to this study came from trials where small pieces of cookie could be exchanged for larger pieces. Some monkeys could not do this at all, whereas others were a little better at handing back the food quality they liked the most, if the next item they could receive was bigger (Fig. 8.2). But, this clearly was a more difficult exchange condition, with quantitative differences in food amount.

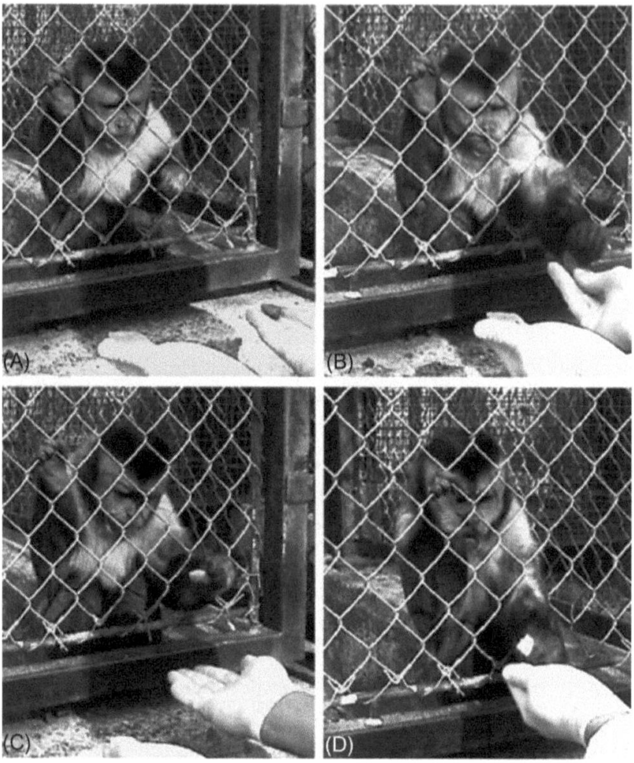

FIGURE 8.1 The exchange sequence used by Drapier et al. (2005) with capuchin monkeys. (A) The experimenter presents a piece of cookie in the left hand and a piece of carrot in the right hand. (B) The experimenter gives the carrot to the subject. (C) The subject puts the carrot back in the hand of the experimenter. (D) The subject is allowed to take the cookie. *From Drapier, M., Chauvin, C., Dufour, V., Uhlrich, P., & Thierry, B. (2005). Food-exchange with humans in brown capuchin monkeys.* Primates, 46, *241–248, reprinted with permission from Springer.*

Drapier et al. (2005) also included a test that I find particularly compelling. It was similar to an earlier experiment that had been done with gorillas, which was one of the few tests ever given to that great ape species to look at their self-control. Chalmeau and Peignot (1998) had first taught gorillas to hand back to experimenters any twigs found in their enclosure in exchange for a peanut. Once they could do this, the experimenters then offered the gorillas a twig if they would find a small piece of fruit in their enclosure, and the gorillas could give back the twig for the peanut. Finally, in a complicated test, the experimenter gave the gorilla a piece of fruit if the gorilla found and exchanged a leaf, and then offered the twig for the fruit back, before finally offering the peanut for the twig back. As you might imagine, this was a complicated series of exchanges, and a lot of information for the gorillas to learn and remember. And, the results reflected that. Some gorillas never learned

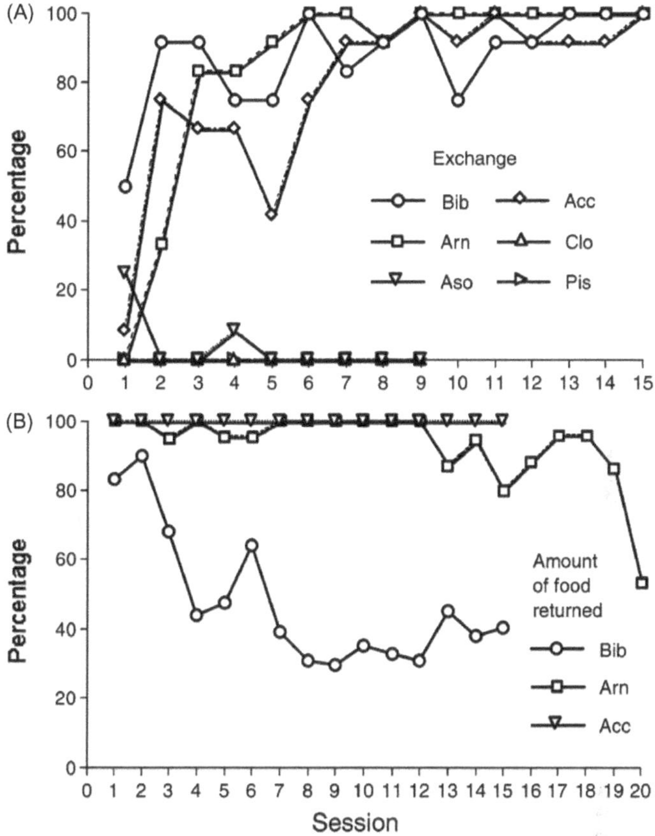

FIGURE 8.2 Performance of capuchin monkeys with the quantitative exchanges in Drapier et al. (2005). The top panel shows the percentage of exchanges throughout sessions (six subjects). The bottom panel shows the amount of food given back (three subjects): sum of the fractions of food items returned in exchanges. *From Drapier, M., Chauvin, C., Dufour, V., Uhlrich, P., & Thierry, B. (2005). Food-exchange with humans in brown capuchin monkeys.* Primates, 46, *241–248, reprinted with permission from Springer.*

the basics of the task. Only three of six could do the double exchange, giving fruit for the twig which they then gave for the peanut. Two succeeded with the even harder triple exchange, suggesting that at least the great apes could perform a series of exchanges of increasing complexity to get to the best reward item.

Returning to Drapier et al. (2005), they also gave monkeys the more difficult double and triple exchange versions of the task. In their test, an experimenter showed a pellet (item 1, less preferred) and a piece of apple (item 2, more preferred) in one hand, and the monkey had to pick up a stone and exchange that with the experimenter to get the pellet. Then, if they refrained from eating the pellet for 5 seconds, they could exchange it for the apple slice. Trials with triple exchanges just added having experimenters first give the stone as the very first exchange, so that now the monkeys had to give stone, pellet, and carrot back in that order to get to the more preferred apple reward. These monkeys flawlessly performed the double exchanges (100% correct), and five of six monkeys were flawless in the triple exchanges. This is an intriguing result because gorillas performed more poorly, although there were some important methodological differences, with one of the main issues being that gorillas were tested when all together and monkeys were tested while isolated. It seems likely that in the latter case, it is easier to give up food and attend to the experimental setting because there are no potential competitors in the test area.

In a variation of exchange task that made use of "symbolic" stimuli, Beran and Evans (2012) and Judge and Essler (2013) combined the use of tokens and the use of real foods as part of the routine. Beran and Evans offered chimpanzees choices between two food items of differing values, two tokens of differing values (where each represented a different food item that was given in exchange for the token), and the combinations of a real food item and a token. In that last case, chimpanzees had to forego taking the immediate food item which could be consumed to instead choose a token that could be exchanged 2 to 3 minutes later when there was a chance to perform token exchanges. These chimpanzees all learned to choose the token over the food item, and to do so repeatedly for blocks of trials before exchange could occur. In the study by Judge and Essler, capuchin monkeys were given choices between real food items, or different kinds of tokens that could later be exchanged for specific foods. On each trial, a monkey started with a token for a low value food item. If the monkey gave back that token, it then was allowed to make a choice between the food represented by that token, or a new token that could then be exchanged for an even better food item. Some of the monkeys used the token value to guide their choices, and in doing so those monkeys often were able to obtain the best possible item on a trial. That meant they had to choose tokens over real foods, suggesting that they truly understood the ultimate value of each token type.

We also were interested in studying sequential exchanges in our chimpanzees (Beran, Rossettie, & Parrish, 2016). We designed a test similar to those of Chalmeau and Peignot (1998) and Drapier et al. (2005) in which chimpanzees could see a sequence of food items on a bench that was out of reach, and the items would be presented in order as long as each distributed item was given back. In our test, on each trial the chimpanzees could see everything that would be given on that trial, lined up in a way that allowed the chimpanzees to see the order as well, with a closer-to-farther orientation on the bench reflecting this. We wanted to be careful to ensure that the person exchanging with the chimpanzees could not know what they were supposed to do, in terms of showing the best responding, so we used a blind between the two experimenters who set up the trials. One experimenter simply handed items to the chimpanzee, and if the chimpanzee handed the item back, that experimenter announced that an exchange had been made. In that case, a second experimenter then handed the first experimenter a new food item to be given to the chimpanzees, and so on through the trial until the chimpanzee kept and ate the item it was holding. Using this method, we could manipulate the order items would be delivered, to ensure that the chimpanzees had to look at the whole sequence rather than just the next thing they might get. In one condition, each newly obtained item for an exchange was a more preferred item than the last one, and so each exchange presented the chance to *upgrade* the quality of the reward one could get. In another condition, things were harder. Each exchange actually led to getting something less preferred than the chimpanzee had just given exchanged, *except that the last item was the best of the whole trial.* So, to do well here, the chimpanzee had to see that there was a best reward at the end, and then keep handing back things to get other, less preferred things. We expected this to be particularly difficult unless the chimpanzees were anticipating the end of the trial as they performed the exchanges. Finally, we had a random condition, where items were placed randomly in an order, to see how this affected behavior. The results showed fairly big differences among the chimpanzees. Lana did not exchange very well, whereas Mercury and Sherman did. In fact, Sherman was good in all cases, and Mercury did well too, although trials where each exchange led to a better next food were the easiest for him (Fig. 8.3). Overall, though, the data showed that another great apes species, chimpanzees, performed more like the monkeys in Drapier et al.

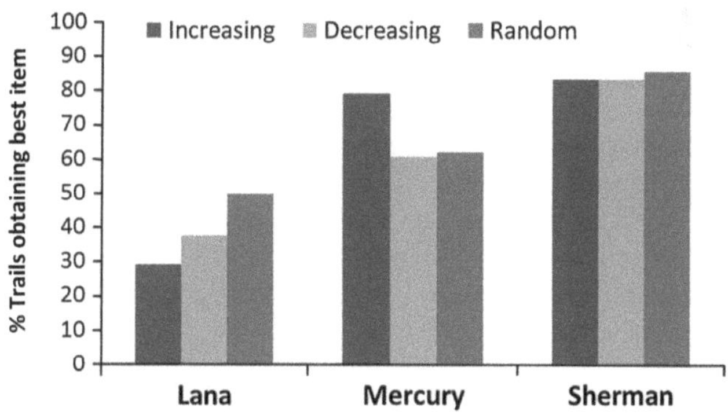

FIGURE 8.3 Performance of each chimpanzee in the first experiment of Beran et al. (2016). *Increasing* trials were those in which each food that the chimpanzee received was better than the one just traded. Decreasing trials involved each item being lower value, *except for the final item* which had the highest overall value. Random trials had no order to the sequence of exchanges. In this experiment, the chimpanzees always could see the full sequence of items yet to be obtained if they continued to exchange. *From Beran, M., Rossettie, M., & Parrish, A. E. (2016). Trading up: Chimpanzees (*Pan troglodytes*) show self-control through their exchange behavior.* Animal Cognition, 19, *109–121, reprinted with permission from Springer.*

(2005) than the gorillas in Chalmeau and Peignot (1998). So, perhaps the setting impacted gorillas' performance, although as I mentioned gorillas are fairly understudied in this area of behavior (as well as others). Another interesting outcome in Beran et al. (2016) came from trials in which the food items were all the same type but differed in size. In this test, two chimpanzees were very good at exchanging smaller pieces of banana up to the point where they got the largest possible piece on a trial, which they promptly ate. But, a third chimpanzee always ate the first banana slice he received, no matter its size, again highlighting the importance of studying individual differences and trying to account for why behavioral choices may vary across individuals.

In addition to the other outcomes I just discussed, in Beran et al. (2016) we wanted to see what role memory might play in choice and self-control during sequential exchange. To do that, we presented the chimpanzees with the sequence of items to be progressively offered with consecutive trades, but then covered those items before starting the sequence, or even made the chimpanzees then wait for 5 minutes before the chance to exchange began. These manipulations required the chimpanzees to remember the best item they could receive on that trial. So, on some trials, the best item was very high preference (e.g., a graham cracker) but on other trials the best item was only of medium preference (e.g., an orange slice). When the delay was short to remember the items, it did not matter whether the best item came after the second, third, or fourth exchange for Lana and Mercury, who were nearly perfect in exchanging until the best item appeared. Sherman, in this case, showed more trouble, often settling for keeping and eating the second most preferred item even when a better item was yet to come on that trial had he continued to exchange (Fig. 8.4). But, overall the chimpanzees could wait for as long as 5 minutes before starting exchange, and then remember what the best item was to come in the sequence. This might suggest a clear future-oriented perspective from the chimpanzees as they faced the task, if one assumes the chimpanzees were viewing the array, then choosing to remember at least the best possible item on that trial, and then later put into play an exchange sequence that could lead to that best item. Of course, it is also possible that the chimpanzees were not anticipating at all, but rather storing the best item in memory and then being willing to do whatever they needed to do until they ate that item. In hindsight, I wish we had used a condition where, during the 5-minute delay, we gave the chimpanzees free foods of different types, to see what effect that might have had on their choice behavior. This remains a type of manipulation rarely used in the comparative literature, to introduce free rewards that might create a conflict with the primary choice task. After all, this is more like what tends to happen in real situations where individuals are delaying gratification. For example, we might decide that we will wait to have dessert until dinner when we can have what we really want (e.g., chocolate cake) instead of having a donut at breakfast, but

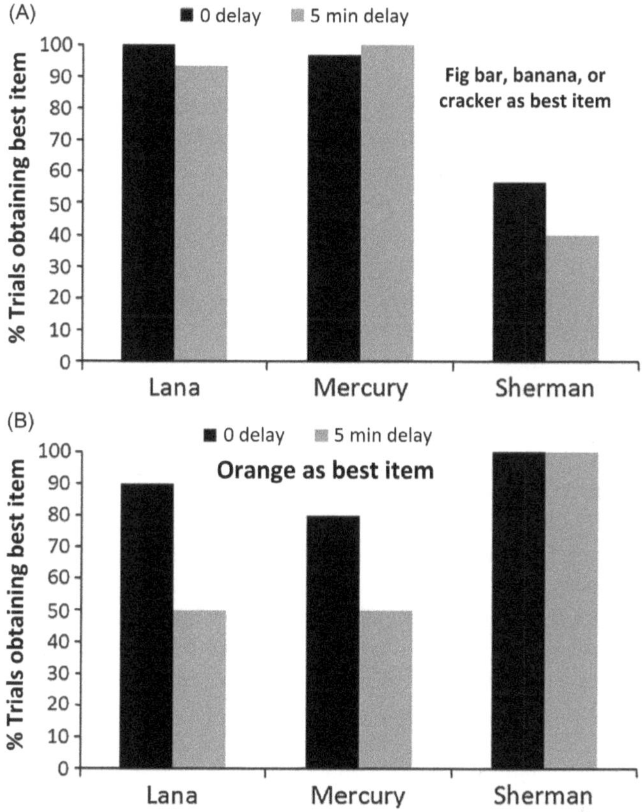

FIGURE 8.4 Performance of each chimpanzee in Experiment 6 of Beran et al. (2016) in which chimpanzees had to remember the best item for 5 minutes before beginning the exchange sequence. The top panel shows performance when the highest preference item in the experiment was available. The bottom panel shows performance on trials in which a medium preference item (orange slice) was the best food item that could be obtained on that trial. *From Beran, M., Rossettie, M., & Parrish, A. E. (2016). Trading up: Chimpanzees (*Pan troglodytes*) show self-control through their exchange behavior.* Animal Cognition, 19, *109–121, reprinted with permission from Springer.*

then at lunch time be faced with the chance to have a cookie. In these cases, what occurs during the delay interval might change how we anticipate future outcomes in a way that changes our preferences somehow. Hopefully, more research will make use of this approach as well. I will talk more about the future-oriented aspects of self-control tasks and self-control behavior in animals in a later chapter.

Returning to exchange tasks, though, I mentioned that the early work used only very short delays. Subsequent tests attempted to use delays more like those used with children, on the scale of minutes or longer. For example, Ramseyer, Pelé, Dufour, Chauvin, and Thierry (2006) also tested some of the same capuchin monkeys tested by Drapier et al. (2005) but now greatly increased the time between when the first food item was handed to a monkey and when the monkey could hand it back for something else. These times ranged from just 10 seconds to as long as 10 minutes, and in some cases the exchange was for a great increase in value (bland food pellets traded for sweet biscuit) versus a smaller increase in value (carrot for sweet biscuit). The results were exactly what you might expect: the monkeys exchanged more pellets for biscuits than carrots for biscuits, and the longer the delay, the more likely the immediate reward was consumed rather than traded. However, it was interesting that the researchers again allowed "nibbling" of foods in these cases, which seemed to really aid how often something could be exchanged. If they instead enforced that an item had to be intact when exchanged, the monkeys then could not hold out for even a minute under the same constraints. This, again, makes a lot of sense, but also suggests a potential "nudge" to aid self-control in some setting. If you are trying, for example, to not eat a whole bag of candy so that later you can enjoy another sweet food for dessert, it might benefit you to eat a single candy. Or, this may even work for nonappetitive rewards. Consider the problem of saving money for later, bigger purchases. These data suggest that one fruitful approach might be to allow yourself a small amount of spending money that you take back from the saved amount, at least on occasion, because that might mitigate some of the aversiveness of wanting to spend now but needing to save for later. Of course, this also introduces the problem of "how much is the right amount of a little cash to spend now." From one perspective, it is *any amount* that would promote saving something over and above what you would otherwise be able to spend. Remember that one does not need to be *perfectly self-controlled* to be wonderfully restrained and goal oriented. The occasional "cheat" actually can be beneficial, and this is true for other animals as well as for humans, as shown in work such as that by Ramseyer et al. (2006).

When Ramseyer et al. (2006) again gave capuchin monkeys the quantitative version of the exchange task, they found that the magnitude of reward increase for exchanging played a role in how often monkeys could wait. Time to wait, though, seemed to really create problems for monkeys when they started trials off being given a food they really liked (the biscuits in this case), and even when the exchange could net *40 times as much biscuit*, these monkeys could not wait for more than a minute to gain that massive increase in reward. Ramseyer et al. anticipated that perhaps the great apes would be better prepared to deal with such long delays, and they were right. Dufour, Pelé, Sterck, and Thierry (2007) gave chimpanzees nearly the same test with quantitative food increases as had been given to capuchins. Chimpanzees had the chance to retain and exchange smaller pieces of cookie for larger pieces, and their performance was markedly different! When the delayed food was two, four, or eight times bigger, the majority of the chimpanzees

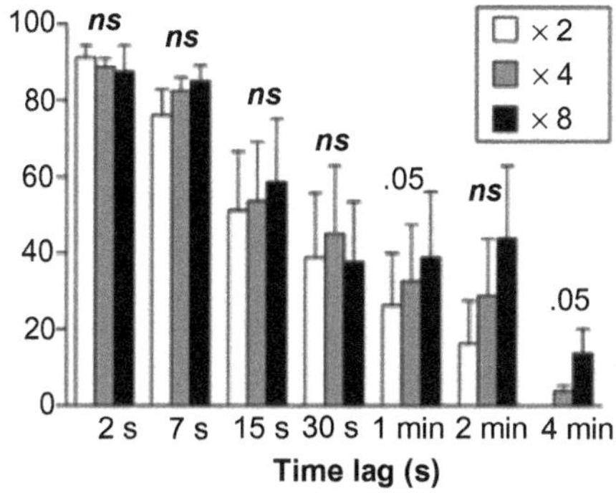

FIGURE 8.5 Percentage of successful returns for each size of cookie (two, four, and eight times the size of the original cookie) at each time lag (from 2 s to 4 min) in Phase 1 of the Dufour et al. (2007) study. The percentage of return increased significantly with the size of the cookies for the time lag of 1 and 4 min. Error bars represent standard errors of the mean. *From Dufour, V., Pelé, M., Sterck, E. H. M., & Thierry, B. (2007). Chimpanzee (*Pan troglodytes*) anticipation of food return: Coping with waiting time in an exchange task.* Journal of Comparative Psychology, 121, *145–155, reprinted with permission of the American Psychological Association.*

would hold the smaller piece and then return it up to 4 minutes later no matter which size of bigger cookie they were offered (Fig. 8.5). If the delayed piece was 40 times bigger, those delays could be stretched to 8 minutes, which is a delay level quite similar to that which we had seen in many of the accumulation tests we had run, and a delay similar to that of many of the various marshmallow tasks given to children.

Dufour et al. (2007) also looked at an interesting aspect of the "failure" trials, where exchange did not occur. They did this to try to examine the degree to which behavior of the chimpanzees was "future oriented" in the sense of seeing whether, at different delay lengths, the chimpanzees anticipated outcome of trials differently. In other words, the researchers wanted to know if the chimpanzees ever acted differently at the outset of trials depending on how long they had learned the delay was going to be (remember, as the study went on, the delays got longer, and the chimpanzees could know this on a session by session basis). The idea here is that perhaps chimpanzees, like humans, sometimes would immediately consume the smaller item right at the start of a trial, as if they did not intend to wait through the delay interval. If this was true, it should have been seen more often when the delay was longer, and this is exactly what Dufour et al. found. As the delays got longer, the chimpanzees were more likely to just eat the small cookie immediately than would have been expected to occur if they had no appreciation of the delay interval. This possibly showed that the chimpanzees were weighing the increase in reward size against the time they had to wait, and perhaps even recognized their fallibility in waiting that long. Of course, there are other possible explanations, such as that the longer delays induced more general frustration with the task, and thus more eating of the first food item. But, these data, along with those we had collected using the toys and accumulation task with chimpanzees (Evans & Beran, 2007), seem to show that chimpanzees are considering their situation within a delayed reward task, and then adjusting their behavior on a trial by trial basis by either avoiding long, and potentially unfruitful, delays, or engaging more in self-distraction during delay of gratification. In the next chapter, I will tell you more about why I think this is the correct interpretation, from newer data that seem to show that chimpanzee intelligence is closely related to delay of gratification in terms of both the ability to delay, and the *choice to only sometimes delay*.

Returning to the question of monkeys and how they perform, other efforts showed some better capacities than those shown by the first capuchin monkeys that were tested. Pelé, Dufour, Micheletta, & Thierry (2010) tested long-tailed macaques, an Old World monkey species (capuchin monkeys are a New World species), and they found that those monkeys were better able to maintain delay of gratification until they could exchange one cookie for another than was two, four, or eight times larger. And, as with chimpanzees, there was some evidence that when monkeys gave up and ate the first item, they did so earlier than would be expected if they were not taking into account the delay time. Then, Pelé et al. tried something new with these monkeys. They gave them the small cookie, and allowed them to give it right back, *before starting the delay* for the larger cookie. So in this case, the monkeys did not have to hold onto the cookie piece for a long time while they waited for a later chance to exchange, and presumably this meant they were under only a very limited time window of temptation to eat that small cookie. The results showed what appear to be very impressive delay times. In that situation, most monkeys would exchange the small cookie even for delays to the larger piece of up to 10 minutes, and some did so even for delays of around 40 minutes! The difference in performance across time delays was striking (Fig. 8.6). But, I think it is important to note that there are two key aspects here. The first is that this variation certainly decreases or largely eliminates any need for what we have called delay maintenance, or the capacity to sustain delay of gratification through time where impulsivity can still occur. Recall that in all previous exchange tests, the smaller or less preferred food item was still in the animal's hand during the delay, and thus was available. Another issue, though, with this new approach is that it is not clear that the subject could know the delay interval when it handed back the smaller cookie. It is true that these delays increased throughout the experiment, and I think that can give us some confidence that the monkeys had recent experience with the delay length that was most relevant to that trial, but I would like to see tests like this somehow explicitly cue the animal as to how long the delay will be. Of course, in that case, the test would operate largely like the intertemporal tests we discussed earlier, in which there was

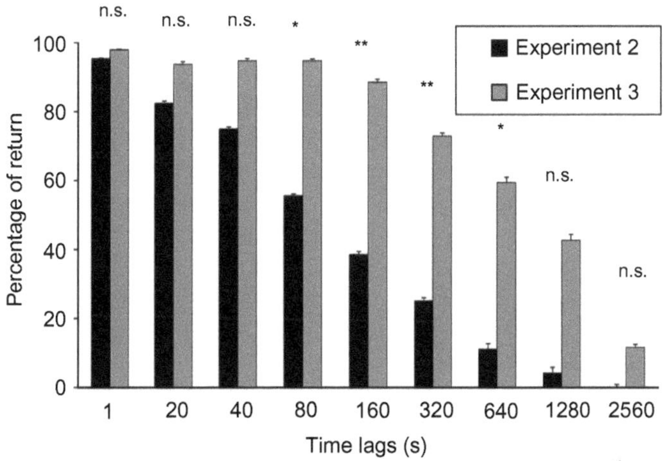

FIGURE 8.6 The comparison of return rates by long-tailed macaques in the two experiments in Pelé et al. (2010). The data are shown for Experiment 2, in which the monkeys had to keep the smaller item and not eat it during the delay, and Experiment 3, where the monkeys could return the smaller item immediately and then wait for the larger item without needing to inhibit eating. The latter case appeared to be much easier for the monkeys, in terms of how often they did what was needed to get the larger cookie. *From Pelé, M., Dufour, V., Micheletta, J., & Thierry, B. (2010). Long-tailed macaques display unexpected waiting abilities in exchange tasks.* Animal Cognition, 13, *263–271, reprinted with permission from Springer.*

no ongoing maintenance but rather a choice and commitment at the outset of a trial to wait or not.

Pelé et al. (2010) also did something that I think is particularly important. They tested the same macaques on an accumulation test. They wanted to see how consistent performance might be across these tasks. They found waiting times in the accumulation test that basically matched those of earlier tests, and also that roughly matched the delay times in the exchange test where delay maintenance was needed. This was a nice convergence of evidence on the approximate delay periods that these monkeys could tolerate when they seemingly had to sustain their delay of gratification throughout trials by not eating food items that were immediately available. In a replication of this approach with Tonkean macaques and capuchin monkeys, Pelé, Micheletta, Uhlrich, Thierry, and Dufour (2011) found similar outcomes. Although the macaques performed slightly better overall, there also was high similarity in delay performance for the exchange and accumulation tasks when delay maintenance was required, and the researchers again found that removing the need for delay maintenance then led to vastly longer delay intervals that these monkeys would tolerate, although I think some of the same concerns still attach to that approach that I already mentioned.

One of the other things that I think is appealing about the exchange task is that it can be used with different kinds of species. And, it has been, with some interesting results. For example, dogs have been given an exchange task (Leonardi, Vick, & Dufour, 2012), in which they first learned to drop inedible items they were holding in their mouths to get a food reward. Then, they were shown two food items, and given one item in their mouth. If they dropped it, they received the other item. Dogs did this when the second item was more highly preferred, but not when the first item was the better item. Dogs also performed the successive exchange task like the one I described earlier, where multiple exchanges needed to be made before the best food item could be obtained. And, they were generally successful when needing to make two or even three exchanges. When delays were introduced, as in the primate tests of exchange, the results were similar to those seen with primates. As the delay interval increased, the dogs made fewer and fewer exchanges, although some dogs showed tolerance of fairly long delays (Fig. 8.7). The behavioral descriptions of what the dogs did in this study were fascinating as well, with some dogs closing their eyes during the delay, and many of them placing the lower preference item on the ground, and out of their mouths during the delay. These behaviors, like those reported for dogs in the Brucks, Soliani, Range, and Marshall-Pescini (2017) study I discussed earlier, again give the feeling that the dogs were attempting to use some kinds of self-distractive strategies, although more would be needed to confirm if this is true. There was also evidence that the dogs more typically would "give up" and eat the lower preference item early in trials where the delay was going to be long, suggesting a nonrandom decision process like that seen in many primates. Given the performance of a couple of dogs with

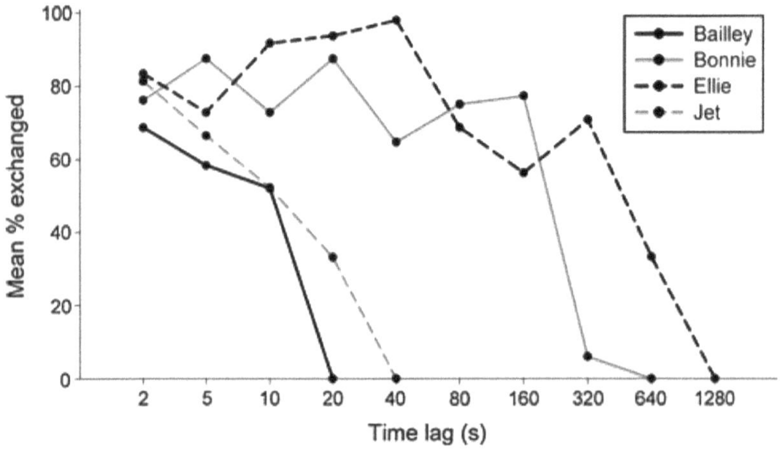

FIGURE 8.7 Mean percentage of exchanges of the item the dogs were first given at the consecutive time delays in Leonardi et al. (2012). *From Leonardi, R. J., Vick, S. J., & Dufour, V. (2012). Waiting for more: The performance of domestic dogs (*Canis familiaris*) on exchange tasks.* Animal Cognition, 15, *107–120, reprinted with permission from Springer.*

really long delays, Leonardi et al. even suggested that delay of gratification may be stronger in dogs than in at least some primates, which is an interesting idea. The methods were fairly comparable across the tasks, lending some support to this idea, but I think that individual differences are more likely to account for what was seen than species differences, something Leonardi et al. also noted. That said, the selective pressures applied to dogs through domestication certainly reflected humans' desire to have an animal companion that could retrieve, track, and even protect prey species, and the ability to do those things would seem to require strong inhibitory tendencies that might lend themselves to more generalized self-control abilities.

Bird species also have been given the exchange task, with differing results depending on the species tested. Dufour, Wascher, Braun, Miller, and Bugnyar (2012) gave crows and ravens the exchange task in which the birds were first given a low preference item and then, after some delay period, could give that piece back for something better (and, the relative value of the better item also varied across trials). Delay periods ranged from 2 to 640 seconds, and an individual bird progressed through these successive delays periods if it made at least one exchange within the six trials given at the current delay period. As with primates, the number of birds that exchanged food items decreased as the delays increased. And, as with some primates there was evidence that those birds who performed best also engaged in behaviors that would seem to support better delay maintenance, such as placing the food item in their possession on the ground or somewhere nearby, a strategy that may have aided in turning attention away from the immediately available reward. Interestingly, both of these species seem to have much more trouble with exchange tasks when there was a quantitative gain to be had by waiting, compared to qualitative gain. Wascher, Dufour, and Bugnyar (2012) offered crows a piece of cheese that could be returned for two, four, or eight pieces, but the crows rarely made such exchanges, even though they would consistently choose the larger of two quantities of cheese in a nondelayed two choice discrimination task (see Fig. 8.8). The same birds were in the Dufour et al. (2012) and Wascher et al. (2012) studies, and yet it was striking to learn that there was not any relation between performance in the two kinds of exchange tasks. One of the two crows that performed best in the qualitative exchange version never exchanged in the quantitative exchange version, and the other exchanged the cheese only once in 108 trials. The most successful bird in the quantitative exchange test (this bird was successful on 13 of 108 trials) was among the worst performers in the quantitative exchange task. To me, this is a very curious result, because it says that perhaps there is something fundamentally different about giving up one thing for another versus giving up a little of something good to get even more of that same good thing. At face value, it is almost as if in the quantitative exchange the birds did not consider food type and food amount, even though this cannot be a result of some kind of overload on their working memory or perceptual

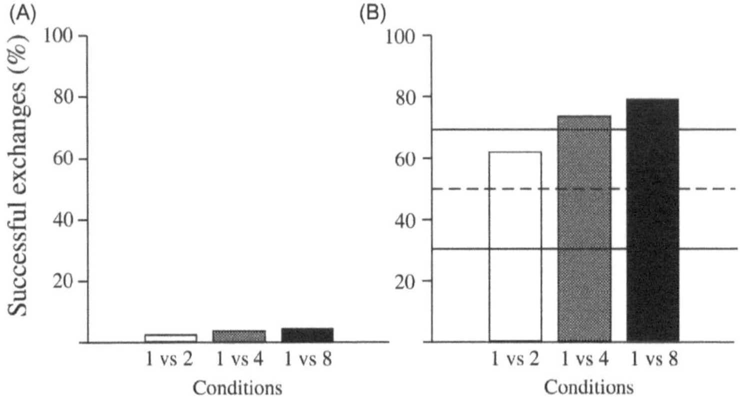

FIGURE 8.8 (A) Performance of crows in the quantitative exchange task and (B) the quantitative discrimination task in Wascher et al. (2012). In the discrimination task, crows chose higher quantities significantly more often than expected by chance for comaprisons of 1 and 4 and 1 and 8. The dashed line represents the 50% chance level, and the full lines represent performance that would differ significantly from that chance level. *From Wascher, C. A. F., Dufour, V., & Bugnyar, T. (2012). Carrion crows cannot overcome impulsive choice in a quantitative exchange task.* Frontiers in Psychology, 3, *Article 118, reprinted with permission of the authors.*

abilities, given that they easily choose the larger amount when the choice was for immediate payoff. Instead, it is almost as if they saw the delayed reward task as being about one type of food they wanted. When that food was not the food they possessed (the qualitative exchange task), they waited. When it was (the quantitative exchange task), they ate it. Note that not all species struggle with this kind of comparison (e.g., Dufour et al., 2007; Pelé et al., 2010; Ramseyer et al., 2006), and at least one bird species (Goffin cockatoos) can wait to exchange for more of a reward as well as a better type of reward, even though in that case exchange was more frequent for a qualitatively better delayed reward (Auersperg, Laumer, & Bugnyar, 2013). But, the relationship between qualitative and quantitative delayed rewards, and how they impact choice behavior and delay maintenance, remains to be more fully understood.

Although accumulation tasks and exchange tasks have tended to be some of the dominant approaches that are used to assess delay of gratification in animals, a number of interesting and creative tasks have been developed. I cannot hope to describe all of those, and so I had to select a few examples that I believe show this creativity and also that show the degree to which task demands might elicit better or worse self-control. Other interesting papers are listed in the Further Reading for this chapter.

One of the things we have tried hard to do in my lab is think about tests that might be more "fair" or intuitive to certain species. I think this is an important point when you work with animals, because there is no chance to verbally instruct them as to what you want to measure, or even as to what the basic rules of the game might be. Rather, the animal has only its sensory and perceptual experiences, to which it might make a response and then observe the consequences of that response. So, for example, you cannot tell an animal that if it waits, it will get something better, you just have to put that contingency into place, and see if the animal comes to recognize it in some way that allows for new behavior to emerge that might be adaptive. Comparative psychologists often think about these constraints as they design their tasks, and this can lead to fascinating new approaches that one would never have considered when thinking only about working with humans. In fact, I think the same thing can be argued for those who study young children, for many of the same reasons. And, perhaps because of this, one sees evidence of comparative tasks that are born from this necessity. Although not directly related to self-control, I think this has been true in the area of studying animal metacognition, and it highlights important points that relate back to studying self-control.

Metacognition is the monitoring of knowledge states (or states of being uncertain) and the adjustment of information-seeking behavior on the basis of that knowledge or ignorance (Nelson, 1992; Nelson & Narens, 1990). You use metacognition when you know that you know the answer to something, or you know that you must Google™ that in order to find the answer. You use metacognition when you decide whether you have studied enough, or need to keep studying, and when you know that although someone's name is still on the tip of your tongue, it is ok to approach them because once you get there, you will remember their name. Although it had long been considered that only humans engaged in metacognition, we now know that some species do seem to engage in similar control and monitoring processes (Basile, Schroeder, Brown, Templer, & Hampton, 2015; Hampton, 2001; Smith, 2009; Templer & Hampton, 2012). Again, this is a whole other story, but the point I want to make here is that in studying animal metacognition, new approaches were developed rather than forcing animals to take tests designed for adult humans. For example, the highly influential information-seeking task involves hiding items and then seeing whether animals (or, in some cases, young children) know when they know or do not know where the hidden item is. If they see the hiding, they can just reach for items, but if they do not, then they probably need to look first. This is simple behavioral measure (i.e., did they look before they responded or just go ahead and respond) that has had a large impact on what we know about how different species seek information when it is needed (Call, 2010; Call & Carpenter, 2001). And, it works because it is intuitive. Animals look for things, and they reach for things. So, this test allows them to just put those behaviors together, if they can, in an intelligent way that allows them to show what they do or do not know (e.g., Marsh & MacDonald, 2012a, 2012b).

A metacognition test we designed took a different approach, again based on thinking about natural behaviors of primates (Beran et al., 2015). We gave chimpanzees a memory test on a computer, and they got food rewards when they were correct. But, we did something special with the food machine. We moved it away from the computer, so that the chimpanzees worked in one place, but got rewarded in another. And, we set it up so that after they finished a memory test, the computer delayed for a few seconds before telling when whether they were correct or incorrect. And, then, if they were correct, it dispensed a treat, but the *chimpanzees had to be at the dispenser to catch that reward, or it would be lost*. This was the key manipulation, and the idea was that there would be no reason to have to run over to the reward location after hearing the computer tell you that you were correct if you already knew that. In that case, you could take your time, walk over early, and be ready for the treat with no chance of losing it. And, this is exactly what chimpanzees did: when they were correct on trials, they were far more likely to walk over early, before any kind of feedback was given, so that they could easily collect their rewards. When they turned out to be incorrect on trials, such early movements were far less likely, and this would seem to show that they would go early when they knew they had done well, but wait to see how they did when they were not so sure.

The point of talking about these metacognition tests is that we try to think about the same intuitive design aspects when we study self-control and delay of gratification. The accumulation and exchange tasks have that quality, but one of my favorite tasks that we have used is called the rotating tray task. The inspiration for that task comes from one of my favorite past times—eating! And, in this case, eating sushi. I was in a restaurant where the sushi options came on plates that were color coded (for price) and that moved through the restaurant on a long conveyor belt (for example, like that shown in Fig. 8.9). The idea was to take those plates that held items you liked, and so that meant sometimes having to let certain plates go by with an enjoyable but not favorite item (e.g., the tuna roll) while you awaited a highly preferred plate (i.e., the salmon roll). Now, I suppose if one had an unlimited budget (or an unlimited stomach) this would not be challenging at all, in terms of showing some restraint. But, if you are hungry, and something pretty good is right in front of you, and you can only afford perhaps five plates, it struck me that this was exactly a short-term self-control task. You have to let something of medium preference go by, so that later something of higher preference can be yours. From this observation came the idea of the rotating tray task (Bramlett, Perdue, Evans, & Beran, 2012).

The apparatus consisted of a circular tray mounted on a motor such that the tray would rotate, similar to what one might see for displaying wedding cakes or something like that. We mounted two "arms" on the tray, so that as it rotated, those arms came in reach of a capuchin monkey subject. The monkey sat and watched what was happening, and could choose to reach out

FIGURE 8.9 An example of a sushi conveyor belt. Different types of sushi pass by the patron sitting at a table, and he or she can select whatever approaches. Sometimes, the person has to wait a little while for the most preferred pieces to make their way to the table. *By cyclonebill from Copenhagen, Denmark (Sushi Uploaded by palnatoke) [CC BY-SA 2.0 (https://creativecommons.org/licenses/by-sa/2.0)], via Wikimedia Commons.*

whenever he or she wanted to grab things on those arms. All the experimenter did was present different kinds of foods, place them on the various arms, and then turn on the motor. As the tray rotated, the monkeys decided when to grab things, but as soon as they took something, the motor was turned off, and nothing else was coming on that trial. So, the game was set—monkeys got to pick one thing off the tray, in much the same way that a budget-constrained person could only select one tray of sushi from the conveyor, and might sometimes have to wait for the best thing. We gave the monkeys a number of different variations. We gave them carrot first, and then banana if they let carrot go by (for all monkeys, banana is much more preferred). We gave them small pieces of banana first, and larger pieces second. Of course, we also gave them easy trials where the best food or biggest size was the first to come within reach. What we found was that nearly all of the monkeys would let carrot go by to get banana. And, many (but not all) of the monkeys also let the smaller piece of the high preference banana go by, if that meant the next piece was even larger. So, it appeared that monkeys could sit and wait for the best food to come.

Next, we made the game harder by introducing reward visibility as something that could change from trial to trial (Perdue, Bramlett, Evans, & Beran, 2015). Now, the rotating apparatus had two opaque boxes on it, rather than arms, and food items could go into those boxes (and be out of view) or sit on top of them (and be in view; see Fig. 8.10). In this case, we used two sizes of banana, 5 grams and 20 grams, and sometimes the small piece was visible on top, whereas the bigger piece was out of view and in the box. This did not seem to disrupt the monkeys, and they would let fully visible, smaller pieces of food go by so that they could reach into the boxes to get the bigger pieces of food. And, we also found that the monkeys did not have to see the

FIGURE 8.10 The rotating tray apparatus used in Bramlett et al. (2012) and Perdue et al. (2015). Food items could be placed either into or on top of the containers on each of the arms, and the tray rotated around to bring those items into reach of the monkeys. *From Perdue, B. M., Bramlett, J. L., Evans, T. A., & Beran, M. J. (2015). Waiting for what comes later: Capuchin monkeys show self-control even for nonvisible delayed rewards.* Animal Cognition, *18, 1105–1112, reprinted with permission from Springer.*

baiting to remember what the best thing was that they could get. If we showed them the two food items that differed in size, and then baited them behind a screen, the monkeys would still let a visible, smaller piece go by, and then reach into the container to get the bigger food item, even though they had not seen it be placed there. Fig. 8.11 shows the cumulative results of that study, in terms of how baiting occurred (in view or out of view, behind the occluder) and where the smaller and larger food pieces were placed. In all cases, the monkeys more often than not were able to gain the bigger food item, and thus showed control over responding in a way that we argued reflected self-control.

Perhaps the most compelling of the efforts to use natural behaviors to examine self-control and delay of gratification makes use of movements through space. I like these approaches because they are, again, highly intuitive for animals in terms of how to obtain the best rewards, if the animals can manage to do that. One of my favorite studies that used this approach was by Stevens, Rosati, Ross, and Hauser (2005). They designed an intertemporal choice test that was tied directly to spatial distances. In some ways, this study would have fit nicely in early chapters where we discussed the two-choice ITC tests, but in my mind, this is more of a delayed gratification test akin to the ones I have discussed in this chapter. The test was given to two monkey species, cotton-top tamarins and marmosets. The way it worked was that the monkeys saw two sets of food items at a distance, but one was closer than the other (and in some cases, much closer, along the lines of being only 35 cm away versus being 245 cm away; Fig. 8.12). The question was whether the monkeys would keep going beyond the closer, smaller

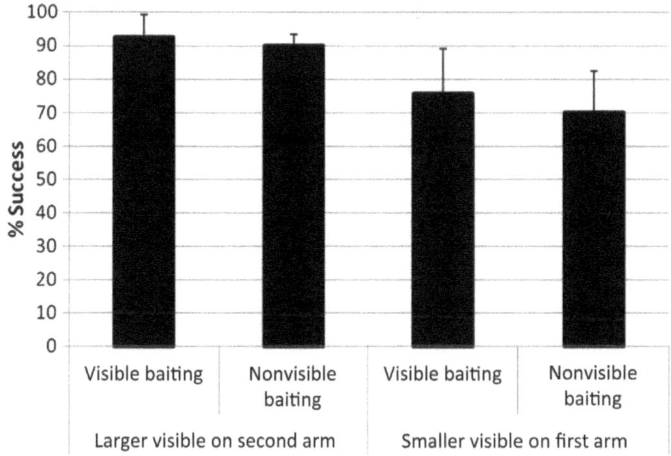

FIGURE 8.11 Average percentage of success (obtaining the better reward) for the critical self-control trials in the visible and nonvisible baiting conditions of Perdue et al. (2015). Error bars indicate the standard error. *From Perdue, B. M., Bramlett, J. L., Evans, T. A., & Beran, M. J. (2015). Waiting for what comes later: Capuchin monkeys show self-control even for nonvisible delayed rewards.* Animal Cognition, 18, *1105–1112, reprinted with permission from Springer.*

number of food items to get the farther, larger number of food items. And, the answer was that they would, although with some interesting species differences. If you recall, in other work that I discussed that used the intertemporal choice paradigm, Stevens, Hallinan, and Hauser (2005) had reported that marmosets waited longer than tamarins when choosing between two sets of food at different delay intervals until delivery, and at that time the researchers suggested that it was not brain size, or life history, that predicted this species difference, but rather feeding ecology. Marmosets relied more on food such as tree sap that takes a while to accumulate, whereas tamarins often had to quickly grab nearby food in the form of insects which would quickly get away otherwise. In the traveling version of the ITC task (Stevens, Rosati, et al., 2005), however, it was the tamarins that showed greater self-control, at least as measured by how often they would walk farther the get the bigger reward (Fig. 8.13). This created an interesting contrast—the same species, given different tests, showed a reversal in relative degrees of self-control. I say relative here, because if you look at Fig. 8.13, you can see that both species often walked farther for more food, so it was not that one species showed self-control and the other did not, it was that one showed greater degrees of self-control. But, in the traveling test, the tamarins held a steady level of choosing the farther option, whereas marmosets appeared to be less willing to travel the farther distances for more food. The researchers considered the role that speed of travel might play in this reversal of performance, and that seemed to be a key issue. Tamarins travel

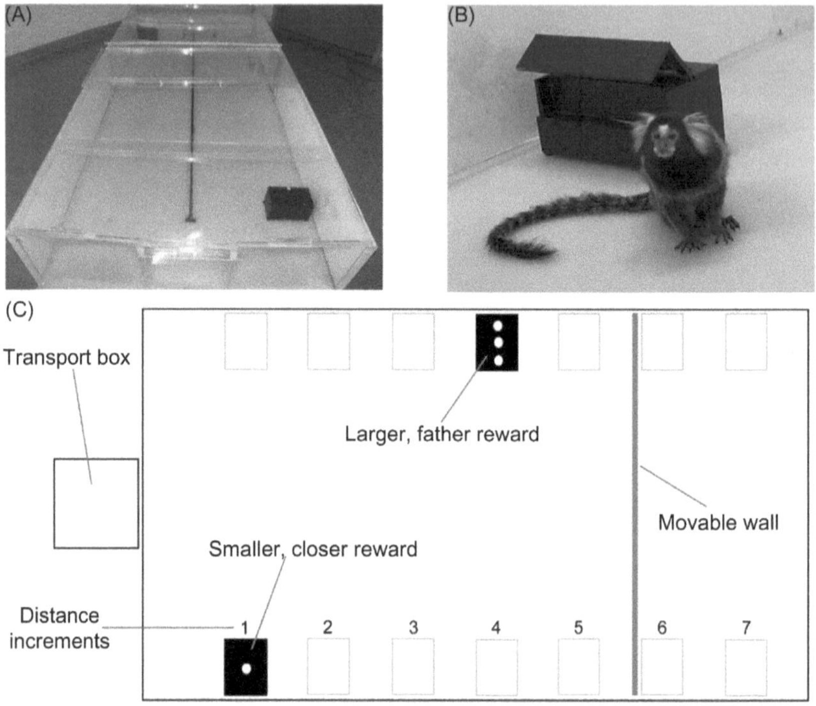

FIGURE 8.12 The design of the traveling self-control test used by Stevens, Rosati, et al. (2005). The monkeys traveled to receive their rewards in a plexiglas enclosure, and the food rewards were lined up in an array on a ledge in the box (A). Panel (B) shows a monkey near a box, and the food reward options were placed at different distances across trials (C). *From Stevens, J. R., Rosati, A. G., Ross, K. R., & Hauser, M. D. (2005). Will travel for food: Spatial discounting in two New World monkeys.* Current Biology, 15, *1855–1860, reprinted with permission from Elsevier.*

faster than marmosets, particularly over longer distances, and so that might have played a role, but perhaps in a complicated way. Using just time itself, for travel, the researchers modeled what the monkeys should have done, and found that marmosets still should have preferred the larger reward even given their longer travel times. This means that something else besides a simple temporal demand (time to travel) factored into the choices of marmosets to sometimes take the smaller, nearer food. The researchers noted that perhaps this was something about being less good at seeing the food amounts, or that satiation levels were a factor. They suggested that space brings its own additional concerns for marmosets more than it does for tamarins. For example, they noted that research on foraging behavior in capuchin monkeys has shown that more distant foods were rapidly devalued by those monkeys, perhaps because of the energy costs required to move to those foods (Janson, 1998, 2000). Perhaps such travel was more energetically

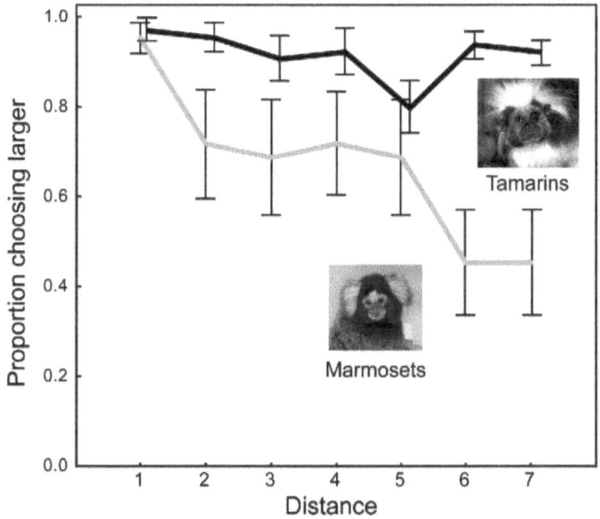

FIGURE 8.13 The results for cotton-top tamarins and marmosets in the study by Stevens, Rosati, et al. (2005). Tamarins appeared to show better self-control, for reasons outlined in the text. *From Stevens, J. R., Rosati, A. G., Ross, K. R., & Hauser, M. D. (2005). Will travel for food: Spatial discounting in two New World monkeys.* Current Biology, 15, *1855–1860, reprinted with permission from Elsevier.*

costly for marmosets. Alternately, it might be that for marmosets travel signifies a greater sense of predation risk. To me, the most compelling argument from these researchers was about reasons for travel in these monkeys. If tamarins have to move over greater distances to obtain insects and other distributed food sources, but marmosets more often stay and forage in one place on slow-emerging food types, then the difference in task performances makes sense. When the choice is a less-now, more-later kind of comparison, a species like tamarins that more rapidly grab at food items might be more inclined to choose the immediate option, whereas when the choice is about traveling more to get more food, those same tamarins might be more inclined to do such travel. Of course, more work is needed to see just how well these ecological pressures relate to choice behavior in lab-based settings, but I think it is a productive and intriguing hypothesis, and one that should be considered by more of us who study self-control and choice behavior across species.

Another study that I found very interesting in its approach involved a truly novel way of asking animals to show self-control: by having them use one edible item to get another (Evans & Westergaard, 2006). In this study, capuchin monkeys were given a piece of celery (a lower preference food for them) or a pretzel (a higher preference food). Sometimes, there was also peanut butter (the highest preference food) placed outside the enclosure, some distance away from where the first food was given. The question was whether monkeys would take those rigid foods and use them as tools to scoop up the peanut butter than was otherwise unavailable. To do this required not eating a food item already in hand before first using it to get the best possible treat on that trial. Fig. 8.14 shows that many monkeys did that, and particularly those monkeys that had some experience using tools in past experiments. What was interesting was that only the experienced tool users transported that food-tool a longer distance to use to get the peanut butter. This suggests that perhaps their experience allowed them to anticipate the value of the food-tool better than the other monkeys, which is an important point when one thinks about how self-control opportunities present themselves. When anyone is offered the chance to delay for a better or larger reward, a key issue is whether the individual understands the necessary conditions for obtaining that reward. For example, saving money in a bank account only makes sense if you understand how banks work, and that the money is safe while there. Or, choosing to skip dessert or choosing a salad over a hamburger so as to lose weight only makes sense if one understands how caloric intake relates to weight gain. In Evans and Westergaard, it appeared that experience directly impacted self-control in capuchin monkeys, and I think this is an important thing to consider when designing experiments.

The last empirical work on self-control in animals that I want to highlight is based on a series of very interesting papers with human participants, by Michael Young at Kansas State University. Young and his students and colleagues make computer games that involve players choosing when and where to shoot at various kinds of targets. They originally designed these games to

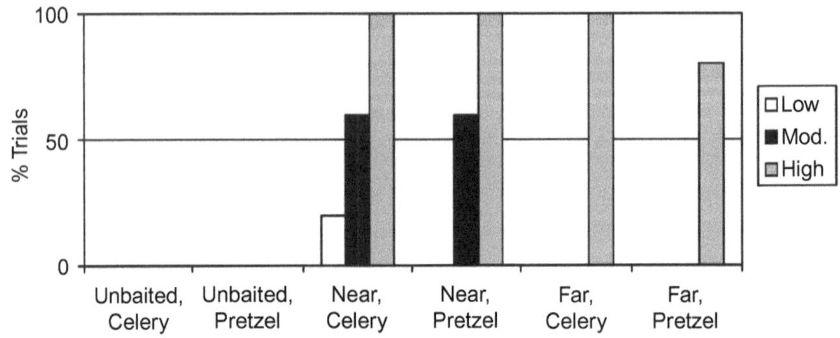

FIGURE 8.14 The results from the food-tool study of Evans and Westergaard (2006). Capuchin monkeys had varying degrees of experience using tools, and the test involved a best reward (peanut butter) sometimes placed close by or far away from where another food was given to the monkey. The graph shows how often monkeys used that first food as a tool to scoop in the peanut butter. *From Evans, T. A., & Westergaard, G. C. (2005). Self-control and tool use in tufted capuchin monkeys (*Cebus apella*).* Journal of Comparative Psychology, 120, *163–166, reprinted with permission of the American Psychological Association.*

look at causal reasoning and how people deal with uncertainty and probabilistic information (e.g., Young, Sutherland, Cole, & Nguyen, 2011), but pretty soon they adapted their games to look at intertemporal choice behavior and self-control. They called these "cash in" games, where the idea was that players had to choose when to fire a weapon when that weapon's power (i.e., effectiveness in gaining advantages in the game) increased the longer it was not fired (Young, Webb, & Jacobs, 2011). Their game always makes me think of something like a snowball fight, where the more effort and time you put into collecting a good amount of packed snow, the more "lethal" the effects on the neighborhood kid you plan to bean with that snowball! In Young's game, this effectiveness of the weapon was something people definitely attended to, and people tended to wait longer to use the weapon when doing so allowed them to eliminate targets more quickly. Subsequent studies validated this game as being highly similar to other intertemporal choice tasks in terms of showing magnitude effects. People showed greater sensitivity to the consequences of their choices to shoot or not when the delay for improving the effectiveness of the weapon was shorter than when the delay was longer, and people waited longer when the damage the weapon generated was doubled for all rewards (Young, Webb, Sutherland, & Jacobs, 2013). And, other interesting effects of using these games were found (see Further Reading).

What I found so compelling about this approach is that it naturally could be adapted for use with animals, something that Young and his colleagues noted as they reported their use of the tasks with humans. My colleague, Ted Evans, designed a task based on this idea of escalating interest, also using a computerized task with rhesus monkeys and capuchin monkeys. Some years earlier, Ted had written a program for monkeys in which they had to select stimuli onscreen in a particular serial order (Evans, 2007). Each time they chose another stimulus within a trial, and in its correct ordinal position in the sequence, they earned another digital reward that later could be "cashed out." Monkeys also had the option to cash out rather than continue to sequence the stimuli on a given trial, and Ted found that delay (in terms of how long it took to get the cursor to contact stimuli) and effort (whether the stimuli were randomly placed on the screen or were placed in highly familiar and repeated locations) both affected whether monkeys would work through the whole sequence, or cash out early and take a smaller number of rewards. So, this suggested that monkeys might make good subjects for a study on nonhuman animal performance in a task like that which Young had developed. Evans and Beran (2014) trained monkeys to use a cursor on the screen as a digital "eraser" that could wipe things from the screen, and when the whole screen was cleared, a reward was given. The trick was that the longer the monkeys waited to move the cursor when it first appeared, the larger it would grow, and the faster it would move. So, waiting made the cursor a more effective tool on that trial. And, as shown in Fig. 8.15, if the cursor got

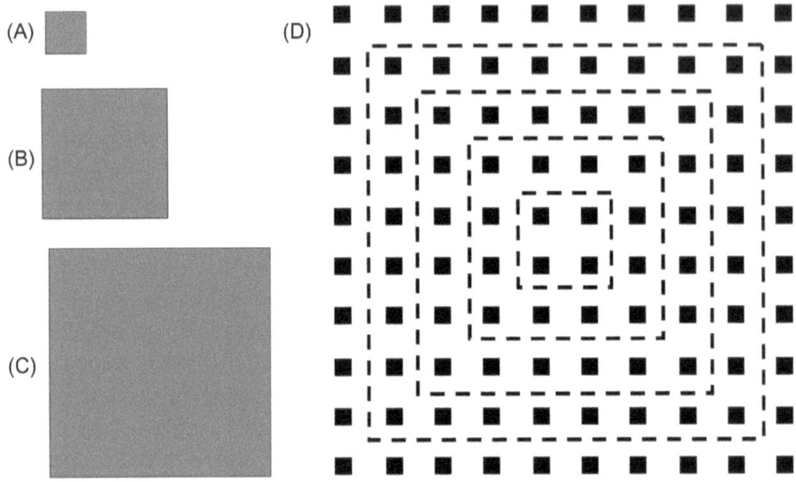

FIGURE 8.15 A schematic of the escalating interest task used by Evans and Beran (2014). The eraser and target array sizes presented throughout the experiment. The size of the eraser was always 8 × 8 mm (panel A) at the start of a trial, and could grow to a maximum size of either 25 × 25 mm (panel B) or 44 × 44 mm (panel C), depending on the experimental phase and how long a monkey waited to begin its response. In all phases, the target array could be presented in one of five sizes (panel D). Here, each array size is represented by a dashed square, but those dashes were not visible during trials. *From Evans, T. A., & Beran, M. J. (2012) Monkeys wait to begin a computer task when waiting makes their responses more effective.* Animal Behavior and Cognition, 1, *36–50, reprinted with permission of the authors.*

big enough, it was really easy to quickly erase all of the targets onscreen. How large the monkeys allowed the eraser to grow was closely related to how many targets they had to erase on a given trial (Fig. 8.16). This suggested that the monkeys closely monitoring the trial difficulty (in terms of effort needed to erase all targets) and adjusted their wait time accordingly, rather than always waiting for a set period of time before starting. And, their choices seemed to be effective, as there was a strong relation between final eraser size and the total time monkeys needed to complete a trial. I think this is a nice example of the synergistic relation between animal and human research. Michael Young, who has done elegant work with humans and nonhuman animals, designed an approach based on what he knew about animal self-control behavior so that he could have a task that looked at the same factors that affect self-control, but in humans. And, the value of that task as a comparative tool then was realized as it was returned to experiments given to nonhuman animals.

As I wrap up discussion of some of the delay of gratification tests used with animals, what should the take-home messages be from all of these studies? I think five important points need to be made, some of which relate to experimental approaches, some of which relate to resulting data, and some of which relate to theoretical issues that need to guide future research in this area.

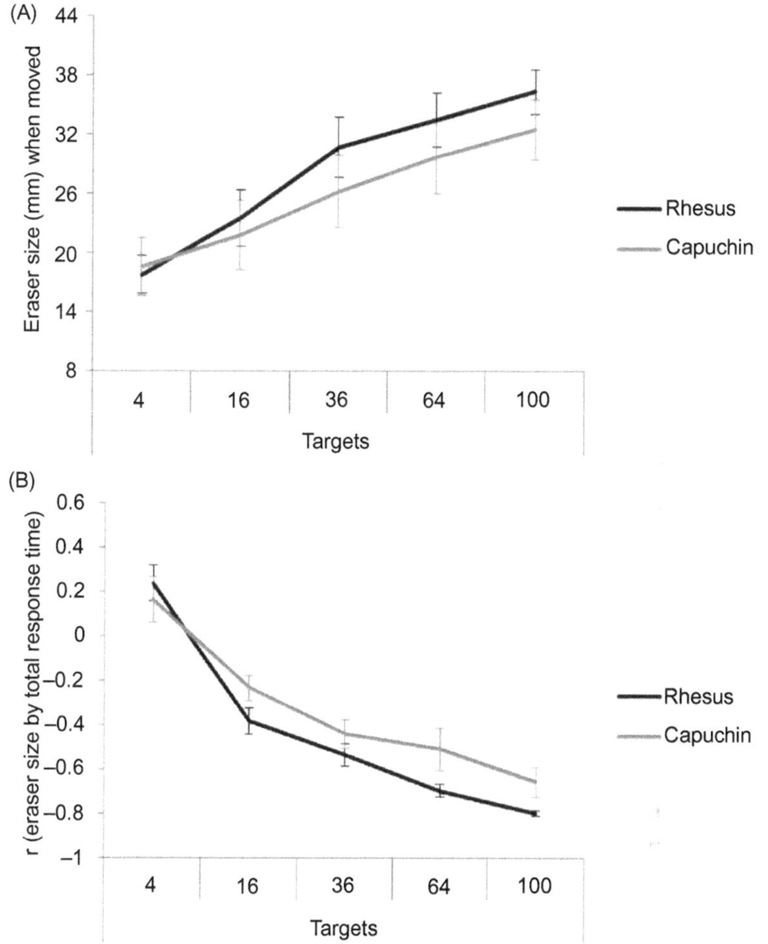

FIGURE 8.16 Monkeys' performance in Evans and Beran (2014), as a function of target array size (*x*-axis) and species (separate lines). Panel (A) illustrates the mean size of the eraser before monkeys attempted to use it. Panel (B) shows the mean relationship (correlation coefficient) between final eraser size and total trial time. *From Evans, T. A., & Beran, M. J. (2012). Monkeys wait to begin a computer task when waiting makes their responses more effective.* Animal Behavior and Cognition, 1, *36–50, reprinted with permission of the authors.*

The first point I think is easy to make is that nonhuman animals are not always impulsive creatures. Although it is true that we have seen cases where pigeons, or rats, or primates tend to take whatever they can most immediately, the idea that humans are uniquely capable of findings ways to wait for better outcomes is simply not true. Diverse nonhuman species (primates, nonprimate mammals, and birds) all have shown at least some evidence that waiting for better rewards is well within the capacity of those species. I think we are at a point of understanding the depth of self-control in other species because we have been creative with how we ask the question. I think about tasks that have animals traveling through space, which mimic natural foraging tendencies, as being a great example of this. Or, other intuitive actions such as handing things out to get things handed back for species such as primates that are used to manipulating foods with their hands. In my opinion, these tasks, more so than tasks that assign arbitrary delays to different choice options, make sense to animals, and so they show self-control by delaying their gratification, when they can. Tasks matter, and the use of only one approach with a species runs the great risk of underestimating what might be learned about the self-control of that species.

The second summary point relates to the first, but in a more cautionary way. Using only one task with a species runs the risk of *overestimating* the self-control of that species if they perform well. For humans, we know that there are relations among degrees of self-control across tasks (i.e., someone who saves money from each paycheck also may be quite likely to shop longer for the best deal rather than buy the first thing they see). But, in other areas, a self-controlled person who maintains a healthy weight and frequently exercises may do other impulsive things (e.g., risky sexual behavior, smoking, etc.). So, one test does not reflect the general self-control of any organism. For developmental researchers, this has been a growing interest, to see how self-control measured in one way (e.g., the marshmallow test) relates to other tests, and to life outcome variables. In animal research, this has barely been attempted. I have discussed a few instances where the same species (and even the same individuals) are given more than one test, as with the tamarins and marmosets in this chapter, but more of this is needed. And, there is a little research on how self-control tests might relate to other aspects of general intelligence or cognition. However, this is improving, as I discuss in the next chapter.

The third point is that there needs to be greater emphasis on considering carefully what we call tests of self-control in animals, particularly with regard to considering how methodological details might bias responses in certain ways, thereby leading to underestimations or overestimations of self-control in animals. The next chapter will also focus on this question, highlighting one case in which I think there is a real risk of confusing why animals may respond the way that they do in some of the tests we give them.

The fourth point I want to raise is about individual differences. For me, this is an issue in many areas of comparative cognition research. Sometimes, we act as if our studies tell us what "chimpanzees do" or "dogs do" or "rats do." But, we do not really mean this, or at least we probably should not mean to do this. In almost every study I have ever conducted, there was the "average" performance of the group of animals that I tested, and then the reality of *what each animal did*. Rarely is the story as simple as the group averages suggest. Some animals succeed immediately at new tests, some get there slowly, and some never do. For choice tests, such as those used in self-control research, there can be wide differences in what individual animals choose to do. In addition, there can even be strong inconsistencies *day to day* in what animals choose to do. Researchers who rely on food preferences, for example, to establish parameters for choice tasks must ensure that those preferences stay consistent through a whole study. And, what I have seen is that a monkey perfectly willing to tolerate delays for more food on one day may not choose to do that at all the next day. I would argue that these kinds of variations in choice behavior reflect exactly the psychology that underlies human self-control as well. What we do in one case, on one day, may well be highly predictive of future decisions, but rarely is it perfectly predictive. More attention should be given to this issue in comparative work, in which we try to understand individual differences, and even differences in choice within the same individuals. We know some of the key factors that affect isolated instances in which self-control is needed, such as delay length, reward magnitude, and environmental aspects such as opportunities to self-distract or precommit to one choice over the other. But, there are certainly factors relating more to the organisms' personality, memory, general intelligence, and social cognitive skills that may add to our ability to predict choice behavior.

The final point is that documenting what animals can do, by way of delaying gratification, making intertemporal choices, and maintaining self-control is just one part of what should be the larger goal of a comparative psychology of self-control. The second part is to use that knowledge to aid in generating potential interventions for improving self-control where it needs to be improved (e.g., reducing gambling, smoking, drug use, impulsive spending, aggression, etc.). The history of ITC tasks with rats and pigeons, for example, has shown the value of looking for broader implications of the work, with some important animal results informing how we consider self-control and impulsivity in humans. Animal research continues to offer that same value in newer areas of investigation in human self-control. In later chapters, I will discuss ideas about self-control as being a type of "limited resource," and how some studies of animals may better inform us about the value of such a conceptualization. I think this is a strong case where a comparative approach can help "ground" claims that are made in research with humans, especially where that research takes an evolutionary perspective. Such efforts to study animals can generate support (or opposition) to hypotheses about human choice behavior, especially when animals are given comparable tests to those used with people that are also fair tests for the animals. Ultimately, knowing what animals can and cannot do, and what role individual differences and environmental features play in animal behavior, can lead to better understanding of human self-control as well.

REFERENCES

Auersperg, A. M. I., Laumer, I. B., & Bugnyar, T. (2013). Goffin cockatoos wait for qualitative and quantitative gains but prefer 'better' to 'more'. *Biology Letters*, *9*, Article 20121092.

Basile, B. M., Schroeder, G. R., Brown, E. K., Templer, V. L., & Hampton, R. R. (2015). Evaluation of seven hypotheses for metamemory performance in rhesus monkeys. *Journal of Experimental Psychology: General*, *144*, 85–102.

Beran, M. J., & Evans, T. A. (2012). Language-trained chimpanzees (*Pan troglodytes*) delay gratification by choosing token exchange over immediate reward consumption. *American Journal of Primatology*, *74*, 864–870.

Beran, M. J., Perdue, B. M., Futch, S. E., Smith, J. D., Evans, T. A., & Parrish, A. E. (2015). Go when you know: Chimpanzees' confidence movements reflect their responses in a computerized memory task. *Cognition*, *142*, 236–246.

Beran, M. J., Rossettie, M. S., & Parrish, A. E. (2016). Trading up: Chimpanzees (*Pan troglodytes*) show self-control through their exchange behavior. *Animal Cognition*, *19*, 109–121.

Bramlett, J. L., Perdue, B. M., Evans, T. A., & Beran, M. J. (2012). Capuchin monkeys (*Cebus apella*) let lesser rewards pass them by to get better rewards. *Animal Cognition*, *15*, 963–969.

Bräuer, J., Call, J., & Tomasello, M. (2009). Are apes inequity averse? New data on the token-exchange paradigm. *American Journal of Primatology*, *71*, 175–181.

Brosnan, S. F., & De Waal, F. B. M. (2004). Socially learned preferences for differentially rewarded tokens in the brown capuchin monkey (*Cebus apella*). *Journal of Comparative Psychology*, *118*, 133–139.

Brosnan, S. F., Schiff, H. C., & De Waal, F. B. (2005). Tolerance for inequity may increase with social closeness in chimpanzees. *Proceedings of the Royal Society of London B: Biological Sciences*, *272*, 253–258.

Brucks, D., Soliani, M., Range, F., & Marshall-Pescini, S. (2017). Reward type and behavioural patterns predict dogs' success in a delay of gratification paradigm. *Scientific Reports*, *7*, 42459.

Call, J. (2010). Do apes know that they could be wrong? *Animal Cognition*, *13*, 689–700.

Call, J., & Carpenter, M. (2001). Do apes and children know what they have seen? *Animal Cognition*, *4*, 207–220.

Chalmeau, R., & Peignot, P. (1998). Exchange of objects between humans and captive western lowland gorillas. *Primates*, *39*, 389–398.

De Waal, F. B. M. (1997). Food transfers through mesh in brown capuchins. *Journal of Comparative Psychology*, *111*, 370–378.

Drapier, M., Chauvin, C., Dufour, V., Uhlrich, P., & Thierry, B. (2005). Food-exchange with humans in brown capuchin monkeys. *Primates*, *46*, 241–248.

Dufour, V., Pelé, M., Sterck, E. H. M., & Thierry, B. (2007). Chimpanzee (*Pan troglodytes*) anticipation of food return: Coping with waiting time in an exchange task. *Journal of Comparative Psychology*, *121*, 145–155.

Dufour, V., Wascher, C. A. F., Braun, A., Miller, R., & Bugnyar, T. (2012). Corvids can decide if a future exchange is worth waiting for. *Biology Letters*, *8*, 201–204.

Evans, T. A. (2007). Performance in a computerized self-control task by rhesus macaques (*Macaca mulatta*): The combined influence of effort and delay. *Learning and Motivation*, *38*, 342–357.

Evans, T. A., & Beran, M. J. (2007). Chimpanzees use self-distraction to cope with impulsivity. *Biology Letters*, *3*, 599–602.

Evans, T. A., & Beran, M. J. (2014). Monkeys wait to begin a computer task when waiting makes their responses more effective. *Animal Behavior and Cognition, 1*, 36–50.

Evans, T. A., & Westergaard, G. C. (2006). Self-control and tool use in tufted capuchin monkeys (*Cebus apella*). *Journal of Comparative Psychology, 120*, 163–166.

Hachiga, Y., Silberberg, A., Parker, S., & Sakagami, T. (2009). Humans *(Homo sapiens)* fail to show an inequity effect in an "up-linkage" analog of the monkey inequity test. *Animal Cognition, 12*, 359–367.

Hampton, R. R. (2001). Rhesus monkeys know when they remember. *Proceedings of the National Academy of Sciences, 98*, 5359–5362.

Horowitz, A. (2012). Fair is fine, but more is better: Limits to inequity aversion in the domestic dog. *Social Justice Research, 25*, 195–212.

Janson, C. H. (1998). Experimental evidence for spatial memory in foraging wild capuchin monkeys, *Cebus apella. Animal Behaviour, 55*, 1229–1243.

Janson, C. H. (2000). Spatial movement strategies: Theory, evidence, and challenges. In S. Boinski & P. A. Garber (Eds.), *On the move: How and why animals travel in groups* (pp. 165–203). Chicago, IL: University of Chicago Press.

Judge, P. G., & Essler, J. L. (2013). Capuchin monkeys exercise self-control by choosing token exchange over an immediate reward. *International Journal of Comparative Psychology, 26*, 256–266.

Leonardi, R. J., Vick, S. J., & Dufour, V. (2012). Waiting for more: The performance of domestic dogs (*Canis familiaris*) on exchange tasks. *Animal Cognition, 15*, 107–120.

Marsh, H. L., & MacDonald, S. E. (2012a). Information seeking by orangutans: A generalized search strategy? *Animal Cognition, 15*, 293–304.

Marsh, H. L., & MacDonald, S. E. (2012b). Orangutans (*Pongo abelii*) "play the odds": Information-seeking strategies in relation to cost, risk, and benefit. *Journal of Comparative Psychology, 126*, 263–278.

Neiworth, J. J., Johnson, E. T., Whillock, K., Greenberg, J., & Brown, V. (2009). Is a sense of inequity an ancestral primate trait? Testing social inequity in cotton top tamarins (*Saguinus oedipus*). *Journal of Comparative Psychology, 123*, 10–17.

Nelson, T. O. (Ed.) (1992). *Metacognition: Core readings*. Toronto: Allyn and Bacon.

Nelson, T. O., & Narens, L. (1990). Metamemory: A theoretical framework and new findings. *The Psychology of Learning and Motivation, 26*, 125–141.

Nissen, H. W., & Crawford, M. P. (1936). A preliminary study of food-sharing behavior in young chimpanzees. *Journal of Comparative Psychology, 22*, 383–419.

Pelé, M., Dufour, V., Micheletta, J., & Thierry, B. (2010). Long-tailed macaques display unexpected waiting abilities in exchange tasks. *Animal Cognition, 13*, 263–271.

Pelé, M., Micheletta, J., Uhlrich, P., Thierry, B., & Dufour, V. (2011). Delay maintenance in Tonkean macaques (*Macaca tonkeana*) and brown capuchin monkeys (*Cebus apella*). *International Journal of Primatology, 32*, 149–166.

Perdue, B. M., Bramlett, J. L., Evans, T. A., & Beran, M. J. (2015). Waiting for what comes later: Capuchin monkeys show self-control even for nonvisible delayed rewards. *Animal Cognition, 18*, 1105–1112.

Price, S. A., & Brosnan, S. F. (2012). To each according to his need? Variability in the responses to inequity in non-human primates. *Social Justice Research, 25*, 140–169.

Ramseyer, A., Pelé, M., Dufour, V., Chauvin, C., & Thierry, B. (2006). Accepting loss: The temporal limits of reciprocity in brown capuchin monkeys. *Proceedings of the Royal Society of London, 273*, 179–184.

Range, F., Horn, L., Viranyi, Z., & Huber, L. (2009). The absence of reward induces inequity aversion in dogs. *Proceedings of the National Academy of Sciences*, *106*, 340–345.

Range, F., Leitner, K., & Virányi, Z. (2012). The influence of the relationship and motivation on inequity aversion in dogs. *Social Justice Research*, *25*, 170–194.

Roma, P. G., Silberberg, A., Ruggiero, A. M., & Suomi, S. J. (2006). Capuchin monkeys, inequity aversion, and the frustration effect. *Journal of Comparative Psychology*, *120*, 67–73.

Silberberg, A., Crescimbene, L., Addessi, E., Anderson, J. R., & Visalberghi, E. (2009). Does inequity aversion depend on a frustration effect? A test with capuchin monkeys (*Cebus apella*). *Animal Cognition*, *12*, 505–509.

Smith, J. D. (2009). The study of animal metacognition. *Trends in Cognitive Sciences*, *13*, 389–396.

Stevens, J. R., Hallinan, E. V., & Hauser, M. D. (2005). The ecology and evolution of patience in two New World monkeys. *Biology Letters*, *1*, 223–226.

Stevens, J. R., Rosati, A. G., Ross, K. R., & Hauser, M. D. (2005). Will travel for food: Spatial discounting in two New World monkeys. *Current Biology*, *15*, 1855–1860.

Talbot, C. F., Freeman, H. D., Williams, L. E., & Brosnan, S. F. (2011). Squirrel monkeys' response to inequitable outcomes indicates a behavioural convergence within the primates. *Biology Letters*, *11*, 680–682.

Templer, V. L., & Hampton, R. R. (2012). Rhesus monkeys (*Macaca mulatta*) show robust evidence for memory awareness across multiple generalization tests. *Animal Cognition*, *15*, 409–419.

Wascher, C. A. F., Dufour, V., & Bugnyar, T. (2012). Carrion crows cannot overcome impulsive choice in a quantitative exchange task. *Frontiers in Psychology*, *3*, Article 118.

Young, M. E., Sutherland, S. C., Cole, J. J., & Nguyen, N. (2011). Waiting to decide helps in the face of probabilistic uncertainty but not delay uncertainty. *Learning & Behavior*, *39*, 115–124.

Young, M. E., Webb, T. L., & Jacobs, E. A. (2011). Deciding when to "cash in" when outcomes are continuously improving: An escalating interest task. *Behavioural Processes*, *88*, 101–110.

Young, M. E., Webb, T. L., Sutherland, S. C., & Jacobs, E. A. (2013). Magnitude effects for experienced rewards at short delays in the escalating interest task. *Psychonomic Bulletin & Review*, *20*, 302–309.

FURTHER READING

Basile, B. M., Hampton, R. R., Suomi, S. J., & Murray, E. A. (2009). An assessment of memory awareness in tufted capuchin monkeys (*Cebus apella*). *Animal Cognition*, *12*, 169–180.

Beran, M. J., Smith, J. D., & Perdue, B. M. (2013). Language-trained chimpanzees (*Pan troglodytes*) name what they have seen but look first at what they have not seen. *Psychological Science*, *24*, 660–666.

Bräuer, J., Call, J., & Tomasello, M. (2006). Are apes really inequity averse? *Proceedings of the Royal Society of London B: Biological Sciences*, *273*, 3123–3128.

Brosnan, S. F., Freeman, C., & De Waal, F. (2006). Partner's behavior, not reward distribution, determines success in an unequal cooperative task in capuchin monkeys. *American Journal of Primatology*, *68*, 713–724.

Crystal, J. D., & Foote, A. L. (2011). Evaluating information-seeking approaches to metacognition. *Current Zoology*, *57*, 531–542.

Dubreuil, D., Gentile, M. S., & Visalberghi, E. (2006). Are capuchin monkeys (*Cebus apella*) inequity averse?. *Proceedings of the Royal Society of London B: Biological Sciences, 273*, 1223–1228.

Massen, J. J., Van den Berg, L. M., Spruijt, B. M., & Sterck, E. H. (2012). Inequity aversion in relation to effort and relationship quality in long-tailed macaques (*Macaca fascicularis*). *American Journal of Primatology, 74*, 145–156.

McAuliffe, K., Chang, L. W., Leimgruber, K. L., Spaulding, R., Blake, P. R., & Santos, L. R. (2015). Capuchin monkeys, *Cebus apella*, show no evidence for inequity aversion in a costly choice task. *Animal Behaviour, 103*, 65–74.

Parrish, A. E., Perdue, B. M., Evans, T. A., & Beran, M. J. (2013). Chimpanzees (*Pan troglodytes)* transfer token repeatedly with a partner to accumulate rewards in a self-control task. *Animal Cognition, 16*, 627–636.

Roberts, W. A., McMillan, N., Musolino, E., & Cole, M. (2012). Information seeking in animals: Metacognition. *Comparative Cognition and Behavior Reviews, 7*, 85–109.

Rung, J. M., & Young, M. E. (2014). Training tolerance to delay using the escalating interest task. *The Psychological Record, 64*, 423–431.

Schwartz, B. L. (1994). Sources of information in metamemory: Judgments of learning and feelings of knowing. *Psychonomic Bulletin and Review, 1*, 357–375.

Smith, J. D., Beran, M. J., Couchman, J. J., Coutinho, M. V. C., & Boomer, J. (2009). Animal metacognition: Problems and prospects. *Comparative Cognition and Behavior Reviews, 4*, 40–53.

Smith, J. D., Coutinho, M. V. C., Church, B. A., & Beran, M. J. (2013). Executive-attentional uncertainty responses by rhesus macaques (*Macaca mulatta*). *Journal of Experimental Psychology: General, 142*, 458–475.

Smith, J. D., Redford, J. S., Beran, M. J., & Washburn, D. A. (2010). Monkeys adaptively monitor uncertainty while multi-tasking. *Animal Cognition, 13*, 93–101.

Suda-King, C. (2008). Do orangutans (*Pongo pygmaeus*) know when they do not remember?. *Animal Cognition, 7*, 239–246.

Thierry, B., Wunderlich, D., & Gueth, C. (1989). Possession and transfer of objects in a group of brown capuchins (*Cebus apella*). *Behaviour, 110*, 294–305.

Tu, H.-W., Pani, A. A., & Hampton, R. R. (2015). Rhesus monkeys (*Macaca mulatta*) adaptively adjust information seeking in response to information accumulated. *Journal of Comparative Psychology, 129*, 147–155.

van Wolkenten, M., Brosnan, S. F., & de Waal, F. B. (2007). Inequity responses of monkeys modified by effort. *Proceedings of the National Academy of Sciences, 104*, 18854–18859.

Westergaard, G. C., Liv, C., Rocca, A. M., Cleveland, A., & Suomi, S. J. (2004). Tufted capuchins (*Cebus apella*) attribute value to foods and tools during voluntary exchanges with humans. *Animal Cognition, 7*, 19–24.

Wolfe, J. B. (1936). Effectiveness of token-rewards for chimpanzees. *Comparative Psychology Monograms, 12*, 1–72.

Young, M. E., Webb, T. L., Rung, J. M., & Jacobs, E. A. (2013). Sensitivity to changing contingencies in an impulsivity task. *Journal of the Experimental Analysis of Behavior, 99*, 335–345.

Young, M. E., Webb, T. L., Rung, J. M., & McCoy, A. W. (2014). Outcome probability versus magnitude: When waiting benefits one at the cost of the other. *PLoS One, 9*, e98996.

Chapter 9

How Do We Know Whether We Are Measuring Self-Control? Methodological Concerns Lead to a New Test

In many areas of psychological study, there are often attempts made to define important theoretical constructs and then tasks are designed that presumably measure and reflect those constructs. Ultimately, in psychology, we are limited to data that must come from observations, but we often are most interested in what we believe those observational data reflect about the components and mechanisms of minds, whether human or nonhuman. In other words, our job is to devise ways of collecting observations that we believe demonstrate the underlying nature of constructs of interest—things like memory, attention, concepts, language, theory of mind, metacognition. . .and self-control. To this point, I have discussed how psychologists and others tend to define self-control, and how we measure things such as intertemporal choices or delay of gratification so that we might use those data to better understand what self-control is, and how it manifests (or fails to manifest) in our species and in others. However, there is still the strong need in this area, like all others, to do what we can to ensure that our empirical tests are truly designed to provide insight into the constructs of interest that motivated the development of those tests. For those who study self-control, this remains an ongoing issue, and one of high importance. As I outlined earlier, there is no agreement on whether some tests truly do measure self-control, or are instead tests of other forms of behavioral inhibition, temporal discounting, or other types of impulsivity or prepotent responding. As I noted, some of the tests that have been called tests of self-control are really more about behavioral inhibition in various forms, or even controlling impulsive responses. They do not have the temporal component that many of us think is necessary to talk about self-control as a capacity for weighing "now and later" aspects of choices that also offer smaller or larger, easier or harder, or less preferred and more preferred outcomes. I have suggested that only those situations in which an individual has to make choices based on more than simply what is

Self-Control in Animals and People. DOI: https://doi.org/10.1016/B978-0-12-812508-3.00009-8
© 2018 Elsevier Inc. All rights reserved.

best now, or what delay or effort is least aversive for the same outcome, should be considered to potentially engage self-control mechanisms.

I think there is still more to be included in a definition of self-control, however, than just making such choices for delayed, better outcomes. As I suggested earlier, some forms of self-control also likely have a maintenance component to them as well as a choice component, or else one might be confusing degrees of delay discounting with self-control. Self-control is more than the measure of how one discounts the future. There must also be a component to which one can sustain the control needed to obtain a larger or better but more delayed reward. If there is agreement that delaying gratification is a form of self-control, then this becomes apparent in thinking about tests such as the marshmallow test. No child at the start of a marshmallow test would choose one marshmallow over two marshmallows (or, at least, no child I have ever met who liked marshmallows!). So of course at the time they are asked, they indicate they want to wait for two marshmallows. In some sense, if this was all we asked, we would claim all children showed good self-control! But, of course, the interesting things happen once the delay begins, and there are factors at work that can aid or sabotage the efforts of the child to wait for the better reward, and sustain their commitment to trying to obtain that better reward. For this reason, I think a test that engages the full suite of cognitive and behavioral mechanisms that are what we call "showing self-control" should engage choice and maintenance components through different aspects of that task's design. The marshmallow test does that, in this sense, by always making sure the child wants two marshmallows instead of one, even before they are put into the test itself. With this in mind, it then becomes clearer how to examine other tests that are used, and whether those tests are sufficient to examine self-control abilities. A number of tests that have been labeled as self-control tests I think fail under this scrutiny, but in some cases perhaps those tests can be combined with others to produce new tests that allow for assessing the role of choice and maintenance within participants who engage those tests.

This chapter is primarily about recent concerns regarding some approaches to using intertemporal choices (ITCs) tasks with animals as measures of self-control, by focusing on how prepotent aspects of stimuli (such as the amount of food in choice options) may bias responding in ways that confound self-control with impulsivity and threaten the validity of such tests. Thus, these tasks are problematic in their design. At the same time, I will suggest that by combining different tests that usually are used in isolation, we can generate new assessments for animals that do engage choice and maintenance mechanisms, to see when and how those may be in agreement in the behavior of animals, and when those mechanisms may be in conflict. I think this approach—examining when choice is matched with maintenance, or cannot be matched—sheds new lights on the nature of how animals and humans attempt to maximize rewards but perhaps overestimate their own abilities or fail to anticipate the aversive nature of delays relative to the attractiveness of immediate gratification.

A focus of this chapter is again on the reverse-reward contingency task that I discussed in Chapter 6, and which has been influential in the comparative literature on self-control and behavioral inhibition. The focus is also on the accumulation task discussed in Chapter 7, which is more equivalent to the marshmallow test, and I think easier to use with a wide range of species. A newer experimental approach, called the Hybrid Delay Task (HDT), is outlined, which combines an ITC test and an accumulation task within the same procedure. The HDT has shown important differences between primate species, and also has been used to highlight that, as in humans, chimpanzee self-control seems to be closely related to general intelligence.

I talked earlier about the variety of ways that ITC test have been used with humans and with nonhuman animals. This chapter focuses on one such approach that specifically involves having animals indicate one of two sets of food items reflecting a smaller-sooner (SS) or larger-later (LL) outcome. I will focus on one of the high profile reports that made use of this approach, in which chimpanzees, bonobos, and humans were tested (Rosati, Stevens, Hare, & Hauser, 2007). However, other studies also used variations on this task, demonstrating that it has become a fairly widely used assessment with nonhuman animals (e.g., Addessi, Paglieri, & Focaroli, 2011; Amici, Aureli, & Call, 2008; Rosati, Stevens, & Hauser, 2006; Stevens, Hallinan, & Hauser, 2005).

The study by Rosati et al. (2007) was an interesting and ambitious design to compare apes and humans in terms of their choices between rewards and delays. In that study, the apes were presented with repeated trials in which they could point to a smaller or a larger set of food items (Fig. 9.1A). The apes were first shown how long it would take to receive the smaller or larger set with some forced trials, in which only one of those options was available. Then, they had both options to choose between, and the researchers gave them enough trials to establish their indifference points between receiving the SS and the LL reward. These indifference points were then used to compare species, and it was found that chimpanzees showed longer indifference points than bonobos, suggesting greater self-control. More strikingly, in a second experiment it was reported that chimpanzees made more choices of the LL option than did humans given the same task of choosing between sets of real food items (Fig. 9.1B). This result suggested that chimpanzees, at least in this test, exhibited more self-control than did humans. This is a big claim, even when one is restricting it to just this particular test. Despite this book being about self-control in humans and other animals, I would argue that there is at least a fairly large quantitative difference in self-control between humans and other species. The argument is not that every human is more self-controlled than any animal, but at the species level, human self-control is ubiquitous enough and so forward-looking in many cases as to

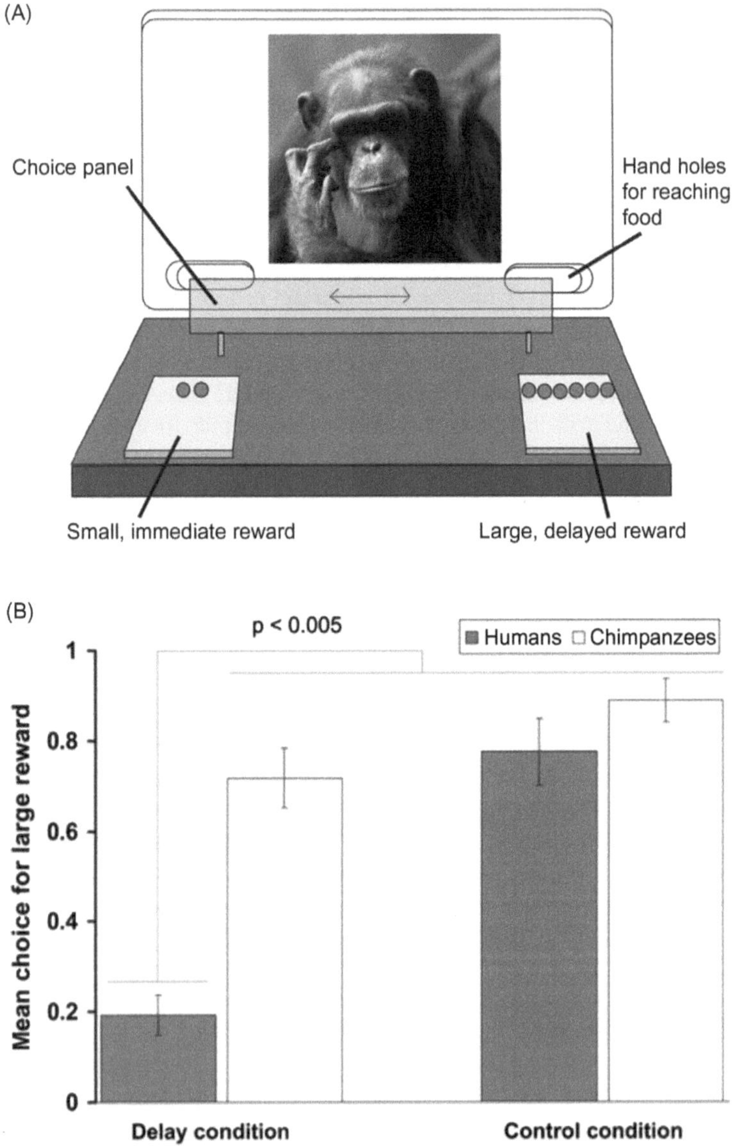

FIGURE 9.1 The top panel shows a drawing of the apparatus used in Rosati et al. (2007). Subjects could choose between a small, immediate reward (two grape halves) and a large, delayed reward (six grape halves). Subjects faced the experimenter (E) through a Plexiglas panel; this panel had hand holes on either side so subjects could insert their fingers to make choices. The experimenter sat in front of a table with two sliding platforms for food rewards. Each trial started when the experimenter removed an occluder blocking access to the table; subjects then had 15 seconds to indicate a choice. Subjects indicated their preference by sliding the

(*Continued*)

have been a key feature in our move to civilization, industry, farming and agriculture, and technological advances. Thus, when it seems that a nonhuman species outdoes our species in a task that *should be* right up our alley, the claim needs to be considered carefully. In this case, the concern seems to center on the nature of using an ITC task with food rewards as the stimuli to be discriminated and chosen.

This approach using reaches toward sets of food items has a number of appealing aspects, allowing one to see why using it might be beneficial. First, because one can present food items or other naturally high-salience stimuli, it is easy to begin to assess choice behavior quickly, without a lot of need of training animals. In many areas of comparative work, we use this *natural choice paradigm* to assess exactly these kinds of natural, spontaneous choices (Silberberg, Widholm, Bresler, Fujita, & Anderson, 1998; see Further Reading for other papers that highlight the value of that approach). Second, such an approach could allow us to test a large number of species, many of whom cannot engage the computerized apparatus or other equipment used in traditional ITC tests such as those reviewed earlier. However, some concerns were raised fairly quickly about this approach. The problem links back to something that was discussed in Chapter 6, where I outlined research on the reverse-reward contingency task. Recall that, for many species, even extensive experience in that task did not allow them to learn to point to smaller amounts of food to get larger amounts. And yet, in some of the tests I just described, researchers were claiming that by pointing to larger rewards, and then having to wait through longer delays as a result, this showed that animals were showing self-control. This struck me as inaccurate, and likely to greatly inflate the degree to which self-control really might be evident, at least in some species. How could one know what to make of a situation where an animal was both unable (or at least highly unlikely) to point away from more food and yet was "scored" as showing self-control by pointing *toward more food*? This seemed like a serious concern, and even more

◀ choice panel to uncover either the left or right hole, and then they could access their chosen food option when the experimenter slid the platform forward (immediately if subjects chose an immediate reward, but after a delay if they chose a delayed reward). The experimenter removed the unchosen option after the subject made a choice. Subjects could take as long as they wanted to eat the food, and a trial ended when the subject placed the last piece of food into his or her mouth. The next trial began after a 30 second inter-trial interval (ITI). Subjects in both studies completed no more than one session per day. The bottom panel shows the performance of human and chimpanzees in the delay condition when subjects chose between two food items available immediately and six food items available after 2 minutes, whereas in the control condition, both reward amounts were available immediately. Chimpanzee data is from their first test session. Error bars represent the standard error of mean proportional choice for the larger reward. *Both panels are from A. G. Rosati, J. R. Stevens, B. Hare, and M. D. Hauser, The evolutionary origins of human patience: Temporal preferences in chimpanzees, bonobos, and human adults.* Current Biology, 17, *1663–1668, copyright 2007, with permission from Elsevier.*

so given the claims for sophisticated self-control in nonhuman animals that seemed to accompany these results (Rosati et al., 2007).

One of the first attempts to see whether performance in ITC tests with food items might be reflective of something other than self-control came from Genty, Karpel, and Silberberg (2012). They argued that the results in Rosati et al. (2007) may have been more about impulsive responding than self-control, and they demonstrated this by giving long-tailed macaques a similar test to that given to the chimpanzees by Rosati et al. They also argued that if this was true, then the same experimental manipulations that positively or negatively affected performance on the reverse-reward task should also affect performance in this ITC task. Genty et al. specifically manipulated the visibility of the food items to see if that affected choice behavior. The idea here is that reverse-reward performance improves when chimpanzees were given symbolic (i.e., nonappetitive) stimuli to choose between because then they could point to smaller-valued stimuli. In the case of ITC tasks, however, this kind of manipulation might work in a different way. If animals have difficulty pointing away from the larger amount of food, they should look particularly self-controlled (i.e., choosing the LL option frequently) when real foods were present, but not maintain that performance when foods were not visible. In the nonvisible case the idea is that without the prepotent stimuli in front of them, animals might then point to the smaller amount associated with the shorter delay. Genty et al. therefore gave monkeys trials in which two visible food sets were the choice options, or those sets were covered with differently colored opaque containers, so that now the monkeys were pointing to the containers, and not directly to the foods. The results were striking—monkeys chose the SS option more when food items were not visible than when they were visible (Fig. 9.2). This kind of result stands in stark contrast to all that we know about how to *improve* delay of gratification in tests like the marshmallow test—by removing or covering the delayed reward one is waiting to receive so that it generates *less impulsivity*. And, Genty et al. reported that their monkeys made the "self-control" response more often in this case, when the food rewards were actually visible. Thus, this test with monkeys suggested that what appeared to be high self-control through frequent choice of the LL option was more the result of a tendency to reach toward greater amounts of food when those were present. Such data may indicate that the chimpanzees in the Rosati et al. (2007) study were not demonstrating the high levels of self-control originally proposed. Of course, these results do not mean that chimpanzees are not performing this kind of ITC test with food items as a test of self-control. The chimpanzees may have considered the time delay for more preferred rewards. But, the design of such tests allows for the influence of factors such as those that dictate reverse-reward performance to also come into play in the ITC task.

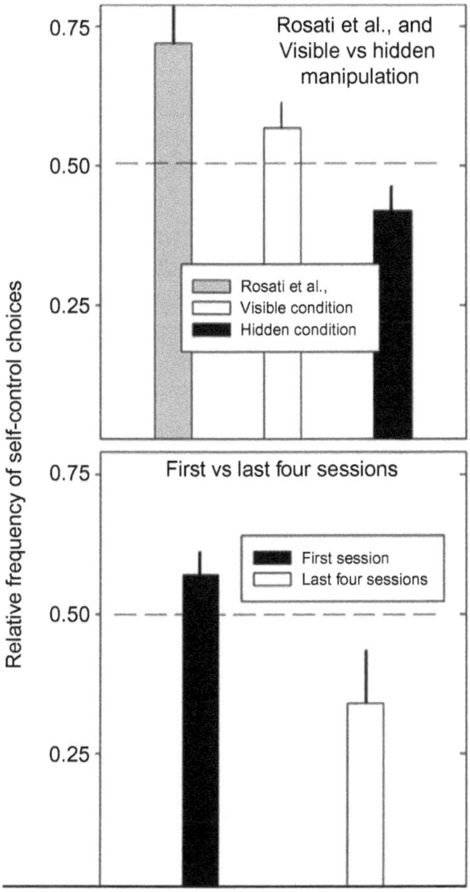

FIGURE 9.2 Top panel: frequency of choices of the larger, delayed alternative divided by all choices in a single session for Rosati et al. (2007) and the visible and hidden conditions of the Genty et al. (2012) study. Bars that end above the horizontal, dashed line evidence more self-control than impulsivity; the bar that ends below this line does not. The vertical lines within bars reflect one standard error of the mean. Bottom panel: change from a propensity toward self-control to impulsivity that occurs across sessions. *Both panels are from E. Genty, H. Karpel, and A. Silberberg, Time preferences in long-tailed macaques (*Macaca fascicularis*) and humans (*Homo sapiens*). *Animal Cognition, *15, 1161–1172, copyright 2012, with permission from Springer.*

As it turns out, other people were worried about this too. Fabio Paglieri is a cognitive scientist who works at the Institute of Cognitive Sciences and Technologies in Italy. I have discussed some of his work earlier, but he plays a central role in this chapter. By chance we met each other at a conference not about self-control. But, we soon were talking about that topic, and about some of the ITC tests that used food items with animals, and he had the same concerns that I had. Fabio is a convincing person when he hooks you onto a topic, and in this case, I was already convinced that this issue needed to be studied in more detail. So, we decided to collaborate, and he soon found his way to Atlanta for what was a very enjoyable and productive visit, working with Ted Evans and I. And, Fabio was working with another Italian researcher, Elsa Addessi, who has made many important discoveries about monkey cognitive abilities, and whose work I have referenced earlier. In fact, Elsa had already been to the Language Research Center (LRC) some years earlier, when she was working on the topic of numerical cognition and quantity judgment skills with capuchins. She had published a number of important studies on that topic (see Further Reading for this chapter), which also interests me a great deal, and so we had the chance to collaborate, and report on some of the numerical cognition abilities of the LRC's capuchin monkeys (e.g., Evans, Beran, & Addessi, 2010). Elsa's inclusion in the new collaboration with Fabio was particularly important because she already had been testing capuchin monkeys on tests of intertemporal choices, which was a big help in what we designed next. And, her work had already shown some evidence that self-control behavior was not as consistently generated even when the same animals were given a variety of tasks that purportedly all were tests of self-control. She had first given 16 capuchin monkeys a version of the adjusting delay procedure I described earlier with SS and LL choice options (e.g., Mazur, 1988) and then compared how the capuchin monkeys performed relative to other primate species tested so far with the same procedure (marmosets and tamarins; Stevens, Hallinan et al., 2005; bonobos and chimpanzees; Rosati et al., 2007). Her monkeys chose between two sets of food items, and over the course of many trials, the delay to the larger amount was varied depending on how frequently the monkeys chose that larger amount. This continued until the monkeys reached a point of equivalence, which then served as the measure of the indifference point, with longer indifference points reflecting greater self-control, or at least the degree of discounting shown by that monkey. The results of that study (Addessi et al., 2011) showed that capuchin monkeys looked much more like apes given the same basic test than like marmosets or tamarins (Fig. 9.3). So, capuchin monkeys seemed like a good species with which to test some of our concerns about general methodological issues in assessing ITCs.

With Fabio visiting Atlanta and the LRC, we thought about how we might show the degree to which pointing to food sets as part of an ITC test was or was not reliable in terms of demonstrating self-control or delay of gratification. Fabio noted that the accumulation test was not subject to the same concerns, because the "failed self-control" response was itself reaching toward and consuming food. He reasoned that we might be able to use one task embedded within the other to sort through these issues, and from those discussions and his creativity we came up with what is called the Hybrid Delay Task (HDT). The HDT is a combination of the two-choice intertemporal test, but with the twist that after that choice is made, one might find oneself in an accumulation trial. The task we designed first offered monkeys a choice—4 food items immediately, or 12 food items with a delay. So, if they reached to the smaller set, we handed that set to them immediately. But, if they reached to the larger set, rather than starting a standard or adjusting delay, we instead began an accumulation phase. For example, in that case, items might be transferred to within reach one at a time, once every 3 seconds. In this way, to get all 12 items involved a delay of 36 seconds, but

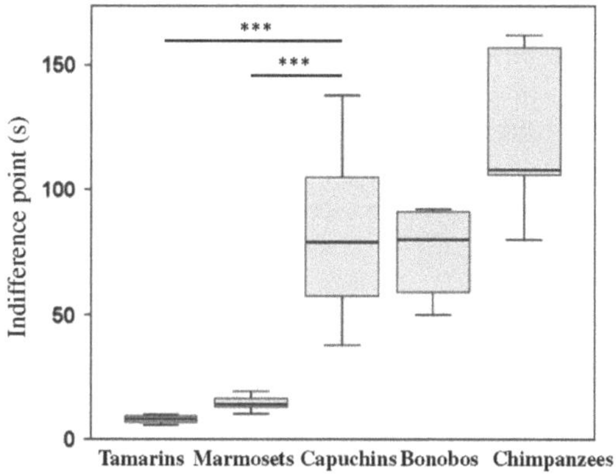

FIGURE 9.3 Indifference points (s) in an intertemporal choice task for five nonhuman primate species. Data are from Stevens et al. (2005) for tamarins and marmosets, from Rosati et al. (2007) for chimpanzees and bonobos, and from Addessi et al. (2011) for capuchins. The line indicates the median, the hinges indicate the first and third quartiles, and the whiskers indicate the minimum and maximum data values. *From E. Addessi, F. Paglieri, and V. Focaroli, The ecological rationality of delay tolerance: Insights from capuchin monkeys.* Cognition, 119, *142–147, copyright 2011, with permission from Elsevier.*

more importantly, it also involved having to inhibit taking those food items or else whatever had not been delivered yet would be forfeited.

The HDT, therefore, is one of the few tests of self-control in which one can objectively define a true error. That is typically hard to do with intertemporal choice tasks because one cannot say whether a person *should* wait 15 minutes for 5 dollars versus waiting 2 minutes for 1 dollar. As discussed earlier, there are too many factors at play for there to be a "right" answer, even if one can define a self-control response or impulsive response. There is an assumption for ITC tasks that, all things considered equal, the individual prefers the larger/better rewards, but one cannot know for sure that choices of the SS reward are not "correct" or choices of the LL reward are not "incorrect." Consider an example: if a person needed only a dollar to get home on a bus leaving in 3 minutes, then for the example above there is a conflict between self-control and needing something now that works *for this particular case*. In the same way, if someone knows they are unlikely to be able to wait through a delay period, taking the SS reward makes more sense. The HDT instantiated these ideas. Now, we could say when a mistake was made. For example, a monkey that chose the set with 12 items, but waited only 6 seconds to get 2 accumulated food items clearly made an error, given that 4 items could have been had immediately! Thus, we now had a task that let us classify choice errors based on poor abilities to show delay maintenance. At the same time, those choices could be "justified" any time an animal then waited long enough to accumulate at least as many items as were in the SS set, even if they could not wait to get all 12 of those items. The key point here is that in the HDT errors could reflect that either (1) the LL choice was not made on the basis of showing self-control but rather reflected a failure to inhibit a prepotent response towards the larger option or (2) the LL choice truly indicated that the subject was committing to a delay for better reward, but then lacked the inhibitory control to sustain that commitment, and thus showed a delay maintenance failure. How to distinguish between these two possibilities depends on the stimuli that one presents in the choice sets, as I will outline later.

So, Fabio, Ted, Elsa, and I set out to test the HDT with capuchin monkeys. We did this with monkeys at the LRC, but also with monkeys that Elsa had previously tested, and for whom she had reported some measures of ITC performance. In those earlier experiments, she had shown that indifference points for capuchin monkeys with an adjusting delay procedure (and responses toward real food items) looked closer to those of apes than other monkey species. However, as we developed and tested the HDT, we also were collaborating on a direct comparison of the delay choice task and a version of the accumulation task to assess whether performances even were related on these two measures of self-control. When we did that study (Addessi et al., 2013), we gave capuchin monkeys in Rome and in Atlanta an ITC task, in which they chose between two food sets. One set was of two items, delivered immediately, and the other was six items delivered after a delay of 80 seconds. The animals reached toward the set they wanted to choose, and they always experienced the two temporal contingencies with forced trials, where they could only pick one of the options. They kept making these ITCs until their relative preference for the options stabilized, meaning they showed a consistent level of preference for one option or the other for multiple days. The same monkeys also performed the accumulation test, where items transferred to within reach every 2 seconds, as long as none were taken. The monkeys had the chance to wait for up to 5 or up to 50 items in different tests, again depending on the degree to which they could demonstrate delay maintenance. Thus, the comparison directly assessed whether delay choice and delay maintenance were correlated in a sample of 18 capuchin monkeys. They were not (Fig. 9.4). This gave us further pause about how well ITC tasks (of this type, at least) and delay maintenance tasks tapped into a presumed common self-control ability in nonhuman primates (also see Addessi et al., 2014).

From this perspective, we began the HDT with 18 capuchin monkeys (Paglieri et al., 2013). In the first phase of the experiment, the delay interval for each accumulating item was 3 seconds, and then the monkeys experienced trials with 6-second delay intervals, and the monkeys reached toward one of two sets of real food item to make a choice (Fig. 9.5). We found that monkeys who reached toward the LL reward sets could not justify those responses with their delaying abilities once accumulation started. In fact, in many cases, we saw real errors—monkeys reached to the larger set of food, but then waited for only one or two items before eating those. To

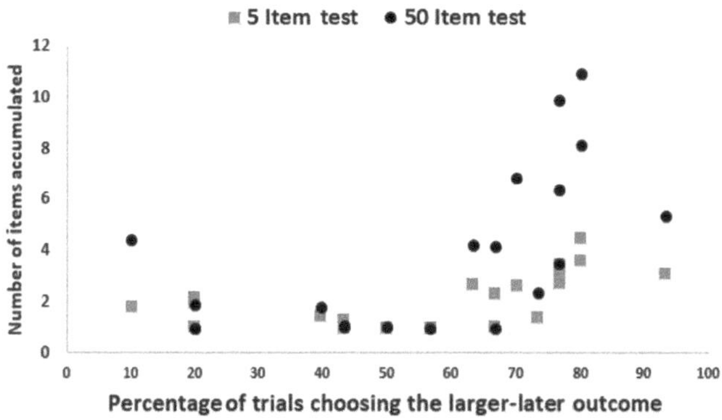

FIGURE 9.4 The relation between choices of larger-later rewards in an ITC task and the performance on accumulation of up to 5 or up to 50 items during the accumulation task. Data are from capuchin monkeys that performed both tasks, and the results show no clear relationship between performance on the two tasks. *Data are redrawn from those reported in Addessi, E., Paglieri, F., Beran, M. Evans, T. Macchitella, L., De Petrillo, F., & Focaroli, V. (2013). Delay choice vs. delay maintenance: Different measures of delayed gratification in capuchin monkeys (Cebus apella). Journal of Comparative Psychology, 127, 392–398.*

FIGURE 9.5 An image of a capuchin monkeys performing the Hybrid Delay Task. *From F. Paglieri, V. Focaroli, J. Bramlett, V. Tierno, J. McIntyre, E. Addessi, T. A. Evans, and M. J. Beran, "The hybrid delay task: Can capuchin monkeys (*Cebus apella*) sustain a delay after an initial choice to do so?"* Behavioural Processes, 94, *45–54, copyright 2013, with permission from Elsevier.*

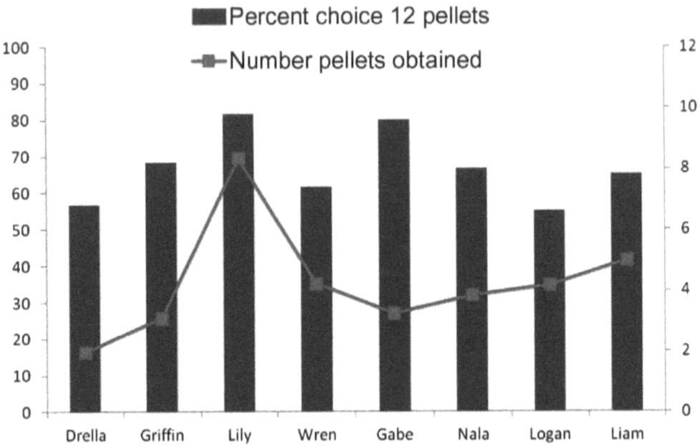

FIGURE 9.6 The performance of capuchin monkeys from the Language Research Center on the Hybrid Delay Task. For each monkey, the bars show the percentage of trials in which the monkey selected the 12-item set, and the line shows the average number of items the monkeys waited to accumulate before taking those items on trials where the 12 item set was selected. Only one monkey (Lily) waited for more items to accumulate (>4) than could have been received by choosing the immediate set, thereby avoiding the need to tolerate a delay period. *These data are redrawn from Paglieri et al. (2013).*

demonstrate this, Fig. 9.6 shows some of the data from the LRC monkeys in terms of how often they choose the LL set in comparison to the average number of items they allowed to accumulate after doing that. As you can see, only one monkey clearly justified those choices (Lily) whereas the rest either only waited to obtain about the same 4 items they could have received immediately, or in some cases waited for even fewer items than they could have received immediately. This was costly not only in terms of loss of food that could have been eaten, but truly suboptimal because the monkeys were *slowing* their rate of food acquisition at the same time that they decreased the amount of food they received by acting this way. And, the original concern about this type of ITC task was clearly evident. Had we only measured the choices between 4 items now and 12 items later, 5 out of these 8 monkeys would have look "self-controlled" (as reflected with asterisks in the figure which indicate significant preference for the LL set). And yet, the results of the accumulation part of the trials made very clear that nearly all of the monkeys had limited self-control in terms of tolerating accumulation and engaging in delay maintenance. These data, along with the finding that other direct comparisons of ITC performance and accumulation performance showed little relation between these two things (Addessi et al., 2013), makes clear that ITC tests with food items may not be the best way to measure self-control in animals, unless one cares only about the technical definition of that term (i.e., as being about choice of LL over SS outcomes). I think most people would agree that self-control, as defined as being the capacity to choose and maintain the path to obtain an objectively better, but more delayed or harder to obtain reward, is not reflected in the performance of most capuchin monkeys in the Paglieri et al. (2013) study. We concluded that capuchin monkeys actually showed limited self-control in this first test, although it was not yet possible to determine the reason for this.

One perspective that I have been discussing is that choices of the LL option may not have reflected anything about intertemporal comparisons by monkeys. What this means is that reaches toward LL sets, when those are made of highly salient food rewards, are difficult to interpret, and likely are not directly related to an underlying self-control construct. Rather, they may well reflect an actual *impulsivity* on the part of subjects, which would be very concerning. Those choices may have reflected only the strong drive to point toward more food. From this perspective, the monkeys tended to point to more food no matter the consequences. In the HDT task, those consequences often were a longer delay to get less food, because the monkeys could not maintain their delay long enough to justify that choice. In this sense, this form of ITC task is an invalid test of self-control. Another perspective, however, gives more control to the monkeys. From that perspective, the monkeys were choosing between 4 and 12 items while taking into account the delays associated with each. Thus, choices were made on the basis of intertemporal properties, but the difficulty came when delay maintenance was required. Here, capuchin monkeys showed little or no ability to maintain their delay of gratification, and so they made many objective errors. However, this perspective allows for the monkeys to be choosing through some degree of temporal comparison, but then failing to maintain delay because another regulatory system faltered. From this perspective, self-control may not be a single construct, but rather a suite of capacities brought to bear on different tasks (or phases within tasks) that we face. Performance on the HDT cannot distinguish between these two possibilities when food items are part of the two choice options, but it does allow one to see within the same individuals (and within the same instance) whether choice and maintenance are aligned in a way that supports maximizing reward.

There is another way one can work to distinguish between the possible causes of failure noted above, and that is to use symbolic stimuli. As I have described in earlier chapters regarding work with humans, such stimuli may operate to remove some of the "hot" features of tasks that promote impulsivity, and instead allow individuals to focus on the choice options and time delays as they really reflect task parameters. Thus, substituting symbolic stimuli for salient and appetitive stimuli might shed might on the nature of the problems that capuchins monkeys seemed to have in their first exposure to the HDT. So, we gave them a symbolic test next (Paglieri et al., 2013). Now, rather than reaching toward one of two sets of food items, they reached toward one of two sets of tokens that they later could exchange for food items. As before, selecting the SS set led to them receiving all tokens immediately, and they could begin to exchange immediately for real food items. But, reaching toward the LL set required them to again sit through an accumulation phase during which those tokens were transferred, one at a time, to within reach. That accumulation again continued until a monkey picked up a token, at which point no more tokens would accumulate in that trial. After giving the monkeys this test, we then returned them to the test with real food items, to see if this experience had any effect on how they performed when they had to reach toward real food items to make choice. This meant that by the end of the study, we had some monkeys that had performed the HDT with real food items to reach toward, but who then had the chance to learn to use tokens in the same task, and then try again with real rewards. The question was whether that symbolic training made a difference, and it appeared to do so. Fig. 9.7 shows the results from monkeys who were in all three phases (food pretest at 3-second delays, symbolic 3-second delays, and food posttest at 3-second delays). As you can see, these monkeys reduced their number of objective errors (choosing the LL set but then not waiting long enough to justify those choices) when symbolic stimuli were introduced, and this continued even more when they were returned to

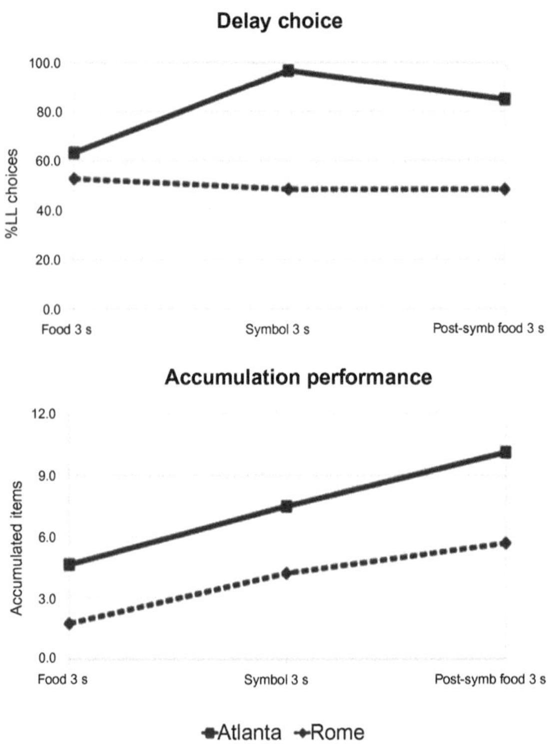

FIGURE 9.7 Mean performance of both groups of capuchin monkeys in the Paglieri et al. (2013) study. The three conditions (Food 3 s, Symbolic 3 s, Postsymbolic food 3 s) are shown for delay choice (top panel) and accumulation (bottom panel). *From F. Paglieri, V. Focaroli, J. Bramlett, V. Tierno, J. McIntyre, E. Addessi, T. A. Evans, and M. J. Beran, "The hybrid delay task: Can capuchin monkeys (*Cebus apella*) sustain a delay after an initial choice to do so?"* Behavioural Processes, 94, *45–54, copyright 2013, with permission from Elsevier.*

choosing between sets of real food rewards. What we also found was that these monkeys improved their accumulation performance at each step of this experiment. This second point is important, because it left us with a bit of an interpretive problem—was the improvement in the last phase where real foods were present the result of the training with token stimuli, which may have allowed the monkeys to approach to choice phase from a more "cool" perspective, or because general experience with the accumulation task itself led to improvement on that component of the HDT, and therefore lower error rates. Both were possibilities in this test, and so we cannot say for sure whether the token intervention aided the animals, or the additional testing time was all they needed. But, in either case, for some monkeys, the increase in experience and the chance to engage the task by responding to symbolic, nonappetitive stimuli in the choice phase aided overall performance in obtaining more rewards. We concluded that the HDT was valuable because delay choices might tell us whether a subject wanted to tolerate a delay interval for a better reward, but we then could see whether that same subject was capable of maintaining that commitment to delay, if faced with tempting alternatives.

In some ways, this last perspective on self-control makes sense, if one thinks about human choices in real situations. For example, a person may choose to autodeposit some portion of their paycheck each month into a savings account rather than take cash that can be carried around and easily spent, but then constantly "raid" that savings account later when they want to make an impulse purchase and do not have cash available. Here, one sees the same dichotomy—choices to save money appear to reflect a degree of good self-control, but after those choices are implemented, maintenance fails, and self-control looks limited and fragile. The question is whether, on the whole, one would argue that this person is showing self-control or not. That is difficult to answer, because in at least trying to save some money instead of immediately taking the full paycheck and making it accessible to spend right away, the person appears to show some future-orientation and some degree of control. However, the repeated raids into the savings account offset that sense rather strongly, and in fact almost make the person look highly ineffective if one assumes there is wasted effort and time in even setting up the automatic transfers to a savings account. My position when I think about these cases is to argue that self-control needs to be defined not only by the choices we make, but also by the capacity we have to justify those choices. Others may disagree, but I think what most people would agree about is that, for our hypothetical person in this example, there is no need to try to aid them in committing more to the act of saving money from each paycheck, because they already do that consistently. Rather, they need help staying away from those savings during the delay period when they had hoped those savings could grow. In other words, self-control failures can be defined when one knows whether the ultimate goals set by someone at choice time are met or not. The idea is that it is not as important what you choose as it is important why you choose it, and whether your subsequent behavior also supports and justifies that choice.

This last point is important, because it helps us understand why there should be times when people (and animals) choose not to wait or choose not to work harder to get more reward or better reward. Very few individuals always make the choice to wait for more, or to wait for better things, compared to taking something of value right now. In some cases, we consider this to be pathological when there is never any enjoyment in the present because everything is pushed off to the future. In fact, there is research suggesting that always focusing on longer-term goals at the expense of enjoying more immediate things (called "hyperopia", as opposed to the "myopia" sometimes invoked as a proxy for impulsivity) causes people to feel regret and remorse in many of the same ways that people who give in to impulsive choices feel regret and remorse (e.g., Kivetz & Keinan, 2006). There is also the added twist that, while regrets about failed self-control tends to fade away over time, regrets for missed opportunities of enjoyment sharpen with the passing of the years—which is also why people on their deathbed usually regret missing out on the pleasures of life (love, family, friends), rather than complaining about not having worked long enough in the office or studied hard enough in school. In fact, people who suffer from hyperopia must work to *force themselves* to indulge using some of the same strategies such as pre-commitment that other people employ when trying to engage in greater delay of gratification (Kivetz & Simonson, 2002)! People who engage in such consistent hyperopia may do so because of societal pressures, given that those around us are much more likely to comment negatively on impulsive choices than comment negatively on consistent choice to put off immediate pleasures. In fact, we elevate those we feel show such wonderful restraint (e.g., Benjamin Franklin) while laughing at or disparaging those who we feel must be in the states they are in because they lack willpower (such as those who are obese, or who engage in unhealthy behaviors even with full knowledge of the dangers). I return to this idea in the next chapter, but for now, it is enough to note that perhaps the ideal existence is one in which people (and animals) can maintain the delay of gratification they need to commit to, while also allowing enough immediate gratification to balance their sense of enjoyment or satisfaction with their lives.

A revised definition of self-control to what I offered earlier actually allows for individuals who show a strong capacity for such self-control to not necessarily be the same individuals who try most often to wait for better things. Those individuals, instead, may likely choose more immediate rewards sometimes, and for good reason. If they have the sense they cannot follow through on the commitment to that delayed reward, or they simply feel compelled in some cases to enjoy something more immediately, they can avoid one of these objective errors such as the HDT can demonstrate.

And, it may be the case that sometimes taking an immediate reward allows one to then reassert choices for more delayed and better rewards at subsequent choice opportunities, a point I will discuss in more detail in Chapter 11 and Chapter 12 where the focus is on the idea of "ego depletion." This perspective may also allow for better understanding of why occasional "cheating" on diets, or exercise regimens, is actually beneficial in the long run, although the key factor in that is being capable of finding the correct balance between "myopic" and "hyperopic" choices on the whole.

As we thought about these issues, and whether the HDT might show us patterns of choice and maintenance for sooner or later rewards, we returned to the original empirical work that led us to develop the HDT. Rosati et al. (2007) had tested chimpanzees and other apes, and as I have discussed, great apes seemed to be substantially better than monkeys in some tests of delayed gratification or other forms of behavioral inhibition. This led us to wonder whether chimpanzees would perform better on the HDT, in terms of justifying their choices. To assess this, we knew we needed more chimpanzees than just those at the LRC. So, we turned to another colleague, Bill Hopkins, who works with chimpanzees at the Yerkes National Primate Research Center, also in Atlanta. Bill has access to a lot more chimpanzees, and also is very interested in how primates control their behaviors, and how that relates to other aspects of cognition, intelligence, and brain development (see Further Reading). He agreed to work with us, testing chimpanzees with the HDT task. And the results were strikingly different.

We tested the 4 chimpanzees at the LRC, and 15 more chimpanzees at the Yerkes Primate Center. The HDT was given to each of these chimpanzees, in much the same way we had tested the capuchin monkeys (Beran et al., 2014). However, the results looked very different. The LRC chimpanzees performed particularly well. They nearly always opted for the delayed, 12-item reward. More importantly, they also exhibited the delay maintenance needed to *justify those choices*. With the same 3-second delay we had used with capuchin monkeys, these chimpanzees waited for nearly all items to accumulate. Then, we moved them to 10-second delays between the transfer of each item into their accumulation, and performance remained largely the same—the chimpanzees chose the LL option, and then waited long enough to gain more food than could have been obtained from the SS set. This pattern also held for 20-second delays, meaning that in this case, obtaining all 12 items required waiting for almost 4 minutes after making that initial choice (Fig. 9.8).

The same pattern emerged with many of the chimpanzees from the Yerkes Primate Center (Fig. 9.9). There was more variability in these chimpanzees, both in terms of their choices, and their delay maintenance, but overall they too typically showed that choices of the LL options were justified through sufficient delay maintenance. If anything, the chimpanzees from the Yerkes Primate Center were less likely to choose the LL option, which

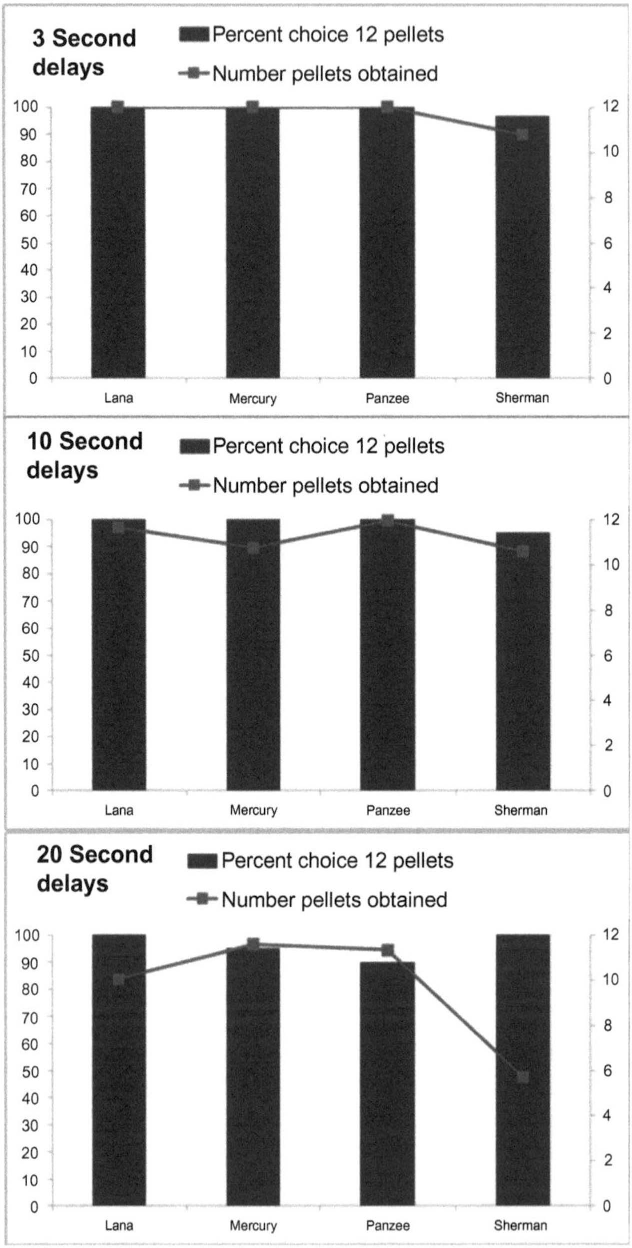

FIGURE 9.8 The performance of LRC chimpanzees on the Hybrid Delay Task, shown as in Fig. 9.3. In contrast to capuchin monkeys, the chimpanzees nearly always selected the 12-item set, but then also showed the delay maintenance needed to obtained most of those items on average. This was true not only for 3-second delays, but also for 10-second delays and 20-second delays. Thus these chimpanzees showed excellent performance on the HDT. *These data are redrawn from Table 1 in Beran, M. J., Evans, T. A., Paglieri, F., McIntyre, J. M., Addessi, E., & Hopkins, W. D. (2014). Chimpanzees (Pan troglodytes) can wait, when they choose to: A study with the hybrid delay task. Animal Cognition, 17, 197–205.*

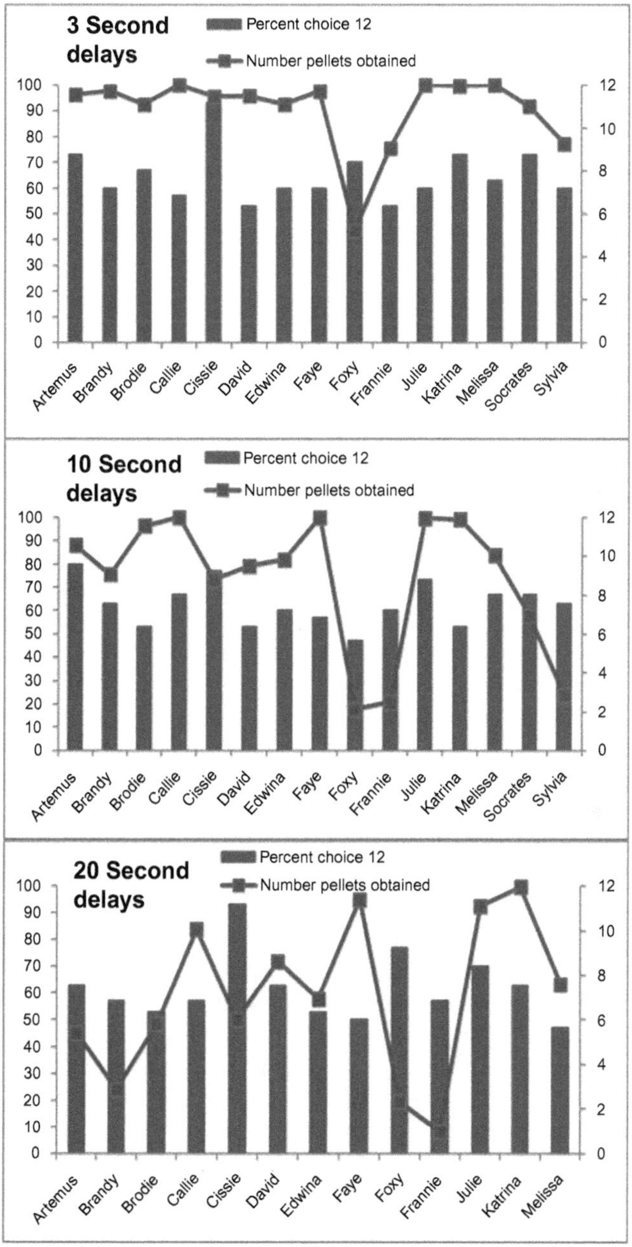

FIGURE 9.9 Data from the Yerkes Primate Center chimpanzees, shown as in Fig. 9.4. Again, one can see that chimpanzees often choose the larger set of items, but also show that they can wait for enough of those items to justify that choice. *These data are redrawn from Table 2 in Beran, M. J., Evans, T. A., Paglieri, F., McIntyre, J. M., Addessi, E., & Hopkins, W. D. (2014). Chimpanzees (*Pan troglodytes*) can wait, when they choose to: A study with the hybrid delay task.* Animal Cognition, 17, *197–205.*

offered us the chance to ask some interesting new questions in later studies. But, for this study, we established that chimpanzees performed the HDT much like one would expect if they approached the task as one in which they had to either commit to waiting through a delay or opt to take a smaller reward more immediately.

In many ways, these results complement the findings of Rosati et al. (2007), adding to the overall sense that chimpanzees (and other great apes) have the capacity to show fairly sophisticated forms of self-control. The value of the HDT, however, is that it allows for choices of a larger set of food items (or other rewards) over a smaller set to be assessed in additional ways *after* recording the intertemporal choice. And, the species contrast in both choice performance and delay maintenance shown by capuchin monkeys and chimpanzees on the HDT offers the promise that expanding the use of this task to other species may help us better understand the capacities and constraints on the different components of self-control shown across primates, and across other nonhuman and nonprimate species. The HDT also could be valuable for asking other questions about the nature of self-control, and how delay choices and delay maintenance may relate to other cognitive capacities, and to other tests of self-control or behavioral inhibition.

Bill Hopkins and I recently looked at one of these possible questions, about the extent to which self-control performance, as measured in the HDT, related to general intelligence in chimpanzees (Beran & Hopkins, 2018). As I mentioned, Bill has done tremendous work with chimpanzees looking at everything from the degree to which they show hand preferences to how their brains are "wired" as a function of their rearing, handedness, and general intelligence. This last issue is the key point here. Bill and others have developed a number of test batteries that can be given to chimpanzees that allow researchers to generate an overall intelligence score, as well as to generate subscores that allow people to see how individual chimpanzees do on various kinds of tasks (Herrmann, Call, Hernandez-Lloreda, Hare, & Tomasello, 2007; Hopkins, Russell, & Schaeffer, 2014; Schmitt, Pankau, & Fischer, 2011). For example, these tests look at aspects of social cognition, such as how well one can follow the gaze of another, or the attentional state of another, as well as tests of other cognitive abilities such as judging quantities, using tools, understanding causal relations, and using spatial memory and object permanence to figure out where things are hidden. Bill had these test scores for 40 chimpanzees, and so we gave all of them the HDT as well. The results were fascinating. We discovered that there was a strong correlation of the chimpanzees' intelligence test scores and how well they performed in the HDT. By "how well" though, I do not mean in terms of how often they chose the larger set. Rather, I mean in how efficiently they waited to accumulate items when they did choose the larger set, combined with when they chose to take the smaller, sooner set. In other words, chimpanzee intelligence as measured in the test Bill used is not most predictive of choices to wait, but is predictive of how well one waits, *when one chooses to wait*, versus taking the smaller set right away. We also found that there was a strong relation between HDT efficiency and specifically those individual tests that Bill gave the chimpanzees that were most closely related to their overall intelligence score. In other words, some tests that best "load" onto overall intelligence in chimpanzees also are most closely related to performance on the HDT. We think this is a fascinating outcome, and I hope more people will begin to study individual differences in animals' self-control as they have with humans for many years (as I outlined in earlier chapters). The results Bill and I found suggest that, as with humans (e.g., Mischel, Shoda, & Peake, 1988; Shamosh & Grey, 2008; Shoda, Mischel, & Peake, 1990), self-control is a key aspect to many other areas of intelligence and cognitive functioning. We think this is because successful inhibitory control seems to be a key aspect of many kinds of cognitive processes. I return to this point later, when I discuss the role that inhibition and self-control play in things like planning and anticipating future needs, as well as in other things such as weighing options before making choices.

Overall, our ongoing work with the HDT has led us to offer the following prescriptions for those working on topics in self-control, and specifically some ideas about methodology (also see Paglieri et al., 2017). First, to ask about ITCs by presenting prepotent, highly valuable items as part of the response mode is problematic. It is difficult in many cases, for many species, to have subjects make responses toward such prepotent stimuli on the basis of anything other than trying to obtain the better of two *immediate* rewards that are presented as part of the choice set. Thus, we need to eliminate such reaching and other motoric responses being made toward items of high value. Instead, we need to focus such reaches or responses toward other aspects of the apparatus (e.g., levers or parts of a computer screen) that are not spatially contiguous with the reward sets that signify the more immediate and more delayed rewards. This will eliminate the chance that a scored "self-control" response is, in fact, a failed inhibitory response in which that attractive larger or better reward naturally drew attention and responding. That said, if one wants to use such stimuli and such reaches, it would be good to build in a secondary measure of self-control capacity by adding something that assesses the delay maintenance component of the task. Something like accumulating the just-chosen reward set. In this way, one can record errors objectively, and also study how animals may justify (or not) their choices in one phase of a self-control task with the necessary delay maintenance. The HDT, or other tasks, could implement this secondary assessment, and therefore provide greater confidence about the relative degree of self-control an organism shows. Self-control is a multifaceted construct, and so we need to design tasks that allow for the best, and clearest, measures of this capacity in the participants that we test. The HDT is one such test, and I think it has a lot of potential for future research efforts across species.

REFERENCES

Addessi, E., Bellagamba, F., Delfino, A., De Petrillo, F., Focaroli, V., Macchitella, L., & Sbaffi, A. (2014). Waiting by mistake: Symbolic representation of rewards modulates intertemporal choice in capuchin monkeys, preschool children and adult humans. *Cognition, 130*, 428–441.

Addessi, E., Paglieri, F., Beran, M., Evans, T., Macchitella, L., De Petrillo, F., & Focaroli, V. (2013). Delay choice vs. delay maintenance: Different measures of delayed gratification in capuchin monkeys (*Cebus apella*). *Journal of Comparative Psychology, 127*, 392–398.

Addessi, E., Paglieri, F., & Focaroli, V. (2011). The ecological rationality of delay tolerance: Insights from capuchin monkeys. *Cognition, 119*, 142–147.

Amici, F., Aureli, F., & Call, J. (2008). Fission–fusion dynamics, behavioral flexibility, and inhibitory control in primates. *Current Biology, 18*, 1415–1419.

Beran, M. J., Evans, T. A., Paglieri, F., McIntyre, J. M., Addessi, E., & Hopkins, W. D. (2014). Chimpanzees (*Pan troglodytes*) can wait, when they choose to: A study with the hybrid delay task. *Animal Cognition, 17*, 197–205.

Beran, M. J., & Hopkins, W. D. (2018). Self-control in chimpanzees relates to general intelligence. *Current Biology, 28*, 574–579.

Evans, T. A., Beran, M. J., & Addessi, E. (2010). Can nonhuman primates use tokens to represent and sum quantities? *Journal of Comparative Psychology, 124*, 369–380.

Genty, E., Karpel, H., & Silberberg, A. (2012). Time preferences in long-tailed macaques (*Macaca fascicularis*) and humans (*Homo sapiens*). *Animal Cognition, 15*, 1161–1172.

Herrmann, E., Call, J., Hernandez-Lloreda, M. V., Hare, B., & Tomasello, M. (2007). Humans have evolved specialized skills of social cognition: The cultural intelligence hypothesis. *Science, 317*, 1360–1366.

Hopkins, W. D., Russell, J. L., & Schaeffer, J. (2014). Chimpanzee intelligence is heritable. *Current Biology, 24*, 1649–1652.

Kivetz, R., & Keinan, A. (2006). Repenting hyperopia: An analysis of self-control regrets. *Journal of Consumer Research, 33*, 273–282.

Kivetz, R., & Simonson, I. (2002). Self-control for the righteous: Toward a theory of precommitment to indulgence. *Journal of Consumer Research, 29*, 199–217.

Mazur, J. E. (1988). Estimation of indifference points with an adjusting-delay procedure. *Journal of the Experimental Analysis of Behavior*, 49, 37–47.

Mischel, W., Shoda, Y., & Peake, P. K. (1988). The nature of adolescent competencies predicted by preschool delay of gratification. *Journal of Personality and Social Psychology, 54*, 687–696.

Paglieri, F., Focaroli, V., Bramlett, J., Tierno, V., McIntyre, J., Addessi, E., … Beran, M. J. (2013). The hybrid delay task: Can capuchin monkeys (*Cebus apella*) sustain a delay after an initial choice to do so?. *Behavioural Processes, 94*, 45–54.

Rosati, A. G., Stevens, J. R., Hare, B., & Hauser, M. D. (2007). The evolutionary origins of human patience: Temporal preferences in chimpanzees, bonobos, and human adults. *Current Biology, 17*, 1663–1668.

Rosati, A. G., Stevens, J. R., & Hauser, M. D. (2006). The effect of handling time on temporal discounting in two New World primates. *Animal Behaviour, 71*, 1379–1387.

Schmitt, V., Pankau, B., & Fischer, J. (2011). Old World monkeys compare to apes in the primate cognition test battery. *PLoS One, 74*, e32024.

Shamosh, N. A., & Gray, J. R. (2008). Delay discounting and intelligence: A meta-analysis. *Intelligence, 36*, 289–305.

Shoda, Y., Mischel, W., & Peake, P. K. (1990). Predicting adolescent cognitive and self-regulatory competencies from preschool delay of gratification: Identifying diagnostic conditions. *Developmental Psychology, 26*, 978–986.

Silberberg, A., Widholm, J. J., Bresler, D., Fujita, K., & Anderson, J. (1998). Natural choice in nonhuman primates. *Journal of Experimental Psychology: Animal Behavior Processes, 24*, 215–228.

Stevens, J. R., Hallinan, E. V., & Hauser, M. D. (2005). The ecology and evolution of patience in two New World primates. *Biology Letters, 1*, 223–226.

FURTHER READING

Addessi, E., Crescimbene, L., & Visalberghi, E. (2007). Do capuchin monkeys (*Cebus apella*) use tokens as symbols? *Proceedings of the Royal Society of London, 274*, 2579–2585.

Addessi, E., Crescimbene, L., & Visalberghi, E. (2008). Food and token quantity discrimination in capuchin monkeys (*Cebus apella*). *Animal Cognition, 11*, 275–282.

Addessi, E., Mancinia, A., Crescimbene, L., Ariely, D., & Visalberghi, E. (2010). How to spend a token? Trade-offs between food variety and food preference in tufted capuchin monkeys (*Cebus apella*). *Behavioural Processes, 83*, 267–275.

Bellagamba, F., Addessi, E., Focaroli, V., Pecora, G., Maggiorelli, V., Pace, B., & Paglieri, F. (2015). False belief understanding and "cool" inhibitory control in 3-and 4-years-old Italian children. *Frontiers in Psychology, 6*, 872.

Evans, T. A., Beran, M. J., Paglieri, F., & Addessi, E. (2012). Delaying gratification for food and tokens in capuchin monkeys (*Cebus apella*) and chimpanzees (*Pan troglodytes*): When quantity is salient, symbolic stimuli do not improve performance. *Animal Cognition, 15*, 539–548.

Gómez-Robles, A., Hopkins, W. D., Schapiro, S. J., & Sherwood, C. C. (2015). Relaxed genetic control of cortical organization in human brains compared with chimpanzees. *Proceedings of the National Academy of Sciences, 112*, 14799–14804.

Hackenberg, T. D., & Pietras, C. J. (2000). Video access as a reinforcer in a self-control paradigm: A method and some data. *Experimental Analysis of Human Behavior Bulletin, 18*, 1–5.

Hackenberg, T. D., & Vaidya, M. (2003). Determinants of pigeons choices in token-based self-control procedures. *Journal of the Experimental Analysis of Behavior, 79*, 207–218.

Hopkins, W. D. (2013). Neuroanatomical asymmetries and handedness in chimpanzees (*Pan troglodytes*): A case for continuity in the evolution of hemispheric specialization. *Annals of the New York Academy of Sciences, 1288*, 17–35.

Jackson, K., & Hackenberg, T. D. (1996). Token, reinforcement, choice, and self-control in pigeons. *Journal of the Experimental Analysis of Behavior, 66*, 29–49.

Latzman, R. D., Hecht, L. K., Freeman, H. D., Schapiro, S. J., & Hopkins, W. D. (2015). Neuroanatomical correlates of personality in chimpanzees (*Pan troglodytes*): Associations between personality and frontal cortex. *NeuroImage, 123*, 63–71.

Latzman, R. D., Taglialatela, J. P., & Hopkins, W. D. (2015). Delay of gratification is associated with white matter connectivity in the dorsal prefrontal cortex: A diffusion tensor imaging study in chimpanzees (*Pan troglodytes*). *Proceedings of the Royal Society of London, 282*, 20150764.

Paglieri, F., Addessi, E., Sbaffi, A., Tasselli, M. I., & Delfino, A. (2015). Is it patience or motivation? On motivational confounds in intertemporal choice tasks. *Journal of the Experimental Analysis of Behavior, 103*, 196–217.

Paglieri, F., Borghi, A. M., Colzato, L. S., Hommel, B., & Scorolli, C. (2013). Heaven can wait. How religion modulates temporal discounting. *Psychological Research, 77*, 738–747.

Paglieri, F., Parisi, D., Patacchiola, M., & Petrosino, G. (2015). Investigating intertemporal choice through experimental evolutionary robotics. *Behavioural Processes, 115*, 1–18.

Parrish, A. E., & Beran, M. J. (2014a). When less is more: Like humans, chimpanzees (*Pan troglodytes*) misperceive food amounts based on plate size. *Animal Cognition, 17*, 427–434.

Parrish, A. E., & Beran, M. J. (2014b). Chimpanzees sometimes see fuller as better: Judgments of food quantities based on container size and fullness. *Behavioural Processes, 103*, 184–191.

Parrish, A. E., Evans, T. A., & Beran, M. J. (2015a). Defining value through quantity and quality - Chimpanzees (*Pan troglodytes*) undervalue food quantities when items are broken. *Behavioural Processes, 111*, 118–126.

Shaw, R. C., & Schmelz, M. (2017). Cognitive test batteries in animal cognition research: Evaluating the past, present and future of comparative psychometrics. *Animal Cognition, 20*, 1003–1018.

Stevens, J. R., & Mühlhoff, N. (2012). Intertemporal choice in lemurs. *Behavioural Processes, 89*, 121–127.

Chapter 10

Is Self-Control Like a Muscle?

My patience is wearing thin!

I am just about out of patience.

It took all I had to avoid eating that cookie at lunch, so I had to choose the chocolate cake at dinner. I had no willpower left.

Quotes like these, and many others, are probably ones you have heard or even said yourself many times. The idea being conveyed here is that our self-control, or as it is sometimes called, willpower, or patience, or ego strength, is finite in its amount, and expendable in a way in which we can seemingly run out of it, at least until we refresh it somehow. This chapter looks at the science behind whether self-control really is like a muscle that fatigues, or whether this conceptualization is incorrect or perhaps incomplete. There are very large implications of determining this, especially for those charged with trying to decrease impulsivity and increase self-control in certain populations, such as young children or adults suffering from a variety of self-control failures.

I think, without question, the manner in which we talk about self-control lends itself perfectly to why this question has been so central to research efforts over the past 15 to 20 years. First, we have come to think of self-control as being a real kind of thing—reification at its finest—rather than as a suite of mechanisms that support inhibitory control, future-oriented perspective taking, and decisional mechanisms for how to engage in behaviors that prevent impulsive responses. Setting that point aside, and assuming here that what we mean by self-control (or willpower, or patience) is, in fact, that suite of behavioral mechanisms that I discussed in Chapter 2, Varieties of Self-Control, and elsewhere, it is still a valid question as to whether those mechanisms are fallible. They could be. After all, perceptual processes are fallible, leading us to experience a wide variety of perceptual illusions. Memory mechanisms are incredibly fallible, right from the outset of perceptual processing, where we seem not to even know and remember what we actually perceived, to the limits we face in working memory, to the long-term memory deficits that occur in areas such as false memory retrieval.

Self-Control in Animals and People. DOI: https://doi.org/10.1016/B978-0-12-812508-3.00010-4
© 2018 Elsevier Inc. All rights reserved.

And, decision processes also take into account information that is not relevant or perhaps even present, or that misleads the decision maker by causing too much focus to be placed on the wrong information. So, why would self-control mechanisms be any less susceptible to limits? I have discussed the issue of temporal discounting, and how humans and other animals cannot accurately represent and reflect the true nature of the temporal delays to future possible outcomes. This impacts self-control strongly. I have talked about the mismatch between our ideas about what strategies might aid delay maintenance and delay of gratification, and how sometimes what we think will work actually does not work, and may even hurt us. This leaves open the question as to whether self-control can weaken in a way that might be analogous to the "weakening" of memory over time, due to decay and interference processes.

The analogy preferred by many of those who have been studying this idea actually comes from exercise physiology and the effect of muscle weakening. The argument is that, just as with repeated use of muscles that slowly fatigue, there is fatigue in self-control. A person doing their fourth set of bench presses in the gym, or sprinting their fourth lap around a track cannot continue at the same strength or pace as they did in the first set or first lap because the muscles that are twitching to generate force must fatigue as a function of use, and must be restored through rest or some other form of intervention. People, it has been suggested, also fatigue their self-control when they sit through a long meeting in which they want to insult their ineffective boss, and then when they leave the meeting, they lack the inhibitory resources to avoid taking two cookies from the conference room even though they are on a diet. Or, perhaps they cut back on their alcohol intake and sugary foods at a party, but then find themselves lacking the willpower to also avoid smoking a cigarette. The question that is the central focus of this chapter is whether this "depletion" is real, whether it is specific to certain kinds of self-control or behavioral inhibition contexts, and what might be done to use what we have learned about depletion of self-control to create interventions that might more rapidly or fully restore our self-control when we are depleted.

As I have noted for other chapters such as those on intertemporal choice tests that are used to study delay discounting, this chapter cannot possibly cover the vast amount of research that has been done on this topic. I have had to be selective, in what I hope is a way that allows the reader to have a general understanding of the hypotheses that are offered, and some of the evidence for and against those hypotheses. There are many other papers I could not cover, some of which are offered in the Further Reading section, and I encourage you to also read some of those, to provide full balance to what has been reported in this area of research about self-control. As you will read, this area has become a contentious aspect of self-control research, and arguably one of the most heavily debated areas within social and experimental psychology.

The core idea behind the *ego depletion hypothesis* is that one's acts of volition draw on some limited resource. That resource can be thought of as being something like a muscle, with its own strength or energy, such that one act of volition will have a detrimental impact on subsequent volition (Baumeister, Bratslavsky, Muraven, & Tice, 1998). Some think of this hypothesis as relating back to Freudian ideas about the ego adjudicating the desires of the id and superego, and doing so in an effortful way that sometimes fails to produce what the ego wants the person to do (Freud, 1923/1961a, 1933/1961b). A more modern conceptualization considers the role of executive functions in controlling behavior and cognition when the person is in a state of conflict. In this framework, *ego depletion* came to be the term used to refer to a temporary reduction in someone's capacity to engage in volitional action (such as controlling how they respond to different aspects of the environment, controlling the self in terms of different desires that were in conflict, making choices, and initiating action). Ego depletion is caused by prior exercise of volition in similar conflicted states (e.g., Baumeister et al., 1998). The notion of ego depletion in self-control was then central to a hypothesis about self-control as being a limited resource. This idea is now called the *strength model*, or *regulatory depletion model*, or *resource depletion model*, or *depletion model*, depending on the groups studying and writing about this hypothesis. Self-control research naturally lends itself to this framework, because any effort to wait for something better, or to work harder for something better, requires aspects of cognitive control and thus depletion and failures of subsequent control might occur.

Although the vast majority of this research has been conducted in the past 20 years, earlier work hinted at this idea. For example, Glass, Singer, and Friedman (1969) conducted an experiment in which they gave women various tasks to perform while also exposing them to reliable interruptions of medium or loud sound bursts, or unreliable bursts. These aversive events were designed to distinguish between conditions in which the noises could be anticipated and presumably relied on less effort to ignore as the subject gained more experience in their timing, compared to random noise interruptions which were likely to require more effort on the part of participants to ignore while working. At the end of this phase, the participants then did two other tasks. One involved an insolvable puzzle, with the measure being how many times participants tried to complete it, and the other was a proofreading task. Glass et al. reported that participants in the random noise conditions made fewer efforts to complete the impossible task (even though participants reported they thought there was a solution), and they made more errors in proofreading. In a second experiment, participants were led to believe they either controlled or did not control the offset of the noise. Here, those who thought they had control over the noise tried far more often to complete the impossible puzzles presented after the noise task. From this study came the basic idea for the methodology that has most often been used for the assessments of the strength model of self-control.

The strength model of self-control[1] consists of three ideas, as outlined by Muraven, Tice, and Baumeister (1998, p. 775): "First, the process of self-regulation consumes some resource, leaving it depleted afterward. Second, success at self-regulation depends on the availability of this resource, and possibly self-regulation may be a linear function of this resource. Third, all forms of self-regulation require some such resource, and indeed they may all draw on the same resource. These assumptions furnish the relevant prediction that an act of self-regulation will be followed by poorer self-regulation even in other, quite different, spheres." Muraven et al. also stated "It is important to note that this depletion of regulatory strength is a short-term effect only; after a period of rest it should return to its previous level. Indeed, much like muscular strength, it is possible that after repeated exertions the overall capacity for self-regulation may increase. This means that self-control in all domains may get easier after repeated attempts at self-control in one specific domain" (p. 775).

There are alternative ideas to the strength model which might also account for changes in performance in back-to-back inhibitory tasks. For example, one could argue that self-control actually improves through each occurrence, if such self-control emerges through knowledge-based schemas about how best to engage mechanisms that promote inhibition and future-oriented choice. Or, one could argue that self-control can be developed as any other skill, with improvements shown as a function of frequent engagement of those mechanisms that support self-control (e.g., Mischel, 2014). Note that in each of these cases, being exposed to back-to-back situations that require inhibition and choice for delayed reward would not affect each other negatively, and so the depletion model often has been contrasted against these ideas (e.g., Muraven et al., 1998). And, there are very different predictions for what might happen to people who are given one task to perform that requires some form of behavioral inhibition or self-control, and then given a second task.

Muraven et al. (1998) measured how long participants would squeeze a handgrip at the start of the experiment. Then, participants were exposed to a movie with difficult-to-watch scenes, and told either to express strongly their emotions or to inhibit showing any emotional reaction (a control group was allowed to watch the movie as they normally would). Then, they were given the handgrip test again. Participants who had to control their emotions as specifically directed showed less effort on the handgrip relative to those that

1. I should note that here, I will frequently use the term self-control depletion, because often that is how the authors of studies referred to it. That said, in many of these tasks, I would argue that self-control is not the appropriate way to label those tasks, as they are more likely tests of behavioral inhibition that do not require self-control as I have defined it earlier.

were allowed to express their emotions normally, and this effect was strongest for those who had to inhibit their emotional responses to the movie. In a second experiment, some participants were told to inhibit thinking about a white bear, some were told to think carefully about a white bear, and some were given no such instructions. All participants then were given unsolvable anagrams to see how long they would try to solve them. People who had to inhibit thinking of the bear showed the least persistence with the anagrams. In a third experiment, some participants performed moderately hard math problems, and others wrote out words while trying to not think about white bears. Both groups then watched comedy skits and were told not to react. Those who had tried to not think of white bears had more trouble not reacting to the comedians. These experiments all hinted toward a depletion of self-regulatory abilities when participants had to engage such abilities in back-to-back tests.

Baumeister et al. (1998) moved this approach closer to tasks that likely involved more traditional measures of self-control. In one experiment, participants were told to eat radishes while forbidden chocolate chip cookies were in view, compared to another group that was told to eat the cookies instead, and a control group that did not see any food. All individuals then were given impossible puzzles to try to solve. Participants who ate cookies or who saw no food worked twice as long at those puzzles than did those who had to inhibit eating the cookie and instead eat undesirable radishes. In another experiment, participants gave a speech either advocating for tuition increases (something these students almost certainly were not in favor of in real life), or for lower tuition, or they gave no speech. Importantly, for those giving speeches, some were allowed to choose which way to argue and others were forced to make one of those arguments (for or against tuition raises). Those who had a choice and agreed to give the speech against their own true attitudes about tuition raises were least likely to keep working at unsolvable problems. Oddly, even those who chose to make a speech in line with their own beliefs were less willing to continue working on the puzzles, leading Baumeister et al. to suggest that making choices are themselves depleting events. A third experiment involved participants watching a comedy skit freely, or while trying to inhibit emotional responses to the skit. Again, those who had to inhibit their emotions showed less persistence when given a subsequent difficult task. Across all of these studies, the manipulations did not seem to differentially affect the moods of participants, suggesting that their persistence was not based on mood differences. And, there were not any differences in reported arousal for the different groups, suggesting this was not the cause of the differences in persistence in the face of difficult effort needed to engage the second tasks. Rather, Baumeister et al. concluded that these experiments showed a common resource was engaged in all tasks, and that this resource could become depleted, to the effect of causing trouble with a second task that relied also on that resource.

Subsequent work produced similar results. For example, Vohs and Heatherton (2000) had participants watch a video while there were snacks present in the room. For some people, the snacks were close by, whereas for others they were farther away in the room. Then, the participants had to fill out a survey about that video. Some were told they could eat the snacks while doing so, but others were told they needed to leave the snacks alone. All participants then moved to another location where they were offered the chance to eat as much ice cream as they wanted while they rated the various flavors of ice cream. A key manipulation was that some participants identified as being on a diet, and others did not. The results showed that people on a diet who had to force themselves not to eat the first snacks of their own choosing when those snacks were close by (i.e., those were told they could have snacks if they wanted), ate far more ice cream later on than dieters who chose not to eat far away snacks during the movie, or those dieters who were explicitly told not to eat any snacks. The pattern was different for nondieters who did not show any differences in ice cream consumption based on the earlier conditions of snack availability (Fig. 10.1). A subsequent experiment showed that the same manipulation of presenting snacks that were off limits, or freely available, led to changes in how long dieters would engage in a difficult later task, in line with the idea that having to inhibit eating freely offered snacks was more detrimental to later perseverance on the hard task. And, another experiment showed that participants who watched a highly emotional movie clip after being told to try to restrain any emotional responses to that clip also ate more ice cream in the subsequent phase of the experiment.

In another study (Muraven, Collins, & Neinhaus, 2002), participants were told they could sample two beers and give ratings of those beers, but this was right before they would take a driving test for which they were rewarded for good performance. Thus, there was a longer-term motivation for not drinking too much alcohol during a free period before the driving test. But, some participants also were made to engage first in a thought suppression test about the white bear (seemingly effortful) or they completed math problems (relatively less effortful in terms of self-control expenditure). Those who had to suppress thoughts of the white bear drank more alcohol that those doing math problems, suggesting that such thought suppression depleted subsequent self-control for inhibiting alcohol consumption (the immediate desire) so as to do well on the driving test (the longer-term goal). Mood states again were similar in the two conditions, confirming that it was not motivational or affective states that led to depletion effects. By the way, if you are wondering, none of these people actually took a real driving test! But, the broader implications are serious ones. Many people choose to be the designated driver, for example, when going to social events. This research might suggest that people who are then challenged in terms of other inhibitory or self-control needs may not be able to deal with continued desire to

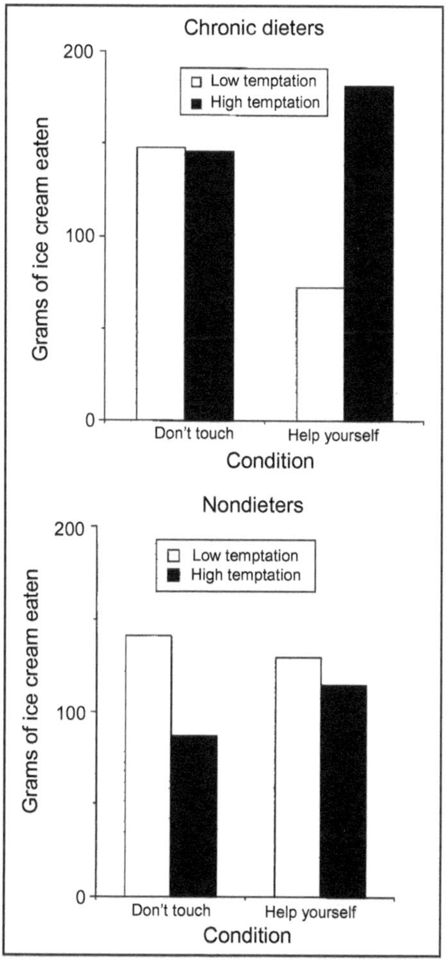

FIGURE 10.1 Effects of dieting status, temptation level, and availability condition on eating behavior (ice cream in grams) in Study 1 of Vohs and Heatherton (2000). Dieters who had to restrain themselves from eating freely available snacks that were close by later ate more ice cream than those with snacks further away, or those who were told to leave the snacks alone. *From Vohs, K. D., & Heatherton, T. F., Self-regulatory failure: A resource-depletion approach.* Psychological Science, 11, *249–254, copyright 2000. Reprinted with permission of Sage.*

consume alcohol. Imagine, for example, being the designated driver and then having to spend time at a party where a former romantic partner was present who you want to talk to, but know you should not. If the depletion model is correct, it is easy to see how such continued inhibition with that ex-partner might lead to increased drinking later in the evening (also see Tice, Bratslavsky, & Baumeister, 2001). Or, something less emotionally arousing may even occur early in the night, such as deciding you are going to avoid the high fat chocolate cake sitting among the party food, and then later trying to stop drinking early so as to be able to drive everyone home. This just might backfire, and in this case, if the depletion model is accurate, having that slice of cake might save your life. But, that would largely depend on whether both of those circumstances really do rely on the same unitary self-control resource.

Other possible explanations for these types of depletion effects also were tested. For example, one idea is that depletion might occur when people feel some sense of failure or frustration at the first task (e.g., having to inhibit eating something they want, or having to try to withhold emotional responding). However, this did not seem to be the case. When people had to perform a difficult inhibitory task in which they either were told how well they were doing or were not told, their subsequent persistence on an impossible figure-tracing task was not affected differentially by getting any feedback (Wallace & Baumeister, 2002).

Moving beyond unsolvable puzzle-type tasks, researchers have investigated the role of ego depletion in financial decision-making in efforts to link the literature to real-world scenarios that occur on a daily basis. For example, purchasing decisions also have been reported as being susceptible to depletion. Vohs and Faber (2007) reported that people made more purchases, spent more money, and were more impulsive in their purchasing choices when depleted by an earlier task. Vohs and Faber noted that Hoch and Loewenstein (1991) had clearly outlined that consumer decisions reflected an ever-shifting conflict between desire and willpower. Specifically, when people have a strong desire for a product, relative to an immediately weaker desire not to spend, impulse buying can occur. Vohs and Faber noted that this might be because the desire to buy allows for more immediate gratification whereas the desire to not buy is based on some type of delayed gratification (e.g., having that money available later, or getting an even better product later). In their study, Vohs and Faber first had people watch videos and either actively inhibit reading words at the bottom of a screen, or not inhibit that behavior and read the words as they chose. Then, they gave ratings for the values of products. Those who inhibited word reading gave higher price values, suggesting a greater willingness to pay more for those products. Other participants performed a first task in which they either avoided thinking of white bears or were told to think of anything they wanted including white bears. Then, they had the unanticipated chance to spend their prize money from being in the experiment on small-cost items. Those who had to inhibit thinking of the bear spent more of their money than those who did not have to inhibit, and this effect was particularly strong for participants who had scored highly on a scale of impulsivity in buying (Fig. 10.2). In a third experiment, participants had to read boring texts either as they chose or with the direction that they had to act excited and highly engaged about reading that text. Those who were forced to maintain

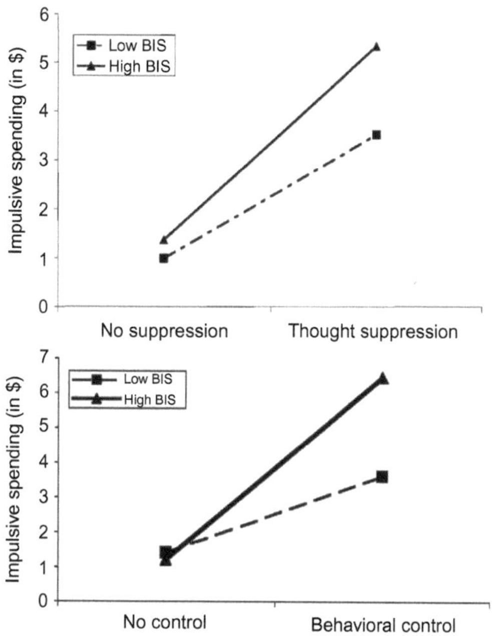

FIGURE 10.2 Results from Vohs and Faber (2007). The top panel shows Experiment 2 results. No Suppression stands for random assignment to a condition in which no self-control demands are placed on the subject. Thought Suppression stands for random assignment to a condition wherein participants are asked to suppress thoughts of a white bear during a thought-listing exercise. The bottom panel shows Experiment 3 results. Behavioral Control stands for random assignment to a condition in which participants are asked to exaggerate facial expressions and gestures while reading aloud a nonemotional text. No Control stands for random assignment to a condition in which participants read aloud the same nonemotional text but were allowed to do so naturally. In both panels, Low buying impulsiveness scores (BIS) and High BIS are categories of participants on the basis of their buying impulsiveness scores, which was split at the median for illustrative purposes. Impulsive Spending (in $) is the mean amount of dollars spent during a buying impulsive spending situation. *From Vohs, K. D., & Faber, R. J., Spent resources: Self-regulatory resource availability affects impulse buying.* Journal of Consumer Research, 33, *537–547, copyright 2007. Reprinted with permission of Oxford University Press.*

excitement about the material subsequently spent more money than the other group (Fig. 10.2).

If the depletion model is valid, and if self-control operates much like a muscle might operate, then an important question is whether self-control can be strengthened through practice in the same way muscles can be strengthened through training. This also had been a lively area of research, with mixed results. In some cases, there do appear to be benefits to "exercising" self-control abilities in one domain and then seeing improvements occur in others. For example, Muraven (2010) had adults perform a stop signal task at the outset of their study. This is a test of inhibition, where ongoing activity must be inhibited when a particular cue occurs. In this case, people had to press the right button if a square appeared on the right side of a fixation point and to press the left button if a square appeared on the left side of a fixation point. The trick was that on some small percentage of trials a tone also sounded. When that happened, people need to suppress any button presses even though a square might be there. After assessing people at the beginning, some then were given exercises such as cutting back on sweets or squeezing a handgrip over a two-week period. Those individuals performed better on the second stop signal task compared to people who had not been instructed to "exercise" self-control. Muraven argued that it was only the practicing of self-control, and not any other intermediate behavioral changes, that led to improvements in the stop signal task. However, it is important to note that this is not a case of depletion, which has been hypothesized to only occur within limited time windows, and so this finding is not at odds with other ideas about how repeated efforts to engage self-control in some contexts can transfer to better self-control in others (e.g., Mischel, 2014). Whether such training of self-control over a few weeks is effective in preventing decrements in second-task performance after self-control and inhibitory mechanisms are engaged in a first task remains to be studied.

Webb and Sheeran (2003) studied the effects of implementing intentions during inhibitory tasks on subsequent depletion. They had participants complete a Stroop task or control task. The Stroop (1935) task involves naming the colors of word letters on a screen rather than reading the color names themselves. So, for example, a particularly hard trial would be one in which the letters were green (the correct answer) but they made up the word YELLOW (the incorrect answer). Half the people given the Stroop test also were told to form and mentally state the intention to carefully ignore the word meaning and attend only to its color. When people formed these intentions during the first task they performed as well or better than control participants on a second task, showing no depletion. Dang, Dewitte, Mao, Xiao, and Shi (2013) also showed that people can adapt to the first test in a way that prevents any kind of depletion. This study is particularly interesting because this adaptation took the form of doing *more of the first task*, which should have truly depleted participants, but it did not. Instead, those participants who did three times as many Stroop trials showed less depletion compared to participants who did less of the Stroop task before moving on to the second task which involved a high-effort search task for strings of numbers. Although these data seem to argue against the depletion model, I am not convinced that the second task is truly a task for which self-control (even in its most liberal definition) is required. Instead, it seems likely that when people work longer on a hard task at which they improve, such as the Stroop test, they may be more focused for subsequent tasks that involve visual search or other perceptual-cognitive mechanisms.

There have been other claims of how to reduce depletion effects. For example, Chow and Lau (2015) reported that exposure to nature scenes offsets depletion effects compared to control conditions with no such exposure. Other research suggests that religious priming (where religious-themed statements are offered during testing) protects against depletion effects and improves some kinds of self-control or delay of gratification (e.g., Rounding, Lee, Jacobson, & Ji, 2012). And, if religion is not your thing, money probably is, and introducing the topic of money between tasks also seems to minimize depletion effects (e.g., Boucher & Kofos, 2012). Other claims were made that when depletion does occur, it likely produces unwanted outcomes, and unethical behaviors, such as cheating (e.g., Gino, Schweitzer, Mead, & Ariely, 2011).

If, at this point, you are beginning to wonder if these depletion effects are ubiquitous, and there is consensus on the strength model of self-control even if there is still debate about the mechanisms that underlie depletion, the answer is a strong No. Although there have been many reports of depletion effects, and numerous reports of how to intervene in those depletion effects with approaches that seem to insulate people from depletion compared to control groups that do not experience the interventions (such as nature images, thoughts of money, etc.), there is an equally influential literature that highlights that no depletion effects were evident in attempted replications and extensions of the two-tasks design.

For example, Xu et al. (2014) reported that in four experiments they failed to find any evidence of depletion effects, using the same tasks from previous experiments such as letter searches, handgrips, and others (e.g., Baumeister et al., 1998). They also assessed different populations (older and younger adults), and overall found that the change from a pretest to a posttest measure of self-control with an attempt to deplete resources in between had little to no effect. In fact, numerically speaking the effects that were observed were in the opposite direction of that expected if depletion were at work (Fig. 10.3).

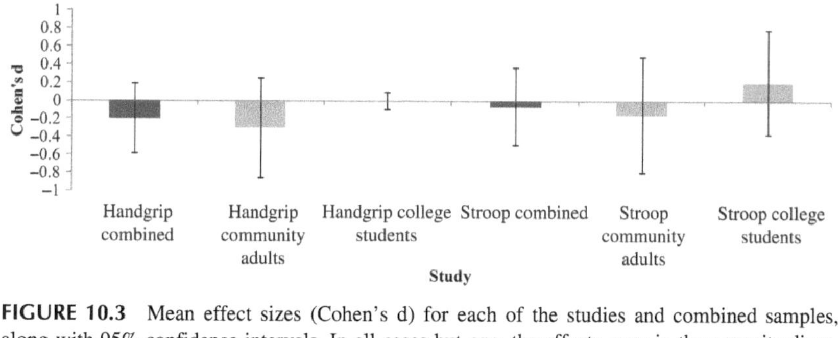

FIGURE 10.3 Mean effect sizes (Cohen's d) for each of the studies and combined samples, along with 95% confidence intervals. In all cases but one, the effects were in the opposite direction from that expected by the depletion hypothesis. *From Xu, X., et al., Failure to replicate depletion of self-control.* PLOS ONE, 9, *e109950, copyright 2014. Reprinted with permission of the authors.*

In other cases, the evidence of depletion effects seems rather strange because that depletion occurs even in tasks that do not assess self-control. For example, people who were asked to make choices between products versus just rate those products showed less willingness to engage in drinking an ill-tasting drink for money, less willingness to leave their hands in cold water, and less willingness to study math problems and other unsolvable problems (Vohs et al., 2008). It is difficult to reconcile the action of making choices with being a self-control response, or even an inhibitory response, and so these effects seem to challenge the idea of self-regulatory depletion as the mechanism at work when people will not engage in a second task that does require some kind of sustained behavior in the face of competing desires to do something else (e.g., not drink the bad beverage, take one's hand out of cold water, or stop doing math problems). An alternative explanation is that people fatigue or even lose motivation in back-to-back tests, regardless of whether those tasks involve self control depletion or not.

Although one might expect that other states would also impact depletion, this does not appear to be the case. For example, one might assume that being sleep deprived would increase depletion. To test this, Vohs, Glass, Maddox, and Markman (2011) sleep deprived some people while allowing others to sleep normally. Then, some participants had to suppress their emotional reactions to a movie while others watched the movie normally. Finally, all participants played a competitive game in which they could decide how loudly a sound was blasted at the opponent when they beat them. The idea was that more aggressive blasts would be chosen when participants were more depleted, which was true, in terms of those people who had to suppress emotions during the movie choosing louder blasts. But, this effect did not interact at all with sleep deprivation (Fig. 10.4), indicating that depletion effects are not the result of sleep-based fatigue.

These results, and many others that I do not have space to describe, led to new ideas about the mechanisms underlying depletion effects. For example, Inzlicht and Schmeichel (2012) suggested that when a person must engage in self-control or some form of inhibition in the first task, this sets in motion a pair of interdependent and iterative processes that lead to weaker self-control in the second task (Fig. 10.5). They argued that this happens because in the first task people experience a shift in motivational orientation and a shift in attentional focus. Those two things then undermine efforts to engage self-control or inhibitory mechanisms in the second task. In other words, after waiting, or inhibiting, or controlling behavior in the first task, people seek easier and faster gratification in the second task. Their motivation to perform well in the second task decreases, because they do not want to continue to engage in self-control. In addition, there is weaker monitoring of those cues that are necessary to inhibiting or delaying gratification, presumably because of attentional shifts. Thus, the "depletion" is less about self-control itself, and more about the motivation and attentional mechanisms

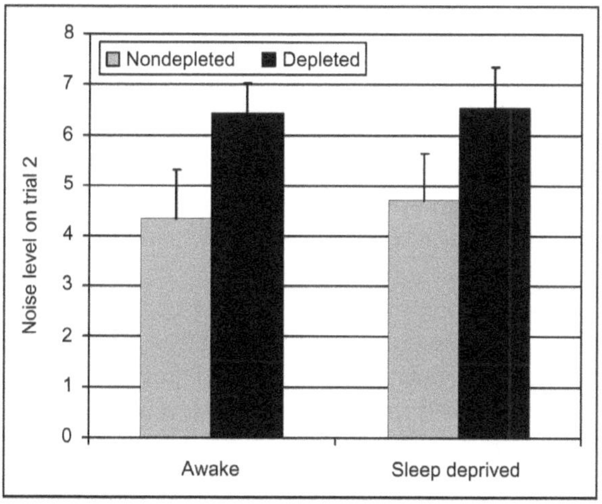

FIGURE 10.4 Noise volume selection in Trial 2 as a function of sleep deprivation condition (rested vs. sleep deprived) and depletion condition (depleted vs. nondepleted). *From Vohs, K. D., Glass, B. D., Maddox, W. T., & Markman, A. B., Ego depletion is not just fatigue: evidence from a total sleep deprivation experiment.* Social Psychological and Personality Science, 2, *166–173, copyright 2011. Reprinted with permission of Sage.*

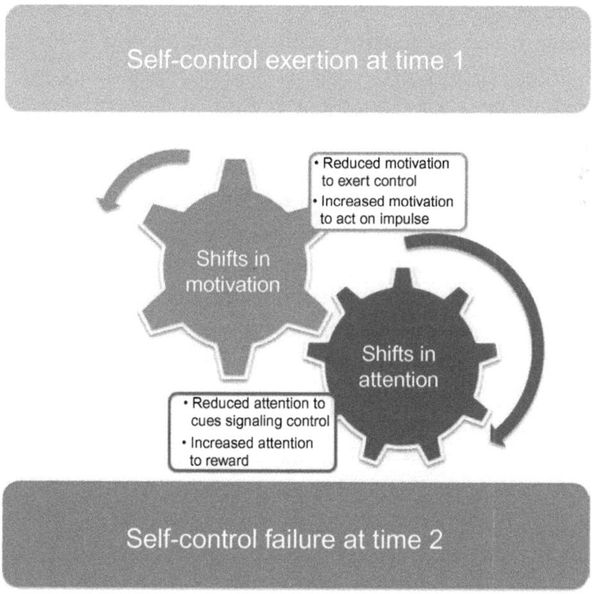

FIGURE 10.5 The process model of ego depletion as outlined by Inzlicht and Schmeichel (2012). Self-control exertion at Time 1 leads to self-control failure at Time 2 by inducing shifts in motivation away from self-regulation and toward self-gratification and attendant shifts in attention away from cues signaling the need for control and toward cues signaling reward. *From Inzlicht, M., & Schmeichel, B. J., What is ego depletion? Toward a mechanistic revision of the resource model of self-control.* Perspectives on Psychological Science, 7, *450–463, copyright 2012. Reprinted with permission of Sage.*

that are necessary for making self-control choices or inhibiting more prepotent responses. Inzlicht, Schmeichel, and Macrae (2014) further argued that self-control deficits from one task to another were not the result of resource limits, but instead occurred because of motivated switching of task priorities. In other words, people came to engage the second task more on the basis of what they wanted than on the basis of what they were supposed to do. Of course, it is not at all clear what determines when people follow "have to do" rules versus "want to do" preferences, and so this does not feel as if it is a truly different perspective on changes in self-control and inhibition with repeated tasks that would require such behaviors.

Other somewhat odd outcomes have been reported. Clarkson, Hirt, Jia, and Alexander (2010) found that how people perceived the idea of resource depletion predicted performance patterns more than did the actual depletion that was seen when back-to-back tasks were completed. Similarly, Job, Dweck, and Walton (2010) found that what seemed to really be the basis for depletion effects were people's *beliefs about how self-control worked* more than any actual depletion that might be based on physiological factors. In that study, people who thought self-control was unlimited did not show depletion effects as strongly as did people who did think about self-control as being limited. And, other research teams found evidence that the depletion effect was more closely related to how people monitored their own behavior rather than being based on actual resource depletion (e.g., Wan & Sternthal, 2008).

With so many empirical reports emerging that assessed depletion effects, it became clear that meta-analyses would be valuable in trying to understand the prevalence and potential mechanisms of depletion effects for self-control. Hagger, Wood, Stiff, and Chatzisarantis (2010) conducted one of the first meta-analyses of ego depletion.[2] While examining published works available at that time, Hagger et al. also examined the role that recovery, training, and conservation might play in this phenomenon. Recovery refers to the time between tasks, and what role that might play if self-control, like a muscle, recovers with the passing of time (e.g., Tyler & Burns, 2008). Conservation refers to the idea that self-control can never be fully depleted, because people always reserve some capacity. For example, when people were told that a third self-control task was still forthcoming, those people showed more depletion than participants not expecting another task to be forthcoming

2. This article very nicely outlined the alternative explanations for the data that were emerging from these studies, including ideas about the role of motivation, fatigue, skill development, self-efficacy, experimenter expectations, and affect. I recommend reading that article to more fully understand the nature of each of those alternate explanations, and to see some of the efforts to discount those alternate ideas, given that I do not have space here to cover those in the detail that they deserve. For my purposes, this paper is relevant because the conclusion from the meta-analysis was that evidence for ego depletion and the strength model was strong.

(Muraven, Shmueli, & Burkley, 2006; Tyler & Burns, 2009). And, training involves the idea that people can actively "build" their self-control through repeated experiences of engaging in forms of inhibition or active cognitive control, as discussed earlier. For example, when people were told to perform programs of academic study, physical exercise routines, and new ways of monitoring their finances for periods of weeks or months, they later reported being more effective in managing other everyday behaviors that presumably required self-control (Oaten & Cheng, 2006a, 2006b, 2007). Thus, these kinds of outcomes would be expected to occur given the major aspects of the strength model of self-control. When Hagger et al. completed the meta-analysis, they found a medium to strong effect of ego depletion, and stated that it was highly unlikely that there were enough null effects in existence to reduce the depletion effect to a trivial level. In addition, training and conservation both showed strong effects, indicating that both played a role in performance on second tasks across studies that included those aspects. Significant effects also were found for ego depletion on effort, perceived difficulty, negative affect, subjective fatigue, and blood glucose, which the authors concluded were reflections of the effortful, aversive nature of self-control tasks. Overall, these authors concluded that there was a depletion effect evident in the available literature.

However, this conclusion was not universally accepted. Carter and McCullough (2014) reported that the meta-analysis of Hagger et al. (2010) was inadequate. Their own application of methods for estimating and correcting for small-study effects led them to conclude that there were strong signals of publication bias, along with concluding that, in fact, there was little evidence to support a depletion effect in the published literature. They argued that we still cannot know whether the depletion effect is real, and more empirical work is needed on this question before we move to trying to elaborate on the model and establish its potential mechanisms. Carter, Kofler, Forster, and McCullough (2015) also tested the depletion effect with data from both published and unpublished experiments. They used improved inclusion criteria, and employed different statistical techniques. They reported that their analysis revealed signals of small-study effects (which occur when larger samples produce smaller effect size estimates). They concluded that "After accounting for small-study effects, we found only scant evidence that the depletion effect is distinguishable from zero" (pp. 796). Of course, these meta-analyses also then faced criticisms, but the point is that this large (and growing) literature is seemingly open to alternate interpretations of the actual role of depletion (if any).

What has really instigated the major debate in this area of research is the idea that ego depletion is the result, at least in part, of a specific physiological change—glucose depletion. From the earliest reports of behaviorally evident depletion effects, researchers kept noting that there was no evidence yet as to what the mechanism(s) might be that supported self-control, and presumably that led to depletion of self-control. However, that changed when researchers began to consider what role blood glucose might play in self-control. Galliott and Baumeister (2007) were among the first to comment on the link between glucose and self-control, a link they argued makes intuitive sense given other things we know about glucose. Alcohol reduces or affects glucose metabolism throughout the brain and body (e.g., Volkow et al., 1990), and of course alcohol use is often associated with reduced inhibition and increased impulsivity. Self-control failures also tend to occur at times when glucose is used least efficiently, such as late at night (Baumeister, Heatherton, & Tice, 1994). From these ideas came the search for direct links between glucose and self-control, as well as glucose depletion and self-control depletion.

Galliott et al. (2007) were the first to report such a link. They also had noted that poor self-control was linked to things such as criminal behavior (Gottfredson & Hirschi, 1990), and criminal behavior has been linked to glucose processing deficits (e.g., Bolton, 1979; Virkkunen & Huttunen, 1982). They also noted the relation that may exist between glucose and aggression and impulsive behavior (Donohoe & Benton, 1999; Lustman, Frank, & McGill, 1991), and so they set out to see how glucose might impact depletion directly. First, Galliott et al. confirmed that people who had to watch a movie while inhibiting looking toward words at the bottom of the screen showed greater decreases in blood glucose levels compared to those who did not have to inhibit behavior that way. Next, they showed that people who had to work harder to try to talk with a person of another race also showed greater decreases in blood glucose, presumably because of the effort required to inhibit saying anything offensive. Next, they presented participants (adults) with back-to-back tasks of inhibitory control and self-control to explicitly examine the link with glucose. They found that across a variety of paired tasks, those people who showed the greatest behavioral depletion in terms of performance on the second task also were most likely to show the largest drops in blood glucose. Then, they intervened in the depletion by giving participants a glucose-rich drink between the two tasks. When people had to watch videos with directed attention away from distracting events, and they were given glucose before performing the second task (a Stroop test), they showed no depletion effects (i.e., Stroop performance as just as good), whereas control participants who drank a placebo drink with no glucose showed depletion as reflected in more errors on the Stroop test (Fig. 10.6). Galliott et al. conducted additional tests, too, showing that various tasks that required controlling behavior or inhibiting natural responses led to depletion, unless glucose was given to offset that depletion.

Given the excitement surrounding these first results with glucose, many additional studies were undertaken, and there was a sense that there could be a "magic bullet" intervention for poor self-control. However, the picture quickly became muddled. For example, Kurzban (2010) reanalyzed the data

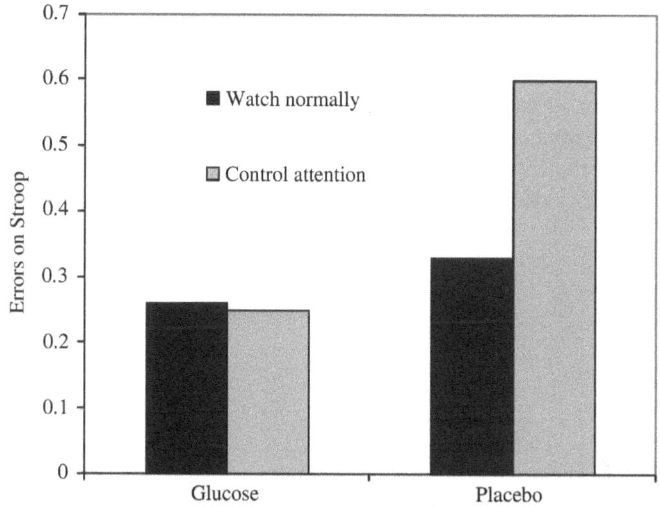

FIGURE 10.6 The degree of depletion seen in participants who drank glucose or did not between an inhibitory task and performance of a Stroop test. *From Gailliot, M. T., et al. "Self-control relies on glucose as a limited energy source: Willpower is more than a metaphor.* Journal of Personality and Social Psychology, 92, *325–336, copyright 2007. Reprinted with permission of the American Psychological Association.*

from Gailliot et al. (2007) and found that only some participants demonstrated the expected drop in glucose level following self-control. Kurzban also noted that some participants actually showed an increase in glucose level, and concluded that there was no relation between changes in glucose level and self-control performance. Other results also appeared to be at odds with the ideas of the depletion model. Molden et al. (2012) found that glucose can enhance self-control even when it is not ingested. Rather than drink liquids with glucose, they had their participants only rinse their mouths, and then engage in a second self-control task. And yet they also found that this manipulation eliminated any depletion effects, even though there was no increase in glucose in the participants' blood. Sanders, Shirk, Burgin, and Martin (2012) also had participants simply gargle with a glucose solution, and they also reported no depletion effects, suggesting that the mere sensing of glucose might be sufficient to offset depletion.

In other cases, however, research teams completely failed to find any effect of glucose offsetting depletion. Lange and Eggert (2014) conducted two studies with large numbers of participants and found no evidence that glucose ingestion or gargling offset depletion effects. This was true, for example, in tests in which participants were at increased risk for making more false alarm responses and more interference effects in a Go–No Go test of inhibition on the second task compared to the first. This was true no matter whether they swished or ingested a glucose drink before one or both tests or did not have any glucose at all (Fig. 10.7). Although there was some question as to whether giving the same test at both times was somehow fundamentally different from giving different kinds of self-control tests at each time (see Chatzisarantis & Hagger, 2015a, b), subsequent work showed the same failure of glucose to offset depletion even when the tasks were different (Lange, Seer, Rapior, Rose, & Eggert, 2014). To me, it would seem that either approach (same tasks given twice, or two different tasks given) should

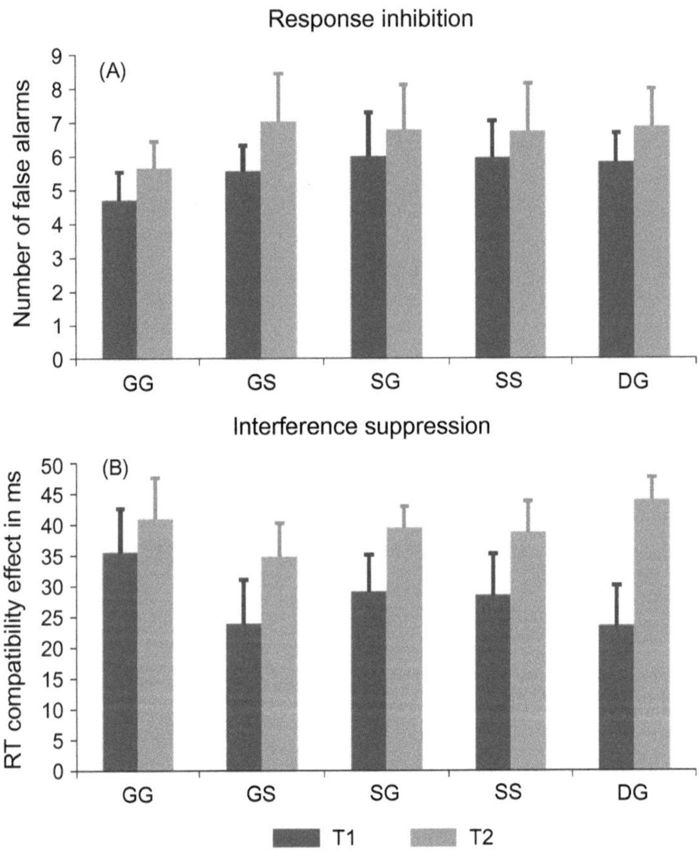

FIGURE 10.7 Self-control performance as a function of group assignment and timing relative to glucose rinsing or consumption in Experiment 2 of Lange and Eggert (2014). Participants rinsed their mouth with a glucose solution directly after the depletion task at T1 (GS), directly before the second self-control task at T2 (SG), on both occasions (GG), or on none of these occasions (SS). Participants in the DG condition drank glucose solution on both occasions. Higher numbers of false alarms (panel A) and higher RT differences between incompatible and compatible conditions (i.e., larger RT compatibility effects) indicate less self-controlled (more impulsive) performances. *From Lange, F., & Eggert, F. Sweet delusion. Glucose drinks fail to counteract ego depletion.* Appetite, 75, *54–63, copyright 2014. Reprinted with permission from Elsevier.*

be equally likely of producing depletion effects, if those are real, and producing resistance to depletion by glucose ingestion, if glucose is the "fuel" for self-control (see Lange, 2015). That said, at present it appears that there may be real problems with the glucose hypothesis. A recent meta-analysis of the role of glucose in depletion found little or no evidence to support that hypothesis, and led to that research team strongly cautioning policy makers about considering the role of glucose as an aid for improving self-control (Vadillo, Gold, & Osman, 2016).

Despite these concerns, other researchers have offered a different perspective on the role of glucose and self-control. For example, Beedie and Lane (2012) argued that it is not depletion that causes failure on subsequent tasks, but rather allocation of resources according to personal priorities. In other words, a person's priorities are as relevant as their present glucose supply, allowing for successful self-control whether glucose is high or low (Fig. 10.8). This perspective may help explain some of the discrepancies in the empirical work. Experiments by Job, Walton, Bernecker, and Dweck (2013) also seemed to indicate that people's beliefs were crucial to the effects of glucose consumption on self-control, suggesting that rather than being a general depletion effect, the real nature of the relation between glucose and self-control is driven by those beliefs.

Finally, the picture becomes very fuzzy on the basis of a recent registered replication report. Registered replications require a team to preregister their methods for conducting a multi-site, large sample replication of some

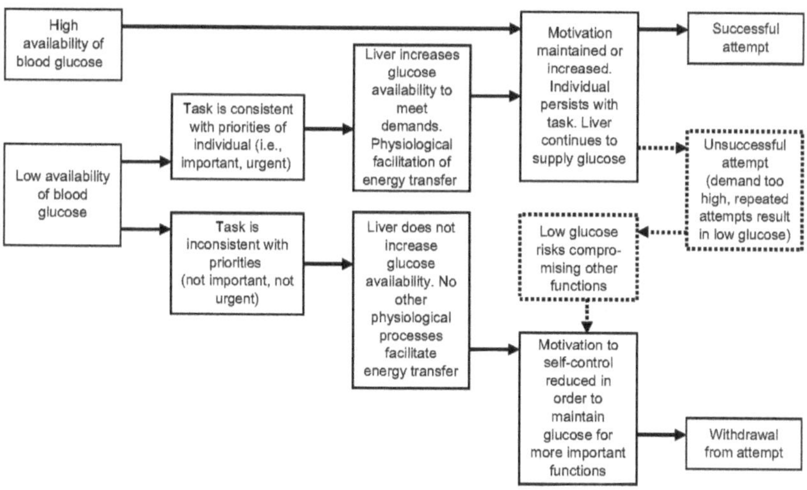

FIGURE 10.8 A resource allocation model of self-control. *From Beedie, C. J., & Lane, A. M., The role of glucose in self-control: Another look at the evidence and an alternative conceptualization.* Personality and Social Psychology Review, 16, *143–153, copyright 2012. Reprinted with permission of Sage.*

phenomenon of interest. In this case, the replication was of depletion effects (Hagger et al., 2016). Data from 2,141 participants from experiments conducted at 23 different sites were subjected to a meta-analysis for depletion effects. Only a small effect was found, and the authors concluded that "Results from the current multi-lab registered replication of the ego-depletion effect provide evidence that, if there is any effect, it is close to zero" (p. 558). However, those authors argued that this did not mean that additional research was not warranted, especially given some of the alternate explanations for depletion effects that had been offered, as well as the promise that neuroscience efforts might yet provide crucial new data in understanding the nature of self-control and inhibitory mechanisms, especially as those may be weakened or strengthened in different ways.

Inzlicht and Berkman (2015) offered the following six questions that they believed should guide future research into the nature and extent of self-control depletion: "(i) Does self-control really wane over time? (ii) Is ego depletion a form of mental fatigue? (iii) What is the resource that is depleted by ego depletion? (iv) How can changes in motivation, perception, and expectations replenish an exhausted resource? (v) Has the revised resource model unwittingly become a model about motivation? (vi) Do self-control exercises increase self-control?" (p. 511). Although I agree that these are important questions, I wish they had anticipated and appreciated that comparative approaches might also be highly illuminating. I would argue that there is good reason to adopt a comparative perspective because the depletion hypothesis and the role of glucose for strength models of self-control would seem to predict similar effects occurring in nonhuman animal models, given that these are perspectives that are biologically driven. And, animal models often can better isolate the role of a variety of mechanisms contributing to depletion, including glucose, motivation, and attention, because of greater control over all aspects of the testing situation. As I have noted in other places, comparative approaches can offer unique insights into human self-control, and to me this is exactly the kind of situation for which data from animals would seem to be highly relevant and warranted. That is the focus of the next chapter.

REFERENCES

Baumeister, R. F., Bratslavsky, E., Muraven, M., & Tice, D. M. (1998). Ego depletion: Is the active self a limited resource? *Journal of Personality and Social Psychology*, *74*, 1252–1265.

Baumeister, R. E., Heatherton, T. F., & Tice, D. M. (1994). *Losing control: How and why people fail at self-regulation*. San Diego, CA: Academic Press.

Beedie, C. J., & Lane, A. M. (2012). The role of glucose in self-control: Another look at the evidence and an alternative conceptualization. *Personality and Social Psychology Review*, *16*, 143–153.

Bolton, R. (1979). Hostility in fantasy: A further test of the hypoglycemia-aggression hypothesis. *Aggressive Behavior*, *2*, 257–274.

Boucher, H. C., & Kofos, M. N. (2012). The idea of money counteracts ego depletion effects. *Journal of Experimental Social Psychology*, *48*, 804–810.

Carter, E. C., & McCullough, M. E. (2014). Publication bias and the limited strength model of self-control: Has the evidence for ego depletion been overestimated? *Frontiers in Psychology*, *5*, 823.

Carter, E. C., Kofler, L. M., Forster, D. E., & McCullough, M. E. (2015). A series of meta-analytic tests of the depletion effect: Self-control does not seem to rely on a limited resource. *Journal of Experimental Psychology: General*, *144*, 796–815.

Chow, J. T., & Lau, S. (2015). Nature gives us strength: Exposure to nature counteracts ego-depletion. *The Journal of Social Psychology*, *155*, 70–85.

Chatzisarantis, N. L., & Hagger, M. S. (2015a). Unsuccessful attempts to replicate effects of self control operations and glucose on ego-depletion pose an interesting research question that demands explanation. *Appetite*, *84*, 328–329.

Chatzisarantis, N. L., & Hagger, M. S. (2015b). Illusionary delusions. Willingness to exercise self-control can mask effects of glucose on self-control performance in experimental paradigms that use identical self-control tasks. *Appetite*, *84*, 322–324.

Clarkson, J. J., Hirt, E. R., Jia, L., & Alexander, M. B. (2010). When perception is more than reality: The effects of perceived versus actual resource depletion on self-regulatory behavior. *Journal of Personality and Social Psychology*, *98*, 29–46.

Dang, J., Dewitte, S., Mao, L., Xiao, S., & Shi, Y. (2013). Adapting to an initial self-regulatory task cancels the ego depletion effect. *Consciousness and Cognition*, *22*, 816–821.

Donohoe, R. T., & Benton, D. (1999). Blood glucose control and aggressiveness in females. *Personality and Individual Differences*, *26*, 905–911.

Freud, S. (1961a). The ego and the id. In J. Strachey & (Ed. & Trans.) *The standard edition of the complete psychological works of Sigmund Freud* (Vol. 19, pp. 12–66). London: Hogarth Press. (Original work published 1923).

Freud, S. (1961b). New introductory lectures on psycho-analysis. In J. Strachey & (Ed. & Trans.) *The standard edition of the complete psychological works of Sigmund Freud* (Vol. 22, pp. 7–182). London: Hogarth Press. (Original work published 1933).

Gailliot, M. T., & Baumeister, R. F. (2007). The physiology of willpower: Linking blood glucose to self-control. *Personality and Social Psychology Review*, *11*, 303–327.

Gailliot, M. T., Baumeister, R. F., DeWall, C. N., Maner, J. K., Plant, E. A., Tice, D. M., ... Schmeichel, B. J. (2007). Self-control relies on glucose as a limited energy source: Willpower is more than a metaphor. *Journal of Personality and Social Psychology*, *92*, 325–336.

Gino, F., Schweitzer, M. E., Mead, N. L., & Ariely, D. (2011). Unable to resist temptation: How self-control depletion promotes unethical behavior. *Organizational Behavior and Human Decision Processes*, *115*, 191–203.

Glass, D. C., Singer, J. E., & Friedman, L. N. (1969). Psychic cost of adaptation to an environmental stressor. *Journal of Personality and Social Psychology*, *12*, 200–210.

Gottfredson, M. R., & Hirschi, T. (1990). *A general theory of crime*. Stanford, CA: Stanford University Press.

Hagger, M. S., Wood, C., Stiff, C., & Chatzisarantis, N. L. D. (2010). Ego depletion and the strength model of self-control: A meta-analysis. *Psychological Bulletin*, *136*, 495–525.

Hagger, M. S., Chatzisarantis, N. L., Alberts, H., Anggono, C. O., Batailler, C., Birt, A. R., & Calvillo, D. P. (2016). A multilab preregistered replication of the ego-depletion effect. *Perspectives on Psychological Science*, *11*, 546–573.

Hoch, S. J., & Loewenstein, G. F. (1991). Time-inconsistent preferences and consumer self-control. *Journal of Consumer Research*, *17*, 492–507.

Inzlicht, M., & Berkman, E. (2015). Six questions for the resource model of control (and some answers). *Social and Personality Psychology Compass*, *9*, 511–524.

Inzlicht, M., & Schmeichel, B. J. (2012). What is ego depletion? Toward a mechanistic revision of the resource model of self-control. *Perspectives on Psychological Science*, *7*, 450–463.

Inzlicht, M., Schmeichel, B. J., & Macrae, C. N. (2014). Why self-control seems (but may not be) limited. *Trends in Cognitive Sciences*, *18*, 127–133.

Job, V., Dweck, C. S., & Walton, G. M. (2010). Ego depletion – Is it all in your head? Implicit theories about willpower affect self-regulation. *Psychological Science*, *21*, 1686–1693.

Job, V., Walton, G. M., Bernecker, K., & Dweck, C. S. (2013). Beliefs about willpower determine the impact of glucose on self-control. *Proceedings of the National Academy of Sciences of the United States of America*, *110*, 14837–14842.

Kurzban, R. (2010). Does the brain consume additional glucose during self-control tasks? *Evolutionary Psychology*, *8*, 244–259.

Lange, F. (2015). If ego depletion cannot be studied using identical tasks, it is not ego depletion. *Appetite*, *84*, 325–327.

Lange, F., & Eggert, F. (2014). Sweet delusion. Glucose drinks fail to counteract ego depletion. *Appetite*, *75*, 54–63.

Lange, F., Seer, C., Rapior, M., Rose, J., & Eggert, F. (2014). Turn it all you want: Still no effect of sugar consumption on ego depletion. *Journal of European Psychology Students*, *5*, 1–8.

Lustman, P. J., Frank, B. L., & McGill, J. B. (1991). Relationship of personality characteristics to glucose regulation in adults with diabetes. *Psychosomatic Medicine*, *53*, 305–312.

Mischel, W. (2014). *The marshmallow test: Understanding self-control and how to master it*. New York: Random House.

Molden, D. C., Hui, C. M., Scholer, A. A., Meier, B. P., Noreen, E. E., D'Agostino, P. R., & Martin, V. (2012). Motivational versus metabolic effects of carbohydrates on self-control. *Psychological Science*, *23*, 1137–1144.

Muraven, M. (2010). Building self-control strength: Practicing self-control leads to improved self-control performance. *Journal of Experimental Social Psychology*, *46*, 465–468.

Muraven, M., Collins, R. L., & Neinhaus, K. (2002). Self-control and alcohol restraint: An initial application of the self-control strength model. *Psychology of Addictive Behaviors*, *16*, 113–120.

Muraven, M., Shmueli, D., & Burkley, E. (2006). Conserving self-control strength. *Journal of Personality and Social Psychology*, *91*, 524–537.

Muraven, M., Tice, D. M., & Baumeister, R. F. (1998). Self-control as a limited resource: Regulatory depletion patterns. *Journal of Personality and Social Psychology*, *74*, 774–789.

Oaten, M., & Cheng, K. (2006a). Improved self-control: The benefits of a regular program of academic study. *Basic and Applied Social Psychology*, *28*, 1–16.

Oaten, M., & Cheng, K. (2006b). Longitudinal gains in self-regulation from regular physical exercise. *British Journal of Health Psychology*, *11*, 717–733.

Oaten, M., & Cheng, K. (2007). Improvements in self-control from financial monitoring. *Journal of Economic Psychology*, *28*, 487–501.

Rounding, K., Lee, A., Jacobson, J. A., & Ji, L. J. (2012). Religion replenishes self-control. *Psychological Science*, *23*, 635–642.

Sanders, M. A., Shirk, S. D., Burgin, C. J., & Martin, L. L. (2012). The gargle effect: Rinsing the mouth with glucose enhances self-control. *Psychological Science*, *23*, 1470–1472.

Stroop, J. R. (1935). Stroop color word test. *Journal of Experimental Physiology, 18*, 643–662.

Tice, D. M., Bratslavsky, E., & Baumeister, R. F. (2001). Emotional distress regulation takes precedence over impulse control: If you feel bad, do it! *Journal of Personality and Social Psychology, 80*, 53–67.

Tyler, J. M., & Burns, K. C. (2008). After depletion: The replenishment of the self's regulatory resources. *Self and Identity, 7*, 305–321.

Tyler, J. M., & Burns, K. C. (2009). Triggering conservation of the self's regulatory resources. *Basic and Applied Social Psychology, 31*, 255–266.

Vadillo, M. A., Gold, N., & Osman, M. (2016). The bitter truth about sugar and willpower: The limited evidential value of the glucose model of ego depletion. *Psychological Science, 27*, 1207–1214.

Virkkunen, M., & Huttunen, M. O. (1982). Evidence for abnormal glucose tolerance test among violent offenders. *Neuropsychobiology, 8*, 30–34.

Vohs, K. D., Baumeister, R. F., Schmeichel, B. J., Twenge, J. M., Nelson, N. M., & Tice, D. M. (2008). Making choices impairs subsequent self-control: A limited-resource account of decision making, self-regulation, and active initiative. *Journal of Personality and Social Psychology, 94*, 883–898.

Vohs, K. D., & Faber, R. J. (2007). Spent resources: Self-regulatory resource availability affects impulse buying. *Journal of Consumer Research, 33*, 537–547.

Vohs, K. D., Glass, B. D., Maddox, W. T., & Markman, A. B. (2011). Ego depletion is not just fatigue: Evidence from a total sleep deprivation experiment. *Social Psychological and Personality Science, 2*, 166–173.

Vohs, K. D., & Heatherton, T. F. (2000). Self-regulatory failure: A resource-depletion approach. *Psychological Science, 11*, 249–254.

Volkow, N. D., Hitzemann, R., Wolf, A. P., Logan, J., Fowler, J. S., Christman, D., et al. (1990). Acute effects of ethanol on regional brain glucose metabolism and transport. *Psychiatry Research, 35*, 39–48.

Wallace, H. M., & Baumeister, R. F. (2002). The effects of success versus failure feedback on further self-control. *Self and Identity, 1*, 35–41.

Wan, E. W., & Sternthal, B. (2008). Regulating the effects of depletion through monitoring. *Personality and Social Psychology Bulletin, 34*, 32–46.

Webb, T. L., & Sheeran, P. (2003). Can implementation intentions help to overcome ego-depletion? *Journal of Experimental Social Psychology, 39*, 279–286.

Xu, X., Demos, K. E., Leahey, T. M., Hart, C. N., Trautvetter, J., Coward, P., . . . Wing, R. R. (2014). Failure to replicate depletion of self-control. *PLoS One, 9*, e109950.

FURTHER READING

Baumeister, R. F. (2002). Yielding to temptation: Self-control failure, impulsive purchasing, and consumer behavior. *Journal of Consumer Research, 28*, 670–676.

DeWall, C. N., Baumeister, R. F., Gailliot, M. T., & Maner, J. K. (2008). Depletion makes the heart grow less helpful: Helping as a function of self-regulatory energy and genetic relatedness. *Personality and Social Psychology Bulletin, 34*, 1653–1662.

DeWall, C. N., Baumeister, R. F., Stillman, T. F., & Gailliot, M. T. (2007). Violence restrained: Effects of self-regulation and its depletion on aggression. *Journal of Experimental Social Psychology, 43*, 62–76.

Dvorak, R. D., & Simons, J. S. (2009). Moderation of resource depletion in the self control strength model. Differing effects of two modes of self-control. *Personality and Social Psychology Bulletin, 35*, 572–583.

Faber, R. J., & Vohs, K. D. (2004). To buy or not to buy? Self-control and self-regulatory failure in purchase behavior. In R. F. Baumeister & K. D. Vohs (Eds.), *Handbook of self-regulation: Research, theory and applications* (pp. 509–524). New York: Guilford Press.

Giacomantonio, M., Jordan, J., Fennis, B. M., & Panno, A. (2014). When motivational consequences of ego depletion collide: Conservation dominates over reward-seeking. *Journal of Experimental Social Psychology*, *55*, 217–220.

Hagger, M. S. (2010). Self-regulation: An important construct in health psychology research and practice. *Health Psychology Review*, *4*, 57–65.

Hagger, M. S., & Chatzisarantis, N. L. D. (2014). It is premature to regard the ego-depletion effect as "Too Incredible". *Frontiers in Psychology*, *5*, 298.

Masicampo, E. J., & Baumeister, R. F. (2008). Toward a physiology of dual-process reasoning and judgment. Lemonade, willpower, and expensive rule-based analysis. *Psychological Science*, *19*, 255–260.

Masicampo, E. J., Martin, S. R., & Anderson, R. A. (2014). Understanding and overcoming self-control depletion. *Social and Personality Psychology Compass*, *8*, 638–649.

Muraven, M., & Baumeister, R. F. (2000). Self-regulation and depletion of limited resources: Does self-control resemble a muscle?. *Psychological Bulletin*, *126*, 247–259.

Muraven, M., Collins, R. L., Shiffman, S., & Paty, J. A. (2005). Daily fluctuations in self-control demands and alcohol intake. *Psychology of Addictive Behaviors*, *19*, 140–147.

Rothbaum, F., Weisz, J. R., & Snyder, S. S. (1982). Changing the world and changing die self: A two-process model of perceived control. *Journal of Personality and Social Psychology*, *42*, 5–37.

Shiv, B., & Fedorikhin, A. (1999). Heart and mind in conflict: Interplay of affect and cognition in consumer decision making. *Journal of Consumer Research*, *26*, 278–282.

Stucke, T. S., & Baumeister, R. F. (2006). Ego depletion and aggressive behavior: Is the inhibition of aggression a limited resource? *European Journal of Social Psychology*, *36*, 1–13.

Wegner, D. M. (1989). *White bears and other unwanted thoughts: Suppression, obsession, and the psychology of mental control.* New York: Viking/Penguin.

Wegner, D. M. (1994). Ironic processes of mental control. *Psychological Review*, *101*, 34–52.

Wegner, D. M., Erber, R., & Zanakos, S. (1993). Ironic processes in the mental control of mood and mood related thought. *Journal of Personality and Social Psychology*, *65*, 1093–1107.

Wegner, D. M., & Pennebaker, J. W. (1993). *Handbook of mental control.* Englewood Cliffs, NJ: Prentice Hall.

Chapter 11

Do Animals Flex Their Own Self-Control "Muscle"?

Given the claims, issues, and theoretical perspectives of those studying whether self-control really is like a muscle and can be depleted, or replenished, it would seem that a concerted effort to look at this question from a comparative perspective would be warranted. However, there has been limited effort to this point to provide such comparative data, which is a shortcoming in this area, and a restriction on our knowledge of the potential biological bases for self-control across species. The claims that are made by those who argue for the depletion model of self-control seem, to me, to be claims that would emerge from an evolutionary progression of behavioral traits based on physiological and psychological mechanisms. In other words, if human self-control suffers in extended or successive instances in which it is required, and this potentially occurs because of metabolic and physiological limitations in terms of producing the glucose-based "fuel" for such self-control, I would think such a relation would be evident in other species as well. There is no reason to assume that this depletion model would be reliant on any uniquely human aspect of metabolic processing of glucose.

Even more so, the inconsistencies in the human literature about depletion, and the lack of consensus about the validity of that model, as well as about the mechanisms that might underlie self-control being shown more strongly or more weakly in differing contexts, seem to beg a comparative approach. As I argued earlier in this book, comparative psychology presents its clear utility in cases where human behavior may be potentially the result of evolutionary pressures that have existed from before the time our own species emerged, and thus studying animals may give unique insights into the role of those pressures on behavioral and cognitive mechanisms still at work in our species. So, it would seem that comparative psychology has a clear and valuable role to play in assessing the depletion hypothesis.

Despite this, to my knowledge, the only extended effort to study depletion and potential mechanisms underlying depletion in other animals has occurred largely in two species—domestic dogs and capuchin monkeys.

Self-Control in Animals and People. DOI: https://doi.org/10.1016/B978-0-12-812508-3.00011-6
© 2018 Elsevier Inc. All rights reserved.

I will outline what we seem to know now, I hope the reader will appreciate that there is a lack of data on this question, especially when one thinks of the large and historically long literature on other aspects of animal self-control. Perhaps more of this research is in progress and will emerge soon. But, at present, we have little information about this issue in animals, and perhaps more confusing is that the information we have seems to speak of sharp differences in what we see in the species that have been tested. These studies largely have focused on the glucose hypothesis for depletion effects, and so I will review what we have learned so far about the role of glucose in depletion, and about those instances in which research teams have assessed whether depletion occurs.

Domestic dogs have shown a number of forms of inhibitory control, as outlined earlier in this book, including some impressive instances in which they delayed gratification and engaged in behaviors that may have been geared toward aiding delay maintenance (e.g., Bray, MacLean, & Hare, 2014; Brucks, Soliani, Range, & Marshall-Pescini, 2017; Leonardi, Vick, & Dufour, 2012). Thus, they seem to make excellent subjects for testing potential depletion-like effects in nonhuman animals, and so it is no surprise that much of the (still limited) work on this question has been done with dogs. They are also good subjects for such assessments because it is easy to introduce one type of inhibitory task that they can perform, and then see how that affects subsequent efforts. An early example of this approach also involved the use of glucose. Miller, Pattison, DeWall, Rayburn-Reeves, and Zentall (2010) first required dogs to sit and stay in one location for 10 minutes, or, in the control condition, the dogs were placed in a kennel instead for 10 minutes. The idea here is that the first group of dogs had to actively obey a command to not move, which was presumed to be effortful and require inhibition, whereas in the second case the control group was forced to stay in one place independent of what the dogs may have wanted to do because of the kennel. This second condition, presumably, would not deplete inhibitory resources. The authors called the activity of the uncaged dogs self-control, although I would argue that this was not self-control and rather was a different form of behavioral inhibition. In any case, it was effortful control over behavior that was most likely contrary to what the dogs naturally wanted to do, which would be to move around. After this 10-minute period, all dogs were released and were given a toy that they had previously learned contained food that only came out of the toy when it was played with. Now, however, there was no food that would come out of the toy, and the researchers measured how long the dogs would persist in playing with the toy (again, presumably so as to get food) before they gave up. Here, again, they called this a second test of self-control, because the dogs needed to persist in the face of unrewarded effort. I would not call this a self-control test either, but it was a second task in which continuous engagement and persistence were required. And, the dogs that were forced to sit of their own volition (in the self-control condition) attempted to get food from the toy for less than a minute, on average, whereas dogs in the control condition persisted for more than 2 minutes (Fig. 11.1). These results were taken as evidence of depletion effects in dogs, in which subjects who had exercised self-control were less likely to persist on an impossible task than those subjects who had not depleted any of their inhibitory resources.

Miller et al. (2010) then proceeded to directly assess the role of glucose in the depletion of inhibition in dogs. Miller et al. noted that there already seemed to be a clear link between glucose and some aspects of behavior and cognition, particularly in rats. For example, they referenced work that

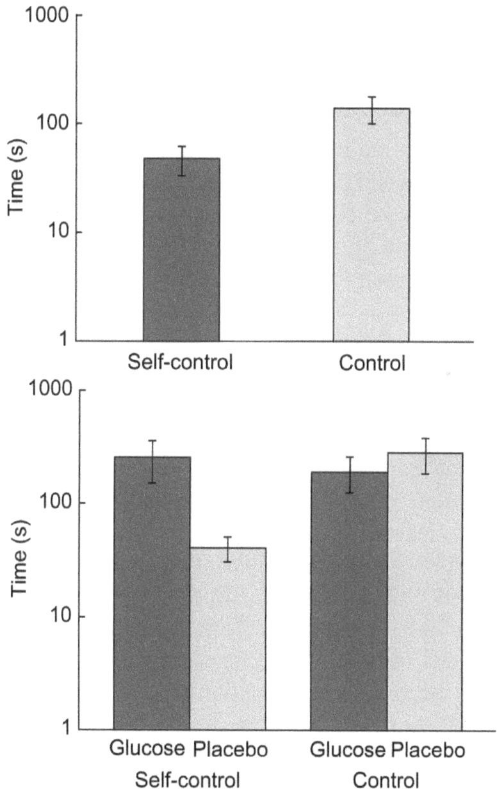

FIGURE 11.1 Mean persistence on the unsolvable toy task as a function of condition in Experiment 1 (top) and Experiment 2 (bottom) in Miller et al. (2010). In both experiments, one dog within each pair was randomly assigned to the self-control condition and the other to the control condition. In Experiment 2, half the dogs in each of these conditions drank a glucose drink prior to the unsolvable task and the other half drank a placebo. Error bars represent ± 1 SEM. *From Miller, H. C., Pattison, K. F., DeWall, C. N., Rayburn-Reeves, R., & Zentall, T. R. (2010). Self-control without a "self"? Common self-control processes in humans and dogs.* Psychological Science, 21, *534–538. Copyright 2010. Reprinted with permission of Sage.*

showed that glucose levels varied in the brains of rats in relation to other measures of neural activity (Fellows, Boutelle, & Fillenz, 1992), and they noted that previous research had found that spatial cognition appeared to tax glucose levels in extracellular fluid in the brains of rats (McNay, Fries, & Gold, 2000). At the same time, it appears that increasing glucose levels may, in some specific circumstances, improve aspects of learning and memory in animals (e.g., Gold, 1995; Hughes, 2003; Wenk, 1989). On the basis of these results, Miller et al. gave dogs the exact same test I described above, but now half of the dogs received a glucose drink before undertaking the impossible toy task, whereas the other dogs drank a sugar-free control drink. Dogs given the glucose after performing the inhibitory sit and stay task persisted with the impossible toy for just as long as dogs who were caged (control group), whereas those given the sugar-free drink spent significantly less time interacting with the toy before giving up (Fig. 11.1). The results seemed to clearly support a glucose-based depletion hypothesis in canines, if glucose was a crucial component to maintaining and sustaining self-control across instances in which it was required. Of course, there are alternate possibilities that were not assessed in this study, in addition to the overarching concern that these may not even be self-control tasks. One possibility is that sugar increases general activity, and with only a toy available, dogs engaged it more. It would be interesting to see if the second task given in this procedure was another inhibitory task rather than an engagement task. For example, after being required to sit for a long period of time, how would dogs perform on a task like the one used by Leonardi et al. (2012) or one like that used by Brucks et al. (2017) that I discussed earlier? Thus, although this study provided some tantalizing results, more effort was required to understand the nature of the relation between glucose consumption and behavioral inhibition, perseverance of effort, and self-control in nonhuman animals.

Miller and her colleagues continued to work on this question, with subsequent studies of dogs' inhibitory skills and the relation of those skills to depletion effects and glucose effects. Miller, DeWall, Pattison, Molet, and Zentall (2012) examined depletion effects in dogs as they might impact social behavior. In this study, dogs performed both conditions. The researchers again gave dogs either a forced 10-minute period of sitting still where the dogs had to refrain from moving or were instead held in a kennel which presumably did not tax inhibitory resources. However, this period of time was made even more difficult for the dogs, because a mechanized "hamster" toy was in the room and it moved randomly around the room (Fig. 11.2). So, you can imagine this was a particularly compelling stimulus for the dogs, and those that had to self-restrain their movements certainly found that to be more effortful in comparison to those dogs in a kennel. Then, the dogs were taken away from that room for a short while, and a dominant dog was brought into the area (Fig. 11.2). The subject dog then returned to the room and had 4 minutes to go wherever it wanted to. So, in this case, during the

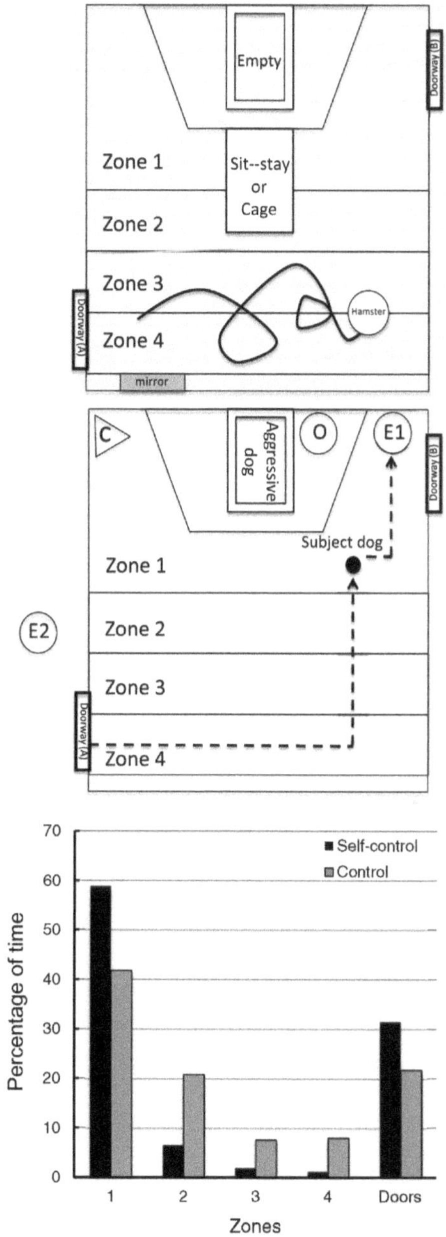

FIGURE 11.2 The top panel shows the first part of the trial, where a dog was given a 10-minute period to observe the "hamster" moving around the room while the dog was either self-restrained in one location or held in a cage. The dog then left, and a dominant other dog came into the room, before the subject dog returned (middle panel), and the experimenters recorded the portion of time the subject dog spent in each zone. The bottom panel shows the results for the group of dogs. *From Miller, H. C., DeWall, C. N., Pattison, K., Molet, M., & Zentall, T. R. (2012). Too dog tired to avoid danger: Self-control depletion in canines increases behavioral approach toward an aggressive threat.* Psychonomic Bulletin & Review, 19, *535–540. Copyright 2012. Reprinted with permission of Springer.*

second "task," rather than engage a toy, there was another dominant dog in the room, and the question was how long the subject dog spent in proximity to this dominant dog. Miller et al. argued that dogs' prepotent response would be to approach the stranger dog, even though this was the riskier option. And the idea here was that depleted dogs would be the ones more likely to approach. This is what they found: although all dogs performed both conditions, they were more likely to go near the dominant individual for longer when they had been forced to self-restrain earlier (Fig. 11.2). Although this was not true for every dog, it did seem to be the case that for many the act of self-restraint then diminished the subsequent capacity for inhibitory action when in the presence of a dominant conspecific.

Another interesting study with dogs took a close look at what role breakfast might play in cognition and inhibition. The idea for this study (Miller & Bender, 2012) was based on past work showing that for humans (children and adults), eating breakfast leads to better cognitive performance (e.g., Benton & Sargent, 1992; Wesnes, Pincock, Richardshon, Helm, & Hails, 2003) including better attentive, better spatial memory, and greater memory for verbal information than in those who did not eat breakfast (Benton & Owens, 1993; Mahoney, Taylor, Kanarek, & Samuel, 2005). These effects even seem to sometimes show up in better test grades for school age children (Rampersaud, Pereira, Girard, Adams, & Metzl, 2005). Miller and Bender considered that eating more food in the morning might impact glucose levels in the brains of dogs, and therefore give them an edge in tasks that followed right after an imposed inhibition task in the same way that ingested glucose from breakfast appears to improve executive functioning in humans (Scholey, Harper, & Kennedy, 2001), and to do so for more extended periods (Ingwersen, Defeyter, Kennedy, Wesnes, & Scholey, 2007). And, this relation seems to hold for rats as well as for humans (e.g., Benton et al., 2003). So, Miller and Bender gave dogs two test sessions, one in which they were fasted before testing and one in which they had a large breakfast (half their daily caloric needs) 30 minutes before testing or 90 minutes before testing. All dogs then had to perform the sit and stay task for 10 minutes, before being given a spatial memory test. This test involved remembering where in an array of containers a food item had been hidden. Dogs performed best in that second test when they were given the test 30 minutes after breakfast, whereas 90 minutes after breakfast they performed similarly to when they were fasted. Miller and Bender suggested that the meal led to increased glucose metabolism which may have helped offset some of the depletion from the inhibition (sit and stay) task. They argued this effect was similar to one seen for spatial memory in rats (Messier, 1997). Unfortunately, there was no condition in this study where the inhibition task was not given, so it is impossible to know what role that task played in general in the subsequent memory performance. And, it is difficult to see whether breakfast led to offsetting depletion or whether recent consumption of food changed the motivation of the dogs to perform the memory task, and depletion was not at work in this experiment.

Miller et al. (2012) stated that the sum total of this work argued for commonalities between animals and humans regarding a link between glucose and self-control that previously has been considered unique to humans. As I noted earlier, in principle I agree with this idea that one should expect to see comparative data that reflect depletion and glucose effects if those effects are real in humans (but see the previous chapter for the arguments over that theoretical position). But, I am not sure all of these studies necessarily reflect a link between self-control and glucose, or that they reflect forms of self-control depletion. As I have noted at various points, I think self-control is a specialized form of broader behavioral inhibition that species may show, and it is not clear that most of the tasks used with dogs to study depletion are self-control tasks. Additionally, I am not sure that depletion, if it is at work in successive performance patterns, is as ubiquitous as to occur in any paired set of tasks that, broadly speaking, tap inhibitory behavioral mechanisms. It seems likely that depletion effects actually should be fairly focused on only those tasks that are most closely related, if the mechanisms of inhibition or self-control are at work for those successive tasks. In fact, we know from other research with some species that have been tested that there is not always a relation between performances of the *same animals* across inhibitory tasks. That is the story of the next chapter.

In an interesting experiment, Bray, MacLean, and Hare (2015) contrasted pet dogs and assistance dogs (specifically bred for low levels of general arousal) on their performance on a detour task where they had to walk around a barrier to get to food rather than try to go directly toward the food. The detour task is a commonly used test of inhibitory control as a subject must resist their natural proclivity to physically move or reach toward the desirable stimuli (such as food) and instead pause to maneuver a transparent barrier to successfully obtain the food. The key manipulation was that dogs first either had their arousal increased by having an experimenter call to them in a highly excited voice or had their arousal kept constant by a dull and monotone experimenter. Then, the dogs were given the detour task, and something fascinating happened. Assistance dogs, which were normally in lower arousal states, actually did *better* on the detour task when their arousal was increased whereas pet dogs did *worse* when their arousal was increased (Fig. 11.3). So, baseline temperamental factors interacted with contextual factors to differentially affect inhibition. And, order of the two arousal-inducing interactions with the experimenter seemed to play a role, where it was better for assistance dogs to engage in the high-arousal condition first, but for pet dogs to engage in the low-arousal condition first. Thus, the temperament of the dogs best predicted how well they would do on the detour task after being more highly aroused or not. Again, I think this shows that experimental context plays a big role in self-control research as it interacts

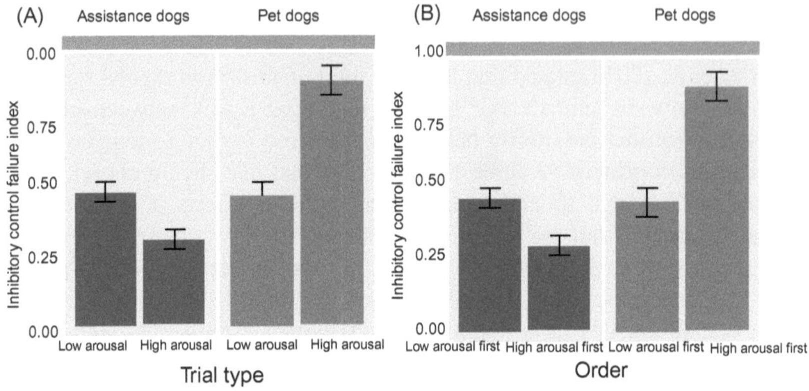

FIGURE 11.3 (A) Cumulative performance of assistance and pet dogs during low-arousal and high-arousal trials in the Bray et al. (2015) study. The interaction between trial type and dog type is significant, with assistance dogs exhibiting optimal levels of inhibitory control during high-arousal trials and pet dogs exhibiting optimal levels during low-arousal trials. (B) Cumulative performance of assistance and pet dogs over the entire task, divided into groups based on those that completed high-arousal trials first and those that completed low-arousal trials first. The bars represent the same as in (A). The interaction between order and dog type is significant, with assistance dogs that completed high-arousal trials first exhibiting optimal levels of inhibitory control on the task overall and pet dogs that completed low-arousal trials first exhibiting optimal levels of inhibitory control on the task overall. *From Bray, E. E., MacLean, E. L., & Hare, B. A. (2015). Increasing arousal enhances inhibitory control in calm but not excitable dogs.* Animal Cognition, 18, *1317–1329. Copyright 2015. Reprinted with permission of Springer.*

with participant-unique factors such as temperament or motivation in explaining a lot about performance in specific inhibitory tasks. To me, these factors seem more relevant than a generalized depletion hypothesis, because they allow for understanding and taking into account individual differences that exist independent of the exertion of inhibition or self-control. Of course, one could argue that depletion and these other factors all matter, and depletion operates differently across individuals (an idea that likely resonates with those who promote ideas such as grit or perseverance, as discussed earlier).

Ultimately, although I appreciate the line of research into depletion effects in dogs, and the efforts to assess nonhuman evidence of depletion and what role glucose might play, I think the resulting data are not sufficient to argue that comparative psychology clearly supports work in social psychology on depletion of self-control in humans. And, as it turns out, work with nonhuman primates on these questions casts more doubt on the conclusion that comparative research supports the ego depletion hypothesis. Or, at the least, the nonhuman primate studies suggest that the jury is still out.

The first experiment to assess the depletion hypothesis with nonhuman primates was conducted by Elsa Addessi and her colleagues (De Petrillo et al., 2015). In their test, capuchin monkeys engaged in many of the same tests I have described previously. These five monkeys were given an accumulation task, in which items were added to a set until the animals took the set, after having either a full meal or before getting a full meal. The idea here was that after meals, glucose levels would be high, and performance should be improved relative to when the monkeys had not yet eaten. In a second experiment, the accumulation test was given after monkeys completed either a low-cognitive-demand task, which consisted of just touching images on a computer screen to earn rewards, or a high-cognitive-demand task that involved using working memory to match a sample image to one of multiple options that had to be identical to that sample to be rewarded (Fig. 11.4). De Petrillo et al. also assessed what relation performance on *each trial* of the accumulation task had on subsequent trials of that task, as well as on subsequent sessions with the accumulation task. What they found was little evidence of depletion effects. Performance on the accumulation task was highly similar within each monkey whether they had eaten or not

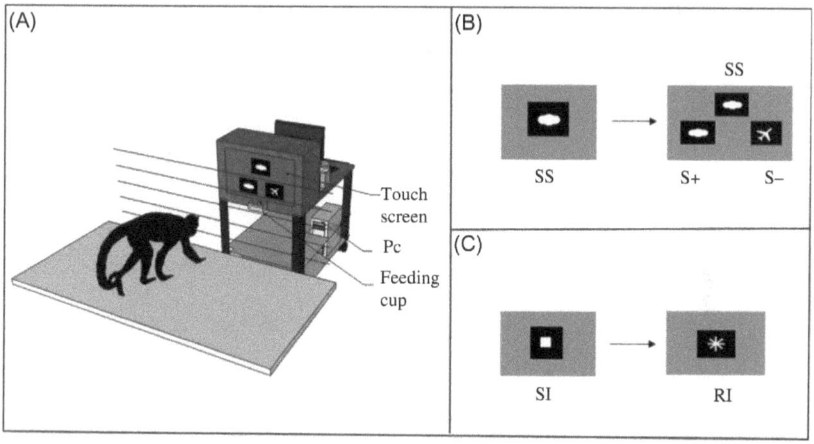

FIGURE 11.4 (A) The apparatus used by De Petrillo et al. (2015) for their cognitive depletion experiment. It consisted of a computerized system mounted on the top shelf of a trolley connected to a 19-in. touchscreen and to an automatic food dispenser. When the subject provided a correct response, the food dispenser delivered one banana-flavored pellet as reward into a Plexiglas feeding cup. (B) High cognitive depletion/identity matching-to-sample task. At the beginning of each trial, an image was presented as a sample stimulus (SS) on the upper central half of the screen. When the subject touched the SS, two comparison stimuli were immediately displayed on the right and on the left, below the sample. The comparison stimuli included one matching stimulus (S +), identical to SS, and one nonmatching stimulus (S−), different from SS. (C) Low-cognitive-depletion/simple touching task. At the beginning of each trial a white square was presented as a starting image (SI) in the center of a black background screen. When the subject touched the SI, it vanished and was immediately replaced by a rewarding image (RI), a white cross. *From De Petrillo, F., Micucci, A., Gori, E., Truppa, V., Ariely, D., & Addessi, E. (2015). Self-control depletion in tufted capuchin monkeys (*Sapajus spp.*): Does delay of gratification rely on a limited resource?* Frontiers in Psychology, 6, *1193. Copyright 2015. Reprinted with permission of the authors.*

(assessment of the glucose hypothesis) and highly similar whether they had just completed the low- or high-cognitive-load task (assessment of the depletion hypothesis, Fig. 11.5). The only slight evidence in favor of the depletion model came from the observed trial-to-trial decrease in accumulation performance, although it is difficult to know whether this is depletion or whether this might be the result of satiation, where monkeys were progressively less

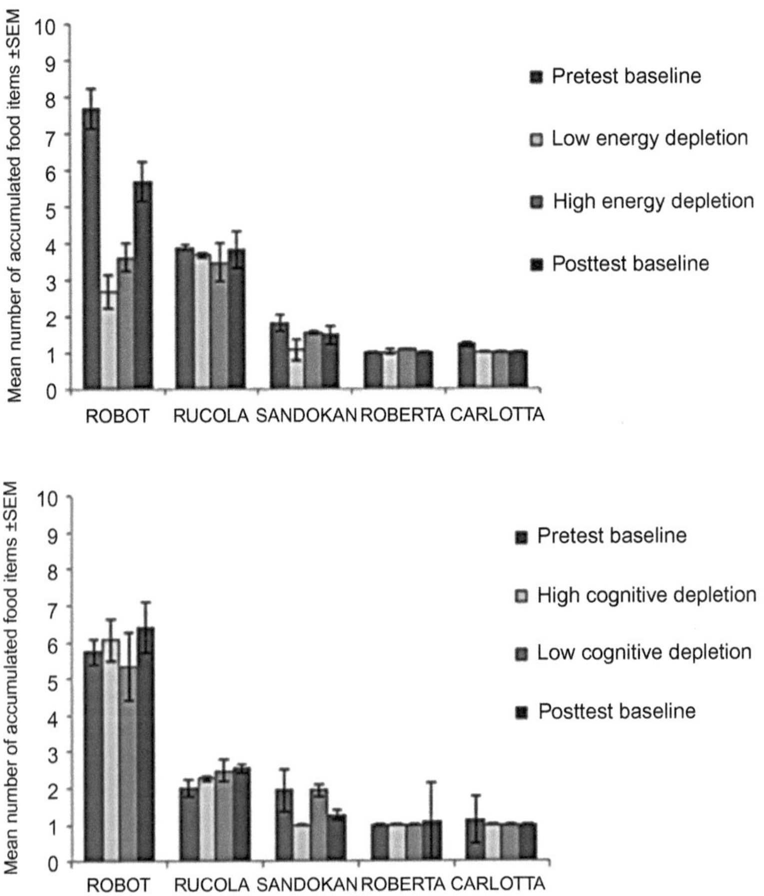

FIGURE 11.5 Performance of each monkey in the energy depletion experiment (top panel) of De Petrillo et al. (2015) in which monkeys performed the accumulation task before or after a meal and performance of each monkey in the cognitive depletion experiment (bottom panel) in which monkeys performed either a cognitive challenging task or a nonchallenging task. The histograms report the mean number of food items accumulated for each condition in the accumulation task. *From De Petrillo, F., Micucci, A., Gori, E., Truppa, V., Ariely, D., & Addessi, E. (2015). Self-control depletion in tufted capuchin monkeys (*Sapajus spp.*): Does delay of gratification rely on a limited resource?* Frontiers in Psychology, 6, *1193. Copyright 2015. Reprinted with permission of the authors.*

interested in maintaining delay of gratification after they had eaten more and more of the same food item. De Petrillo et al. concluded that their results were more in agreement with human studies that had showed glucose depletion *did not* affect self-control performances (e.g., Kurzban, 2010; Lange & Eggert, 2014; Molden et al., 2012).

The second study conducted with nonhuman primates to directly assess the glucose hypothesis came from my lab, and it was conducted by Audrey Parrish. In her study (Parrish, Emerson, Rossettie, & Beran, 2016), we used the accumulation test as well, with capuchin monkeys that were tested in the morning, having not eaten since the previous evening. In the morning, monkeys were given either a heavily glucose-enriched breakfast meal or a low-glucose breakfast meal, where caloric intake was equated in both conditions. One possible limitation of the De Petrillo et al. (2015) study was that it lacked a control condition in which the caloric intake was equated independent of the delivery of glucose. By carefully equating the number of calories in both meals (high and low glucose), we were able to investigate the effects of glucose on the accumulation task performance of monkeys while not having to worry about differential motivational factors such as hunger or satiation. Each monkey participated in both conditions, eating a breakfast meal that consisted of either honey-roasted peanuts coated with additional raw honey or unsalted peanuts, with one honey-roasted peanut consumed last so that we could ensure in both conditions the monkeys had experienced the taste of the sweetened food. In each session, the monkeys had one forced-accumulation trial where they had to experience the item-by-item addition of raisins into the collection pan, but could not take the pan until five items were given, and a free-choice trial where they determined when to take the accumulating raisins. They could obtain as many as 50 raisins in the free-choice trial, and the prediction if glucose served to facilitate self-control was that they would accumulate more raisins after the high-glucose meal than after the low-glucose meal. After 20 sessions for each monkey, 10 in each condition, the results were clear and did not support the depletion model or the idea that glucose serves as fuel for self-control (Fig. 11.6). Monkeys looked nearly identical in their performances across the two conditions, even with high variability in terms of individual differences in their general ability to delay gratification. To us, these results would seem to argue strongly against the idea that ingesting glucose following a depleted state (such as a breakfast meal) may offset self-control difficulties. However, it should be noted that we did not attempt to "deplete" self-control in the monkeys with a first task before giving them the second task. Perhaps that would have led to a difference between meal conditions. We assessed that possibility next.

Parrish et al. (2018) gave capuchin monkeys back-to-back self-control tests in order to assess depletion effects. Monkeys first completed the accumulation test, and then an exchange test in which they had to hand back lower preference items in order to receive higher preference items. Exchange

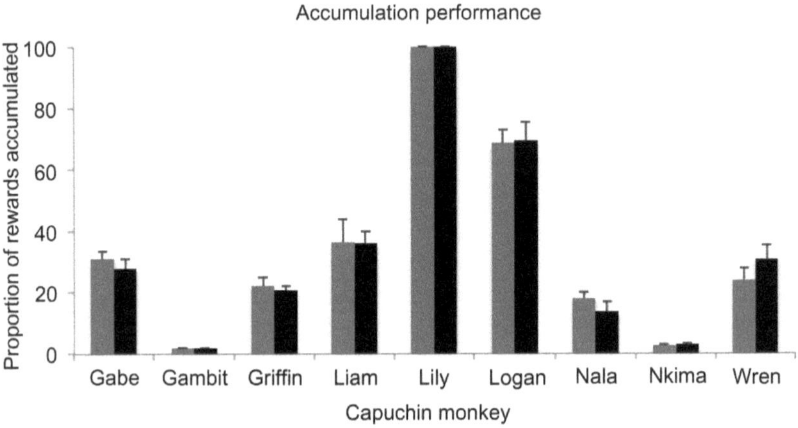

FIGURE 11.6 Accumulation performance for individual capuchin monkeys for the low-glucose (gray bars) and high-glucose (black bars) conditions in Parrish et al. (2016). Bars represent the mean proportion of rewards accumulated in each condition. Error bars depict standard error of the mean. *From Parrish, A. E., Emerson, I. D., Rossettie, M. S., & Beran, M. J. (2016). Testing the ego-depletion hypothesis among capuchin monkeys: Does glucose boost self-control?* Behavioral Sciences, 6, *16. Copyright 2016. Reprinted with permission of the authors.*

tests are frequently used to test self-control in animals because a subject is required to inhibit consumption of a food item in lieu of receiving a potentially tastier reward (e.g., exchange an apple for a cookie). The key depletion manipulation occurred during the accumulation test within each session. On some sessions, the monkeys had to inhibit taking the accumulating food items, or else the accumulation would end. On other sessions, the number of food items that accumulated was yoked to a free-choice trial, but monkeys *could not* access the accumulation while it was occurring. The idea here was that the free-choice condition required self-control and inhibition of taking the foods, whereas the yoked condition had all of the same features (potential frustration at needing to wait to eat, potential excitement to see food accumulating, etc.) without requiring any actual inhibition as the accumulation food pan was inaccessible but visible to the monkey. In both cases, monkeys then received a series of exchange opportunities to see how often they would hand back the first food received to get the second food. Those exchange opportunities included chances to trade a low-preference item for a very high preference item (carrot for marshmallow), medium-preference item for a high-preference item (apple for marshmallow), low-preference item for medium-preference item (carrot for apple), and a control condition where apple could be traded for carrot (but such a trade would be against food preference values). Although there was a lot of variation in terms of those different exchange conditions and how individual monkeys performed on the two tasks, with regard to self-control depletion effects, there was again little evidence that such depletion occurred. In other words, exchange task performances for the monkeys were very similar, no matter whether inhibition was required in the free-choice accumulation task or was not required in the yoked trials. Instead, the individual monkeys' performances in the food exchange task were consistent across these conditions (Fig. 11.7). A second experiment replicated this outcome even when both tasks (accumulation and exchange) were varied session to session in terms of their order, with little evidence that performance on one task depleted performance on the second.

Thus, it seems that there is conflicting evidence about the nature of self-control depletion in nonhuman animals. The work with dogs (Miller & Bender, 2012; Miller et al., 2010, 2012) shows some examples of situations where depletion appears to be evident, and may even be offset by glucose consumption. However, none of the work with nonhuman primates supports this hypothesis, despite some approaches similar in design to those used with humans. Clearly, more research is needed on this topic. I again would suggest that the construct of self-control is not as unitary as to lend itself cleanly to the idea of a depletion model. Self-control as a construct really refers to a suite of mechanisms that control responding, that evaluate current and future reward opportunities, and that interact with subject variables such as personality, motivation, and perhaps other cognitive abilities that relate to future-orientation or outcome weighing processes. And, the field (human and nonhuman) still must contend with the inconsistency in performance of the same individuals across tasks that are often lumped together as being self-control tasks or inhibition tasks, an issue I discuss in the next chapter. This is to me another important concern moving forward. I already discussed the need for more careful consideration of terms, and how those are applied to tasks in Chapter 2, Varieties of Self-Control, but the issue here is less about terminology and more about considering the psychology of task demands. This is more difficult, because at face value a task may appear to be one that should require an animal (or a human) to show self-control, or to inhibit a response, but that does not mean all such tasks rely on the same mechanisms to control behavior and generate responses.

Clearly, the Depletion Model or Strength Model of self-control has generated a lot of research interest. In its infancy, the results were striking and seemed to point to an almost "magical" solution to at least some problems that occur when people are faced with the need to exhibit self-control repeatedly in a short period of time, or when people are forced to inhibit actions they want to perform. There were claims that glucose or other fairly easy to implement remedies might be valuable interventions, and perhaps even improve cognitive functioning in some cases. And, that may be true in some contexts and circumstances. Despite some failed replications, there are plenty of reports of clear depletion effects and protection against depletion by glucose ingestion or other interventions. I suspect it will take some time not only to work out the physiological mechanisms that are at work when food

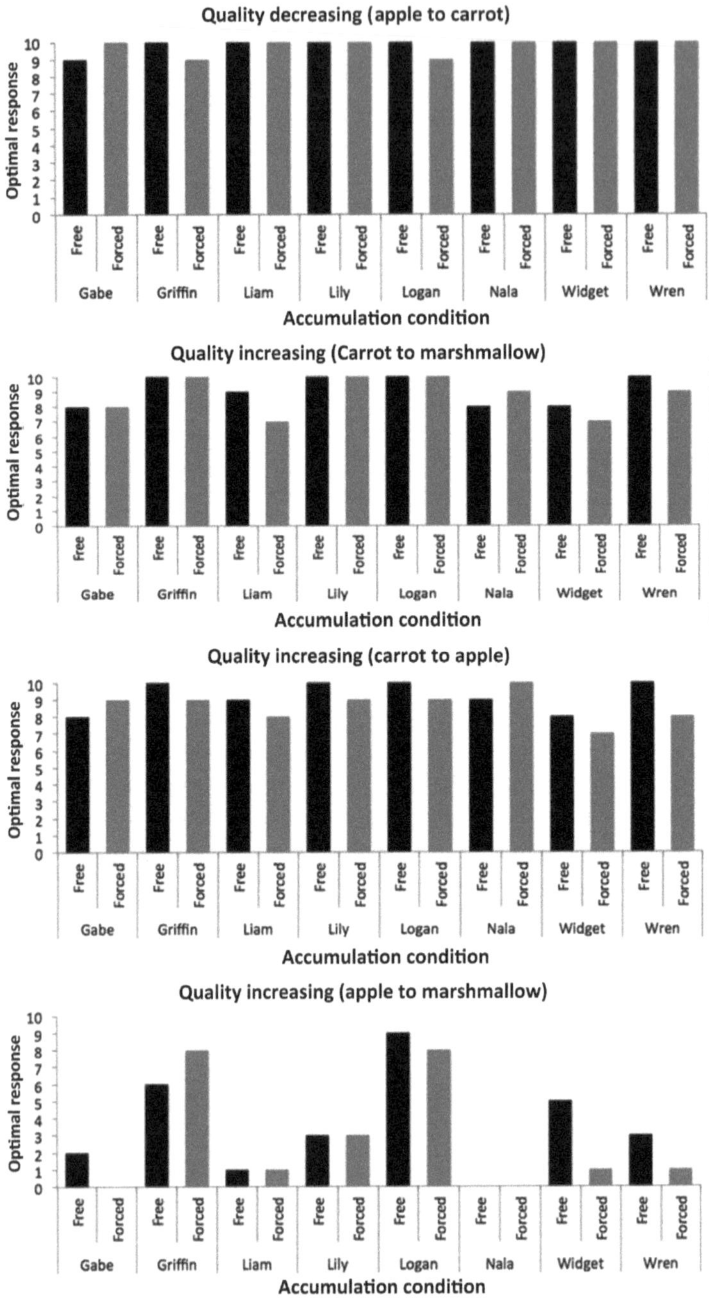

FIGURE 11.7 Test performance for the food exchange self-control task in Experiment 1 of Parrish et al. (2018). Each graph shows a different exchange opportunity, for each monkey, after each of the two accumulation test conditions. (A) Quality-decreasing trial type—apple to carrot, (B) quality-increasing trial type—carrot to marshmallow, (C) quality-increasing trial type—carrot to apple, (D) quality-increasing trial type—apple to marshmallow. *From Parrish, A. E., James, B. T., Rossettie, M. S., Smith, T. R., Otalora-Garcia, A., & Beran, M. J. (2018) Investigating the depletion effect: Self-control does not waiver in capuchin monkeys.* Animal Behavior and Cognition, 5, *118–138. Reprinted with permission of the authors.*

impacts choice behavior, inhibition, and self-control, but also to determine what role depletion of self-control or inhibitory control plays in other aspects of cognitive functioning, and particularly executive functioning. My own conclusion, that is undoubtedly biased by my own work in this area, and perhaps a bit of a primate-centric perspective, is that comparative efforts to document depletion and the positive role of glucose in behavioral inhibition have not done so, and thus I do not think there is good reason to promote those ideas. The work with dogs is highly suggestive of such evidence occurring in other animals, but primates are more closely related to humans, and therefore should also be giving us some similar evidence. Instead, they do not, at least to this point. This may be a methodological shortcoming (as I discuss in the next chapter), or it may be that the depletion/strength model is inconsistently at work in different kinds of tests for reasons we have not yet discerned. My guess is that we will have a clearer picture about this within the next few years, as more studies are conducted with a larger number of species, an outcome which may require me to change my opinion, or stick more strongly to it.

REFERENCES

Benton, D., & Owens, D. S. (1993). Blood glucose and human memory. *Psychopharmacology, 113*, 83–88.

Benton, D., Ruffin, M., Lassel, T., Nabb, S., Messaoudi, M., Vinoy, S., ... Lang, V. (2003). The delivery rate of dietary carbohydrates affects cognitive performance in both rats and humans. *Psychopharmacology, 166*, 86–90.

Benton, D., & Sargent, J. (1992). Breakfast blood glucose and memory. *Biological Psychology, 33*, 207–210.

Bray, E. E., MacLean, E. L., & Hare, B. A. (2014). Context specificity of inhibitory control in dogs. *Animal Cognition, 17*, 15–31.

Bray, E. E., MacLean, E. L., & Hare, B. A. (2015). Increasing arousal enhances inhibitory control in calm but not excitable dogs. *Animal Cognition, 18*, 1317–1329.

Brucks, D., Soliani, M., Range, F., & Marshall-Pescini, S. (2017). Reward type and behavioural patterns predict dogs' success in a delay of gratification paradigm. *Scientific Reports, 7*, 42459.

De Petrillo, F., Micucci, A., Gori, E., Truppa, V., Ariely, D., & Addessi, E. (2015). Self-control depletion in tufted capuchin monkeys (*Sapajus spp.*): Does delay of gratification rely on a limited resource?. *Frontiers in Psychology, 6*, 1193.

Fellows, L. K., Boutelle, M. G., & Fillenz, M. (1992). Physiological stimulation increases nonoxidative glucose metabolism in the brain of the freely moving rat. *Journal of Neurochemistry, 75*, 325–337.

Gold, P. E. (1995). Role of glucose in regulating the brain and cognition. *American Journal of Clinical Nutrition, 61*, 987–995.

Hughes, R. N. (2003). Effects of glucose on responsiveness to change in young adult and middle-aged rats. *Physiology & Behavior, 78*, 529–534.

Ingwersen, J., Defeyter, M. A., Kennedy, D. O., Wesnes, K. A., & Scholey, A. B. (2007). A low glycaemic index breakfast cereal preferentially prevents children's cognitive performance from declining throughout the morning. *Appetite, 49*, 240–244.

Kurzban, R. (2010). Does the brain consume additional glucose during self-control tasks?. *Evolutionary Psychology, 8*, 244–259.

Lange, F., & Eggert, F. (2014). Sweet delusion. Glucose drinks fail to counteract ego depletion. *Appetite, 75*, 54–63.

Leonardi, R. J., Vick, S. J., & Dufour, V. (2012). Waiting for more: The performance of domestic dogs (*Canis familiaris*) on exchange tasks. *Animal Cognition, 15*, 107–120.

Mahoney, C. R., Taylor, H. A., Kanarek, R. B., & Samuel, P. (2005). Effect of breakfast composition on cognitive processes in elementary school children. *Physiology & Behavior, 85*, 635–645.

McNay, E. C., Fries, T. M., & Gold, P. E. (2000). Decreases in rat extracellular hippocampal glucose concentration associated with cognitive demand during a spatial task. *Proceedings of the National Academy of Sciences, USA, 97*, 2881–2885.

Messier, C. (1997). Object recognition in mice: Improvement of memory by glucose. *Neurobiology of Learning Memory, 67*, 172–175.

Miller, H. C., & Bender, C. (2012). The breakfast effect: Dogs (*Canis familiaris*) search more accurately when they are less hungry. *Behavioural processes, 91*, 313–317.

Miller, H. C., DeWall, C. N., Pattison, K., Molet, M., & Zentall, T. R. (2012). Too dog tired to avoid danger: Self-control depletion in canines increases behavioral approach toward an aggressive threat. *Psychonomic Bulletin & Review, 19*, 535–540.

Miller, H. C., Pattison, K. F., DeWall, C. N., Rayburn-Reeves, R., & Zentall, T. R. (2010). Self-control without a "self"? Common self-control processes in humans and dogs. *Psychological Science, 21*, 534–538.

Molden, D. C., Hui, C. M., Scholer, A. A., Meier, B. P., Noreen, E. E., D'Agostino, P. R., et al. (2012). Motivational versus metabolic effects of carbohydrates on self-control. *Psychological Science, 23*, 1137–1144.

Parrish, A. E., Emerson, I. D., Rossettie, M. S., & Beran, M. J. (2016). Testing the ego-depletion hypothesis among capuchin monkeys: Does glucose boost self-control?. *Behavioral Sciences, 6*, 16.

Parrish, A. E., James, B. T., Rossettie, M. S., Smith, T. R., Otalora-Garcia, A., & Beran, M. J. (2018). Investigating the depletion effect: Self-control does not waiver in capuchin monkeys. *Animal Behavior and Cognition, 5*, 118–138.

Rampersaud, G. C., Pereira, M. A., Girard, B. L., Adams, J., & Metzl, J. D. (2005). Breakfast habits, nutritional status, body weight, and academic performance in children and adolescents. *Journal of the American Dietary Association, 105*, 743–760.

Scholey, A., Harper, S., & Kennedy, D. O. (2001). Cognitive demand and blood glucose. *Physiology & Behavior, 73*, 585–592.

Wenk, G. (1989). An hypothesis on the role of glucose in the mechanism of action of cognitive enhancers. *Psychopharmacology, 99*, 431–438.

Wesnes, K. A., Pincock, C., Richardshon, D., Helm, G., & Hails, S. (2003). Breakfast reduces declines in attention and memory over the morning in schoolchildren. *Appetite, 41*, 329–331.

FURTHER READING

Baumeister, R. F., Bratslavsky, E., Muraven, M., & Tice, D. M. (1998). Ego depletion: Is the active self a limited resource? *Journal of Personality and Social Psychology*, *74*, 1252–1265.

Benton, D., Owens, D. S., & Parker, P. Y. (1994). Blood glucose influences memory and attention in young adults. *Neuropsychologia*, *32*, 595–607.

Benton, D., & Parker, P. Y. (1998). Breakfast, blood glucose, and cognition. *American Journal of Clinical Nutrition*, *67*, 772S–778S.

Benton, D., Parker, P. Y., & Donohoe, R. T. (1996). The supply of glucose to the brain and cognitive functioning. *Journal of Biosocial Science*, *28*, 463–479.

Mayack, C., & Naug, D. (2015). Starving honeybees lose self-control. *Biology letters*, *11*, 20140820.

Miklósi, Á. (2007). *Dog behaviour, evolution, and cognition*. Oxford, UK: Oxford University Press.

Miller, H. C., Bourrasseau, C., & Blampain, J. (2015). Self-regulatory depletion in dogs: Insulin release is not necessary for the replenishment of persistence. *Behavioural Processes*, *110*, 22–26.

Wright, H. F., Mills, D. S., & Pollux, P. M. (2012). Behavioural and physiological correlates of impulsivity in the domestic dog (*Canis familiaris*). *Physiology & Behavior*, *105*, 676–682.

Chapter 12

Are Animal Tests of Self-Control All Measuring the Same Thing?

Are all self-control and inhibition studies given to nonhuman animals "created equal"? This is the question that is beginning to be asked by some research teams, and that I will focus on for this fairly short chapter, given how early we are in the process of asking this question. To this point, I have noted that in many cases, researchers have found that what people do in one instance in which inhibition or self-control is needed does not necessarily predict what they might do in another. Lempert and Phelps (2016) discussed this issue at length as it pertains to human intertemporal choices and self-control decisions. They noted that although there has been a longstanding notion that impulsivity and self-control are traits that might be genetically influenced (e.g., Anokhin, Grant, Mulligan, & Heath, 2015; Bickel, 2015; MacKillop, 2013; Odum, 2011), behavioral research seems to suggest otherwise. Reference points such as those commonly described as crucial to economic decisions (e.g., Loewenstein, 1988) play a role in intertemporal choice, as do things such as the endowment effect, and various emotional states that people might be in when they make choices (e.g., Lempert, Glimcher, & Phelps, 2015). How people consider time, and the nearness in time of the future rewards, also impacts intertemporal choices (DeHart & Odum, 2015; Gibbon, Church, Fairhurst, & Kacelnik, 1988; Kim & Zauberman, 2009; Zauberman, Kim, Malkoc, & Bettman, 2009). And, the extent to which people are future oriented in their thinking impacts intertemporal choices (Daniel, Said, Stanton, & Epstein, 2015; Kwan et al., 2015; Lin & Epstein, 2014; Liu, Feng, Chen, & Li, 2013), an issue that will be the focus of Chapter 14. Thus, it is an open question as to how best to predict what a person might choose in each instance in which intertemporal choices are offered. Even knowing what people might do in one test may not give reliable predictions of what they do in another test, no matter how closely related those tests may seem to be.

For example, Young and McCoy (2015) adapted a first person shooter game to be played in either a delay of gratification condition or a delay discounting condition. In the delay of gratification condition, the power of the weapon used would increase as long as the player avoided shooting it while

Self-Control in Animals and People. DOI: https://doi.org/10.1016/B978-0-12-812508-3.00012-8
© 2018 Elsevier Inc. All rights reserved.

it charged up. In the delay discounting condition, the player had one second to shoot the weapon, or else they were forced to allow it to build to a greater strength. So, in the first case, delay maintenance was needed, whereas in the second case the choice phase occurred early in the trial, and then locked the player into that outcome based on that choice. As you might expect, people were more likely to lock into the delayed reward of a stronger weapon in the delay discounting variation of the task, compared to the delayed gratification version where defection (i.e., changing their mind and shooting the weapon) was a possibility. In that experiment, however, people were in one task or the other, not both tasks, so we do not know a lot about how the same people would do in both kinds of tests. It would be interesting to see if people were consistent in their choices (whether to delay or not) in both tests given at different points in the experiment.

Forzano, Michels, Carapella, Conway, and Chelonis (2011) also gave children an intertemporal delay discounting task and a delay of gratification task, and in this case each child was given each test. In the discounting task, children chose repeatedly between one candy more immediately, and three candies after a longer delay. They also completed a delay of gratification trial where they had to wait 20 minutes for a large reward or they could end the trial by pressing a bell and instead get a small reward. Forzano et al. found a strong correlation between performances on these two tasks, suggesting that both tapped into a common self-control mechanism. One important point about this study was that, for the intertemporal choice task, children had the option to stop waiting, and instead take the smaller reward at any time. So, this was a task that also had a maintenance component to it, like the commonly used delay of gratification test where children had to wait through a delay to improve the reward. This likely accounts for why there was such similarity in performance across the tasks. Other efforts, with more variable tasks, have often shown little or no correspondence between performance on one task of self-control or impulsivity and others (Olson, 1989; Reynolds & Stark, 1986; Soreni, Crosbie, Ickowicz, & Schachar, 2009), although some studies do find similar performances across tasks (e.g., Avila, Cuenca, Félix, Parcet, & Miranda, 2004). Because of this inconsistency, it is difficult to argue that there is a generalized self-control capacity within people that is as readily applied to one task or context as to another.

Work with nonhuman animals appears to show some of the same constraints on our ability to argue for generalized self-control abilities and generalized capacities for behavioral inhibition. I will discuss tasks I have already described in earlier chapters, but now I will focus on studies where more than one of those tasks have been given to the same individuals of a species, in an effort to see whether there are relations between the resulting performances of animals in those tasks. There have not been many such efforts to give a diverse set of inhibitory and self-control tasks to the same animals, but I think those studies have highlighted important issues for understanding the nature of self-control.

One of the earliest attempts to assess performance in the same animals on different tests was conducted with rats and involved delay of gratification and delay discounting tasks. Reynolds and Schiffbauer (2005) had written an article about human self-control, and they argued that although the two kinds of tasks were related, there were also important differences. Unlike Rachlin (2000), who had argued that delay of gratification tasks were measures of delay discounting functions in subjects who did those tests (such as the marshmallow test), Reynolds and Schiffbauer stated that too much behavioral evidence argued against that idea. They noted that in studies like Mischel and Metzner (1962) in which children were asked delay discounting questions about future events, children did not show much preference for later rewards until around 9 years of age, whereas good performance on the marshmallow task emerges much earlier. In their own work, children younger than 9 also seemed not to show typical discounting functions when given choices between real-world rewards like nickels at different delays. Reynolds and Schiffbauer also argued, as have I, that the delay of gratification tests involved an aspect of maintenance that is not present in typical delay discounting tests. And, in delay of gratification tests, one of the best predictors of delay length is not time estimation accuracy, but rather behavioral strategies to deal with temptation.

From these arguments, Reynolds, de Wit, and Richards (2002) directly assessed the performance of rats given both a delay of gratification test and a delay discounting task. In the delay of gratification test, rats could choose a smaller, immediate reward or a larger, delayed reward, *and during the delay they could change that choice*. So, there was a maintenance component. In the delay discounting test, however, the same procedure was in place, but with no chance to change the initial response for smaller-sooner or larger-later reward. What I find most compelling is that rats made fewer "defection-like" responses when in the delay of gratification test than in the delay discounting task. These responses, where rats contacted the immediate reward option during the delay period as they waited for the delayed reward, would have been costly in the delay of gratification test because they would mean the rat essentially put itself into a longer delay to get the same smaller reward it could have had immediately. So, inhibiting those responses during delay maintenance was crucial. But, in the delay discounting test, those kinds of secondary behaviors were unrelated to the outcome of the trial, and the delay had to be tolerated no matter. This means rats treated the two tests differently, even though both procedures were largely identical. However, rats also responded to the two kinds of tests in a highly similar way when one looked at how they discounted the delayed reward. Both tasks produced rates of discounting that were not significantly different from each other, although the rats in the delay of gratification task discounted at a higher rate (Fig 12.1). In both tasks, the discounting was well described by the hyperbolic function I discussed earlier. Reynolds et al. concluded that delay of

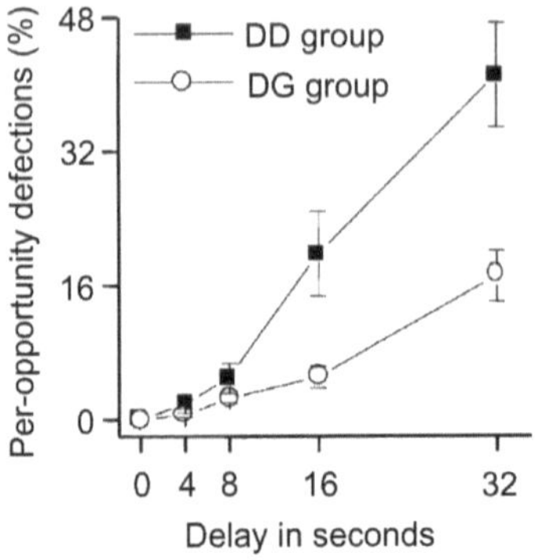

FIGURE 12.1 The per-opportunity percentage of defections for the rats given the delay of gratification (DG) or delay discounting (DD) tasks in Reynolds et al. (2002). *From Reynolds, B., de Wit, H., & Richards, J. B. (2002). Delay of gratification and delay discounting in rats.* Behavioural Processes, 59, *157–168. Copyright 2002. Reprinted with permission from Elsevier.*

gratification tests and delay discounting tests measure different aspects of impulsive behavior, and specifically that inhibitory mechanisms are brought to bear in delay of gratification tasks that are not activated in delay discounting tasks.

Some other studies have directly assessed the performance of animals on multiple delay of gratification and self-control tests. I have already discussed one of these studies in detail in Chapter 9 (Addessi et al., 2013), that involved capuchin monkeys who were given an intertemporal choice test and the accumulation test. In that study, there was no relation between performance on the two tasks. In a subsequent study with capuchin monkeys in my lab, we were looking for improved performance in one task after getting improved performance in another. Specifically, we gave capuchin monkeys a series of rotating tray tasks and accumulation tasks (Beran et al., 2016). The first thing we wanted to do was to build a version of each task that was as close to identical as we could, in terms of how rewards were viewed, the temporal demands of waiting for the better item, and so forth (Fig. 12.2). In Experiment 1 of that study, the delayed rewards were always visible, either slowly moving around the rotating tray or being held as part of the set of items that could be accumulated. And, both tasks had "forced" trials where the monkeys could not act impulsively, and had to see what would happen as the delay elapsed and more food was rewarded. In these tasks, the accumulation or rotating tray movement brought more food, not different food, so it was a quantitative gain from waiting. And, it was progressive. In Experiment 1, each "unit" of delay led to the food set that could then be eaten increasing from 1 reward, to 3 rewards, and then to 6, 12, 20, and 40 rewards (these were small banana-flavored pellets). This meant that as the tray arms came within reach on a trial, there would be a substantial

FIGURE 12.2 A capuchin monkey sitting in front of the rotating tray test (left) and the accumulation apparatus (right). *From Beran, M. J., Perdue, B. M., Rossettie, M. S., James, B. T., Whitham, W., Walker, B...., & Parrish, A. E. (2016). Self-control assessments of capuchin monkeys with the rotating tray task and the accumulation task.* Behavioural Processes, 129, *68–79. Copyright 2016. Reprinted with permission from Springer.*

proportional gain, and the same was true for new amounts added at each time interval in the accumulation task. Given past results with these same monkeys (Addessi et al., 2013; Bramlett, Perdue, Evans, & Beran, 2012; Perdue, Bramlett, Evans, & Beran, 2015), we predicted that the rotating tray task would lead to better performance in terms of gaining more rewards. We were wrong. The monkeys performed equally well in both tasks, and the only real effect of that experiment was that they improved in both tasks across sessions, which is what one might expect to see—that experience helps. We considered that the use of such big changes in amount might have contributed to this, so we replicated this with the more traditional addition of the same number of items at each rotation or each accumulation point. We found the same results. Monkeys performed equally well. This was again surprising, because here was a situation where we predicted that the two tasks *were not equally demanding* in terms of what monkeys could see during trials. The rotating tray task keeps giving the subject a chance to see an even bigger reward on its way, whereas the accumulation task is more passive in terms of not presenting a bigger, distant reward but only a growing, close reward. But, the good news was that these data suggested the two tasks were engaging the same inhibitory mechanisms in these monkeys. However, we then tested a new group of monkeys, and we found no indication that improving performance on one of these tasks predicted improving performance on the other. Instead, it was clear that *specific task parameters* such as delay intervals or reward increases (in terms of relative amounts) were crucial features. Overall, we concluded that the two tasks likely share some common engagement with certain self-control mechanisms, but they are not so closely related as to be interchangeable.

This conclusion seems to hold for nonprimate species as well. Hillemann, Bugnyar, Kotrschal, and Wascher (2014) gave the same crows and ravens an exchange task and the accumulation task, as well as, in each case, offering qualitative and quantitative "upgrades" in reward type if the birds waited. In the exchange tasks, delays to getting the better or larger reward varied from only 2 seconds to as long as 1,280 seconds, depending on whether birds would exchange at whatever current delay they were at. The accumulation task they used allowed for as many as four items to accumulate, and they again increased the inter-item delays on the basis of how well the birds could wait, again up to a longest possible delay of 1,280 seconds. The maximum delay condition reached was 640 seconds, achieved in the qualitative exchange task, and 320 seconds in the accumulation task. As with past work with birds, performance generally was better for the qualitative reward "upgrades" compared to the quantitative ones (Fig. 12.3). Although Hillemann et al. did not report a direct assessment of performance between tasks (e.g., a correlation of successful trial numbers across their subjects), the general group performance supported the idea that birds performed comparably in exchange and accumulation (Fig. 12.3). Thus, it would seem that in birds also, exchange and accumulation tasks appear to recruit similar mechanisms underlying self-control.

In contrast, Bray, MacLean, and Hare (2014) showed another clear example of limited connection between task performances when they gave dogs three different inhibition tasks. Although these are not tests of self-control, as I explained in Chapter 2, I think they highlight the same issue of knowing whether tasks all measure the same thing they may "feel" like they must be measuring. In the first task, dogs had to learn that one experimenter was stingy and would not give the dogs the better food that the experimenter held, and so the dogs needed to inhibit going toward the person with better food, and instead approach a person with the lower preference item. In what is called the A-not-B task, dogs had to learn to inhibit going back to a location where they last found food, and instead go to a new location where they saw food moved from that original location (i.e., they could not perseverate on the previous location where food had been placed). And, the dogs were given the cylinder task I described earlier, in which they had to detour around to the end of the cylinder rather than try to reach directly at the food through the transparent tube because it was not accessible this way. Dogs learned to perform all three of these tasks, but there did not seem to be any relation between performances on the tasks within the same dogs. This suggests that not all "inhibition" tasks are equally taxing of the same behavioral, cognitive, and neural mechanisms, which of course I discussed earlier as also being true for people. In fact, we know this intuitively, because we know that people can show wonderful inhibitory and self-control capacities in some contexts while being highly impulsive in others (e.g., the cigarette smoking marathon runner). Bray et al. discussed this idea at length, noting

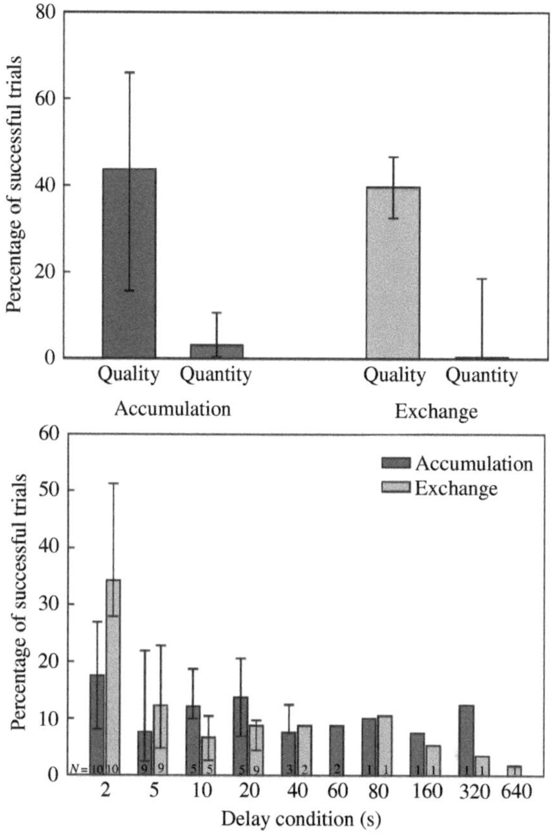

FIGURE 12.3 Result from Hillemann et al. (2014). The top panel shows the percentage of successful trials in each task depending on reward type. Bars represent medians; error bars are based on interquartile ranges (25th and 75th percentiles) and indicate individual variation. The bottom panel shows the number of subjects tested (inside bars) and median percentage of successful trials per delay condition. Interindividual variation is presented as interquartile ranges (25th and 75th percentiles). *From Hillemann, F., Bugnyar, T., Kotrschal, K., & Wascher, C. A. F. (2014) Waiting for better, not for more: Corvids respond to quality in two delay maintenance tasks.* Animal Behaviour, 90, *1–10. Copyright 2014. Reprinted with permission of Elsevier.*

research that supports the idea that inhibitory control is highly variable between contexts and individuals. For example, Tsukayama et al. (2010) reported that people who reported that they are easily tempted by food are more likely to be impulsive when it comes to dietary decisions (which makes sense), but not in other scenarios, such as in their alcohol consumption or in their daily finance decisions. This highlights the earlier contrast I discussed between those who argue that there is support for more generalized inhibitory capacities within individuals (e.g., Baumeister, Bratslavsky, Muraven, & Tice, 1998; Duckworth & Seligman, 2005) and those who claim that the individual differences we see in performance across tasks may also reflect the large role that context plays in inhibitory behavior (Tsukayama & Duckworth, 2010). Because of this, there may not be clear relations between different tasks that should seem to elicit a common mechanism (or mechanisms) for making intertemporal choices or demonstrating self-control. Rather, one might best think of self-control, for example, as being a multidimensional construct that will be best understood when it is studied through a range of methodologies such as delay of gratification, intertemporal choice tasks, and others (Duckworth & Kern, 2011).

Of course, this does not mean that *no inhibitory tasks* are related in their design and response requirements. We know that they are, and I discussed earlier some of the longitudinal work that showed relations between self-control and other positive life outcomes. This simply means that the nature of inhibitory control processes, including self-control mechanisms, are not unitary, but are likely a suite of subprocesses that may or may not be brought to bear by different individuals on specific environmental contexts that require inhibition or self-control for the best objective outcome to occur. This idea perhaps explains some of the discrepancies in the ego depletion literature, because it could be the case that the depletion is a real phenomenon, but also one that is heavily dependent on context, individual differences in participants' natural tendencies, and other sources of variance. From this, it seems the conservative interpretation is that sometimes exerting self-control or some other type of behavioral inhibition affects subsequent choice behavior, or perseverance in the face of difficulty, but this relation is more fragile than that used in the analogy of self-control as a muscle. Physical muscles fatigue, and there is nothing about the second exercise (assuming it uses the same muscle) that affords possible differences in recovery strength after performing a first exercise to exhaustion, but in the psychological realm this may not be the case. There may be other factors that dictate the degree of consequence on the second task from performing the first, and one of the clearest factors may be the nature of the tasks themselves. Some tasks require only temporally guided choice behavior, and of a form where a quick, discrete response is made (e.g., a bar press, poke, or screen touch), others require motoric inhibition (e.g., detour tasks), and yet others require a sustained maintenance of the attempt to delay gratification by not eating items already present (e.g., the accumulation test, exchange tasks). Each of these tests has unique response properties, and the mechanisms supporting those properties likely are recruited *in addition to* a general desire on the part of the subject to wait for a better reward (or, in many cases, to not wait, and take what is available now).

Another recent series of independent studies, all conducted with dogs, highlights this issue very nicely. Marshall-Pescini, Virányi, and Range (2015) presented dogs and wolves with two tasks that would seem to be highly similar in their inhibitory demands. The detour task required both species to go around a fence to obtain a reward rather than go toward the central part of the fence where the food was on the other side. The cylinder task involved a food reward in the center of a cylinder, which required the dogs and wolves to go to one end to get into it and retrieve the reward. In some cases, the cylinder was transparent, and so the measure of inhibition pertained to whether dogs and wolves tried to reach directly at the food before going around to the end. Both species showed levels of success in both tasks, but the key issue here pertained to whether performance was related *between tasks*. It was not. There was no significant correlation of success in the cylinder task and duration of staying at the fence in either species, and there was no significant correlation of success in the cylinder task and latency to obtain the reward in the detour task. Marshall-Pescini et al. did a very nice job of considering why these two tasks might not correlate. They noted that perhaps the detour task required more than just inhibition, but also some greater understanding of the nature of spatial relationships. Or perhaps the cylinder task required greater attentional control on the part of subjects as they needed to watch what the experimenter was doing. Marshall-Pescini concluded that it may be difficult to develop and promote one "clean" inhibition task, given that inhibitory control may instead be a collection of processes (as noted also by Friedman & Miyake, 2004; Miyake et al., 2000). I think it is a very important comment that needs to be remembered in future research.

Müller, Riemer, Virányi, Huber, and Range (2016) did find some relations among three inhibition tasks given to dogs. They used a "wait-for-treat" task in which the dogs had to avoid eating a treat right on the ground in front of them after receiving a "wait" command. They also used a "middle cup task" where three transparent cups were lined up and treats were placed under two of them. The dogs only got to displace two cups, and so when there was no treat under the middle cup the dogs had to inhibit knocking over cups in a row and instead skip past the middle one. And they used a "leash task," in which the dogs could see that a leash attached to their collar or harness could get caught on an obstacle such as a tree if they were not careful to move around that obstacle when called by an owner. For these three tasks, Müller et al. found only weak correlations in terms of dogs' performances, again perhaps because of different response demands as well as different motivational demands.

Brucks, Marshall-Pescini, Wallis, Huber, and Range (2017) made the important point that an crucial step in understanding inhibitory control in any species requires some assessment of the categorization of behaviors into motor inhibition, cognitive inhibition, and self-control to see whether that categorization holds for that species in the way it does for others. They also noted that we must do more to validate that individual tests we give to animals actually capture the specific aspects of inhibition we claim we are studying. I could not agree more, and I also agree with Brucks et al. that until we put in the work to better understand these relations, we are not on solid ground to be making claims about how inhibitory control plays a role in other aspects of animal behavior (and human behavior). Brucks et al. took a big step in that direction with a study they conducted with dogs.

In that study, they gave dogs three tasks designed to assess inhibitory control, to see whether the performance of individual dogs held constant across those tasks or if there was no consistent performance, to determine what mechanisms might underlie responding in each task (Fig. 12.4.). The first inhibition task is called "the box test," and it was originally a task used with children (Diamond & Gilbert, 1989; Lockman & Adams, 2001) that later was adapted to use with nonhuman species such as cotton-top tamarins (Santos, Ericson, & Hauser, 1999), rhesus monkeys (Diamond, 1990), and squirrel monkeys (Parker et al., 2005). In this task, a reward is visible in the center of a clear box. But, reaching right toward it will not be effective, because the box gets in the way. Instead, the subject has to reach around to the side to gain the item, as in the cylinder task I discussed earlier

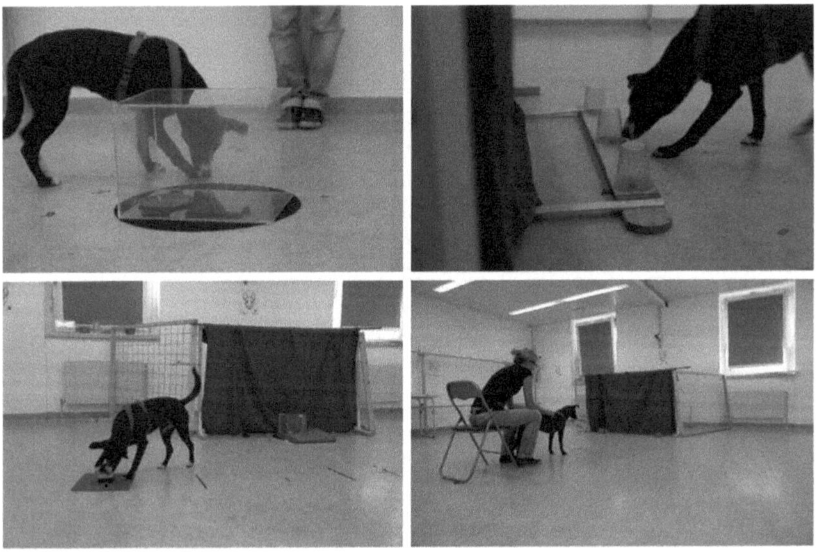

FIGURE 12.4 Inhibition tasks in the Brucks et al. (2017) experiment. Top left: Setup in the box test. The reward is positioned deep in the box on a lid and the box is open on the right side. The experimenter stands behind the box. Top right: Setup for middle cup test. The left and middle cups are baited in this trial. Bottom left: Setup for test trials in the buzzer test. The dog presses the buzzer and the box containing the reward is opened. Bottom right: Setup for reversal learning test. Rewards were hidden under either the orange or the blue object depending on the test group. The owner sat and held the dog 2 m behind the objects. *From Brucks, D., Marshall-Pescini, S., Wallis, L. J., Huber, L., & Range, F. (2017) Measures of dogs' inhibitory control abilities do not correlate across tasks.* Frontiers in Psychology, 8, *Article 849. Copyright 2017. Reprinted with permission of the authors.*

(MacLean et al., 2014; Marshall-Pescini et al., 2015). The unique aspect to this version of a detour/reaching task is that the experimenter can move where the reward is located inside the box to vary the difficulty in terms of the inhibitory component. The second task was the "middle cup test" that I also already described. The third task is called the "buzzer test." This task involved first teaching dogs that they had to press a buzzer next to an opaque box in order to open that box and get a reward. Then, the buzzer was moved *over to the side some distance* and the reward was now in a clear box. So, the dogs had to go to the buzzer, and not toward the visible food in the box. This test combines the motoric inhibition component with a learning component, in terms of the dogs needing to remember how the buzzer works while also inhibiting moving toward the food. The delay of gratification test was the one I described in Chapter 7, where one reward was in reach of the dog for some period of time before another, better reward was moved into reach (if the dog inhibited eating the first reward). Finally, dogs did a reversal learning task, which was originally designed for use with primates to assess their cognitive flexibility and capacity to use rule-based learning in the face of new kinds of problems (e.g., Rumbaugh, 1971). In a reversal learning task, the subject first learns that one of two arbitrary stimuli is the one to choose to gain reward, whereas the other leads to no reward. After becoming good at choosing that rewarded stimulus, the experimenter then *reverses* the task contingencies, so that the previously rewarded stimulus is no longer rewarded, and the previously unrewarded stimulus now is the one that needs to be selected. So, if you think about what is happening at reversal, the animal has to use what it learned about rewarded and nonrewarded stimuli and also inhibit choosing the stimulus it has been choosing. As Brucks et al. (2017) noted, this task has been used with a lot of species to assess their flexibility in what they learn about stimulus relations (e.g., pigeons: Laude, Pattison, Rayburn-Reeves, Michler, & Zentall, 2016; Laude, Stagner, Rayburn-Reeves, & Zentall, 2014; Reid, 1958; rats: Rayburn-Reeves, Stagner, Kirk, & Zentall, 2013; corvids: Bond, Kamil, & Balda, 2007; honeybees: Komischke, Giurfa, Lachnit, & Malun, 2002; cats: Warren, 1966; monkeys: Beran et al., 2008; Hauser, Santos, Spaepen, & Pearson, 2002; Rayburn-Reeves, James, & Beran, 2017; Rumbaugh & McQueeney, 1963; Rumbaugh & Pate, 1984; Rumbaugh & Pournelle, 1966; chimpanzees: Nissen, Riesen, & Nowlis, 1938; Schusterman, 1962), including dogs (Laude et al., 2016; Tapp et al., 2003).

After all of the data were collected, Brucks et al. (2017) found that none of the inhibition tests correlated with each other or with the delay of gratification test or the learning task. Given this outcome, and in order to understand whether any underlying structure exists in dogs' performance across tasks, they next conducted an analysis on the various measures in each task to see if there were any component mechanisms that might underlie these tasks' performances. They reported that three components—which they called persistency, compulsivity, and decision time—best captured the underlying structure of the test battery. However, none of these components were, themselves, a measure of inhibitory control. Brucks et al. had also asked the dogs' owners to do a survey about the dogs' impulsivity, but this questionnaire only modestly captured the variance in the three-component model they proposed. One thing that was interesting was that the underlying components that Brucks et al. found best explained the dogs' performance in the inhibition tests (persistency, compulsivity, decision time) were similar to those sometimes described in the human literature on inhibitory control (e.g., Miller, Joseph, & Tudway, 2004; also see Evenden, 1999, for a review).

A final study I want to mention involved a number of inhibition and intertemporal choice tasks and was conducted by Amici, Aureli, and Call (2008). They gave spider monkeys, capuchin monkeys, macaques, chimpanzees, gorillas, orangutans, and bonobos fives tests (Fig. 12.5). The A-not-B task involved three trials where a reward was placed under the same container, but then in a critical fourth trial it was placed and then moved to another container, to see if the primates could inhibit reaching to the same place for a fourth time. They also used a middle cup task where three cups were aligned in a row, and on each trial the primate could touch two of those. Baseline (non-inhibition) trials were those where the rewards were under adjacent cups, but the crucial inhibition trial left the middle location empty, so the primate had to inhibit touching it and instead go around that cup to the other one on the end. In the third task, food rewards were placed

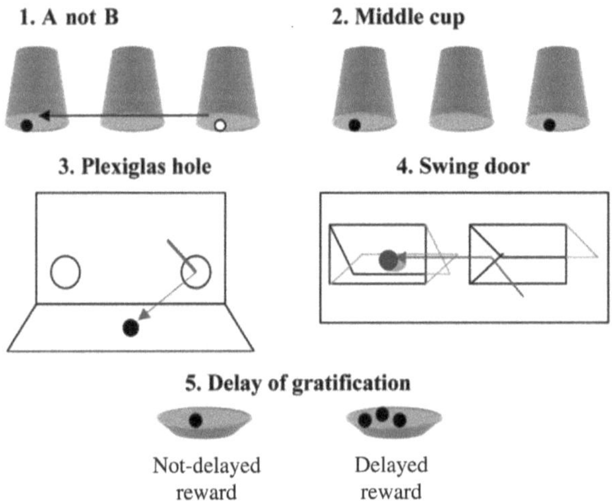

FIGURE 12.5 Illustration of the five tasks in Amici et al. (2008). *From Amici, F., Aurelli, F., & Call, J. (2008). Fission-fusion dynamics, behavioral flexibility, and inhibitory control in primates.* Current Biology, 18, *1415–1419. Copyright 2008. Reprinted with permission from Elsevier.*

right behind one of two holes in a transparent panel for six consecutive trials, but then on the last trial the reward was placed in the middle so that now the subject had to reach around rather than directly at the reward. In the last inhibition task, a detour movement was also needed with an apparatus where two doors could be displaced, but if food was behind one of those, the only way to get it was to reach through the other door or else it would be lost. The last test was a choice test with a smaller-sooner or larger-later option, as I have described in detail earlier. Amici et al. reported a number of interesting species differences in terms of how task performance was rank ordered, and what I find most interesting is that there seemed to be little relation *between tasks*. For example, one might assume the A-not-B and middle cup tasks would be closely related, but gorillas performed perfectly on the A-not-B task but were the worst species at the middle cup task. The tasks requiring detouring around the panel or reaching through the opposite door would also seem to be highly similar, and in some cases they appeared to produce similar results. Orangutans and chimpanzees, respectively, were best and second best at each of those tasks, but bonobos were third best at the panel task and *never succeeded* on any trials with the doors task. Amici et al. did not report their data at the individual level, but I suspect the species-level inconsistencies might also be present within individuals.

So, what is the take-home message from all of this research? In agreement with Brucks et al. (2017), I think the key message is that inhibitory control, or self-control, is not a unitary process but is best conceived of as being a context- and domain-specific process. This is true for humans and for nonhuman animals. There is evolutionary convergence of these capacities, both in their individual manifestations and in their theoretical nature of being as much domain specific as being domain general. My hope is that additional studies will present batteries of inhibitory tasks and self-control to the same individuals, of as many species as we can test. We can fill out a phylogenetic map of these individual performances and relations among performances, and hopefully begin to better understand when specific domains elicit specific mechanisms versus more general mechanisms that are sometimes called "inhibition" or "self-control."

For the remainder of this book, I will focus on what I see as some additional understudied aspects of self-control, and how the integration of more research on those questions may help us better understand what we mean by self-control contexts, and what might explain some of the differences we see in performance across tasks, or between different individuals. This includes considering what role social contexts may play in self-control, and particularly how being alone or in groups might impact choice behavior where self-control is warranted. Then, I will discuss what role future-oriented cognition might play in self-control, and whether that might account for some of the results seen in animals, young children, and even adult humans. The idea that animals could anticipate the future, or even project themselves into that future, was once largely discounted in comparative psychology, but recent evidence suggests that future-oriented decision making may occur in some species, and I think the ideas about how animals anticipate the future have natural links to when and how animals show self-control.

REFERENCES

Addessi, E., Paglieri, F., Beran, M., Evans, T., Macchitella, L., De Petrillo, F., & Focaroli, V. (2013). Delay choice vs. delay maintenance: Different measures of delayed gratification in capuchin monkeys (*Cebus apella*). *Journal of Comparative Psychology*, *127*, 392–398.

Amici, F., Aurelli, F., & Call, J. (2008). Fission-fusion dynamics, behavioral flexibility, and inhibitory control in primates. *Current Biology*, *18*, 1415–1419.

Anokhin, A. P., Grant, J. D., Mulligan, R. C., & Heath, A. C. (2015). The genetics of impulsivity: Evidence for the heritability of delay discounting. *Biological Psychiatry*, *77*, 887–894.

Avila, C., Cuenca, I., Félix, V., Parcet, M. A., & Miranda, A. (2004). Measuring impulsivity in school-aged boys and examining its relationship with ADHD and ODD ratings. *Journal of Abnormal Child Psychology*, *32*, 295–304.

Baumeister, R. F., Bratslavsky, E., Muraven, M., & Tice, D. M. (1998). Ego depletion: Is the active self a limited resource? *Journal of Personality and Social Psychology*, *74*, 1252–1265.

Beran, M. J., Klein, E. D., Evans, T. A., Chan, B., Flemming, T. J., Harris, E. H., & Rumbaugh, D. M. (2008). Discrimination reversal learning in capuchin monkeys (*Cebus apella*). *Psychological Record*, *58*, 3–14.

Beran, M. J., Perdue, B. M., Rossettie, M. S., James, B. T., Whitham, W., Walker, B., ... Parrish, A. E. (2016). Self-control assessments of capuchin monkeys with the rotating tray task and the accumulation task. *Behavioural Processes*, *129*, 68–79.

Bickel, W. K. (2015). Discounting of delayed rewards as an endophenotype. *Biological Psychiatry*, *77*, 846–847.

Bond, A. B., Kamil, A., & Balda, R. P. (2007). Serial reversal learning and the evolution of behavioral flexibility in three species of north American Corvids (*Gymnorhinus cyanocephalus, Nucifraga columbiana, Aphelocoma californica*). *Journal of Comparative Psychology*, *121*, 372–379.

Bramlett, J. L., Perdue, B. M., Evans, T. A., & Beran, M. J. (2012). Capuchin monkeys (*Cebus apella*) let lesser rewards pass them by to get better rewards. *Animal Cognition*, *15*, 963–969.

Bray, E. E., MacLean, E. L., & Hare, B. A. (2014). Context specificity of inhibitory control in dogs. *Animal Cognition*, *17*, 15–31.

Brucks, D., Marshall-Pescini, S., Wallis, L. J., Huber, L., & Range, F. (2017). Measures of dogs' inhibitory control abilities do not correlate across tasks. *Frontiers in Psychology*, *8*, Article 849.

Daniel, T. O., Said, M., Stanton, C. M., & Epstein, L. H. (2015). Episodic future thinking reduces delay discounting and energy intake in children. *Eating Behaviors*, *18*, 20–24.

DeHart, W. B., & Odum, A. L. (2015). The effects of the framing of time on delay discounting. *Journal of the Experimental Analysis of Behavior*, *103*, 10–21.

Diamond, A. (1990). Developmental time course in human infants and infant monkeys, and the neural bases of, inhibitory control in reaching. *Annals of the New York Academy of Sciences*, *608*, 637–676.

Duckworth, A. L., & Kern, M. L. (2011). A meta-analysis of the convergent validity of self-control measures. *Journal of Research in Personality*, *45*, 259–268.

Duckworth, A. L., & Seligman, M. E. (2005). Self-discipline outdoes IQ in predicting academic performance of adolescents. *Psychological Science*, *16*, 939–944.

Evenden, J. L. (1999). Varieties of impulsivity. *Psychopharmacology*, *146*, 348–361.

Forzano, L. B., Michels, J. L., Carapella, R. K., Conway, P., & Chelonis, J. J. (2011). Self-control and impulsivity in children: Multiple behavioral measures. *The Psychological Record*, *61*, 425–448.

Friedman, N. P., & Miyake, A. (2004). The relations among inhibition and interference control functions: A latent-variable analysis. *Journal of Experimental Psychology: General*, *133*, 101–135.

Gibbon, J., Church, R. M., Fairhurst, S., & Kacelnik, A. (1988). Scalar expectancy theory and choice between delayed rewards. *Psychological review*, *95*, 102–114.

Hauser, M. D., Santos, L. R., Spaepen, G. M., & Pearson, H. E. (2002). Problem solving, inhibition and domain-specific experience: experiments on cottontop tamarins, *saguinus oedipus*. *Animal Behaviour*, *64*, 387–396.

Hillemann, F., Bugnyar, T., Kotrschal, K., & Wascher, C. A. F. (2014). Waiting for better, not for more: Corvids respond to quality in two delay maintenance tasks. *Animal Behaviour*, *90*, 1–10.

Kim, B. K., & Zauberman, G. (2009). Perception of anticipatory time in temporal discounting. *Journal of Neuroscience, Psychology, and Economics*, *2*, 91–101.

Komischke, B., Giurfa, M., Lachnit, H., & Malun, D. (2002). Successive olfactory reversal learning in honeybees. *Learning & Memory*, *9*, 122–129.

Kwan, D., Craver, C. F., Green, L., Myerson, J., Gao, F., Black, S. E., & Rosenbaum, R. S. (2015). Cueing the personal future to reduce discounting in intertemporal choice: Is episodic prospection necessary? *Hippocampus*, *25*, 432–443.

Laude, J. R., Pattison, K. F., Rayburn-Reeves, R. M., Michler, D. M., & Zentall, T. R. (2016). Who are the real bird brains? Qualitative differences in behavioral flexibility between dogs (*Canis familiaris*) and pigeons (*Columba livia*). *Animal Cognition*, *19*, 163–169.

Laude, J. R., Stagner, J. P., Rayburn-Reeves, R. M., & Zentall, T. R. (2014). Midsession reversals with pigeons: Visual versus spatial discriminations and the intertrial interval. *Learning & Behavior*, *42*, 40–46.

Lempert, K. M., Glimcher, P. W., & Phelps, E. A. (2015). Emotional arousal and discount rate in intertemporal choice are reference dependent. *Journal of Experimental Psychology: General*, *144*, 366–373.

Lempert, K. M., & Phelps, E. A. (2016). The malleability of intertemporal choice. *Trends in Cognitive Sciences*, *20*, 64–74.

Lin, H., & Epstein, L. H. (2014). Living in the moment: effects of time perspective and emotional valence of episodic thinking on delay discounting. *Behavioral Neuroscience*, *128*, 12–19.

Liu, L., Feng, T., Chen, J., & Li, H. (2013). The value of emotion: How does episodic prospection modulate delay discounting? *PloS One*, *8*, e81717.

Lockman, J. J., & Adams, C. D. (2001). Going around transparent and grid-like barriers: Detour ability as a perception-action skill. *Developmental Science*, *4*, 463–471.

Loewenstein, G. F. (1988). Frames of mind in intertemporal choice. *Management Science*, *34*, 200–214.

MacKillop, J. (2013). Integrating behavioral economics and behavioral genetics: delayed reward discounting as an endophenotype for addictive disorders. *Journal of the Experimental Analysis of Behavior, 99*, 14–31.

MacLean, E. L., Hare, B., Nunn, C. L., Addessi, E., Amici, F., Anderson, R. C., & Boogert, N. J. (2014). The evolution of self-control. *Proceedings of the National Academy of Sciences, 111*, E2140–E2148.

Marshall-Pescini, S., Virányi, Z., & Range, F. (2015). The effect of domestication on inhibitory control: Wolves and dogs compared. *PLoS ONE, 10*, 0118469.

Miller, E., Joseph, S., & Tudway, J. (2004). Assessing the component structure of four self-report measures of impulsivity. *Personality and Individual Differences, 37*, 349–358.

Mischel, W., & Metzner, R. (1962). Preference for delayed reward as a function of age, intelligence, and length of delay interval. *Journal of Abnormal and Social Psychology, 64*, 425–431.

Miyake, A., Friedman, N. P., Emerson, M. J., Witzki, A. H., Howerter, A., & Wager, T. D. (2000). The unity and diversity of executive functions and their contributions to complex 'frontal lobe' tasks: A latent variable analysis. *Cognitive Psychology, 41*, 49–100.

Müller, C. A., Riemer, S., Virányi, Z., Huber, L., & Range, F. (2016). Inhibitory control, but not prolonged object-related experience appears to affect physical problem-solving performance of pet dogs. *PloS one, 11*, e0147753.

Nissen, H. W., Riesen, A. H., & Nowlis, V. (1938). Delayed response and discrimination learning by chimpanzees. *Journal of Comparative Psychology, 26*, 361–386.

Odum, A. L. (2011). Delay discounting: trait variable? *Behavioural Processes, 87*, 1–9.

Olson, S. L. (1989). Assessment of impulsivity in preschoolers: Cross-measure convergences, longitudinal stability, and relevance to social competence. *Journal of Clinical Child Psychology, 18*, 176–183.

Parker, K. J., Buckmaster, C. L., Justus, K. R., Schatzberg, A. F., & Lyons, D. M. (2005). Mild early life stress enhances prefrontal-dependent response inhibition in monkeys. *Biological Psychiatry, 57*, 848–855.

Perdue, B. M., Bramlett, J. L., Evans, T. A., & Beran, M. J. (2015). Waiting for what comes later: Capuchin monkeys show self-control even for nonvisible delayed rewards. *Animal Cognition, 18*, 1105–1112.

Rachlin, H. (2000). *The science of self-control*. Cambridge, MA: Harvard University Press.

Rayburn-Reeves, R. M., James, B. J., & Beran, M. J. (2017). Within-session reversal learning in rhesus macaques (*Macaca mulatta*). *Animal Cognition, 20*, 975–983.

Rayburn-Reeves, R. M., Stagner, J. P., Kirk, C. R., & Zentall, T. R. (2013). Reversal learning in rats (*Rattus norvegicus*) and pigeons (*Columba livia*): qualitative differences in behavioral flexibility. *Journal of Comparative Psychology, 127*, 202–211.

Reid, R. L. (1958). Discrimination-reversal learning in pigeons. *Journal of Comparative and Physiological Psychology, 51*, 716–720.

Reynolds, B., de Wit, H., & Richards, J. B. (2002). Delay of gratification and delay discounting in rats. *Behavioural Processes, 59*, 157–168.

Reynolds, B., & Schiffbauer, R. (2005). Delay of gratification and delay discounting: A unifying Feedback model of delay-related impulsive behavior. *The Psychological Record, 55*, 439–460.

Reynolds, W. M., & Stark, K. D. (1986). Self-control in children: A multimethod examination of treatment outcome measures. *Journal of Abnormal Child Psychology, 14*, 13–23.

Rumbaugh, D. M. (1971). Evidence of qualitative differences in learning processes among primates. *Journal of Comparative and Physiological Psychology, 76*, 250–255.

Rumbaugh, D. M., & McQueeney, J. A. (1963). Learning-set formation and discrimination reversal: learning problems to criterion in the squirrel monkey. *Journal of Comparative and Physiological Psychology*, *56*(2), 435.

Rumbaugh, D. M., & Pate, J. L. (1984). The evolution of cognition in primates: A comparative perspective. In H. L. Roitblat, T. G. Bever, & H. S. Terrace (Eds.), *Animal Cognition* (pp. 569–587). Hillsdale, NJ: Erlbaum.

Rumbaugh, D. M., & Pournelle, M. B. (1966). Discrimination-reversal skills of primates: The reversal/acquisition ratio as a function of phyletic standing. *Psychonomic Science*, *4*, 45–46.

Santos, L. R., Ericson, B. N., & Hauser, M. D. (1999). Constraints on problem solving and inhibition: Object retrieval in cotton-top tamarins (*Saguinus oedipus oedipus*). *Journal of Comparative Psychology*, *113*, 186–193.

Schusterman, R. J. (1962). Transfer effects of successive discrimination-reversal training in chimpanzees. *Science*, *137*, 422–423.

Soreni, N., Crosbie, J., Ickowicz, A., & Schachar, R. (2009). Stop signal and conners' continuous performance tasks: Test—retest reliability of two inhibition measures in adhd children. *Journal of Attention Disorders*, *13*, 137–143.

Tapp, P. D., Siwak, C. T., Estrada, J., Head, E., Muggenburg, B. A., Cotman, C. W., & Milgram, N. W. (2003). Size and reversal learning in the beagle dog as a measure of executive function and inhibitory control in aging. *Learning & Memory*, *10*, 64–73.

Tsukayama, E., Toomey, S. L., Faith, M. S., & Duckworth, A. L. (2010). Self-control protects against overweight status in the transition from childhood to adolescences. *Archives of Pediatrics and Adolescent Medicine*, *164*, 631–635.

Tsukayama, E., & Duckworth, A. L. (2010). Domain-specific temporal discounting and temptation. *Judgment and Decision Making*, *5*, 72–82.

Warren, J. M. (1966). Reversal learning and the formation of learning sets by cats and rhesus monkeys. *Journal of Comparative and Physiological Psychology*, *61*, 421–428.

Young, M. E., & McCoy, A. W. (2015). A delay discounting task produces a greater likelihood of waiting than a deferred gratification task. *Journal of the Experimental Analysis of Behavior*, *103*, 180–195.

Zauberman, G., Kim, B. K., Malkoc, S. A., & Bettman, J. R. (2009). Discounting time and time discounting: Subjective time perception and intertemporal preferences. *Journal of Marketing Research*, *46*, 543–556.

FURTHER READING

Brucks, D., Range, F., & Marshall-Pescini, S. (2017). Dogs' reaction to inequity is affected by inhibitory control. *Scientific Reports*, *7*, 15802.

Crockett, M. J., Braams, B. R., Clark, L., Tobler, P. N., Robbins, T. W., & Kalenscher, T. (2013). Restricting temptations: Neural mechanisms of precommitment. *Neuron*, *79*, 391–401.

Essock-Vitale, S. M. (1978). Comparison of ape and monkey modes of problem solution. *Journal of Comparative and Physiological Psychology*, *92*, 942–957.

Kim, B. K., & Zauberman, G. (2012). Can Victoria's Secret change the future? A subjective time perception account of sexual-cue effects on impatience. *Journal of Experimental Psychology General*, *142*, 328–335.

Rayburn-Reeves, R. M., & Cook, R. G. (2016). The organization of behavior over time: insights from mid-session reversal. *Comparative Cognition & Behavior Reviews*, *11*, 103–125.

Rayburn-Reeves, R. M., Molet, M., & Zentall, T. R. (2011). Simultaneous discrimination reversal learning in pigeons and humans: Anticipatory and perseverative errors. *Learning & Behavior, 39*, 125–137.

Richards, J. B., Zhang, L., Mitchell, S., & de Wit, H. (1999). Delay and probability discounting in a model of impulsive behavior: Effect of alcohol. *Journal of the Experimental Analysis of Behavior, 71*, 121–143.

Rumbaugh, D. M., & Jeeves, M. A. (1966). A comparison of two discrimination-reversal indices intended for use with diverse groups of organisms. *Psychonomic Science, 6*, 1–2.

Rumbaugh, D. M., & Pate, J. L. (1984). Primates' learning by levels. In G. Greenberg, & E. Tobach (Eds.), *Behavioral evolution and integrative levels* (pp. 221–240). Hillsdale, NJ: Erlbaum.

Rumbaugh, D. M., Savage-Rumbaugh, E. S., & Washburn, D. A. (1996). Toward a new outlook on primate learning and behavior: Complex learning and emergent processes in comparative perspective. *Japanese Psychological Research, 38*, 113–125.

Rumbaugh, D. M., & Washburn, D. A. (2003). *Intelligence of apes and other rational beings.* New Haven: Yale University Press.

Rumbaugh, D. M., Washburn, D. A., & Hillix, W. A. (1996). Respondents, operants, and emergents: Toward an integrated perspective on behavior. In K. Pribram, & J. King (Eds.), *Learning as a self-organizing process* (pp. 57–73). Hillsdale, NJ: Erlbaum.

Van den Bergh, B., Dewitte, S., & Warlop, L. (2008). Bikinis instigate generalized impatience in intertemporal choice. *Journal of Consumer Research, 35*, 85–97.

Warren, J. M. (1965). Primate learning in comparative perspective. In A. M. Schrier, H. F. Harlow, & F. Stollnitz (Eds.), *Behavior of nonhuman primates Vol 1* (pp. 249–281). New York: Academic Press.

Warren, J. M. (1974). Possibly unique characteristics of learning by primates. *Journal of Human Evolution, 3*, 445–454.

Wilson, M., & Daly, M. (2004). Do pretty women inspire men to discount the future? *Proceedings of the Royal Society of London B: Biological Sciences, 271*, S177–S179.

Chapter 13

Self-Control and Social Settings

To this point, nearly all of the research that I have discussed has involved investigators studying one individual in isolation. One rat choosing the smaller-sooner or larger-later reward. One chimpanzee waiting for food items to accumulate in a bowl. One child sitting alone in a room with a marshmallow, hoping to get another, but also increasingly tempted to eat the one that is already there. In all of these cases, the idea is to see what that rat, that chimpanzee, or that child does in that situation, as a way of assessing the self-control of that creature. And yet, all of these tests fail to capture one of the most important and salient contextual aspects of self-control choices or impulsive choice—what those around us are doing! This chapter discusses the role of social settings on self-control behavior, an area of inquiry that is almost as sparsely covered in this literature as the solo-testing approaches have been so densely covered!

So many of our decisions that involve self-control or impulsive choices are made in the presence of others. Think back to my story from the first chapter, about that fried cannonball of ice cream. In isolation, every one of us at the table would have done the right thing and passed on that caloric tidal wave. And yet, together, we all were more at risk for giving in, because any weakness was going to lead to total weakness. I suspect every reader of this book can think of a recent example of such failures in their own choices, made when in a group compared to when made alone. And, it is not just about food. We do this when we shop together, when we hang out around friends who smoke while we are trying to quit, when we choose to cheat on exams or skip classes to be with friends, and when we spend our paychecks on social events rather than saving for things like rent and other longer-term needs. In many cases, we increase our risk-taking behaviors because of social influences, but I am not going to talk about that here. I will restrict my discussion to cases where social influences change how we choose between more immediate and more delayed (or harder to obtain) and also better outcomes.

Not all such social influences lead to impulsivity. In fact, for each of the cases above, one can offer examples where social influences improve self-control choices. For those fighting addiction, having a sponsor or group to whom one can turn to when feeling vulnerable or fallible can help lead to good choices. A dieting friend, a running or workout buddy, or a roommate

Self-Control in Animals and People. DOI: https://doi.org/10.1016/B978-0-12-812508-3.00013-X
© 2018 Elsevier Inc. All rights reserved.

who stays on the path toward good class participation and performance all can as easily evoke self-control from us as can their devil-on-the-shoulder counterparts who would lead us astray. I suspect that, had any of us at dinner that night talked more about how many calories that dessert contained or how sick to the stomach we would have felt later, we might have passed on ordering. (Ok, probably not—you were not there, so you cannot really understand just how good it looked!).

Despite these examples, and the fact that we all know that social pressures (good and bad) can steer our choices, little research has been conducted on the role of social partners or social influence in our intertemporal choices or our ability to choose delayed gratification or longer-term goals. At the outset, I want to propose that this needs to become a research priority going forward, for two reasons: first, the lack of attention to this area means we have an incomplete understanding of choice behavior and what environmental factors impact that behavior. Second, I believe that with the increasing reliance of so many people on forms of social media, there is a greater need than ever before to understand how social influences impact self-control and impulsivity. I suspect (although I do not know of any data to confirm this) that fewer and fewer of our choices are made without social input. I cannot count the number of Facebook posts I see each week from friends commenting on what they are about to eat (although I have noticed it is almost never a picture of grilled chicken with broccoli!) or what they are about to do that is impulsive and not well thought out. And, sometimes within seconds, there are responses that are made approvingly or disapprovingly of those posts. Add together the other forms of social media, many of which are designed to have users comment on what is going on right this second, and you can see a future in which we are almost continuously aware of what those around us think of our present and near-future choices. We need to better understand what role group decision making and social influence more broadly play in our intertemporal choices.

The simplest way to do this experimentally, of course, is to continue to use all of those methods I have been discussing, but see how people (and animals) change when another individual or group of individuals is around. There is almost no work, to date, on this, although I will review those few studies that have looked at these questions. A little more research has focused on other kinds of tasks that I think tap into self-control mechanisms and how social versus solitary contexts influence behavior and choices. And, some research has looked at the role that the experimenter or a social model may play in self-control.

For example, Bandura and Mischel (1965) were among the first to present children with models who showed choice responses opposite to those shown by the children when given scenarios of choosing between a better, more delayed reward and a lower preference, less-delayed reward. The models had large impacts on all children. Children who, on their own, chose to take the sooner rewards became more likely to wait after seeing a model make those choices and explain those choices. At the same time, children who initially showed self-control, choosing the delayed reward, became more likely to choose the more immediate reward when the model did that and talked about that choice. So, we know that models for self-control and for impulsive choice are both effective at influencing what the observer does.

There is other evidence that social modeling can impact self-control in young children, nicely linking back to the massive anecdotal evidence that all of us are familiar with. Corriveau, Min, Chin, and Doan (2016), for example, reported that children would tend to copy the actions of a model who presented a specific choice and strategy when offered an intertemporal choice. Children watched as an adult was presented with the standard one-now, two-later delay of gratification task (using stickers rather than marshmallows). The adult either verbally announced that she would choose to wait or would choose not to wait, and then in half of cases truly did wait or truly did not wait. In all cases, the model then exhibited behaviors that were like those known to help maintain delay of gratification. She sang a song to distract herself or pushed away the reward so that it was not close. Children then were given the same delay task, and when that was finished, they were given another inhibition task that involved being taken to a room with a bag of toys, but being told they needed to not touch those toys until the experimenter returned. Children were more likely, when they took the choice test, to adopt the behavioral strategy of the model when the model was successful in waiting to get the second sticker. And, more children were successful in their own tests when seeing a successful model. It was also true that children who were successful in waiting in the first task were nearly three times as likely to wait and not touch the toys in the second task. This study shows nicely that seeing what others plan to do (waiting or not) is less important that what they actually do during the delay maintenance phase, and how things turn out. In other words, it is outcome, not the stated intention, that seems to impact subsequent choices *and performance* of the observer. And, this holds not only for identical contexts, but also for other contexts that are encountered close in time to the observation period. It would be very interesting to see how modeling effects like these persist over longer time frames and to determine how many observations of a model are needed to create persistent increases in a subject's own intertemporal choices for delayed rewards and delay maintenance abilities.

It is also important to see if other forms of modeled behavior would be equally effective, including forms that could be more widely disseminated, as through books or movies. Kumst and Scarf (2015) gave children a delay maintenance task where they were presented with one gift box and told that if they did not peek, they would also get a second gift. Children did this task two times, approximately 1 week apart, and in between they took a book home that was read to them each day. The book offered a number of different scenarios in terms of the text, although the pictures were identical. The control (no self-control) story involved two princes or princesses walking in the forest and meeting a magical character. This character gives the hungry child a lollipop and gives the other child a toy that the child had lost earlier. The self-control modeling stories were different. The children in these stories are given a choice by the magical character—a small gift now or a large gift later. One child is impatient and takes the small gift now (the lollipop), and the other child chooses to wait (the toy). There were two versions of this book, one in which the prince or princess who chose to wait was named after the child in the study and one in which the name was different from the child. Kumst and Scarf reported no difference in delay maintenance performance at the second test depending on the book the child had been read for a week. Children did improve from the first test to the second, but that did not appear to be the result of whether the children heard the story that modeled self-control choices or did not. Kumst and Scarf noted a number of reasons they may not have found an effect, and it may be the case that this simply will not be an effective approach to improving self-control (also see Lee, Lan, Wang, & Chiu, 2008). I think that future work addressing some of the limitations of these few past studies will be important as we try to develop techniques that could easily be integrated into normal daily routines (such as reading with children), if those techniques can change choice behavior in situations in which self-control would be important. But, it may be the case also that some approaches simply are not effective.

We also know that children's decisions to delay gratification can be biased by how experimenters act, in terms of being reliable or not. Being willing to wait, and delaying one's gratification, only makes sense in a test where someone tells you about a delayed reward if you trust that person. If you do not believe the delayed reward is forthcoming, then this is a situation in which self-control mechanisms play a secondary role in decision making, and instead there is reliance on cognitive mechanisms that gauge trustworthiness (e.g., Kidd, Palmeri, & Aslin, 2013; Mahrer, 1956; Mischel & Ayduk, 2004). Michaelson and Munakata (2016) showed this by having children first observe an experimenter behaving in a trustworthy manner or not. In each case, the experimenter damaged an art project that had just been completed by the child and another experimenter. The trustworthy experimenter confessed to that action, but the untrustworthy experimenter denied doing this, although in both cases the child saw what happened. Children then were given the instructions for the marshmallow test by whichever of these experimenters they had just seen damage the art. This included being told that the experimenter would return to give two marshmallows. Children who had observed the untrustworthy experimenter performed more poorly on the marshmallow test in terms of shorter delay maintenance (Fig. 13.1).

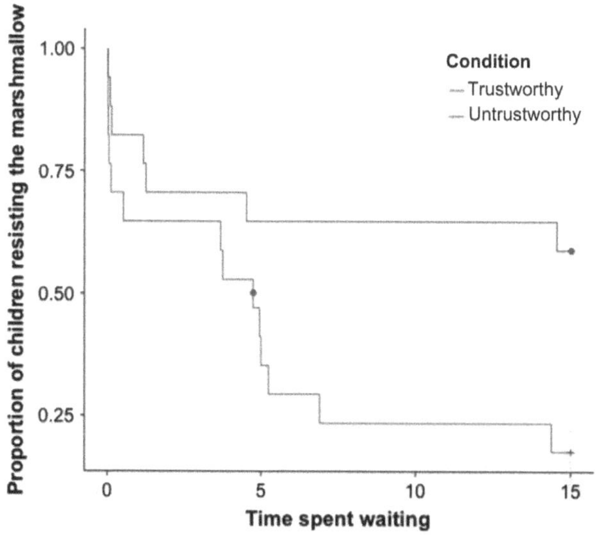

FIGURE 13.1 Performance of children on the marshmallow test in Michaelson and Munakata (2016) after observing a trustworthy or untrustworthy experimenter. *From Michaelson, L. E., & Munakata, Y. (2016). Trust matters: Seeing how an adult treats another person influences preschoolers' willingness to delay gratification.* Developmental Science, 19, *1011–1019. Copyright 2016. Reprinted with permission from John Wiley and Sons, Ltd.*

These results extend to other cases, as Michaelson and Munakata (2016) noted. For example, when adolescents reported that their parents were not reliable in terms of giving promised, delayed rewards, those adolescents also were more likely to devalue future rewards more steeply, and adults who were given games of choice and who were less trusting of the experimental context also devalued the offered delayed rewards more steeply (Harris & Madden, 2002; Schneider, Peters, Peth & Büchel, 2014). Michaelson, de la Vega, Chatham, and Munakata (2013) also reported that adults were less willing to delay gratification for hypothetical rewards if untrustworthy characters were part of the scenario than when trustworthy ones were part of the scenario. These results highlight an important aspect of social context on choice behavior. Humans take into account what others are doing, in terms of their trustworthiness, when they determine the relative values of immediate and delayed rewards, and such social evaluation can change the nature of discounting future rewards more steeply or more shallowly.

It appears that, at least in one case, even the touch of another person can affect delay of gratification. Leonard, Berkowitz, and Shusterman (2014) gave children a delay of gratification test that involved children being told that, while an experimenter was gone, they were not to look at or search for candy that was present in the room. Half of the children were told this without being touched, but the other half were touched on the back during

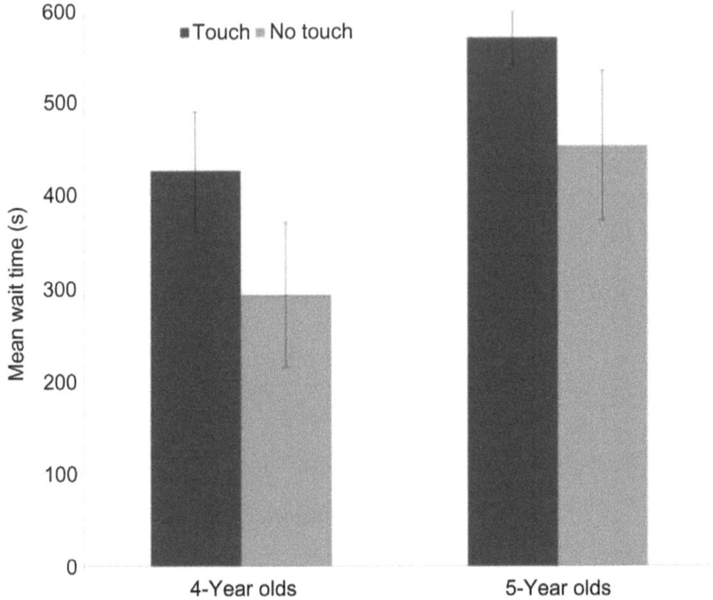

FIGURE 13.2 The effects of touch and age on mean waiting times in a delay of gratification task given by Leonard et al. (2007). *From Leonard, J. A., Berkowitz, T., & Shusterman, A. (2014). The effect of friendly touch on delay-of-gratification in preschool children.* The Quarterly Journal of Experimental Psychology, *67, 2123–2133. Copyright 2014. Reprinted with permission of Sage.*

instructions. The measure of delay was how long the children waited until they called the experimenter back into the room, and Leonard et al. found that children waited almost 2 minutes longer when they had been touched (Fig. 13.2). This suggested that a friendly form of touch may have served to reduce stress in the children, which would aid in delaying, or that touch increased the "bond" between the child and the experimenter toward the end of motivating children to want to do what they were told to do. It was also possible that such touch served as a means of making the experimenter more authoritative. Some research has indicated that children who perform better on delay of gratification tasks come from homes in which mothers show a more authoritative parenting style rather than a permissive parenting style (Mauro & Harris, 2000), although this is only one aspect of the home environment. We still know very little about what might explain the individual differences in children's ability to delay gratification in terms of studying their home environments. But, there seems to be a clear role for the parents and caregivers in terms of how their behavior and even physical contact levels with children might impact self-control.

In one major study of self-regulation in children tested alone or in groups, McCabe and Brooks-Gunn (2007) found large differences between those contexts. In one task, called the snack delay, children were told they had to wait until the experimenter blew a whistle to eat a snack, and then the experimenters measured how long the children waited before they broke the rule and took the treat early. In another test called the gift wrap test, children were told they would be given a gift, but that while it was being wrapped they were not to peek at it. Again, what was measured was how long and how well children stuck to that rule, and avoided peeking. Sometimes, children were tested alone, whereas other times they were in groups of four peers who knew each other. The results showed that peer groups performed less well, waiting less time and peeking more often in these tasks (Fig. 13.3). And, this difference became more magnified as children got older. Although older children, in general, were better at the tasks, those tested in groups showed less self-control than those tested alone. McCabe and Brooks-Gunn noted the importance of these findings for assessments of children. When tested alone, a child's performance may or may not reflect how that child

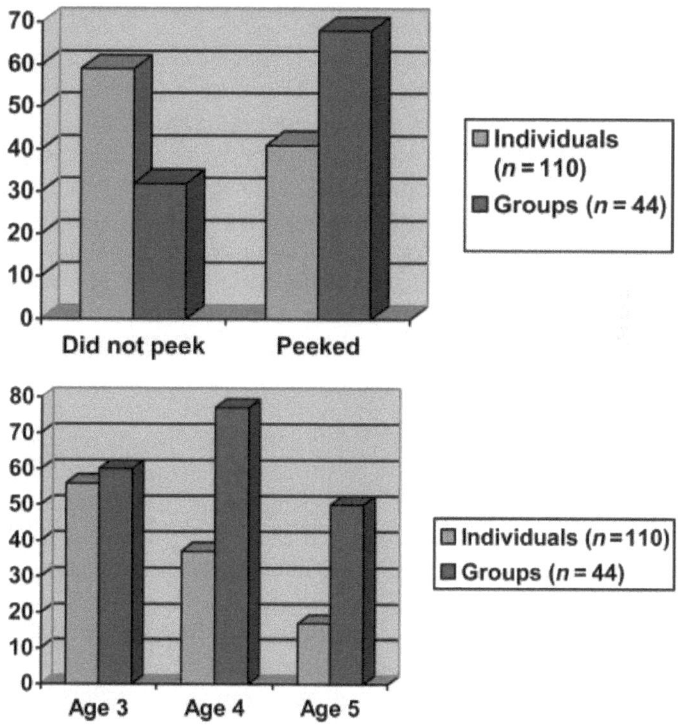

FIGURE 13.3 The performance of children in the group and solo conditions in the gift wrap experiment in McCabe and Gunn (2007). The top panel shows peeking behavior in both conditions, and the bottom panel shows peeking also as a function of children's age. *From McCabe, L. A., & Brooks-Gunn, J. (2007). With a little help from my friends?: Self-regulation in groups of young children.* Infant Mental Health Journal, 28, *584–605. Copyright 2007. Reprinted with permission of Elsevier.*

will behave in the same kind of situation but with peers present. What I find really interesting is that, in groups, some of the effects of behavioral strategies appear to be less consistent. There was no clear relationship between peeking behavior, for example, and the engagement of various delay facilitation strategies. Even those children who engaged in such strategies or even initiated such strategies (such as reminding everyone of the rules they were supposed to follow) tended to peek as often as those who did not engage in such strategies. It would appear that social pressure or influence can override some of the usual positive benefits of strategies that are used in solo.

The results from McCabe and Brooks-Gunn (2007) are somewhat at odds with other work looking at group decisions. Nisan (1976) gave children the choice between one piece of candy now or two pieces the next day. In some cases, three children were told to come to a group decision first and then after that to make their own personal (independent) choice. In other cases, the independent choice was made first, before the group choice. Although girls tended not to vary too much in their group versus solo decisions, boys were found to make *more* delayed reward choices when deciding in groups than when deciding alone. This study would suggest that making group decisions may lead at least some individuals to choose more often for delayed rewards. However, this is one of the few studies to assess the same children in both conditions, and the sample size was fairly small. There is a strong need for more work along these lines, because it is an important question whether group decision making truly induced more future-oriented thinking and more choices for delayed reward. For example, one could envision having new employees discuss in a group their thoughts on retirement planning and voluntary withdrawals to fund retirement plans, toward the end of having more of them make the smart choice to invest for their retirement. Or, even having groups decide what should be ordered for lunch may lead to healthier choices. That said, I am not sure that more delayed-reward choices would consistently emerge from such group decisions. Such results may be limited to young children or perhaps only to those who already know each other well. It is easy to envision situations where groups easily and readily choose now over later, as in the many corporate shareholder decisions that reflect desire for more immediate stock gains than longer-term fiscal strength. And, of course, we return to cannonballs of ice cream as a reminder that groups do not always make the right choice when it comes to more delayed but better outcomes over more hedonically pleasing and more immediate outcomes.

What about cases of intertemporal choice made in collaboration with others? Again, little research has been done on this topic, but what we have learned is very interesting. Bixter, Trimber, and Luhmann (2017) studied how the intertemporal preferences of individual group members affected what those same people chose when put into a group decision making situation. They also studied whether the experience of making group decisions then influenced the decisions those people made when they were alone again.

Thus, the question is how individual choices might affect what groups do, and then to see how those group choices might change what *the same individuals* later chose when given the same options again. In the first experiment by Bixter et al., in the first phase, people completed an intertemporal choice task by themselves. Then, they were put into groups that had two other people in them and were allowed to discuss and make the same choices. Then, they were tested alone one more time. The choices were between varying hypothetical reward amounts (money) at varying delays to each option, and in each case one reward amount was left blank, so that the subject (or the group) had to fill in that amount to indicate what would then create a choice that had two equally preferred options. What Bixter et al. found was that when people came together into groups, the values they gave for equivalence of the options converged toward the *average of their individual choices earlier*. And, when they answered the same questions again, but alone, their new values were much closer to the group values than to their own original values (Fig. 13.4). So, working together in a group to determine intertemporal choices seemed to have an impact on, and to really change, individual preferences.

Think about what this means. No matter how you choose between options on your own—whether you are highly impulsive or strongly self-controlled—being around other people and having to work together leads to something akin to an averaging of everyone's preferences. That result perhaps is not unexpected: People were asked to collaborate on these choices and come to a consensus, and the averaging effect would seem to indicate that everyone's personal preference was accounted for in a way that avoided anyone being too extremely different in their personal choice compared to the group choice. But, the truly interesting (and, I think, exciting) effect is that, when people were then allowed to make a choice *only for themselves*, they relied a lot more on the groups' decision about equivalence of value in the two choices than in their own past decisions. So, the group decision seemed to change their own preferences, at least in this case.

Bixter et al. (2017) then repeated their test with pairs of people rather than larger groups as the collaborative portion of the experiment, and they also included a dichotomous intertemporal choice test where participants chose either smaller-sooner or larger-later rewards. Once again, individuals' second choices made when by themselves were more closely aligned with what the pair had chosen compared to what the individual people had chosen on their first solo effort. Thus, collaborative effort overrode people's earlier choices and preferences just a short while later. This is only one study, but I think there are some potentially very important implications of this research. First, it seems to be the case that what a person might choose when alone is not necessarily something they feel so strongly about that they are unwilling to compromise when choosing in groups. This might be related to how group input informs individuals as to how closely their own estimates of value

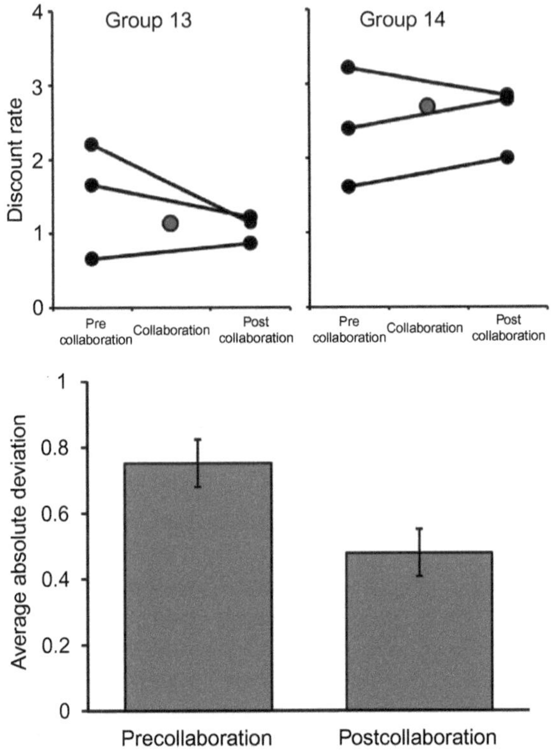

FIGURE 13.4 The top panels show two groups of people, and how they valued options when tested alone, then in a group, and then alone again in Bixter et al. (2017). Group decisions led individuals more toward an average discount rate, which then appeared to influence subsequent discounting by people when they were alone. The bottom panels show the average absolute deviations between discount rates in the precollaboration/postcollaboration phases and groups' discount rates during the collaboration phase. Discount rates during the postcollaboration phase converged toward groups' discount rates during the collaboration phase. *From Bixter, M. T., Trimber, E. M., & Luhmann, C. C. (2017). Are intertemporal preferences contagious? Evidence from collaborative decision making.* Memory & Cognition, *1–15. Copyright 2017. Reprinted with permission of Springer.*

were to other people, and from that they may have wanted to move more toward what other people estimated (Cialdini, 2001; Deutsch & Gerard, 1955). Another potential implication is that having impulsive people spend time around more self-controlled individuals, and work with those individuals to make choices, could have long-lasting effects in terms of reducing future impulsive choices. The caveat to this is that someone who shows high levels of self-control and future-oriented behavior might change somewhat when spending time collaboratively making decisions with people who are less self-controlled. In essence, group-think weighs heavily on the individual, even for intertemporal choices, and it may be that people have more confidence in group choices than in their own choices. More work is needed to see how robust these effects are, and what I would really like to see is whether collaborative decision making about intertemporal choices might change the subsequent choices of individuals, in ways that generalize to new choice situations that might be encountered days or even weeks later. We know that individual temporal discounting rates tend to be consistent and long lasting (e.g., Beck & Triplett, 2009; Kirby, 2009), but also that choices made for groups rather than for individuals tend to discount the future less steeply (e.g., Charlton et al., 2013). Perhaps social interventions hold the key to changing some of that consistency within the individual.

Would similar results to any of those found with humans also occur with nonhuman animals? At the moment, we really do not know. Very little research on intertemporal choices, delay of gratification, or other forms of behavioral inhibition has been conducted with nonhuman species tested in social settings versus solo settings. But, the little work that has been done seems to suggest a continuity in some of the main findings between humans and nonhuman animals. For example, domestic chicks that were raised to either learn to peck for food reward in isolation or to peck in groups showed very different discounting functions when given the chance to choose smaller-sooner or larger-later rewards. In the test phase where they made these choices, they were alone, but those birds that had faced a more competitive training environment tended to discount the future more steeply (Amita, Kawamori, & Matsushima, 2010). In later research (Amita & Matsushima, 2011), this difference with increased impulsivity in chicks trained in competition was long lasting, even as chicks improved in both conditions over time by choosing the larger-later option more often (Fig. 13.5).

We have conducted one study to see what effect working with each other at the same time might have on chimpanzees' performance on the accumulation task (Evans et al., 2012). The results were interesting, but somewhat difficult to interpret. Sometimes, a chimpanzee worked alone, waiting to accumulate candies in the container that was within reach. In other cases, the chimpanzee worked on the task while another chimpanzee also worked on the same task, at the same time. So, in that case, although they each had their own accumulating piles of treats in front of them, they could also see that they were each waiting (they were in separate test areas, so that we could ensure that no one would try to steal treats from the partner). Here, we predicted that self-control would be weaker when both were playing the game than when playing alone. In another condition, we allowed the partner animal to freely eat their rewards throughout the trial, so that the subject had to inhibit eating rewards while they saw the partner freely eating. We expected this to be particularly troubling for the focal subject, in terms of delay maintenance. And, in a final condition, the continued accumulations were contingent on each other—if either chimpanzee ended a trial by eating a reward, the trial was ended for both chimpanzees at that point. So, in that case, they

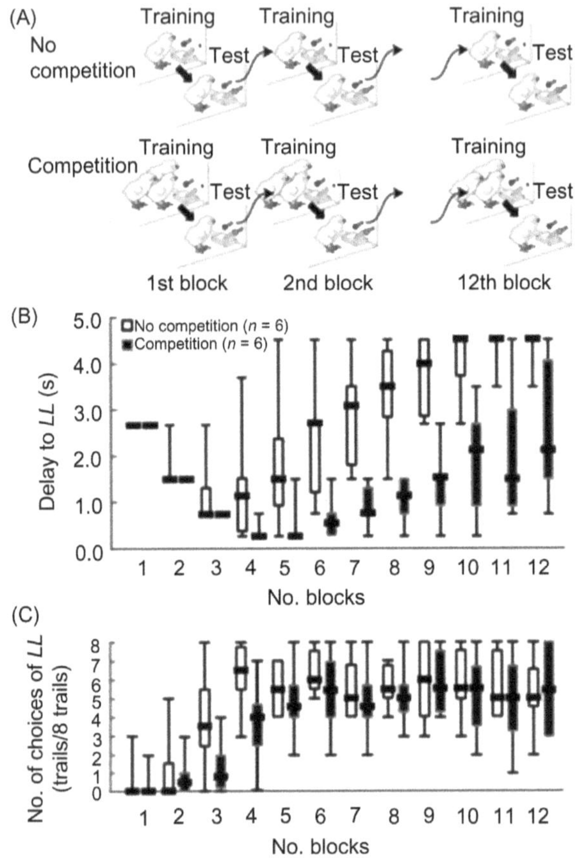

FIGURE 13.5 Competition caused lasting and cumulative effects on impulsiveness in the chicks tests by Amita and Matsushima (2011). Panel A shows the experimental procedure of the behavioral titration. Chicks were trained and tested for 12 days. In the no-competition group, chicks were trained in isolation. In the competition group, chicks were trained in a group of three chicks. Note that chicks were tested in isolation in both groups. Panel B shows the delay to the larger-later reward at which there was equivalence preference for both choices at each testing block. Short horizontal bars indicate the median, boxes the 25–75% range, and whiskers the min–max range, respectively. Panel C shows the number of choices of LL was similarly plotted. *From Amita, H., & Matsushima, T. (2011). Instantaneous and cumulative influences of competition on impulsive choices in domestic chicks.* Frontiers in Neuroscience, *5, Article 101. Copyright 2011 by the authors. Reprinted with permission as Open Access.*

both had to keep waiting in order for them both to keep accumulating treats. We had hoped to find some clear indication that working together in this case might improve self-control, and this test condition was our attempt at something like a "workout buddy"—someone else in the same situation as you, who might help bolster your self-control. What we found, unfortunately, were only slight differences in performance across these different manipulations.

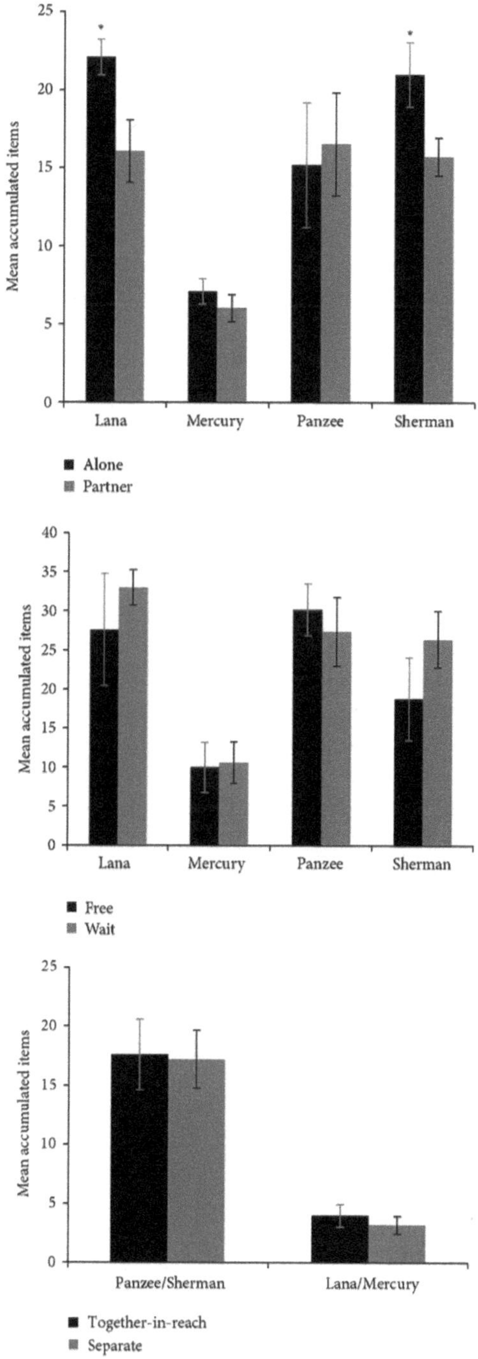

FIGURE 13.6 The top panel shows the performance of chimpanzees in Evans et al. (2012) when the partner chimpanzee was also working on the task independently or when the focal subject chimpanzee worked alone. Asterisks indicate a significant difference between conditions. The middle panel showed performance when the partner chimpanzee received either continuous free rewards while the subject had to inhibit eating their own rewards, or the partner had to wait until the end of the trial to eat the rewards. The bottom panel shows performance when chimpanzees were tested either alone or in the same enclosure as the partner chimpanzee. In all panels, the error bars are standard errors of the mean. *From Evans, T. A., Perdue, B. M., Parrish, A. E., Menzel, E., Brosnan, S. F., & Beran, M. J. (2012). How is chimpanzee self-control influenced by social setting?* Scientifica, *Article ID 654094. Copyright 2012. Reprinted with permission of the authors.*

We did find that two of four chimpanzees waited longer and accumulated more rewards when they were tested alone compared to when they were tested together, but the other two did not (Fig. 13.6). However, there was not any relation between when the partner ended their trial and when the focal subject ended the trial. In other words, it did not seem as if what the partner did had much of an impact on what each chimpanzee subject did, in terms of waiting. By way of analogy, this means that having a friend give in and smoke a cigarette would have no effect on whether you smoked at that time. What was more surprising was that it did not matter if the partner got free food during a subject's delay interval compared to when the partner did not. The focal subject waited just as long in both cases (Fig. 13.6). By way of analogy, this would suggest that a friend being given a free dessert from the dessert tray would not cause you to then give in and eat dessert. Finally, we gave two chimpanzees access to each other on each trial, to see whether performance or the behaviors exhibited during delay maintenance were different with partners together during trials versus being tested alone. Again, we did not find any difference (Fig. 13.6). Thus, at least in this series of manipulations, the chimpanzees did not seem to be affected at all by the social context in which they had to inhibit eating food items to allow their accumulations to grow. However, we have to be cautious in how we interpret these results, because these chimpanzees had spent decades of their lives participating in cognitive studies with each other in proximity, meaning that they may have learned long ago not to pay attention to what was going on with other chimpanzees during testing. We hope to continue to study this question with new species to see whether these results with chimpanzees are also seen with those other species, or whether these results are not reflective of what role social context plays on nonhuman primate self-control in joint testing situations. Future research could show more evidence that social contexts affect animals much as they do humans, but as we have read in earlier chapters, the nonhuman animal and human outcomes do not always align with each other.

REFERENCES

Amita, H., Kawamori, A., & Matsushima, T. (2010). Social influences of competition on impulsive choices in domestic chicks. *Biology Letters*, *6*, 183–186.

Amita, H., & Matsushima, T. (2011). Instantaneous and cumulative influences of competition on impulsive choices in domestic chicks. *Frontiers in Neuroscience*, *5*, Article 101.

Bandura, A., & Mischel, W. (1965). Modifications of self-imposed delay of reward through exposure to live and symbolic models. *Journal of Personality and Social Psychology*, *2*, 698–705.

Beck, R. C., & Triplett, M. F. (2009). Test–retest reliability of a group administered paper–pencil measure of delay discounting. *Experimental and Clinical Psychopharmacology*, *17*, 345–355.

Bixter, M. T., Trimber, E. M., & Luhmann, C. C. (2017). Are intertemporal preferences contagious? Evidence from collaborative decision making. *Memory & Cognition*, 1–15.

Charlton, S. R., Yi, R., Porter, C., Carter, A. E., Bickel, W., & Rachlin, H. (2013). Now for me, later for us? Effects of group context on temporal discounting. *Journal of Behavioral Decision Making*, *26*, 118–127.

Cialdini, R. B. (2001). Harnessing the science of persuasion. *Harvard Business Review*, *79*, 72–79.

Corriveau, K. H., Min, G., Chin, J., & Doan, S. (2016). Do as I do, not as I say: Actions speak louder than words in preschoolers learning from others. *Journal of Experimental Child Psychology*, *143*, 179–187.

Deutsch, M., & Gerard, H. B. (1955). A study of normative and informational social influences upon individual judgment. *Journal of Abnormal and Social Psychology*, *51*, 629–636.

Evans, T. A., Perdue, B. M., Parrish, A. E., Menzel, E., Brosnan, S. F., & Beran, M. J. (2012). How is chimpanzee self-control influenced by social setting?. *Scientifica*, Article ID 654094.

Harris, A. C., & Madden, G. J. (2002). Delay discounting and performance on the prisoner's dilemma game. *The Psychological Record*, *52*, 429–440.

Kidd, C., Palmeri, H., & Aslin, R. N. (2013). Rational snacking: Young children's decision-making on the marshmallow task is moderated by beliefs about environmental reliability. *Cognition*, *126*, 109–114.

Kirby, K. N. (2009). One-year temporal stability of delay-discount rates. *Psychonomic Bulletin & Review*, *16*, 457–462.

Kumst, S., & Scarf, D. (2015). Your wish is my command! The influence of symbolic modelling on preschool children's delay of gratification. *PeerJ*, *3*, e774.

Lee, P. L., Lan, W., Wang, C. L., & Chiu, H. Y. (2008). Helping young children to delay gratification. *Early Childhood Education Journal*, *35*, 557–564.

Leonard, J. A., Berkowitz, T., & Shusterman, A. (2014). The effect of friendly touch on delay-of-gratification in preschool children. *The Quarterly Journal of Experimental Psychology*, *67*, 2123–2133.

Mahrer, A. R. (1956). The role of expectancy in delayed reinforcement. *Journal of Experimental Psychology*, *52*, 101–106.

Mauro, C. F., & Harris, Y. R. (2000). The influence of maternal child-rearing attitudes and teaching behaviors on preschoolers' delay of gratification. *The Journal of Genetic Psychology*, *161*, 292–306.

McCabe, L. A., & Brooks-Gunn, J. (2007). With a little help from my friends? Self-regulation in groups of young children. *Infant Mental Health Journal*, *28*, 584–605.

Michaelson, L., de la Vega, A., Chatham, C. H., & Munakata, Y. (2013). Delaying gratification depends on social trust. *Frontiers in Psychology*, *4*, Article 355.

Michaelson, L. E., & Munakata, Y. (2016). Trust matters: Seeing how an adult treats another person influences preschoolers' willingness to delay gratification. *Developmental Science*, *19*, 1011–1019.

Mischel, W., & Ayduk, O. (2004). Willpower in a cognitive–affective processing system: the dynamics of delay of gratification. In K. D. Vohs, & R. F. Baumeister (Eds.), *Handbook of self-regulation: Research, theory, and applications* (pp. 99–129). New York: Guilford.

Nisan, M. (1976). Delay of gratification in children: Personal versus group choices. *Child Development*, *47*, 195–200.

Schneider, S., Peters, J., Peth, J. M., & Büchel, C. (2014). Parental inconsistency, impulsive choice and neural value representations in healthy adolescents. *Translational Psychiatry*, *4*, e382.

FURTHER READING

Albrecht, K., Volz, K. G., Sutter, M., Laibson, D. I., & von Cramon, D. Y. (2011). What is for me is not for you: Brain correlates of ntertemporal choice for self and other. *Social Cognitive and Affective Neuroscience, 6*, 218–225.

Crusco, A. H., & Wetzel, C. G. (1984). The Midas touch: The effects of interpersonal touch on restaurant tipping. *Personality and Social Psychology Bulletin, 10*, 512–517.

Fitzsimons, G. M., & Finkel, E. J. (2010). Interpersonal influences on self-regulation. *Current Directions in Psychological Science, 19*, 101–105.

Kidd, C., Palmeri, H., & Aslin, R. N. (2013). Rational snacking: Young children's decision-making on the marshmallow task is moderated by beliefs about environmental reliability. *Cognition, 126*, 109–114.

Kleinke, C. L. (1977). Compliance to requests made by gazing and touching experimenters in field settings. *Journal of Experimental Social Psychology, 13*, 218–223.

McCabe, L. A., Cunnington, M., & Brooks-Gunn, J. (2004). The development of self-regulation in young children: Individual characteristics and environmental contexts. In R. F. Baumeister, & K. D. Vohs (Eds.), *Handbook of self-regulation: Research, theory, and applications* (pp. 340–356). New York: Guilford.

McCabe, L. A., Hernandez, M., Lara, S., & Brooks-Gunn, J. (2000). Assessing preschoolers' self-regulation in homes and classrooms: Lessons from the field. *Behavioral Disorders, 26*, 53–69.

McCabe, L. A., Rebello-Britto, P., Hernandez, M., & Brooks-Gunn, J. (2004). Games children play: Observing young children's self-regulation across laboratory, home, and school settings. In R. DelCarmen-Wiggins, & A. Carter (Eds.), *Handbook of infant, toddler, and preschool mental health assessment* (pp. 491–521). New York: Oxford University Press.

Mischel, W. (1961). Preference for delayed reinforcement and social responsibility. *Journal of Abnormal and Social Psychology, 62*, 1–7.

Mizuyama, R., Uno, L., & Matsushima, T. (2016). Food variance and temporal discounting in socially foraging chicks. *Animal Behaviour, 120*, 143–151.

Righetti, F., & Finkenauer, C. (2011). If you are able to control yourself, I will trust you: The role of perceived self-control in interpersonal trust. *Journal of Personality and Social Psychology, 100*, 874–876.

Salvy, S. J., Howard, M., Read, M., & Mele, E. (2009). The presence of friends increases food intake in youth. *The American Journal of Clinical Nutrition, 90*, 282–287.

Sniezek, J. A., & Henry, R. A. (1989). Accuracy and confidence in group judgment. *Organizational Behavior and Human Decision Processes, 43*, 1–28.

Sniezek, J. A., & Henry, R. A. (1990). Revision, weighting and commitment in consensus group judgment. *Organizational Behavior and Human Decision Processes, 45*, 66–84.

Chapter 14

Mental Time Travel: What Is It, and How Does It Relate to Self-Control?

Throughout this book, I have been discussing examples of choices such as these:

> Do I eat a big dessert right now and skip the gym or try to get into shape for my beach vacation?
> Should I spend my money now on shoes and a new watch or keep saving it so that I can buy a new house in a few years?
> Would I rather work at a job with my friends this summer or take that unpaid internship that makes me a better candidate for graduate school next year?

Inherent in these kinds of choices is the clear sense that one is considering the future and perhaps seeing oneself in that future. What I mean is that these choices have a quality to them that is often called "mental time travel" (Corballis, 2013; Suddendorf & Busby, 2003; Suddendorf & Corballis, 1997, 2007). You imagine yourself either about to eat, spend, or have fun in your near future, or you imagine the consequences of waiting and delaying, in terms of how your future self will be healthier and skinnier, or happier in a new house, or better qualified to get into graduate school. I suspect that throughout your reading of this book, you framed nearly all of the example choices in this kind of way. Humans do this naturally. We think about the future, and we simulate what we might want in the future. When we do this, we may actually frame choices as being for our immediate selves and our future selves (see Manning, 2016). Thus, self-control choices could be considered choices between what the current self wants the most, and what the future self would want, when that future arrives. In this conceptualization, one immediately sees the problem. The future self is always in the future, and the current self is always the one making the choice! From this perspective, the future self needs the present self to decide against its own interests,

Self-Control in Animals and People. DOI: https://doi.org/10.1016/B978-0-12-812508-3.00014-1
© 2018 Elsevier Inc. All rights reserved.

with the hope that when a person chooses to wait or work harder or forego more immediate pleasure for future pleasure, this works out in the long run.[1] That is not always an easy thing to do, but there are certain qualities that one might possess in terms of being more future oriented that lend themselves to making more choices to demonstrate self-control. If those qualities relate to how future oriented a person is, this could reflect important issues in child development and how to intervene on behalf of those who need to make more choices to delay gratification, by giving them better ways of thinking about the future. And, studies with nonhuman animals also could offer insights into the relation of self-control to future-oriented cognition, as I will discuss later in the chapter.

Some theorists who have studied delay of gratification in children have referred to such delay as being future-oriented self-control (e.g., Mischel, Shoda, & Rodriguez, 1989). This perspective stands in contrast to a position where one might be faced with an intertemporal choice, for example, and not need to anticipate the future to make a self-control response or an impulsive. Asking me whether I want a $100 now or $1,000 tomorrow does not require that I think about how I will spend $100 now or how I will spend $1,000 later (although I probably would think about that). It does not even require that I think about getting money today or tomorrow for me to choose between those options. And so, one can argue that humans and animals do not need a future-oriented perspective to show self-control. But, I think it is more likely that although some choices with different time outcomes (beyond a few seconds or minutes) can be made without need of any future orientation, there are many such cases in which it is difficult to frame the choice options *without* an orientation toward the future. The important issue is how to define such future orientation (see Michaelian, Klein, & Szpunar, 2016; Szpunar, Spreng, & Schacter, 2016).

This is an issue not only in self-control research, but also in other areas of psychological study (Michaelian et al., 2016). For example, there is an extensive literature on planning abilities in humans, and the extent to which plans must include anticipation of the future versus a simpler orientation toward a goal that cannot presently be obtained. This debate largely centers on how one defines planning (e.g., Miller, Galanter, & Pribram, 1986). I will work from the assumption that planning occurs whenever present behavior cannot immediately generate the goal that initiated that behavior, and that

---

1. Note that it does not really matter whether this is a "battle between two selves" or instead is about one chooser with two time perspectives for different outcomes. I actually prefer thinking of this struggle as being more like the second case, where a person has two goals in conflict, not two selves in conflict. In either case, though, there is a difference between what one wants now and what one knows he or she will want at a future time, if that future time was here. No rational person with the money in hand to purchase a home today would instead walk away and go buy a home's value worth of smaller items like shoes and watches. The trouble is in waiting to get to the goal.

present behavior cannot generate an outcome of any discernible value in the present moment. What makes this tricky is that many behaviors can be seen from two perspectives. Imagine tying your shoes. Each step in the process must be followed in the correct order, as a sequence, and so this has the feel of planned behavior. But, having done it many times, you are unlikely to be forming the plan each day to loop, swoop, and then pull. However, that is what you do. From the perspective of wanting the shoes to stay on your feet, tying them is not at all future oriented, and likely did not involve a plan to ties shoes so they stay on your feet. You wanted shoes on your feet so you tied them on. But, if what you truly wanted was to go to the park to run, then tying your shoes is part of the plan to get dressed appropriately for running and then go for a run. That is future oriented.

EPISODIC FUTURE THINKING

A key issue in thinking about future-oriented cognition and its role in self-control is to make a distinction between *episodic future thinking* and *semantic future thinking* (Atance and O'Neill, 2001). This distinction, adapted from work on episodic memory research (e.g., Tulving, 1984, 2001), centers on the role that an individual sees for themselves in the future event. In both cases, there is the need to anticipate the future, and perhaps to make some plan for obtaining something in the future. And, there might be the need to implement that plan at the right time. These processes, for anticipating and remembering future needs, are what we call *prospective memory* (Einstein & McDaniel, 2005; Hicks, Marsh, & Cook, 2005; Kliegel, Mackinlay, & Jager, 2008; Kliegel, McDaniel, & Einstein, 2000; Marsh, Hancock, & Hicks, 2002; McDaniel & Einstein, 2007). Prospective memory is relevant to future-oriented decision making whenever someone has to form an intention to do something that will benefit the future self rather than the present self. In episodic future thinking, however, one does more than just anticipate a need and then set up a scenario where that need will be met. The individual also *imagines* themselves in that future need state. Consider this example: I am taking medication each morning before I leave for work. From a semantic future-thinking perspective, I may place the medicine bottle right next to my car keys, knowing I cannot leave without those and knowing I will see the pill bottle. There is no need to imagine my future self as taking the pill to accomplish the goal. But, now imagine that after finishing the last pill, I realize I need to go by the pharmacy for a refill. Because all I have is the pill bottle, and the same routine (setting it next to my keys), I might also form the intention to remember, the next morning, to see myself taking a detour to the pharmacy on the way to work (and perhaps also think about how that will impact what time I need to leave and what route I will take). This makes that prospective memory episodic rather than semantic.

To many theorists, episodic thinking is a more complicated cognitive process than semantic thinking (Atance & O'Neill, 2001), and it is also a process that might help individuals avoid some kinds of errors and biases. For example, people who engage more in semantic future thinking sometimes underestimate the time it will take to complete something because they rely on past experience rather than imagine the more exceptional possible future situation, and they underestimate how well they will be able to remember what they have just planned to do (e.g., Buehler, Griffin, & Ross, 1994; Buehler, Griffin, & MacDonald, 1997). In addition, a more episodically encoded intention is more likely to be implemented, perhaps because it is specific rather than generalized (e.g., seeing yourself take the pill the *next morning* vs forming the intention to take a pill *each morning*: Gollwitzer, 1999; Sheeran & Orbell, 1999). And, we know that episodic future thinking can sometimes improve how well people engage in prospective memory and accurately implement their intentions (e.g., Altgassen et al., 2015). However, *why* such episodic prospection works is not entirely clear in terms of the mechanism that promotes longer-term thinking. Do people have to be engaged in actual mental time travel (i.e., seeing themselves in the future) to make more future-oriented choices, or does merely framing a choice in the context of being about the future work well enough to engender more of those choices? It seems that mental time travel is not a requirement for choosing delayed rewards, although it also seems that mental time travel certainly can help support such choices.

Kwan et al. (2012) reported a fascinating study in which they gave hypothetical intertemporal choices to a participant named K.C. This individual shows little or no ability to think about the future or reflect on how the future might unfold. However, K.C. showed clear discounting of future rewards, with steeper discounting as a function of longer delays to the bigger monetary reward. In fact, K.C. fell well within the range of normal control subjects (see Fig. 14.1). This would seem to show a dissociation between imagining the future and making decisions involving the future since K.C. does not imagine the future. When he was asked about his strategy, K.C. reported relying on a gut feeling to choose "the best deal." The normal participants reported relying on both episodic (e.g., "I thought about how I might spend the money in my retirement") and non-episodic (e.g., "I estimated accumulated interest") future-oriented thoughts. This case shows that although mental time travel may impact decisions about future rewards, one does not need to engage in mental time travel to still make decisions that look like those made by people who do consider the future. In a subsequent report (Kwan et al., 2015), 6 amnesic participants and 20 participants without amnesia were given two versions of an intertemporal choice test: A standard version, but also a version where they were prompted to imagine specific personal future events that were aligned in time with the receipt of hypothetical delayed rewards. In the normal

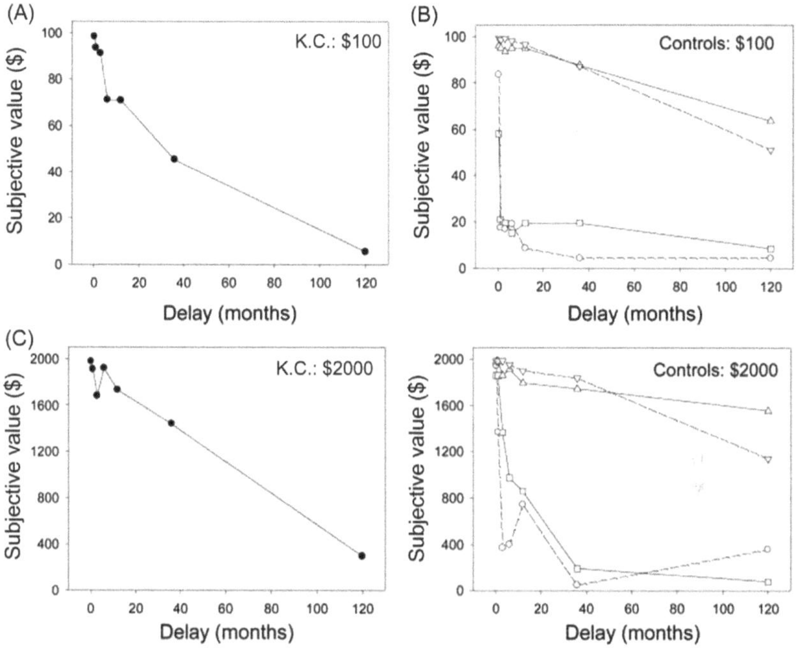

FIGURE 14.1 Discounting of $100 and $2000 delayed rewards by K.C. and control participants in the study by Kwan et al. (2012). (A) Mean subjective values at each delay to the $100 reward for K.C. (B) Mean subjective values at each delay to the $100 reward for the two control participants who showed the steepest and the two who showed the shallowest discounting. (C) Mean subjective values at each delay to the $2,000 reward for K.C. (D) Mean subjective values at each delay to the $2,000 reward for the two control participants who showed the steepest discounting and the two who showed the shallowest discounting. *From Kwan, D., Craver, C. F., Green, L., Myerson, J., Boyer, P., & Rosenbaum, R. S. (2012). Future decision-making without episodic mental time travel. Hippocampus, 22, 1215–1219. Copyright 2012. Reprinted with permission of John Wiley & Sons.*

condition, the two groups looked similar in their discounting of delayed rewards. More surprising was that the amnesic participants showed less discounting in the future-oriented prompting condition, even though those participants do not actually engage in episodic prospective cognition (or, at least, do not report being aware of doing so). This suggests that the framing of intertemporal choices in the context of episodic prospection can produce behavioral changes even in people who do not think much about the future. This is exciting, I think, because it highlights another contextual effect on self-control that could be manipulated fairly easily when people are offered choices.

So, what happens when people are explicitly "nudged" to think about the future? In some cases, explicit prompts lead them to discount the future less steeply (e.g., Peters & Büchel, 2010). For example, when people made choices between a consistent smaller/sooner amount of money and varying larger/later amounts, they more often chose the delayed amounts on those trials where a participant-specific episodic tag was added (e.g., they might be reminded that the larger amount was available on the date of a friend's birthday party; see Fig. 14.2). Thus, the comparisons of amount and delay were the same across choices, but sometimes there was episodic prompting that was designed to get participants to engage in mental time travel. In addition, fMRI results showed that the episodic prompts led to greater activation of brain networks related to episodic future thinking (confirming the manipulation worked), and that these networks likely contributed to the changes in discounting. And, the effect of episodic prompts worked best on those who reported the highest levels of imagery for the episodes. High-imagery subjects reduced their discount rate by on average 16% in the episodic condition (i.e., they chose the delayed reward more often), whereas low-imagery subjects did not reduce their rate much at all (also see Benoit, Gilbert, & Burgess, 2011; Ersner-Hershfield, Wimmer, & Knutson, 2009).

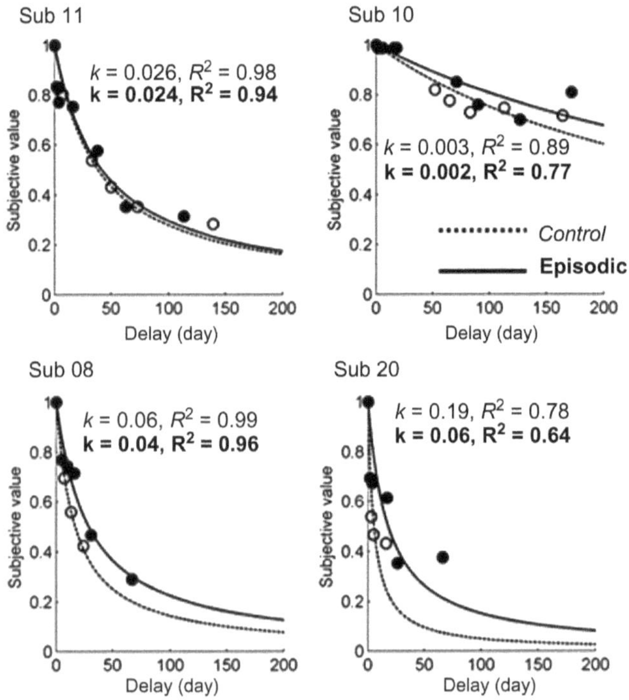

FIGURE 14.2 Hyperbolic functions were fit to the indifference points separately for the control (dashed lines) and episodic (solid lines, filled circles) conditions, and the best-fitting *k*-parameters (discount rates) and R^2 values are shown for each subject. The log-transformed difference between discount rates was taken as a measure of the effect of the episodic tags on choice preferences. *From Peters, J., & Büchel, C. (2010). Episodic future thinking reduces reward delay discounting through an enhancement of prefrontal-mediotemporal interactions. Neuron, 66, 138–148. Copyright 2010. Reprinted with permission of Elsevier.*

These effects of episodic future thinking are found in real-world settings as well as in hypothetical judgments. One area that has been investigated extensively is food consumption, with evidence that episodic future thinking allows people to focus on future health goals rather than the pleasure associated with a decision that is highly gratifying in the present moment. For example, when women are steered toward imagining the future, they stick to longer-term weight-based goals in their food choices by reducing caloric intake relative to women who are not steered toward thinking about the future (Daniel, Stanton, & Epstein, 2013a, 2013b). O'Neill, Daniel, and Epstein (2016) gave overweight women the chance to spend a gift card on food. Some women also listened to themselves on an audio recording where they discussed future-oriented goals and events relevant to their own lives, and those women made healthier food choices and consumed less calories compared to women who listened to themselves talk about general habits that were important to them, but that were not future oriented (Fig. 14.3). These effects were fairly large for that meal, suggesting that approaches that focus on future-oriented goals can have measurable and substantial impacts on real-world choices. And, this is true also for children, especially those

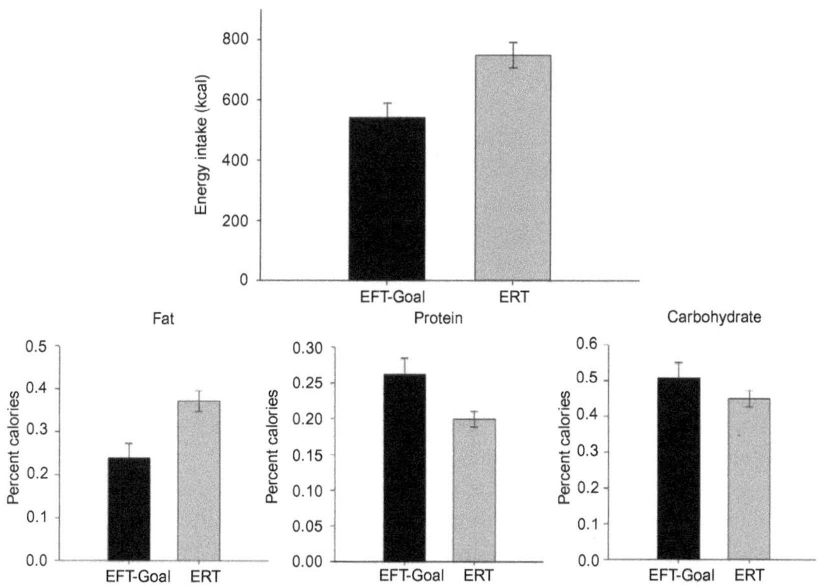

FIGURE 14.3 The top panel shows the difference in caloric intake for participants in O'Neill et al. (2016) on the basis of whether they heard future-oriented prompts (EFT) or not (ERT) during choice or food and consumption. The bottom panels show the between-group differences in percent of calories consumed from fat, protein, and carbohydrate. Values reflect the means and standard errors of the mean. *From O'Neill, J., Daniel, T. O., & Epstein, L. H. (2016). Episodic future thinking reduces eating in a food court. Eating Behaviors, 20, 9–13. Copyright 2016. Reprinted with permission of Elsevier.*

who are highly motivated to lose weight. When those children were given the same kinds of episodic future-oriented cues versus episodic, nonfuture-oriented cues, they consumed fewer calories from available treats. Those children also were less likely to discount delayed hypothetical monetary rewards compared to children who were not prompted to think about the future, showing that such prompts can have broad impacts on self-control and behavioral restraint (Daniel, Said, Stanton, & Epstein, 2015). The same effect was seen in female undergraduate students and was especially pronounced for those who engaged in food-related future-oriented imagery (Dassen, Jansen, Nederkoorn, & Houben, 2016).

There are other connections between future-oriented cognition and self-control. A large study of individuals between the ages of 10 and 30 years showed that younger people were less inclined to think about the future, in general, and they also showed greater discounting of future rewards (Steinberg et al., 2009). Bromberg, Wiehler, and Peters (2015) reported that when adolescents thought about the future, the vividness of those thoughts was negatively correlated with their delay discounting rate, meaning that the more vivid their future-oriented thoughts were, the less impulsive they were in their choices. Smallwood, Ruby, and Singer (2013) also found that there was a relation between mind-wandering (which often takes the form of thinking about the future) and reduced delay discounting. Bulley, Henry, and Suddendorf (2016) argued that although future-oriented episodic memory may not be a requirement for showing self-control, it certainly is a big benefit to the goal of demonstrating such self-control. Simulating the future through episodic imagining allows one to envision what needs to be done now to better prepare for or bring about that future. Bulley et al. discussed evidence that supports the idea that working memory is responsible for valuing future rewards on the basis of how easily they are brought to consciousness when one thinks about those rewards (see Kurth-Nelson, Bickel, & Redish, 2012). Prospective episodic thoughts increase the value of delayed rewards because they are easier for working memory to "find" when they are being considered as part of the future. In an interesting connection to this idea, Hinson, Jameson, and Whitney (2003) reported that working memory limitations and working memory load (i.e., how much one is trying to remember or mentally manipulate at a given time) increase discounting rates. And, it may even be that training working memory could lead to reduced discounting rates (Bickel, Yi, Landes, Hill, & Baxter, 2011). I think this is an interesting connection that merits more research, because it could have large implications for improving self-control. Bulley et al. also reviewed a number of other factors that link future-oriented episodic thought to intertemporal choices. For instance, they noted that when an imagined future is grim or negative, this may lead to more choices for more immediate rewards, and that this could be seen as highly adaptive. The same is true when episodic future thinking leads to recognizing probabilistic aspects of choices

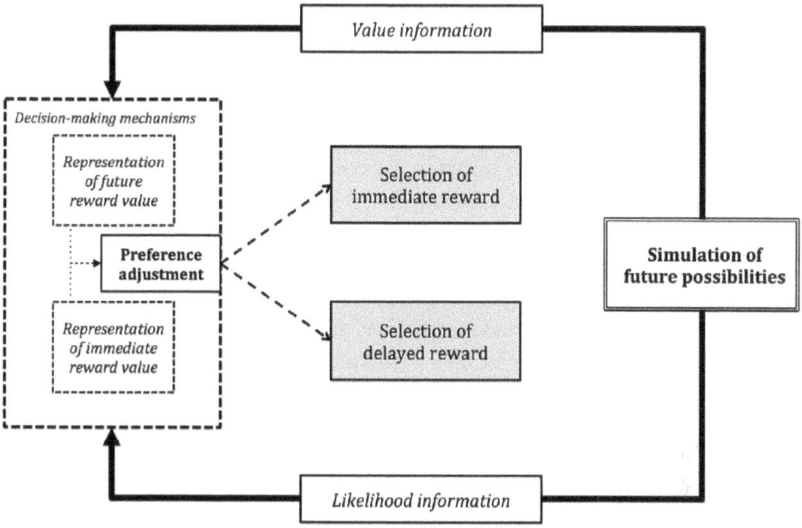

FIGURE 14.4 The model from Bulley et al. (2016) describing how simulations of future reward outcomes and contexts feed back value and likelihood information into decision-making mechanisms. These mechanisms are responsible for executing the behavioral selection of immediate or delayed rewards, and preferences for these rewards may shift differentially depending on what is simulated. *From Bulley, A., Henry, J., & Suddendorf, T. (2016). Prospection and the present moment: The role of episodic foresight in intertemporal choices between immediate and delayed rewards. Review of General Psychology, 20, 29–47. Copyright 2016. Reprinted with permission of the American Psychological Association.*

that may lend themselves to choosing a more immediate and more guaranteed outcome. And, they offered a model for how episodic simulation of the future impacts the valuation and estimation of probabilities of different outcomes (Fig. 14.4).

FUTURE-ORIENTED COGNITION IN CHILDREN

The preschool years for children would seem to be a time ripe with possibilities for future-oriented cognition to emerge, and to be heavily supported and/or taxed by their daily lives. Children at this age, at least in western and industrialized cultures, are beginning new routines such as getting ready for school or organized activities, aiding in chores around the home, and self-regulating some of their basic hygiene behaviors such as brushing teeth or washing hands. All of these behaviors seem to require some capacity for planning and for remembering what needs to be done. And, experimental research shows that planning abilities begin to emerge at this age (e.g., Carlson, Moses, & Claxton, 2004; Klahr & Robinson, 1981). Children also show the ability to make and implement plans in tasks in which travel routes have to be organized to collect items (Fabricius, 1988; Wellman, Fabricius, & Sophian, 1985), such as in a grocery store (e.g., Gauvain & Rogoff, 1989), or to get through a maze (e.g., Beran, Parrish, Futch, Evans, & Perdue, 2015; Gardner & Rogoff, 1990). For example, when children had to imagine going to the beach or store, and then plan for familiar parts of those trips (Hudson, Shapiro, & Sosa, 1995), it was around 3 to 5 years that planning really improved for these kinds of events.

Preschool children also are being asked more and more by parents and caregivers to "remember to do" different kinds of things—exactly the commands that should promote prospective cognition. And, research has shown that prospective memory begins to emerge at this age, as children begin to form future intentions, and then carry those out (e.g., Guajardo & Best, 2000; Kerns, 2000; Kretschmer, Voigt, Friedrich, Pfeiffer, & Kliegel, 2014; Kvavilashvili, Messer, & Ebdon, 2001; Mahy & Moses, 2011; Mahy, Moses, & Kliegel, 2014; Perdue, Beran, Williamson, Gonsiorowski, & Evans, 2014). At this age, children begin to get choices over "now or later" outcomes. In my family, this was the age at which my daughters began to choose whether they wanted smaller, sooner treats (such as a popsicle), or something more enticing later, perhaps like a big slice of cake after dinner. And, they began to learn that they needed to behave in certain ways now, to gain rewards later. Finally, we know that this is the age at which children begin to engage in mental time travel (e.g., Atance, 2008; Busby & Suddendorf, 2005; Hayne, Gross, McNamee, Fitzgibbon, & Tustin, 2011; Payne, Taylor, Hayne, & Scarf, 2015), and by the early school years they readily anticipate the future as much as they recall the past (e.g., Perner, Kloo, & Rohwer, 2010). For these reasons, it is a natural question as to whether the psychological mechanisms of planning, prospective memory, and self-control show relations among themselves through development. And, to ask whether children's capacity for mental time travel plays a role in these other processes. The evidence that these capacities all begin to emerge in the preschool years suggests that there should be links, and so these potential relationships between various forms of future-oriented cognition have recently drawn excitement and attention. However, the results have been somewhat mixed in terms of the empirical findings, particularly when such assessments have been done with young children.

Atance and Jackson (2009) looked carefully at the relation of all of these future-oriented behaviors. Children between 3 and 5 years of age were given a battery of tasks that measured important aspects of future orientation, including mental time travel ability, delay of gratification, planning, and prospective memory. The picture book task involved showing children color photographs of four locations—a river, a desert, a waterfall, and a mountain—and the children had to decide from three photos of objects which one they would take with them to each of those locations. Only one thing would be useful there, even though other things would make sense there (e.g., a fish makes sense at the river, but the correct choice was a band-aid in case of injury). Children had to explain why they chose what they did. Children were also asked about what they were going to do the next day, and then those answers were checked against what parents told the experimenters was likely, to see how well the children anticipated their real futures. Children also did the marshmallow test, as described earlier. To assess planning, children did the Tower of Hanoi task that involves moving a stack of wooden disks from one peg to another, but with a rule that only one disk could be moved at a time and smaller disks could sit on larger ones but not vice versa. This makes the task hard, because you have to think through how to move everything, and in some cases you have to make choices that seem to move away from the goal in order to finally reach it. In the truck loading task, children played the role of a mail carrier who needed to deliver party invitations. But, a series of rules about how the truck could navigate the streets and which invitations needed to go where and in what order meant that children had to really plan their routes. The task varied in terms of children delivering two to five invitations, to vary the difficulty of the delivery routes that needed to be planned. Children also completed two prospective memory tasks. In one (based on Kvavilashvili et al., 2001), children named images of items on flash cards, but also had to remember that any animal pictures that appeared needed to be hidden away so as to not scare a stuffed dog toy named "Scruffles." Such cards appeared infrequently, to see whether children remembered to implement that rule when the time was right. The second prospective memory test was based on Guajardo and Best (2000) and involved a small, colorful finger puppet. Children were told they could have the puppet, but only if they remembered to ask for it after completing a measure of their verbal abilities. The puppet was placed out of sight, and so children had to remember to ask for it later. What Atance and Jackson found was that, if you controlled for the age of the children, and their general verbal abilities, there were few relations between performance on any of these tasks. They concluded that although mental time travel, delay of gratification, planning, and prospective memory all are considered to be future-oriented capacities, they do not appear to be held together by this common component—at least in this age range. One possibility is that some of these tasks actually did not require the children to think about the future, at least in an episodic way. As I noted earlier, this could be an important factor, given that episodic future thinking offers stronger benefits to things like intertemporal choices. Another possibility is that the tasks may have required future orientation but they also differed in terms of the additional cognitive components involved, with some of those other components being more critical (e.g., working memory span). An important idea here is that future-oriented cognition may consist of a suite of capacities, rather than one thing that is "tapped" across a wide range of tasks. But, again, this is also where the idea of episodic versus semantic prospection may be important to recognize. The pictures task, the question about what the child would do tomorrow, and the marshmallow test likely were the only tasks to really force children to think about the future, and so future work will need to use a lot more tasks, and to consider the actual requirements for semantic and episodic prospection involved in each.

FUTURE-ORIENTED COGNITION IN NONHUMAN ANIMALS

This leaves us with the question of future-oriented cognition in other species and the question of mental time travel by animals. There is no question in my mind that animals remember past personal events and anticipate future outcomes. They do this in a number of domains, including foraging behavior, social behavior, and perhaps even in cases in which they anticipate future needs and plan for those needs in the present. This is a highly studied question, and a number of good reviews have been written (e.g., Cheke and Clayton, 2010; Clayton, Bussey, & Dickinson, 2003; Raby & Clayton, 2009; Roberts, 2002; Suddendorf & Busby, 2003; Suddendorf & Corballis, 2007; Tulving, 2005; Zentall, 2006). I will focus on only a few reports here, largely to demonstrate the parallels between humans and nonhuman animals for the key cognitive processes of planning and prospective memory, and then to discuss how confident we might feel about episodic future planning as a form of mental time travel in animals.

Among the best examples of prospective memory in animals comes from studies of rats by Jon Crystal and his colleagues. In one study conducted by that group, rats learned to classify a tone as either short or long in duration. At the same time, during sessions, the rats learned when a large food meal would become available, and soon the rats showed anticipatory behaviors (e.g., they began poking their noses into the food trough) right around the time that the big meal approached (Wilson & Crystal, 2012). This behavior seems similar to the time-based prospective memory tasks used in humans in which people have to remember that something is going to appear at a certain time in the future. In addition, rats showed decreases in their ongoing performance levels when they were maintaining a prospective intention to disengage from that primary task and go consume the large meal (Wilson, Pizzo, & Crystal, 2013; see Fig. 14.5). In a study from my lab, we gave the language-trained chimpanzee, Panzee, a choice between two food items (Beran, Perdue, Bramlett, Menzel, & Evans, 2012). The chosen item was immediately scattered around an adjacent outdoor yard and the unselected item remained in a container indoors. Panzee then was allowed to go into the outdoor yard and forage for the chosen food reward for 30 minutes. In addition to the scattered food, there were also lexigram tokens (images representing various food types) in the same space. The key issue was that one of those tokens was the name for the *other food item* that Panzee had not chosen, and if she brought that token in to give to a naïve experimenter, she could get the other item as well. Panzee consistently remembered, after eating all of the preferred items, to then go get the correct token and bring it in,

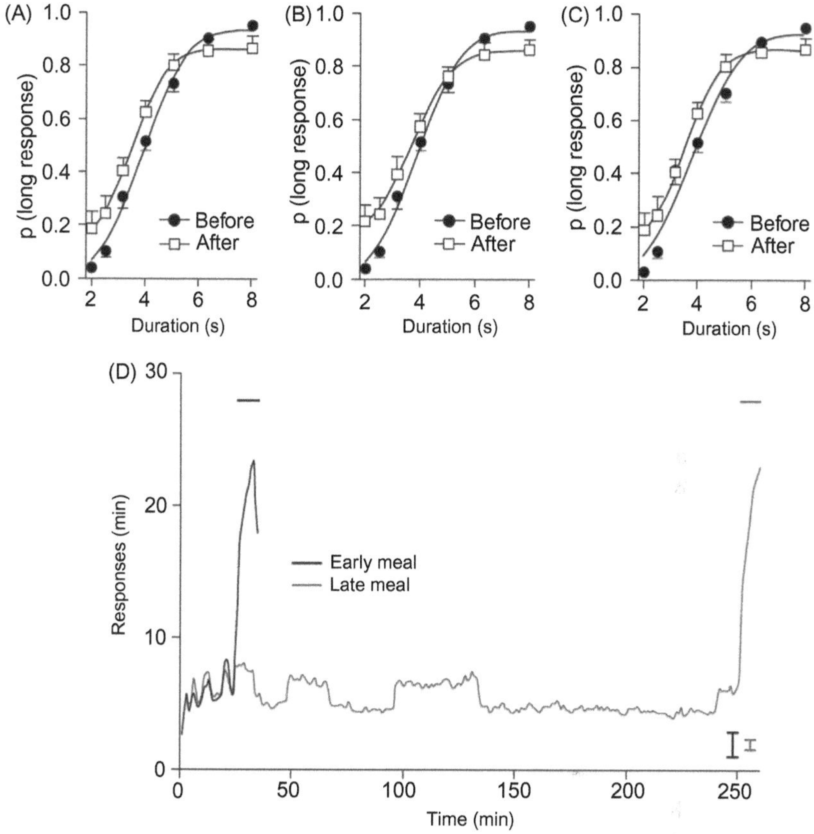

FIGURE 14.5 Testing rats in a prospective memory test. Anticipation of early (A) and late (B) meals severely disrupted performance in an ongoing task (an auditory discrimination) after the event, relative to excellent performance at an earlier time point. (C) When event and time were dissociated (using data from 25 to 34 min, with and without the event), performance was severely disrupted by the event. (D) Rats anticipated the arrival of the meal, as shown by the increase in food-trough responses when the event provided information that the meal could be obtained soon; the meal could be obtained early or late (beginning at 35 or 260 min, respectively), which was randomly determined on each day. Horizontal lines indicate the last 10-min before the meal when the event was presented. *From Wilson, A. G., Pizzo, M. J., & Crystal, J. D. (2013). Event-based prospective memory in the rat. Current Biology, 23, 1089–1093. Copyright 2013. Reprinted with permission of Elsevier.*

in much the same way that you might remember, after finishing the nice meal you prepared for yourself, to then go make the grocery list for next week (also see Evans, Perdue, & Beran, 2014).

Of course, the above examples are of prospective memory, but they do not have to involve seeing oneself in a future event. Rather, they can reflect semantic prospection only. So, what about mental time travel in animals? This is obviously a more difficult thing to demonstrate than simply showing future-oriented cognition, because it requires some demonstration that actions are undertaken *as if the animal anticipates its own future needs as being in the future*. But, I think there is still good evidence of such possible mental time travel in animals, especially if one is willing to allow that it may never be possible to know for certain that a nonverbal subject actually sees itself in a future scenario. If, instead, we consider that future-oriented, situation-unique anticipatory planning reflects episodic-like prospective cognition, then I think a number of species qualify. Extensive and impressive work with birds has shown this in foraging contexts. Across a wide variety of task variations, birds that cache different kinds of food items (some that perish and some that do not) seem to then retrieve those items in a manner that suggests they anticipate which items might still be viable to eat. Even the choices of what to cache may be future oriented in some of these cases (e.g., Clayton & Dickinson, 1999; Correia, Dickinson, & Clayton, 2007; Raby, Alexis, Dickinson, & Clayton, 2007). In addition, we know that monkeys also plan travel routes of hundreds of meters when looking for food sites (Chauvin & Thierry, 2005; Janson, 1998, 2007; Noser & Byrne, 2007).

As I noted in Chapter 2, I believe that some instances of tool use by animals reflect future-oriented cognition, especially when tools must be collected and then used in sequences to accomplish goals. We know that chimpanzees do this, for example, when they crack nuts (e.g., Boesch & Boesch, 1983, 1984). Great apes show other forms of future-oriented cognition as well. Chimpanzees spontaneously saved tokens to use them in the near future, indicating that they anticipated a delayed opportunity to exchange them for food (Sousa & Matsuzawa, 2001). And, we know that chimpanzees can learn to obtain and then later trade tokens or real food items to obtain something better (e.g., Dufour, Pelé, Sterck, & Thierry, 2007). Or, to allow items to accumulate before taking those items (e.g., Beran, 2002). This does not mean that these animals are seeing themselves in the future with better rewards or larger amounts of reward, but I do not think one can exclude that possibility. We certainly allow that when children wait for a second marshmallow or when we work to obtain money to then exchange for food or other pleasurable things that we may be engaging in mental time travel. Of course, researchers must do the best they can to show that other animals are also engaging in such mental time travel, but I do not think this precludes us from starting from a perspective that in some cases animals are thinking about their own, unique future, and then organizing behavior to best accomplish a future goal.

I often like to think of a specific example of episodic prospection in my own life that involves making lunch for my children. Each evening, we decide if they will have school lunch or take a lunch, and if they plan to take a lunch, I make the sandwiches ahead of time (we put everything together in the lunch box in the morning, though). I do this because I know I will not have time in the morning and will want to have the sandwiches ready to go, and I am imagining how much easier the morning will be if we do have them ready. We do other things like this, such as setting out our clothes the night before or packing for a vacation a few days ahead of time or even doing things like putting an umbrella in the car because we see that it will rain tomorrow and we are going to have to walk across campus a few times that day. I think these examples offer insights into what might be analogous events to nonhuman species, and then we can look to see if they do any kind of anticipatory behavior. Turns out, they sometimes do!

For example, chimpanzees in the wild show a number of behaviors that appear to reflect either planning or prospective cognition, including instances in which present behavior seems to be organized in a way that reflects anticipated future activity. One instance of this is in the coordinated way in which chimpanzee hunt monkeys and other prey species (e.g., Stanford, Wallis, Mpongo, & Goodall, 1994), which suggests some degree of planning and anticipation that impacts how coordination of the hunt occurs. Individual chimpanzees take on what appear to be specific roles, which can vary a lot in terms of where they are located and what they do. But, more impressive to me is a report about wild chimpanzees' nest building activity in the evenings. It turns out that chimpanzees may be choosing nest sites and the direction of nest orientation based on where they will go early the next day (Janmaat, Polansky, Ban, & Boesch, 2014). When highly preferred and fairly infrequently available fruits are ripening, chimpanzees will move closer toward the locations where those foods are located before bedding down for the night, compared to where they make their beds when other, less preferred foods are the main diet source for breakfast. So, the sites they choose for their nightly nests allow for some prediction over where they will go the next day. And, the time at which they would rise and travel also varied depending on what fruit was ripe and how far away that food was. This feels a lot like when we set the alarm to wake up extra early because we know we have a long drive ahead of us (also see Ban, Boesch, & Janmaat, 2014), or how I make sandwiches the night before, because I know we have to leave early for school. The chimpanzees also seem to anticipate where they will go the next day, and use their evening time to get better ready for that.

We see other examples of such planning and potential episodic prospection in laboratory tasks, and with animals in captive settings. In one case, a chimpanzee was reported to collect stones in advance of visitors coming to see him in his zoo exhibit, at which point he would have those stones available to throw at visitors (Osvath, 2009).[2] Other observations suggested this chimpanzee even attempted to conceal those collections of projectiles

2. This is one of the great "joys" of working with great apes. Their intelligence, matched with their mischievousness and occasional ill-temperedness, leads to their infamy as throwers of all kinds of things. But, I think it is fascinating that such behavior seems to beg anticipation of the future by the apes to achieve the greatest effect on those at whom such things are aimed!

(Osvath & Karvonen, 2012). More controlled tests confirmed this kind of anticipatory behavior in great apes. For example, Mulcahy and Call (2006) reported a strong case for anticipation of future needs in great apes. When given the chance to collect and transport tools from one location in the laboratory to another, the apes more selectively transported tools that could function to gain rewards, but *only at a later time*. So, these apes determined what tools were needed, and then chose those tools even though they could not be used at that time. A subsequent study showed that apes could choose a tool needed in the future even against a more immediate, less preferred food reward (Osvath & Osvath, 2008). This suggests future orientation and self-control in the same context. These studies, and others, make the strong case that at least the great apes show future-oriented, anticipatory behaviors (see Osvath & Martin-Ordas 2014), and in many ways these claims very closely approximate the kinds of behaviors that we would typically say involve mental time travel when humans perform them. In recent years, we have begun to learn even more about nonprimate species in this regard as well. And, it seems clearer and clearer that apes are not the only species to engage in such anticipation and planning, as other reports of planning and future-oriented behavior have emerged with bird species (e.g., Kabadayi & Osvath, 2017).

I think these data from other species, from different kinds of tests, with different time periods, goal states, and task structures, all support the argument that animals sometimes anticipate what they need to do. They can generate and remember goals. They sometimes then structure present behavior in a way that seems to maximize overall later goals rather than only immediate desires, and perhaps through that process even experience some sense of their future selves. We cannot say whether that experience includes mental time travel, where animals think about their future selves. That does not matter. What matters is that they show many of the same foundational future-oriented cognitive processes that humans show. And, as I have explained in earlier chapters, they engage in similar choice behavior in the face of competing options and in the face of temptations that sometimes must be overcome to obtain the best possible outcome. Sometimes, they show self-control, and I think that often occurs in situations where they are considering the future. I think the developmental and comparative literatures converge on the idea that self-control serves future-oriented cognition, to the extent that choices of now versus later are felt to be those kinds of choices. I think for many species this is true, and that decision makers (whether human, monkey, great ape, rat, dog, pigeon, etc.) weigh "present" and "future" along with "better" and "worse" when making choices. Of course, as I have discussed, a lot of contextual factors and individual traits also play a role in what one chooses. But, the main point of summary for this chapter is to argue that a productive future line of comparative research is to match the growing interest in studying the relation of future-oriented cognition and self-control developmentally in humans. In the next chapter, I will conclude by offering some prescriptions for what I hope will be the next 20 years of research into self-control, and also offer some thoughts on how to frame the big questions that might guide that research.

REFERENCES

Altgassen, M., Rendell, P. G., Bernhard, A., Henry, J. D., Bailey, P. E., Phillips, L. H., & Kliegel, M. (2015). Future thinking improves prospective memory performance and plan enactment in older adults. *The Quarterly Journal of Experimental Psychology*, *68*, 192–204.

Atance, C. M. (2008). Future thinking in young children. *Current Directions in Psychological Science*, *17*, 295–298.

Atance, C. M., & Jackson, L. K. (2009). The development and coherence of future-oriented behaviors during the preschool years. *Journal of Experimental Child Psychology*, *102*, 379–391.

Atance, C. M., & O'Neill, D. K. (2001). Episodic future thinking. *Trends in Cognitive Sciences*, *5*, 533–539.

Ban, S. D., Boesch, C., & Janmaat, K. R. (2014). Taï chimpanzees anticipate revisiting high-valued fruit trees from further distances. *Animal Cognition*, *17*, 1353–1364.

Benoit, R. G., Gilbert, S. J., & Burgess, P. W. (2011). A neural mechanism mediating the impact of episodic prospection on farsighted decisions. *The Journal of Neuroscience*, *31*, 6771–6779.

Beran, M. J. (2002). Maintenance of self-imposed delay of gratification by four chimpanzees (*Pan troglodytes*) and an orangutan (*Pongo pygmaeus*). *Journal of General Psychology*, *129*, 49–66.

Beran, M. J., Parrish, A. E., Futch, S. E., Evans, T. A., & Perdue, B. M. (2015). Looking ahead? Computerized maze task performance by chimpanzees (*Pan troglodytes*), rhesus monkeys (*Macaca mulatta*), capuchin monkeys (*Cebus apella*), and human children (*Homo sapiens*). *Journal of Comparative Psychology*, *129*, 160–173.

Beran, M. J., Perdue, B. M., Bramlett, J. L., Menzel, C. R., & Evans, T. A. (2012). Prospective memory in a language-trained chimpanzee (*Pan troglodytes*). *Learning and Motivation*, *43*, 192–199.

Bickel, W. K., Yi, R., Landes, R. D., Hill, P. F., & Baxter, C. (2011). Remember the future: Working memory training decreases delay discounting among stimulant addicts. *Biological Psychiatry*, *69*, 260–265.

Boesch, C., & Boesch, H. (1983). Optimisation of nut-cracking with natural hammers by wild chimpanzees. *Behaviour*, *83*, 265–286.

Boesch, C., & Boesch, H. (1984). Mental map in wild chimpanzees: An analysis of hammer transports for nut cracking. *Primates*, *25*, 160–170.

Bromberg, U., Wiehler, A., & Peters, J. (2015). Episodic future thinking is related to impulsive decision making in healthy adolescents. *Child Development*, *86*, 1458–1468.

Buehler, R., Griffin, D., & MacDonald, H. (1997). The role of motivated reasoning in optimistic time predictions. *Personality and Social Psychology Bulletin*, *23*, 238–247.

Buehler, R., Griffin, D., & Ross, M. (1994). Exploring the "planning fallacy": Why people underestimate their task completion times. *Journal of Personality and Social Psychology*, *67* (3), 366–381.

Bulley, A., Henry, J., & Suddendorf, T. (2016). Prospection and the present moment: The role of episodic foresight in intertemporal choices between immediate and delayed rewards. *Review of General Psychology*, *20*, 29–47.

Busby, J., & Suddendorf, T. (2005). Recalling yesterday and predicting tomorrow. *Cognitive Development, 20*, 362–372.

Carlson, S. M., Moses, L. J., & Claxton, L. J. (2004). Individual differences in executive functioning and theory of mind: An investigation of inhibitory control and planning ability. *Journal of Experimental Child Psychology, 87*, 299–319.

Chauvin, C., & Thierry, B. (2005). Tonkean macaques orient their food search from olfactory cues conveyed by group mates. *Ethology, 111*, 301–310.

Cheke, L. G., & Clayton, N. S. (2010). Mental time travel in animals. *Wiley Interdisciplinary Reviews: Cognitive Science, 1*, 915–930.

Clayton, N. S., Bussey, T. J., & Dickinson, A. (2003). Can animals recall the past and plan for the future? *Nature Reviews Neuroscience, 4*, 685–691.

Clayton, N. S., & Dickinson, A. (1999). Scrub jays (*Aphelocoma coerulescens*) remember the relative time of caching as well as the location and content of their caches. *Journal of Comparative Psychology, 113*, 403–416.

Corballis, M. C. (2013). Mental time travel: A case for evolutionary continuity. *Trends in Cognitive Sciences, 17*, 5–6.

Correia, S. P. C., Dickinson, A., & Clayton, N. S. (2007). Western scrub-jays anticipate future needs independently of their future motivational state. *Current Biology, 17*, 856–861.

Daniel, T. O., Said, M., Stanton, C. M., & Epstein, L. H. (2015). Episodic future thinking reduces delay discounting and energy intake in children. *Eating Behaviors, 18*, 20–24.

Daniel, T. O., Stanton, C. M., & Epstein, L. H. (2013a). The future is now: Comparing the effect of episodic future thinking on impulsivity in lean and obese individuals. *Appetite, 71*, 120–125.

Daniel, T. O., Stanton, C. M., & Epstein, L. H. (2013b). The future is now: Reducing impulsivity and energy intake using episodic future thinking. *Psychological Science, 24*, 2339–2342.

Dassen, F. C., Jansen, A., Nederkoorn, C., & Houben, K. (2016). Focus on the future: Episodic future thinking reduces discount rate and snacking. *Appetite, 96*, 327–332.

Dufour, V., Pelé, M., Sterck, E. H. M., & Thierry, B. (2007). Chimpanzee (*Pan troglodytes*) anticipation of food return: Coping with waiting time in an exchange task. *Journal of Comparative Psychology, 121*, 145–155.

Einstein, G. O., & McDaniel, M. A. (2005). Prospective memory: Multiple retrieval processes. *Current Directions in Psychological Science, 14*, 286–290.

Ersner-Hershfield, H., Wimmer, G. E., & Knutson, B. (2009). Saving for the future self: Neural measures of future self-continuity predict temporal discounting. *Social Cognitive and Affective Neuroscience, 4*, 85–92.

Evans, T. A., Perdue, B. M., & Beran, M. J. (2014). The relationship between event-based prospective memory and ongoing task performance in chimpanzees (*Pan troglodytes*). *PLoS One, 9*, e112015.

Fabricius, W. V. (1988). The development of forward search planning in preschoolers. *Child Development, 59*, 1473–1488.

Gardner, W., & Rogoff, B. (1990). Children's deliberateness of planning according to task circumstances. *Developmental Psychology, 26*, 480–487.

Gauvain, M., & Rogoff, B. (1989). Collaborative problem solving and children's planning skills. *Developmental Psychology, 25*, 139–151.

Gollwitzer, P. M. (1999). Implementation intentions. *American Psychologist, 57*, 493–503.

Guajardo, N. R., & Best, D. L. (2000). Do preschoolers remember what to do? Incentive and external cues in prospective memory. *Cognitive Development, 15*, 75–97.

Hayne, H., Gross, J., McNamee, S., Fitzgibbon, O., & Tustin, K. (2011). Episodic memory and episodic foresight in 3-and 5-year-old children. *Cognitive Development, 26*, 343–355.

Hicks, J. L., Marsh, R. L., & Cook, G. I. (2005). Task interference in time-based, event-based, and dual intention prospective memory conditions. *Journal of Memory and Language, 53*, 430–444.

Hinson, J. M., Jameson, T. L., & Whitney, P. (2003). Impulsive decision making and working memory. *Journal of Experimental Psychology: Learning, Memory, and Cognition, 29*, 298–306.

Hudson, J. A., Shapiro, L. R., & Sosa, B. B. (1995). Planning in the real world: Preschool children's scripts and plans for familiar events. *Child Development, 66*, 984–998.

Janmaat, K. R. L., Polansky, L., Ban, S. D., & Boesch, C. (2014). Wild chimpanzees plan their breakfast time, type, and location. *Proceedings of the National Academy of Sciences USA, 111*, 16343–16348.

Janson, C. H. (1998). Experimental evidence for spatial memory in foraging wild capuchin monkeys, *Cebus apella. Animal Behaviour, 55*, 1229–1243.

Janson, C. H. (2007). Experimental evidence for route integration and strategic planning in wild capuchin monkeys. *Animal Cognition, 10*, 341–356.

Kabadayi, C., & Osvath, M. (2017). Ravens parallel great apes in flexible planning for tool-use and bartering. *Science, 357*, 202–204.

Kerns, K. A. (2000). The CyberCruiser: An investigation of development of prospective memory in children. *Journal of the International Neuropsychological Society, 6*, 62–70.

Klahr, D., & Robinson, M. (1981). Formal assessment of problem-solving and planning processes in preschool children. *Cognitive Psychology, 13*, 113–148.

Kliegel, M., Mackinlay, R., & Jager, T. (2008). Complex prospective memory: Development across the lifespan and the role of task interruption. *Developmental Psychology, 44*, 612–617.

Kliegel, M., McDaniel, M. A., & Einstein, G. O. (2000). Plan formation, retention, and execution in prospective memory: A new approach and age-related effects. *Memory & Cognition, 28*, 1041–1049.

Kretschmer, A., Voigt, B., Friedrich, S., Pfeiffer, K., & Kliegel, M. (2014). Time-based prospective memory in young children—Exploring executive functions as a developmental mechanism. *Child Neuropsychology, 20*, 662–676.

Kurth-Nelson, Z., Bickel, W., & Redish, A. D. (2012). A theoretical account of cognitive effects in delay discounting. *The European Journal of Neuroscience, 35*, 1052–1064.

Kvavilashvili, L., Messer, D. J., & Ebdon, P. (2001). Prospective memory in children: The effects of age and task interruption. *Developmental Psychology, 37*, 418–430.

Kwan, D., Craver, C. F., Green, L., Myerson, J., Boyer, P., & Rosenbaum, R. S. (2012). Future decision-making without episodic mental time travel. *Hippocampus, 22*, 1215–1219.

Kwan, D., Craver, C. F., Green, L., Myerson, J., Gao, F., Black, S. E., & Rosenbaum, R. S. (2015). Cueing the personal future to reduce discounting in intertemporal choice: Is episodic prospection necessary. *Hippocampus, 25*, 432–443.

Mahy, C. E., & Moses, L. J. (2011). Executive functioning and prospective memory in young children. *Cognitive Development, 26*, 269–281.

Mahy, C. E., Moses, L. J., & Kliegel, M. (2014). The development of prospective memory in children: An executive framework. *Developmental Review, 34*, 305–326.

Manning, L. (2016). Future mental time travel and the me-self. In K. Michaelian, S. B. Klein, & K. K. Szpunar (Eds.), *Seeing the future: Theoretical perspectives on future-oriented mental time travel* (pp. 183–198). Oxford, UK: Oxford University Press.

Marsh, R. J., Hancock, T. W., & Hicks, J. L. (2002). The demands of an ongoing activity influence the success of event-based prospective memory. *Psychonomic Bulletin & Review, 9*, 604–610.

McDaniel, M. A., & Einstein, G. O. (2007). *Prospective memory: An overview and synthesis of an emerging field*. Los Angeles, CA: Sage Publications.

Michaelian, K., Klein, S. B., & Szpunar, K. K. (Eds.), (2016). *Seeing the future: Theoretical perspectives on future-oriented mental time travel*. Oxford, UK: Oxford University Press.

Miller, G.A., Galanter, E., & Pribram, K.H. (1986). *Plans and the structure of behavior*. Adams Bannister Cox.

Mischel, W., Shoda, Y., & Rodriguez, M. L. (1989). Delay of gratification in children. *Science, 244*, 933–938.

Mulcahy, N. J., & Call, J. (2006). Apes save tools for future use. *Science, 312*, 1038–1040.

Noser, R., & Byrne, R. W. (2007). Travel routes and planning of visits to out-of-sight resources in wild chacma baboons, *Papio ursinus*. *Animal Behaviour, 73*, 257–266.

O'Neill, J., Daniel, T. O., & Epstein, L. H. (2016). Episodic future thinking reduces eating in a food court. *Eating Behaviors, 20*, 9–13.

Osvath, M. (2009). Spontaneous planning for future stone throwing by a male chimpanzee. *Current Biology, 19*, R190–R191.

Osvath, M., & Karvonen, E. (2012). Spontaneous innovation for future deception in a male chimpanzee. *PloS One, 7*, e36782.

Osvath, M., & Martin-Ordas, G. (2014). The future of future-oriented cognition in non-humans: Theory and the empirical case of the great apes. *Philosophical Transactions of the Royal Society B, 369*, 20130486.

Osvath, M., & Osvath, H. (2008). Chimpanzee (*Pan troglodytes*) and orangutan (*Pongo abelii*) forethought: Self-control and pre-experience in the face of future tool use. *Animal Cognition, 11*, 661–674.

Payne, G., Taylor, R., Hayne, H., & Scarf, D. (2015). Mental time travel for self and other in three-and four-year-old children. *Memory, 23*, 675–682.

Perdue, B. M., Beran, M. J., Williamson, R. A., Gonsiorowski, A., & Evans, T. A. (2014). Prospective memory in children and chimpanzees. *Animal Cognition, 17*, 287–295.

Perner, J., Kloo, D., & Rohwer, M. (2010). Retro-and prospection for mental time travel: Emergence of episodic remembering and mental rotation in 5-to 8-year old children. *Consciousness and Cognition, 19*, 802–815.

Peters, J., & Büchel, C. (2010). Episodic future thinking reduces reward delay discounting through an enhancement of prefrontal-mediotemporal interactions. *Neuron, 66*, 138–148.

Raby, C. R., Alexis, D. M., Dickinson, A., & Clayton, N. S. (2007). Planning for the future by western scrub jays. *Nature, 445*, 919–921.

Raby, C. R., & Clayton, N. S. (2009). Prospective cognition in animals. *Behavioural Processes, 80*, 314–324.

Roberts, W. A. (2002). Are animals stuck in time? *Psychological Bulletin, 128*, 473–489.

Sheeran, P., & Orbell, S. (1999). Implementation intentions and repeated behaviors: Augmenting the predictive validity of the theory of planned behavior. *European Journal of Social Psychology, 29*, 249–370.

Smallwood, J., Ruby, F. J. M., & Singer, T. (2013). Letting go of the present: Mind-wandering is associated with reduced delay discounting. *Consciousness and Cognition, 22*, 1–7.

Sousa, C., & Matsuzawa, T. (2001). The use of tokens as rewards and tools by chimpanzees (*Pan troglodytes*). *Animal Cognition, 4*, 213–221.

Stanford, C. B., Wallis, J., Mpongo, E., & Goodall, J. (1994). Hunting decisions in wild chimpanzees. *Behaviour, 131*, 1–18.

Steinberg, L., Graham, S., O'Brien, L., Woolard, J., Cauffman, E., & Banich, M. (2009). Age differences in future orientation and delay discounting. *Child Development, 80*, 28–44.

Suddendorf, T., & Busby, J. (2003). Mental time travel in animals? *Trends in Cognitive Sciences*, *7*, 391–396.

Suddendorf, T., & Corballis, M. C. (1997). Mental time travel and the evolution of the human mind. *Genetic, Social, and General Psychology Monographs*, *123*, 133–167.

Suddendorf, T., & Corballis, M. C. (2007). The evolution of foresight: What is mental time travel and is it unique to humans? *Behavioral and Brain Sciences*, *30*, 299–351.

Szpunar, K. K., Spreng, N., & Schacter, D. L. (2016). Toward a taxonomy of future thinking. In K. Michaelian, S. B. Klein, & K. K. Szpunar (Eds.), *Seeing the future: Theoretical perspectives on future-oriented mental time travel* (pp. 21–38). Oxford, UK: Oxford University Press.

Tulving, E. (1984). Précis of elements of episodic memory. *Behavioral and Brain Sciences*, *7*, 223–268.

Tulving, E. (2001). The origin of autonoesis in episodic memory. In H. L. Roediger, J. S. Nairne, I. Neath, & A. M. Suprenant (Eds.), *The nature of remembering: Essays in honor of Robert G. Crowder* (pp. 17–34). Washington, DC: American Psychological Association.

Tulving, E. (2005). Episodic memory and autonoesis: Uniquely human? In H. S. Terrace, & J. Metcalfe (Eds.), *The missing link in cognition: Origins of self-reflective consciousness* (pp. 3–56). New York: Oxford University Press.

Wellman, H. M., Fabricius, W. V., & Sophian, C. (1985). The early development of planning. In H. M. Wellman (Ed.), *Children's searching* (pp. 123–149). Hillsdale, NJ: Lawrence Erlbaum.

Wilson, A. G., & Crystal, J. D. (2012). Prospective memory in the rat. *Animal Cognition*, *15*, 349–358.

Wilson, A. G., Pizzo, M. J., & Crystal, J. D. (2013). Event-based prospective memory in the rat. *Current Biology*, *23*, 1089–1093.

Zentall, T. R. (2006). Mental time travel in animals: a challenging question. *Behavioural Processes*, *72*(2), 173–183.

FURTHER READING

Atance, C. M., & Mahy, C. E. V. (2016). Episodic future thinking in children: Methodological and theoretical approaches. In K. Michaelian, S. B. Klein, & K. K. Szpunar. (Eds.), *Seeing the future: Theoretical perspectives on future-oriented mental time travel* (pp. 367–388). Oxford, UK: Oxford University Press.

Atance, C. M., & Meltzoff, A. N. (2005). My future self: Young children's ability to anticipate and explain future states. *Cognitive Development*, *20*, 341–361.

Atance, C. M., & Meltzoff, A. N. (2006). Preschoolers' current desires warp their choices for the future. *Psychological Science*, *17*, 583–587.

Barresi, J., & Moore, C. (1997). The development of future-oriented prudence and altruism in preschoolers. *Cognitive Development*, *12*, 199–212.

Boyer, P. (2008). Evolutionary economics of mental time travel? *Trends in Cognitive Sciences*, *12*, 219–224.

Busby, J., & Suddendorf, T. (2005). Recalling yesterday and predicting tomorrow. *Cognitive Development*, *20*, 362–372.

Epstein, L. H., Jankowiak, N., Fletcher, K. D., Carr, K. A., Nederkoorn, C., Raynor, H., et al. (2014). Women who are motivated to eat and discount the future are more obese. *Obesity*, *22*, 1394–1399.

Fawcett, T. W., McNamara, J. M., & Houston, A. I. (2012). When is it adaptive to be patient? A general framework for evaluating delayed rewards. *Behavioural Processes*, *89*, 128–136.

Feeney, M. C., Roberts, W. A., & Sherry, D. F. (2011). Black-capped chickadees (Poecile atricapillus) anticipate future outcomes of foraging choices. *Journal of Experimental Psychology: Animal Behavior Processes*, *37*, 30–40.

Griskevicius, V., Tybur, J. M., Delton, A. W., & Robertson, T. E. (2011). The influence of mortality and socioeconomic status on risk and delayed rewards: A life history theory approach. *Journal of Personality and Social Psychology*, *100*, 1015–1026.

Janson, C. H., & Byrne, R. (2014). What wild primates know about resources: Opening up the black box. *Animal Cognition*, *10*, 357–367.

Kliegel, M., Ropeter, A., & Mackinlay, R. (2006). Complex prospective memory in children with ADHD. *Child Neuropsychology*, *12*, 407–419.

Klineberg, S. L. (1968). Future time perspective and the preference for delayed reward. *Journal of Personality and Social Psychology*, *8*, 253–257.

Mackinlay, R. J., Kliegel, M., & Mäntylä, T. (2009). Predictors of time-based prospective memory in children. *Journal of Experimental Child Psychology*, *102*, 251–264.

Menzel, C. R. (1999). Unprompted recall and reporting of hidden objects by a chimpanzee (*Pan troglodytes*) after extended delays. *Journal of Comparative Psychology*, *113*, 426–434.

Moore, C., & Lemmon, K. (2001). *The self in time: Developmental perspectives*. Mahwah, NJ: Lawrence Erlbaum Associates.

Osvath, M., & Persson, T. (2013). Great apes can defer exchange: A replication with different results suggesting future oriented behavior. *Frontiers in Psychology*, *4*, 698.

Sayers, K., & Menzel, C. R. (2012). Memory and foraging theory: Chimpanzee utilization of optimality heuristics in the rank-order recovery of hidden foods. *Animal Behaviour*, *84*, 795–803.

Scullin, M. K., Kurinec, C. A., & Nguyen, K. (2017). The effects of implementation intention strategies on prospective memory cue encoding. *Journal of Cognitive Psychology*, *29*, 929–938.

Stephens, D. W., & Anderson, D. (2001). The adaptive value of preference for immediacy: When shortsighted rules have farsighted consequences. *Behavioral Ecology*, *12*, 330–339.

Suddendorf, T. (2010). Episodic memory versus episodic foresight: similarities and differences. *WIREs Cognitive Sciences*, *1*, 99–107.

Suddendorf, T., Addis, D. R., & Corballis, M. C. (2009). Mental time travel and the shaping of the human mind. *Philosophical Transactions of the Royal Society B: Biological Sciences*, *364*, 1317–1324.

Suddendorf, T., & Busby, J. (2005). Making decisions with the future in mind: Developmental and comparative identification of mental time travel. *Learning and Motivation*, *36*, 110–125.

Szpunar, K. K. (2010). Episodic future thought: An emerging concept. *Perspectives on Psychological Science*, *5*, 142–162.

Weller, R. E., Cook, E. W., Avsar, K. B., & Cox, J. E. (2008). Obese women show greater delay discounting than healthy-weight women. *Appetite*, *51*, 563–569.

Wiese, J., Buehler, R., & Griffin, D. (2016). Backward planning: Effects of planning direction on predictions of task completion time. *Judgment and Decision Making*, *11*, 147–167.

Chapter 15

Worth Waiting For: Final Thoughts on Self-Control and the Future of Future-Oriented Research With People and Animals

> *... because as we know, there are known knowns; there are things we know we know. We also know there are known unknowns; that is to say we know there are some things we do not know. But there are also unknown unknowns – the ones we don't know we don't know.*
>
> US Secretary of Defense Donald Rumsfeld, February 12, 2002.

I really like this quote, not for any reason connected to the historical context in which Secretary Rumsfeld said this, but for the wording itself. As someone who also studies metacognition (Beran, 2017; Beran, Brandl, Perner, & Proust, 2012), I think this quote reflects exactly the kind of self-awareness that we hold to be one of humans' most sophisticated intellectual abilities. However, people reacted fairly harshly to this quote, arguing that it reflected poorly on the Secretary and the administration at the time in terms of how they were operating. But, in and of itself, it is a perfectly logical statement about the state of the world. And, for my present purposes, it is a perfect way of thinking about most areas of psychological research. As we do research, we add more to the *known knowns* category, while sometimes having to revise that category by moving a former *known known* back to the category of uncertain or inconsistently supported ideas. And, of course, science is driven by the *known unknowns*—these generate hypotheses to be tested so that we might resolve some of what we know we do not yet know. The *unknown unknowns*... those are the coolest things to scientists (if I can speak for all of us!). The things we do not yet know to study as unknowns are the things we hope to be inspired to realize, because then we are on to something truly new.

Self-Control in Animals and People. DOI: https://doi.org/10.1016/B978-0-12-812508-3.00015-3
© 2018 Elsevier Inc. All rights reserved.

For research into self-control, here is what I think are the most important *known knowns*:

First, self-control is not a thing. One does not "have it" or "not have it," and one does not exhaust it or replenish it. Self-control is the behavioral result of a suite of psychological mechanisms that include perceptual and learning mechanisms, cognitive mechanisms, and motivational systems (and perhaps other things such as grit).

Second, these capacities can be "turned on" in the moment in which a choice must be made, but even here such "turning on" is not dichotomous. The employment of self-control responses is not like turning on a light switch, where the room goes from darkness to light. It is like a dimmer switch, allowing for the room to be barely lit all the way to fully illuminated. And, as with light controlled by a dimmer, it can be adjusted in the moment, sharpened, or diminished. This is why delayed gratification falters, or why intertemporal choices are reversed.

Third, the sharpening or diminishing of self-control across instances can be predicted by knowing something about the individual who is making those choices, by knowing about the environment in which options are presented, and by understanding the nature of the interaction between these two things. Regarding individuals, it seems clear that your species matters, with differences in self-control between species being a real phenomenon. For humans, your age matters (at least through childhood), as do a number of other factors that may represent particular traits that lend themselves to making (or not making) good decisions for better rewards. But, environment is just as important. There are things that affect people's choices that involve their socioeconomic status, their access to education, their diet, the nature of their home life, and the role of positive social influences instead of negative ones. Having access to ways to distract oneself, or present choice options in ways that minimize steeply discounting the future will aid in self-control. But even then, the individual has to recognize at some level how to make use of contextual aids, and avoid contextual temptations. For example, I have described how the individual has to know to look away from the reward, to engage in other activities, to transform how they are thinking about the task, or to sharpen how they represent future time intervals.

We know we have impulsivity problems, and for many of us, these can lead to devastating consequences. But, the above *known knowns* show us that there are multiple paths to intervene, and to help those who struggle to achieve long term goals because of the temptations of shorter-term or easier to obtain pleasures. I have outlined the ways in which self-control responses can be increased in children and in other species. Comparative approaches have been highly influential in this pursuit, with the well-developed animal models of intertemporal choice, for example. I firmly believe that psychological research on self-control can and has impacted human behavior in measurable and important ways. What is perhaps lacking is a "full court press" to take this knowledge and apply it broadly through "nudges" to get people to make more self-control choices while being happy to do so. These nudges often work to change behavior for the better in many areas of life (Thaler & Sunstein, 1999), and so I hope to see more research integrating what we have learned in the laboratory into actual real-world applications.

This is not complicated, to generate such nudges for self-control. All we need is for someone else to give us instructions to influence what we are thinking when we are choosing to wait, or not. Perhaps these instructions can be the simplest of things. Imagine if you are saving money for a new car. Place a photo of the car right in front of your credit card in your wallet. Or, perhaps have that photo appear each morning somewhere in your digital world, such as through email or social media. I could easily envision a service that lets you choose now to get such prompts later, when you are at risk for failing to delay gratification. A human version of the pigeons' precommitment button. Some services are starting to appear that nudge us toward better self-control. Google Chrome, for example, has in beta testing a delay device, to make sure you really want to spend time on that website you just entered. When you attempt to log in to a site that you have put onto your personal "bad" list, it makes you wait for 10 to 30 seconds during which time you can decide whether you really need to be browsing that site or not. Normally, the immediate reward of being back on that time-sucking site you like is more tempting than the delayed reward of instead finishing your paper on time, or finishing that spreadsheet you have been working on. But, we know that if both events are pushed further off in time (which the delay timer does in this case), we can see more preference shifts toward the more delayed response. If you really want to be on that website, you will still wait, but you might otherwise shift to going back to the paper or spreadsheet you need to be working on now.

Here is what I think are the most important *known unknowns*:

Can focal interventions in one area of choice behavior, that improve self-control in that particular context, also pay off in other choice situations? This would be a huge benefit, to find out how to train people to engage in self-control in one specific context and have that training feed through all of life's choices. So far, we have not found a way to do this reliably.

How do social groups affect self-control choices? As I noted earlier, it is shocking how little research has been done on this question relative to the hundreds of studies testing one participant at a time on some variation of intertemporal choice test or delayed gratification test. We need more research that puts groups of people (or animals) into situations where self-control is needed. I think perhaps our intuition is that groups lend themselves to more impulsivity, but we have to think harder about this. There are too many examples of support groups, athletic training groups, and groups of experts in music or other areas where having more people together lends itself to better, more delayed outcomes rather than short-term outcomes. One really interesting animal result comes from a study by Fruteau, Van Damme, and Noë (2013). The researchers trained low ranking monkeys in bigger social groups to open a box of a large amount of preferred food. Those monkeys would do so only when all other monkeys sat *far away from the box*. So, a classic test of inhibition for all participants. The food is naturally highly salient, and dominant monkeys should want to be near it. But, to get it, they have to move away, and they *all have to move away*. If anyone stays near the food, the low ranking animal will not feel secure enough to open it. The monkeys learned to do this, and by the end of the study, were very quickly moving away as a group so that they could all later come back as a group to get the big reward.

Other *known unknowns* include understanding the true link between future-oriented cognition and self-control. We continue to learn new things about how animals anticipate the future, and how much they can orient present choices toward future goals. We need to do much more in this area, although I am encouraged by the recent attempts to address this relation between future-oriented cognition and self-control in children and in other species. What about links between specific forms of cognitive control and self-control? And, what is the true nature of the relation between self-control and "general intelligence"? Can that relationship be modified through some form of intervention on one link within that connection?

I leave to you, the reader, the charge of thinking about the *unknown unknowns*. They exist, and they may push us as far forward as did the marshmallow test, or the intertemporal choice test. The *unknown unknowns* will provide questions that we cannot even begin to think to answer right now, and I suspect overcoming the *unknown unknowns* will lead to another series of fascinating tasks that we will use. For now, I hope that I have highlighted how our own capacity to show self-control, as well as our susceptibility to impulsivity, come from our evolutionary history and emerge through development. Showing self-control in one context, or at one choice point, does not guarantee success at the next, and comparative research shows that although animals can show similar performances to those of humans, they also show limitations in their self-control. Self-control is fallible, within and across species. However, a developmental/comparative perspective demonstrates that certain principles for improving self-control appear to be universal, whereas others remain to be tested further. My ultimate hope is for there to be continued support for research on this topic and continued appreciation for testing many species on fair, valid tests of self-control, so that a fuller evolutionary picture of this important ability can emerge alongside a fuller developmental picture within our own species.

REFERENCES

Beran, M. J. (2017). To err is (not only) human: Fallibility as a window into primate cognition. *Comparative Cognition & Behavior Reviews*, *12*, 57–81.

Beran, M. J., Brandl, J., Perner, J., & Proust, J. (Eds.) (2012). *Foundations of metacognition*. Oxford, UK: Oxford University Press.

Fruteau, C., Van Damme, E., & Noë, R. (2013). Vervet monkeys solve a multiplayer "forbidden circle game" by queuing to learn restraint. *Current Biology*, *23*, 665–670.

Thaler, R. H., & Sunstein, C. R. (1999). *Nudge: Improving decisions about health, wealth, and happiness*. New Haven: CT Yales University Press.

Index

Note: Page numbers followed by "*f*" and "*t*" refer to figures and tables.

FSC
www.fsc.org
MIX
Papier | Fördert gute Waldnutzung
FSC® C083411

Kolibri 360 GmbH
Ferdinand-Jühlke-Straße 7
99095 Erfurt, Deutschland
produktsicherheit@kolibri360.de